Au

AutoCAD Architecture 2013 Fundamentals

Elise Moss

ISBN: 978-1-58503-745-2

SDC PUBLICATIONS

Schroff Development Corporation

www.SDCpublications.com

Schroff Development Corporation
P.O. Box 1334
Mission, KS 66222
(913) 262-2664
www.SDCpublications.com

Publisher: Stephen Schroff

Moss, Elise
Autodesk AutoCAD Architecture 2013 Fundamentals
Elise Moss
ISBN: 978-1-58503-745-2

Printed and bound in the United States of America.

Preface

No textbook can cover all the features in any software application. This textbook is meant for beginning users who want to gain a familiarity with the tools and interface of AutoCAD Architecture before they start exploring on their own. By the end of the text, users should feel comfortable enough to create a standard model, and even know how to customize the interface for their own use. Knowledge of basic AutoCAD and its commands is helpful, but not required. I do try to explain as I go, but for the sake of brevity I concentrate on the tools specific to and within AutoCAD Architecture.

The files used in this text are accessible from the Internet at www.schroff.com/resources. They are free and available to students and teachers alike.

We value customer input. Please contact us with any comments, questions, or concerns about this text.

Elise Moss
elise_moss@mossdesigns.com

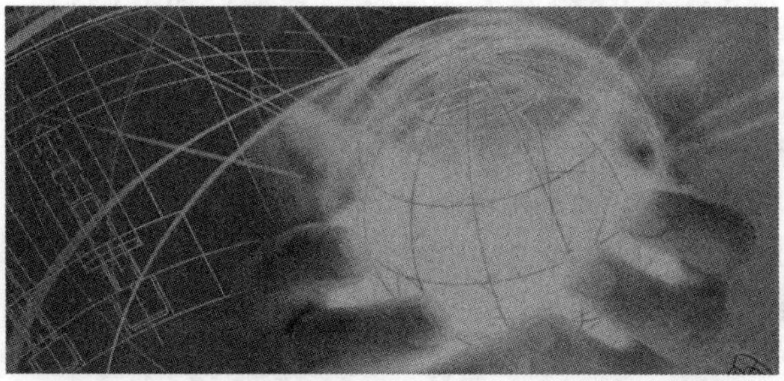

Acknowledgements from Elise Moss

This book would not have been possible without the support of some key Autodesk employees.

The effort and support of the editorial and production staff of Schroff Development Corporation is gratefully acknowledged. I especially thank Stephen Schroff for his helpful suggestions regarding the format of this text.

Finally, truly infinite thanks to Ari for his encouragement and his faith.

- Elise Moss

About the Author

Elise Moss has worked for the past thirty years as a mechanical designer in Silicon Valley, primarily creating sheet metal designs. She has written articles for Autodesk's Toplines magazine, AUGI's PaperSpace, DigitalCAD.com and Tenlinks.com. She is President of Moss Designs, creating custom applications and designs for corporate clients. She has taught CAD classes at DeAnza College, Silicon Valley College, and for Autodesk resellers. She is currently teaching CAD at SFSU, in the College for Extended Learning campus and at Laney College in Oakland. Autodesk has named her as a Faculty of Distinction for the curriculum she has developed for Autodesk products. She holds a baccalaureate degree in Mechanical Engineering from San Jose State.

She is married with three sons. Her older son, Benjamin, is an electrical engineer. Her middle son, Daniel, works with AutoCAD Architecture in the construction industry. His designs have been featured in architectural journals. Her youngest son, Isaiah, is in high school, but shows signs of being a budding engineer. Her husband, Ari, is retired from a distinguished career in software development.

Elise is a third generation engineer. Her father, Robert Moss, was a metallurgical engineer in the aerospace industry. Her grandfather, Solomon Kupperman, was a civil engineer for the City of Chicago.

She can be contacted via email at elise_moss@mossdesigns.com.

More information about the author and her work can be found on her website at www.mossdesigns.com.

Autodesk
Certified Instructor

<u>Other books by Elise Moss</u>

Autodesk Revit Architecture 2013 Basics

Table of Contents

Lesson 1:
Desktop Features

AutoCAD Architecture (ACA) enlists object oriented process systems (OOPS). That means that ACA uses intelligent objects to create a building. This is similar to using blocks in AutoCAD. Objects in AutoCAD Architecture are blocks on steroids. They have intelligence already embedded into them. A wall is not just a collection of lines. It represents a real wall. It can be constrained, has thickness and material properties, and is automatically included in your building schedule.

AEC is an acronym for Architectural/Electrical/Construction.
BID is an acronym for Building Industrial Design.
BIM is an acronym for Building Information Modeling.
AIA is an acronym for the American Institute of Architects.
MEP is an acronym for Mechanical/Electrical/Plumbing.

The following table describes the key features of objects in AutoCAD Architecture:

Feature Type	Description
AEC Camera	Create perspective views from various camera angles. Create avi files.
AEC Profiles	Create AEC objects using polylines to build doors, windows, etc.
Anchors and Layouts	Define a spatial relationship between objects. Create a layout of anchors on a curve or a grid to set a pattern of anchored objects, such as doors or columns.
Annotation	Set up special arrows, leaders, bar scales.
Ceiling Grids	Create reflected ceiling plans with grid layouts.
Column Grids	Define rectangular and radial building grids with columns and bubbles.
Design Center	Customize your AEC block library.
Display System	Control views for each AEC object.
Doors and Windows	Create custom door and window styles or use standard objects provided with the software.
Elevations and Sections	An elevation is basically a section view of a floor plan.
Layer Manager	Create layer standards based on AIA CAD Standards. Create groups of layers. Manage layers intelligently using Layer Filters.
Masking Blocks	Store a mask using a polyline object and attach to AEC objects to hide graphics
Model Explorer	View a model and manage the content easily. Attach names to mass elements to assist in design.
Multi-view blocks	Blocks have embedded defined views to allow you to easily change view.

Feature Type	Description
Railings	Create or apply different railing styles to a stair or along a defined path.
Roofs	Create and apply various roof styles.
Floorplate slices	Generate the perimeter geometry of a building.
Spaces and Boundaries	Spaces and boundaries can include floor thickness, room height, and wall thickness.
Stairs	Create and apply various stair types.
Tags and Schedules	Place tags on objects to generate schedules. Schedules will automatically update when tags are modified, added, or deleted.
Template Files	Use templates to save time. Create a template with standard layers, text styles, linetypes, dimension styles, etc.
Walls	Create wall styles to determine material composition. Define end caps to control opening and end conditions. Define wall interference conditions.

AutoCAD Architecture sits on top of AutoCAD. It is helpful for users to have a basic understanding of AutoCAD before moving to AutoCAD Architecture. Users should be familiar with the following:

- AutoCAD toolbars and ribbons
- Zoom and move around the screen
- Manage blocks
- *Draw* and *Modify* commands
- *Model* and *Paper space* (layout),
- Dimensioning and how to create/modify a dimension style

If you are not familiar with these topics, you can still move forward with learning AutoCAD Architecture, but you may find it helpful to have a good AutoCAD textbook as reference in case you get stuck.

TIP: The best way to use AutoCAD Architecture is start your project with massing tools (outside-in design) or space planning tools (inside-out design) and continue through to construction documentation.

The AEC Project Process Model

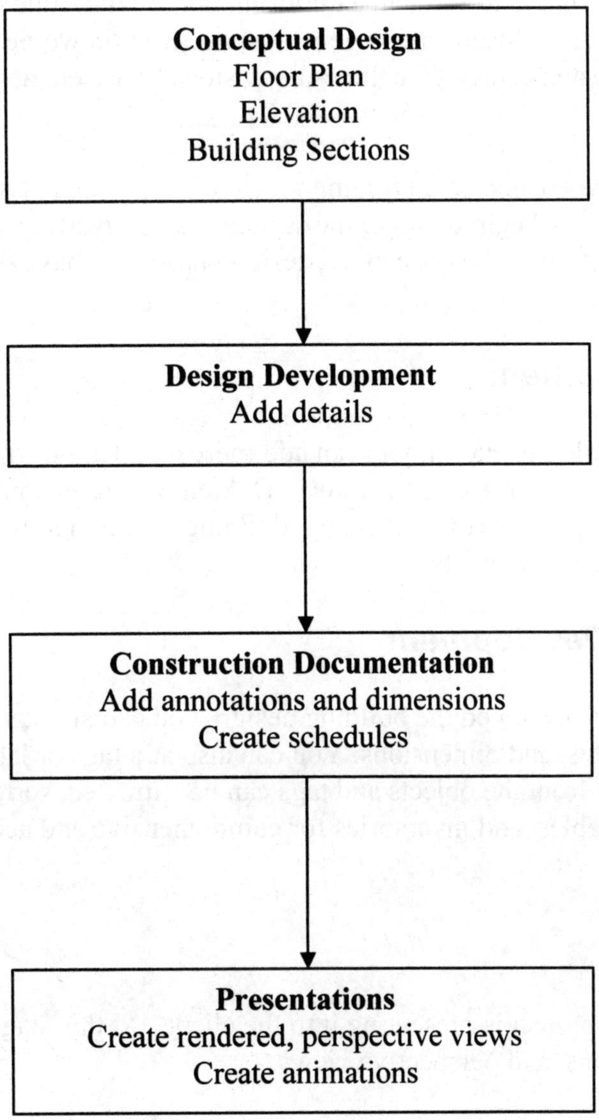

Conceptual Design

In the initial design phase, you can assemble AutoCAD Architecture mass elements as simple architectural shapes to form an exterior model of your building project. You can also lay out interior areas by arranging general spaces as you would in a bubble diagram. You can manipulate and consolidate three-dimensional mass elements into massing studies.

Later in this phase, you can create building footprints from the massing study by slicing floorplates, and you can begin defining the structure by converting space boundaries into walls. At the completion of the conceptual design phase, you have developed a workable schematic floor plan.

Design Development

As you refine the building project, you can add more detailed information to the schematic design. Use the features in AutoCAD Architecture to continue developing the design of the building project by organizing, defining, and assigning specific styles and attributes to building components.

Construction Development

After you have fully developed the building design, you can annotate your drawings with reference marks, notes, and dimensions. You can also add tags or labels associated with objects. Information from the objects and tags can be extracted, sorted, and compiled into schedules, reports, tables, and inventories for comprehensive and accurate construction documentation.

Presentations

A major part of any project is presenting it to the client. At this stage, you develop renderings, animations, and perspective views.

> **TIP:** If you use the **QNEW** tool, it will automatically use the template set in the Options dialog.

Express Tools

By default, Express Tools are not installed with AutoCAD Architecture.

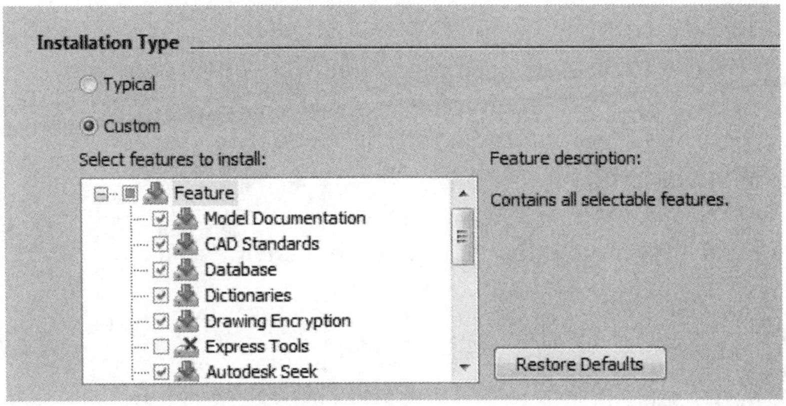

In order to install the Express Tools, you need to select the Custom Installation Type.

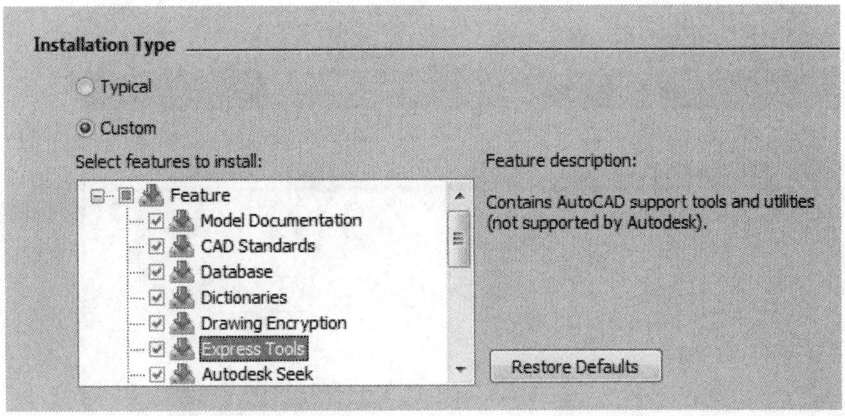

Place a check next to Express Tools to enable the installation and continue with the installation.

Express Tools can be used to create custom line types, control layers, and many other useful functions.

If you forgot to check Custom and install the Express Tools, they can be installed at any time. Refer to the next lesson for further guidance on installing the Express Tools after ACA has been installed.

Exercise 1-1:

Exploring the User Interface

Drawing Name: New
Estimated Time: 15 minutes

Note: This exercise requires the user to be connected to the internet. Some help and support features require web-browsing.

This exercise reinforces the following skills:

- ❑ Getting the user familiar with tools and the ACA environment

1. Launch ACA.

2. 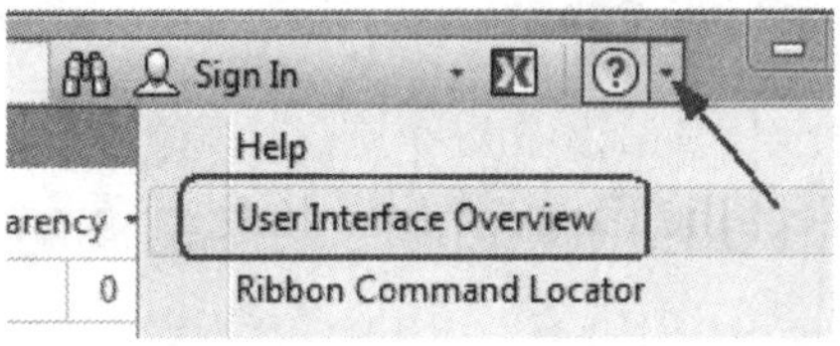

Select the down arrow next to the Help tool.

Select **User Interface Overview**.

3. Mouse over each number to identify the tools.

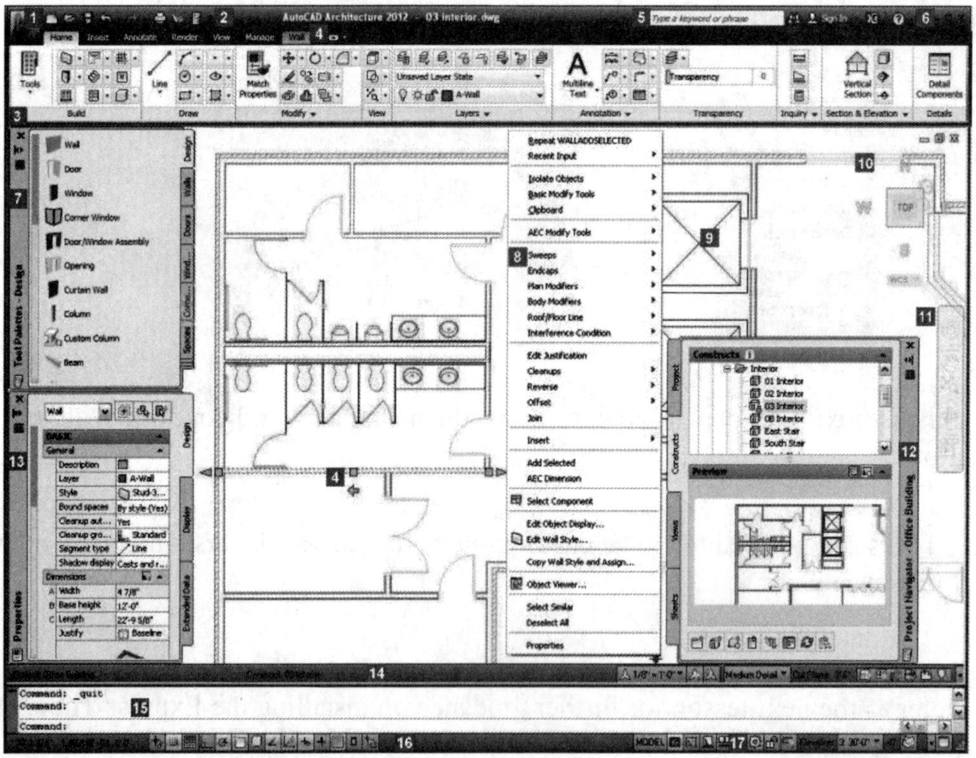

4. 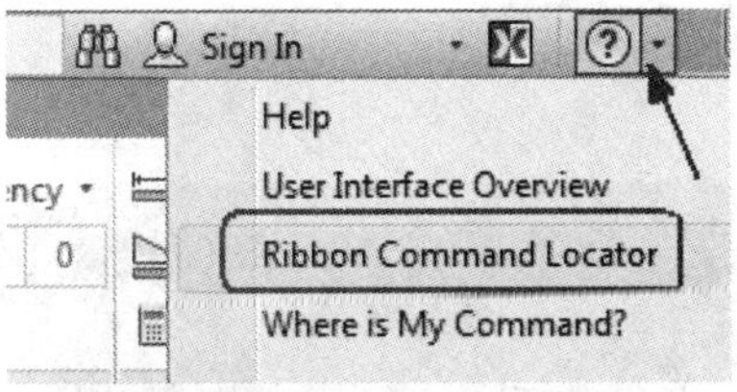

Select the down arrow next to the Help tool.

Select **Ribbon Command Locator**.

5. 

If you used older versions of AutoCAD or AutoCAD Architecture, you may wish to use this tool if you get stuck looking for a command.

Click on the link.

6. A webpage will load.

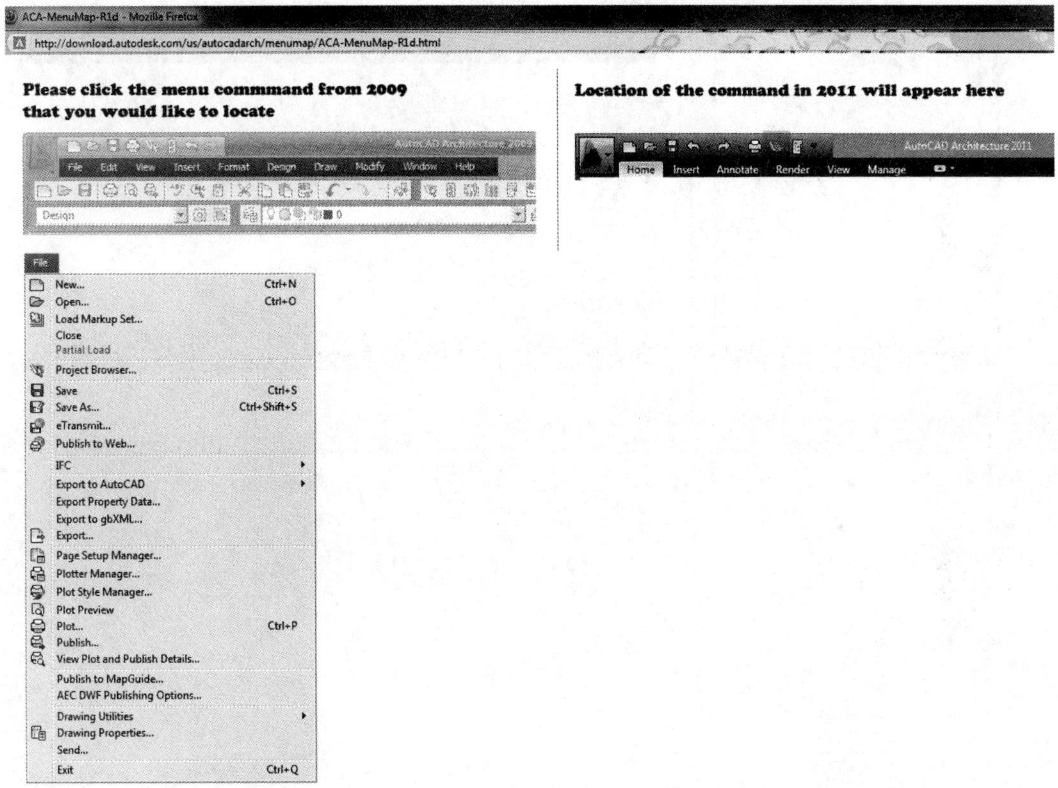

Look for a command using the old interface and the page will show you where to locate it in 2013.

7. 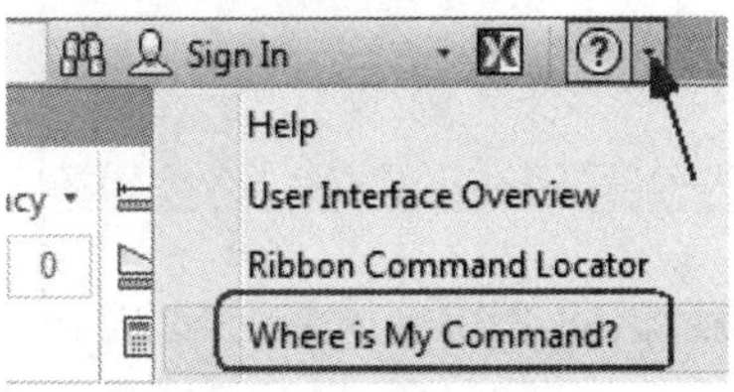

Select the down arrow next to the Help tool.

Select **Where is My Command?**

8. This help file allows you to locate where commands can be found in 2013.

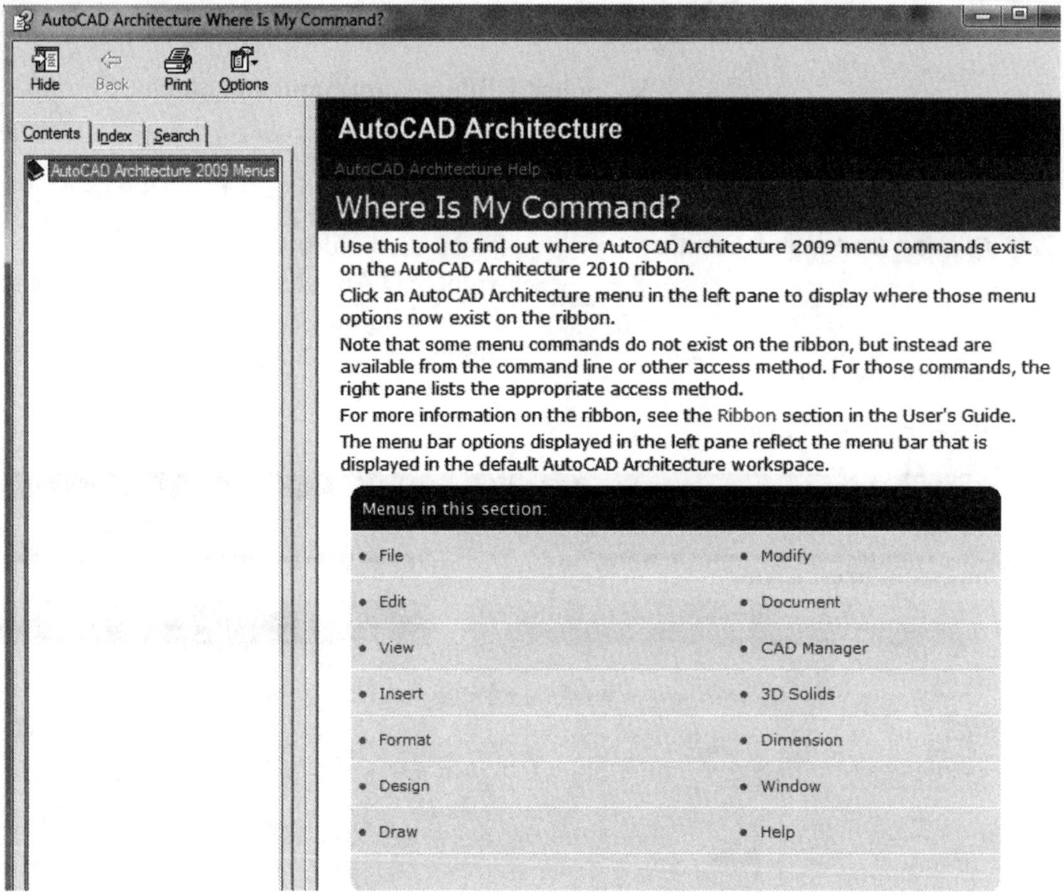
AutoCAD Architecture Where Is My Command?
Hide
Back
Print
Options
Contents
Index
Search
AutoCAD Architecture 2009 Menus
AutoCAD Architecture
AutoCAD Architecture Help
Where Is My Command?
Use this tool to find out where AutoCAD Architecture 2009 menu commands exist on the AutoCAD Architecture 2010 ribbon.
Click an AutoCAD Architecture menu in the left pane to display where those menu options now exist on the ribbon.
Note that some menu commands do not exist on the ribbon, but instead are available from the command line or other access method. For those commands, the right pane lists the appropriate access method.
For more information on the ribbon, see the Ribbon section in the User's Guide.
The menu bar options displayed in the left pane reflect the menu bar that is displayed in the default AutoCAD Architecture workspace.
Menus in this section:
File
Modify
Edit
Document
View
CAD Manager
Insert
3D Solids
Format
Dimension
Design
Window
Draw
Help

Exercise 1-2:

Setting the Template for QNEW

Drawing Name: New
Estimated Time: 15 minutes

This exercise reinforces the following skills:

- Use of templates
- Getting the user familiar with tools and the ACA environment

1. Launch ACA.

2. Place your cursor on the command line.

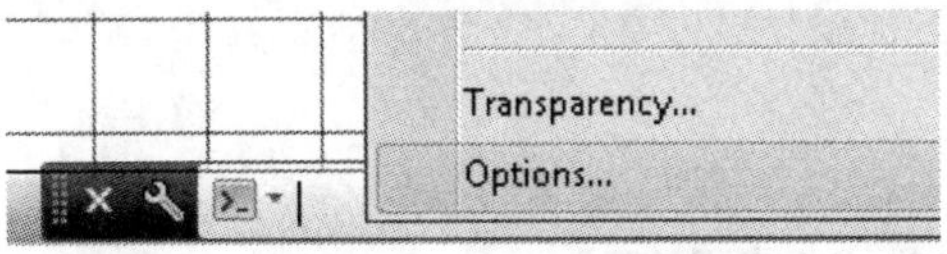

Right click the mouse.

Select **Options** from the short-cut menu.

3. Select the **Files** tab.
Locate the *Template Settings* folder.

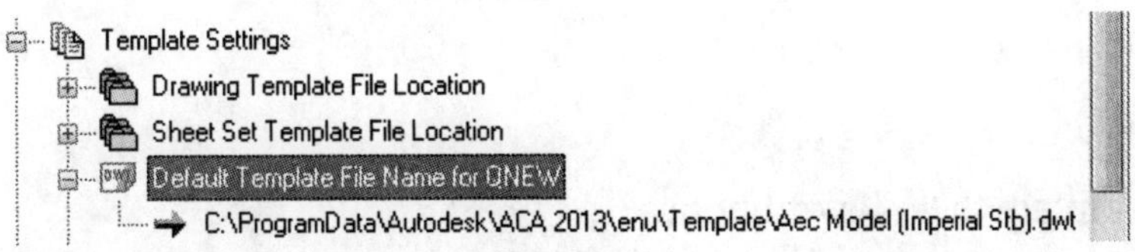

Click on the + symbol to expand.
Locate the Default Template File Name for QNEW.

4. 

Highlight the path and file name listed and select the **Browse** button.

5. Browse to the *Template* folder.

This should be listed under
Documents & Settings\[user name]\Application Data\ Autodesk\ACD-A 2013\enu
or
Program Data/Autodesk/ ACA 2013/enu

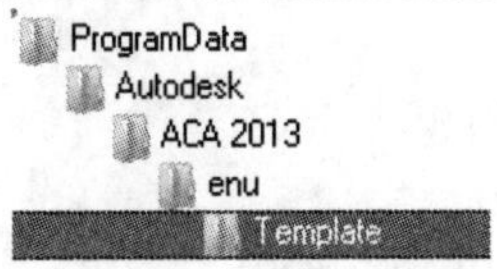

6. 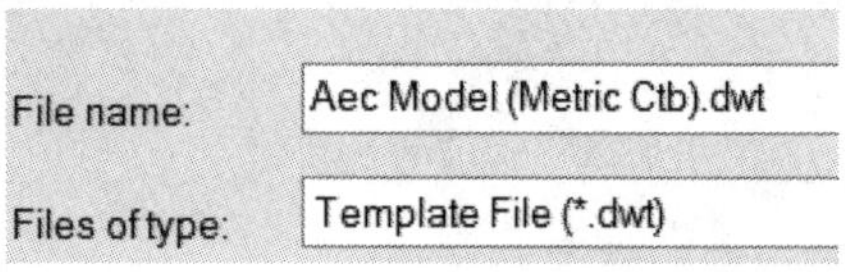

Locate the *Aec Model (Imperial Ctb).dwt [Aec Model (Metric Ctb).dwt]* file.

Press **Open**.

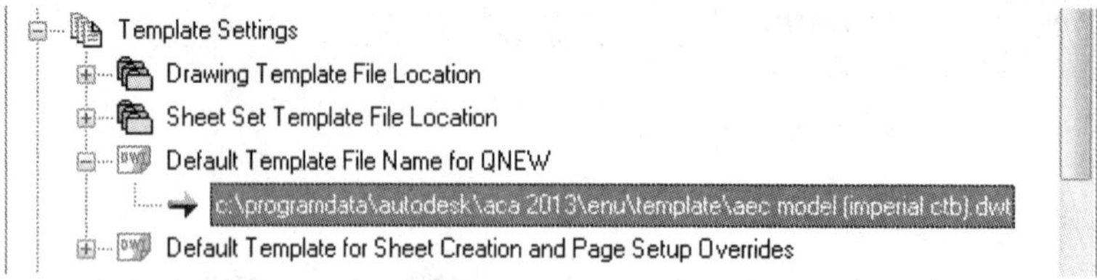

7. Note that you can also set where you can direct the user for templates. This is useful if you want to create standard templates and place them on a network server for all users to access.

   You can also use this setting to help you locate where your template files are located.

8. Press **Apply** and **OK**.

9. 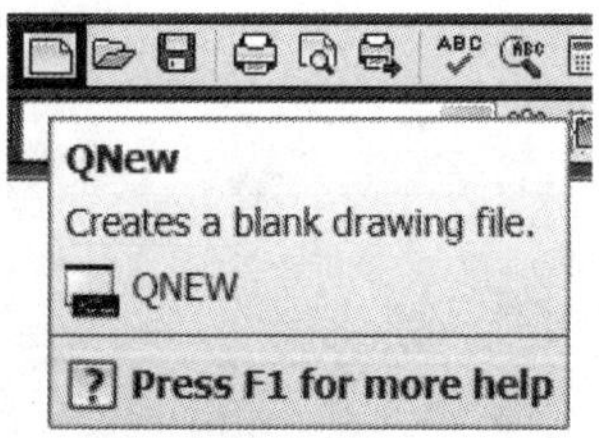

Select the **QNEW** tool button.

10. 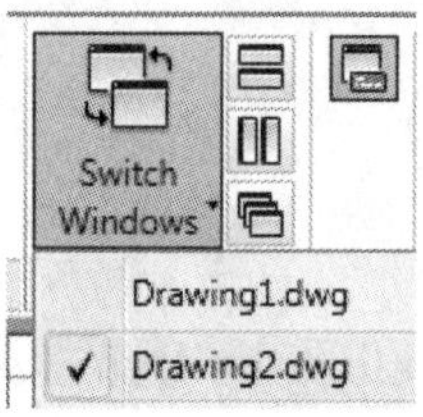

Activate the **View** ribbon.

Under **Switch Windows**, you see that you have two files open now. A check mark appears next to the active file.

11. 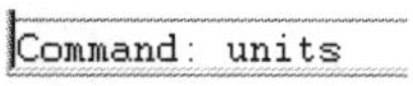

Type **units** on the *Command* line.

12. 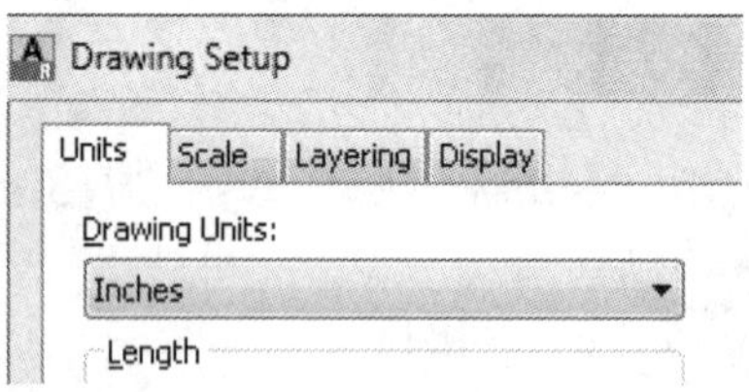

Note that the units are in inches [millimeters].

The units are determined by the template you set to start your new drawing.

13. Close the drawing without saving.

TIP: Templates can be used to preset layers, property set definitions, dimension styles, units, and layouts.

Setting AEC Drawing Options

Menu	Tools→Options
Command line	Options
Context Menu→Options	Place Mouse in the graphics area and right click
Shortcut	Place mouse in the command line and right click

Access the Options dialog box.

ACA's Options includes five additional AEC specific tabs.
They are AEC Editor, AEC Content, AEC Object Settings, AEC Dimension, and AEC Project Defaults.

AEC Editor

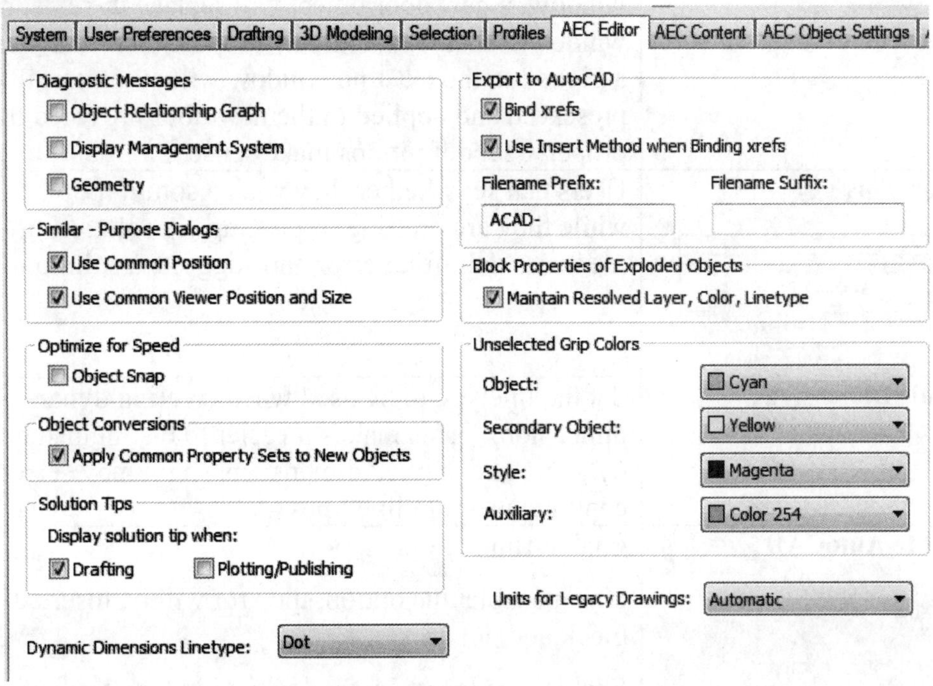

Diagnostic Messages	All diagnostic messages are turned off by default.
Similar-Purpose Dialogs	Options for the position of dialog boxes and viewers.
Use Common Position	Sets one common position on the screen for similar dialog boxes, such as door, wall, and window add or modify dialog boxes. Some dialog boxes, such as those for styles and properties, are always displayed in the center of the screen, regardless of this setting.

Use Common Viewer Position and Sizes	Sets one size and position on the screen for the similar-purpose viewers in AutoCAD Architecture. Viewer position is separately controlled for add, modify, style, and properties dialog boxes.
Optimize for Speed	Options for display representations and layer loading in the Layer Manager dialog.
Object Snap	Enable to limit certain display representations to respond only to the Node and Insert object snaps. This setting affects stair, railing, space boundary, multi-view block, masking block, slice, and clip volume result (building section) objects.
Apply Common Property Sets to New Objects	Property sets are used for the creation of schedule tables. Each AEC object has embedded property sets, such as width and height, to be used in its schedule. AEC properties are similar to attributes. Size is a common property across most AEC objects. Occasionally, you may use a tool on an existing object and the result may be that you replace the existing object with an entirely different object. For example, if you apply the tool properties of a door to an existing window, a new door object will replace the existing window. When enabled, any property sets that were assigned to the existing window will automatically be preserved and applied to the new door provided that the property set definitions make sense.
Solution Tips 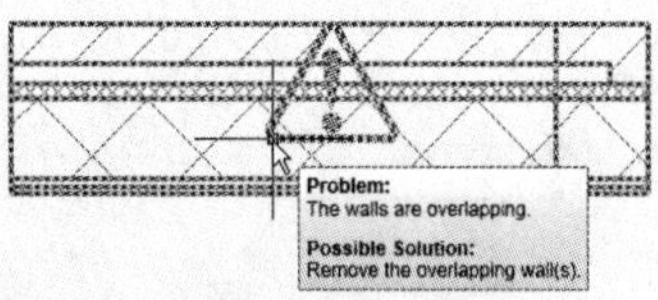	Users can set whether they wish a solution tip to appear while they are drafting or plotting. A solution tip identifies a drafting error and suggests a solution.
Dynamic Dimensions Linetype	Set the linetype to be used when creating dynamic dimensions. This makes it easier to distinguish between dynamic and applied dimensions. You may select either continuous or dot linetypes.
Export to AutoCAD 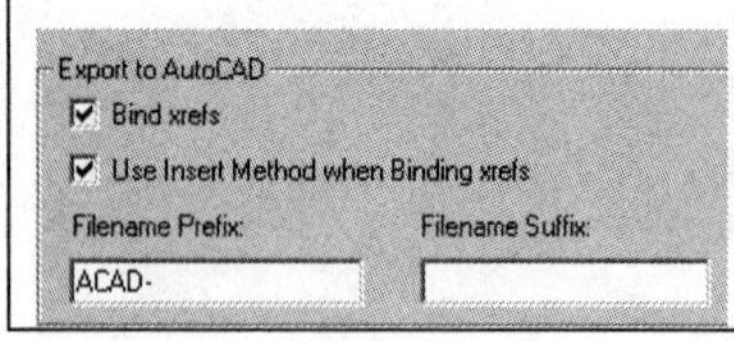	Enable Bind Xrefs If you enable this option, the xref will be inserted as a block and not an xref. Enable Use Insert Method when binding Xrefs if you want all objects from an xref drawing referenced in the

	file you export to be automatically exploded into the host drawing. If you enable this option, the drawing names of the xref drawings are discarded when the exported drawing is created. In addition, their layers and styles are incorporated into the host drawing. For example, all exploded walls, regardless of their source (host or xref) are located on the same layer. Disable Use Insert Method when binding Xrefs if you want to retain the xref identities, such as layer names, when you export a file to AutoCAD or to a DXF file. For example, the blocks that define walls in the host drawing are located on A-Wall in the exploded drawing. Walls in an attached xref drawing are located on a layer whose name is created from the drawing name and the layer name, such as Drawing1|WallA. Many architects automatically bind and explode their xrefs when sending drawings to customers to protect their intellectual property. Enter a prefix or a suffix to be added to the drawing filename when the drawing is exported to an AutoCAD drawing or a DXF file. In order for any of these options to apply, you have to use the Export to AutoCAD command. This is available under the Files menu.
Unselected Grip Colors	Assign the colors for each type of grip
Units for Legacy Drawings	Determines the units to be used when opening an AutoCAD drawing in AutoCAD Architecture. Automatic – uses the current AutoCAD Architecture units setting Imperial – uses Imperial units Metric – uses Metric units

TIP: Option Settings are applied to your current drawing and saved as the default settings for new drawings. Because AutoCAD Architecture operates in a Multiple Document Interface, each drawing stores the Options Settings used when it was created and last saved. Some users get confused because they open an existing drawing and it will not behave according to the current Options Settings.

AEC Content

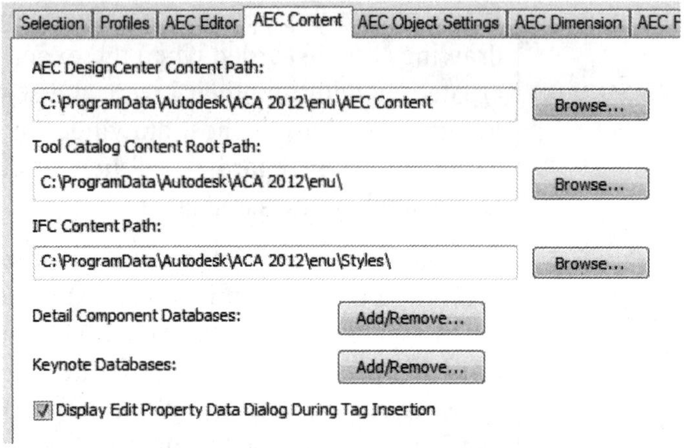

AEC DesignCenter Content Path	Type the path and location of your content files, or click Browse to search for the content files.
Tool Catalog Content Root Path	Type the path and location of your Tool Catalog files, or click Browse to search for the content files.
IFC Content Path	Type the path and location of your Tool Catalog files, or click Browse to search for the content files.
Detail Component Databases	Select the **Add/Remove** button to set the search paths for your detail component files.
Keynote Databases	Select the **Add/Remove** button to set the search paths for your keynote database files.
Display Edit Schedule Data Dialog During Tag Insertion	To attach schedule data to objects when you insert a schedule tag in the drawing, this should be ENABLED.

IFC Content is an object-based building data model that is non-proprietary. It uses open-source code developed by the IAI (International Alliance for Interoperability) to promote data exchange between CAD software. IFC Content might be created in Autodesk Revit, Inventor, or some other software for use in your projects.

Using AEC Content

AutoCAD Architecture uses several pre-defined and user-customizable content including:

- Architectural Display Configurations
- Architectural Profiles of Geometric Shapes
- Wall Styles and Endcap geometry
- Door styles
- Window styles
- Stair styles
- Space styles
- Schedule tables

Standard style content is stored in the AEC templates subdirectory. You can create additional content, import and export styles between drawings.

AEC Object Settings

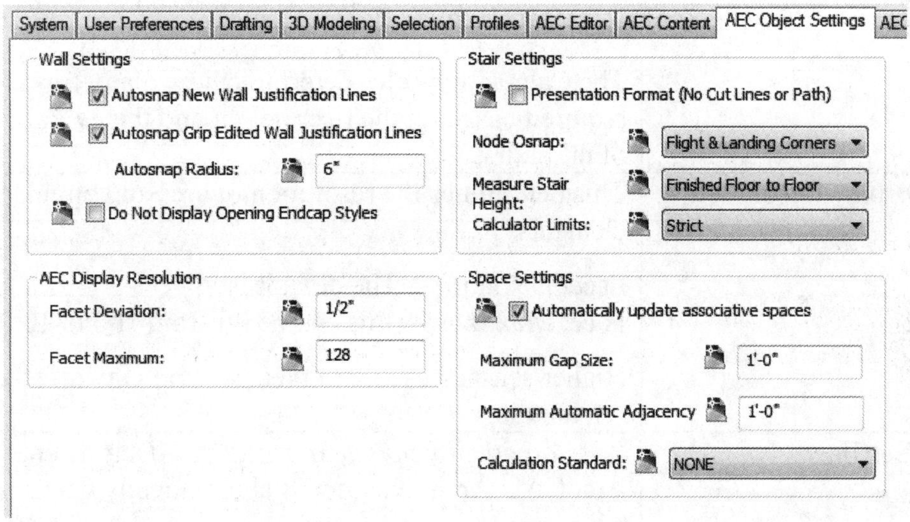

Wall Settings	
Autosnap New Wall Justification Lines	Enable to have the endpoint of a new wall that is drawn within the Autosnap Radius of the baseline of an existing wall automatically snap to that baseline. If you select this option and set your Autosnap Radius to 0, then only walls that touch, clean up with each other.
Autosnap Grip Edited Wall Justification Lines	Enable to snap the endpoint of a wall that you grip edit within the Autosnap Radius of the baseline of an existing wall. If you select this option and set your Autosnap Radius to 0, then only walls that touch clean up with each other.

Autosnap Radius	Enter a value to set the snap tolerance.
Do not display opening end cap styles	Enable Do Not Display Opening Endcap Styles to suppress the display of endcaps applied to openings in walls. Enabling this option boosts drawing performance when the drawing contains many complex endcaps.
Stair Settings	
Presentation Format (No Cut Lines or Path)	If this is enabled, a jagged line and directional arrows will not display.
Node Osnap	Determines which snap is enabled when creating stairs: Vertical Alignment Flight and Landing Corners
Measure Stair Height	Rough floor to floor – ignore offsets Finished floor to floor – include top and bottom offsets
Calculator Limits	Strict – stair will display a defect symbol when an edit results in a violation of the Calculation rules. Relaxed – no defect symbol will be displayed when the stair violates the Calculation rules. The Calculation rules determine how many treads are required based on the riser height and the overall height of the stairs.
AEC Display Resolution	This determines the resolution of arcs and circular elements. Facet Deviation – The default is ½″. Facet Maximum – this can be set from 100 to 10,000. Higher settings use more memory and may affect screen refresh rates
Space Settings  	If *Automatically update associative spaces* is enabled, AutoCAD Architecture will automatically determine which spaces are adjacent to each other and update their association accordingly. The Maximum Gap Size is the allowable distance between spaces. The Maximum Automatic Adjacency sets the gap allowance between spaces for spaces to be considered adjacent. The Floor Boundary Thickness sets the value of the Floor Boundary Thickness. The Calculation Standard determines how the space values are calculated.

AEC Dimension

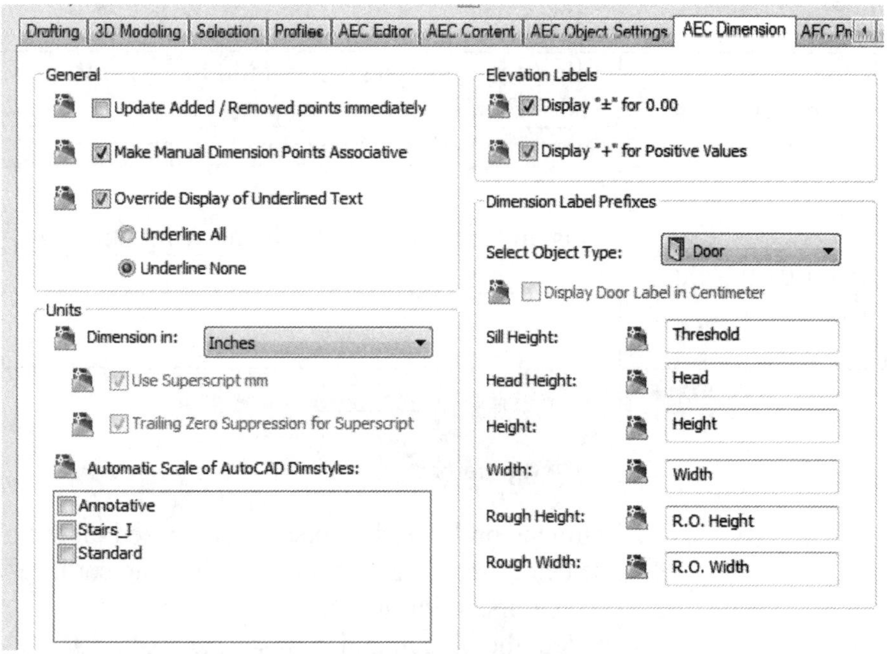

General	
Update Added/Removed points immediately	Enable to update the display every time you add or remove a point from a dimension chain.
Make Manual Dimension Points Associative	Enable if you want the dimension to update when the object is modified.
Override Display of Undefined Text	Enable to automatically underline each manually overridden dimension value.
Underline All	Enable to manually underline overridden dimension values.
Underline None	Enable to not underline any overridden dimension value.
Units	
Dimension in:	Select the desired units from the drop-down list.
Use Superscript mm	If your units are set to meters or centimeters, enable superscripted text to display the millimeters as superscript. 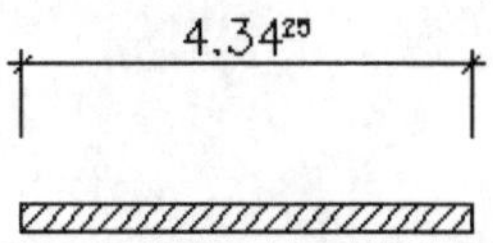
Trailing Zero Suppression for Superscript	To suppress zeros at the end of superscripted numbers, select Trailing Zeros Suppression for Superscript. You can select this option only if you have selected Use Superscript mm and your units are metric.

	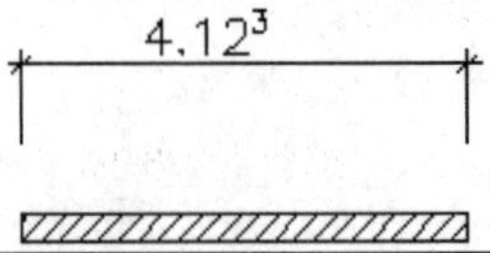
Automatic Scale of AutoCAD Dimstyles	Select the dimstyles you would like to automatically scale when units are reset.
Elevation Labels	Select the unit in which elevation labels are to be displayed. This unit can differ from the drawing unit.
Display +/- for 0.00 Values	
Display + for Positive Values	
Dimension Label Prefixes	 Dimension Label Prefixes are set based on the object selected from the drop-down. You can set label prefixes for Doors, Windows, Openings, and Stairs. Select the object, and then set the prefix for each designation. The designations will change based on the object selected.

AEC Project Defaults

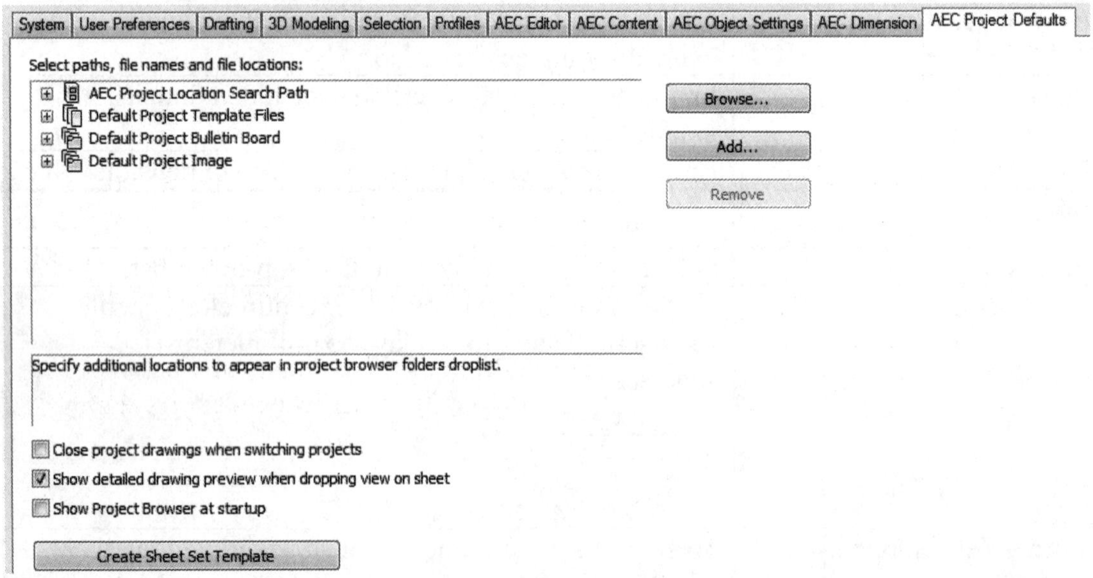

Most BID/AEC firms work in a team environment where they divide a project's tasks among several different users. The AEC Project Defaults allows the CAD Manager or team leader to select a folder on the company's server to locate files; set up template files with the project's title blocks; and even set up a webpage to post project information.

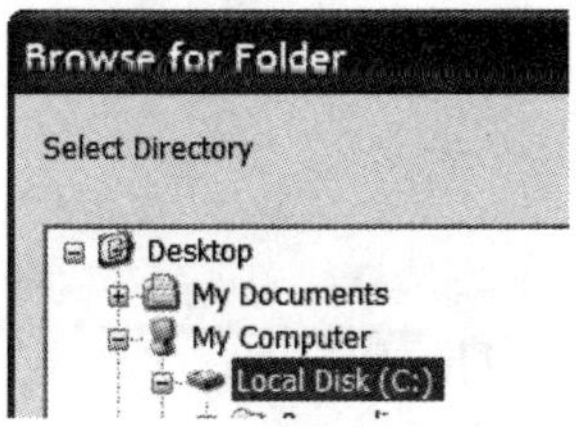

To add a path, simply expand the folder and use the Browse button to locate the desired folder.

You can add more than one path to the AEC Project Location Search Path. All the other folders only allow you to have a single location for template files, the project bulletin board, and the default project image.

TIP: I highly recommend that you store any custom content in a separate directory as far away from AutoCAD Architecture as possible. This will allow you to back up your custom work easily and prevent accidental erasure if you upgrade your software application.

You should be aware that AutoCAD Architecture currently allows the user to specify only ONE path for custom content, so drawings with custom commands will only work if they reside in the specified path.

☐ Close project drawings when switching projects	If enabled, when a user switches projects in the Project Navigator, any open drawings not related to the new project selected will be closed. This conserves memory resources.
☑ Show detailed drawing preview when dropping view on sheet	If enabled, then the user will see the entire view as it is being positioned on a sheet. If it is disabled, the user will just see the boundary of the view for the purposes of placing it on a sheet.
☐ Show Project Browser at startup	If enabled, you will automatically have access to the Project Browser whenever you start AutoCAD Architecture.

Accessing the Project Browser

Command line	AECProjectBrowser
Quick Access Toolbar	
Files Menu	Project Browser

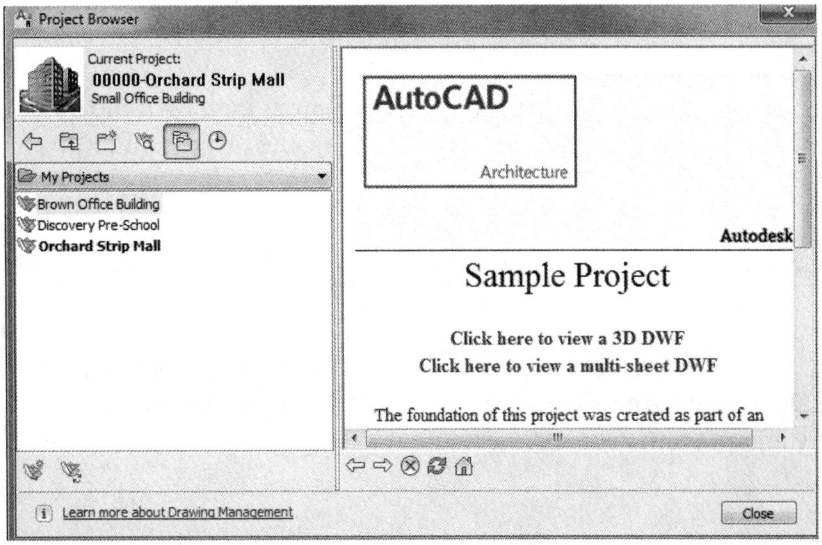

The Project Browser allows you to manage your project, similar to the old Today window in 2002, but more powerful. Projects have two parts: the building model and the reports generated from the building model.

The building model is made of two drawing types: constructs and elements. A construct is any unique portion of a building. It can be a flight of stairs, a specific room, or an entire floor. Constructs are assigned to a level (floor) and a division within a project. Elements are any AEC object or content that is used multiple times in a model. For example, furniture layouts or lavatory layouts. Elements can be converted into constructs if you decide that they will not be used repeatedly.

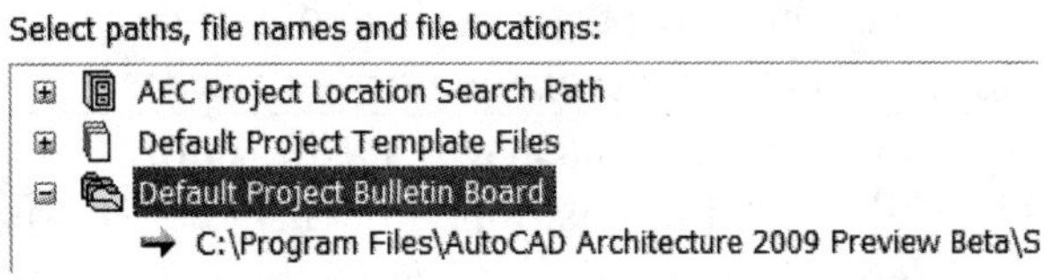

The text you see in the right window is actually an html file. The path to this file is controlled in the path for the Default Project Bulletin Board. This is set on the AEC Project Defaults tab in the Options dialog.

Architectural Profiles of Geometric Shapes

You can create mass elements to define the shape and configuration of your preliminary study, or mass model. After you create the mass elements you need, you can change their size as necessary to reflect the building design.

- **Mass element**: A single object that has behaviors based on its shape. For example, you can set the width, depth, and height of a box mass element, and the radius and height of a cylinder mass element.

Mass elements are parametric, which allows each of the shapes to have very specific behavior when it comes to the manipulation of each mass element's shape. For example, if the corner grip point of a box is selected and dragged, then the width and depth are modified. It is easy to change the shape to another form by right-clicking on the element and selecting a new shape from the list.

Through Boolean operations (addition, subtraction, intersection), mass elements can be combined into a mass group. The mass group provides a representation of your building during the concept phase of your project.

- **Mass group**: Takes the shape of the mass elements and is placed on a separate layer from the mass elements.
- **Mass model**: A virtual mass object, shaped from mass elements, which defines the basic structure and proportion of your building. A marker appears as a small box in your drawing to which you attach mass elements.

As you continue developing your mass model, you can combine mass elements into mass groups and create complex building shapes through addition, subtraction, or intersection of mass elements. You can still edit individual mass elements attached to a mass group to further refine the building model.

To study alternative design schemes, you can create a number of mass element references. When you change the original of the referenced mass element, all the instances of the mass element references are updated.

The mass model that you create with mass elements and mass groups is a refinement of your original idea that you carry forward into the next phase of the project, in which you change the mass study into floor plates and then into walls. The walls are used to start the design phase.

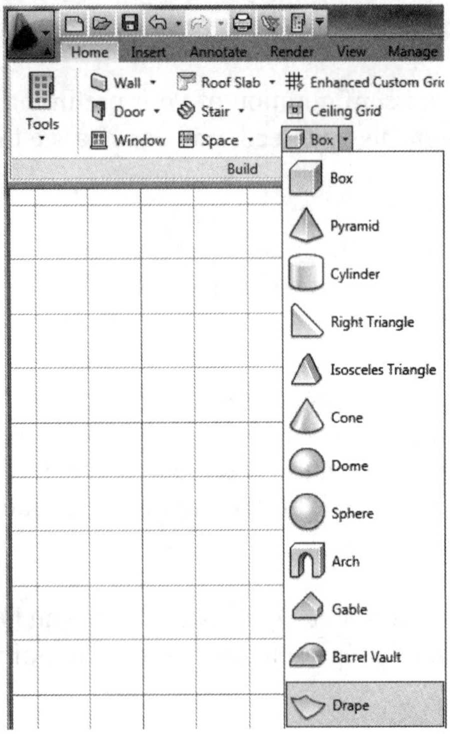

Mass Elements are accessed from the Home ribbon.

Mass Elements that can be defined include Arches, Gables, Doric Columns, etc.

The Style Manager

Menu

Access the Style Manager from the Manage ribbon.

The Style Manager is a Microsoft® Windows Explorer-based utility that provides you with a central location in Autodesk AutoCAD Architecture where you can view and work with styles in drawings or from Internet and intranet sites.

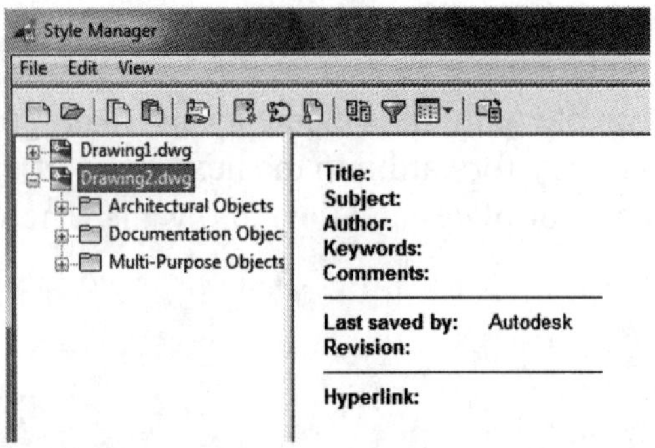

Styles are sets of parameters that you can assign to objects in Autodesk AutoCAD Architecture to determine their appearance or function. For example, a door style in Autodesk AutoCAD Architecture determines what door type, such as single or double, bi-fold or hinged, a door in a drawing represents. You can assign one style to more than one object, and you can modify the style to change the all the objects that are assigned that style.

Depending on your design projects, either you or your CAD Manager might want to customize existing styles or create new styles. The Style Manager allows you to easily create, customize, and share styles with other users. With the Style Manager, you can:

- Provide a central point for accessing styles from open drawings and Internet and intranet sites
- Quickly set up new drawings and templates by copying styles from other drawings or templates
- Sort and view the styles in your drawings and templates by drawing or by style type
- Preview an object with a selected style
- Create new styles and edit existing styles
- Delete unused styles from drawings and templates
- Send styles to other Autodesk AutoCAD Architecture users by email

Objects in Autodesk AutoCAD Architecture that use styles include 2D sections and elevations, AEC polygons, curtain walls, curtain wall units, doors, endcaps, railings, roof slab edges, roof slabs, schedule tables, slab edges, slabs, spaces, stairs, structural members, wall modifiers, walls, window assemblies, and windows.

Additionally, layer key styles, schedule data formats, and cleanup group, mask block, multi-view block, profile, and property set definitions are handled by the Style Manager.

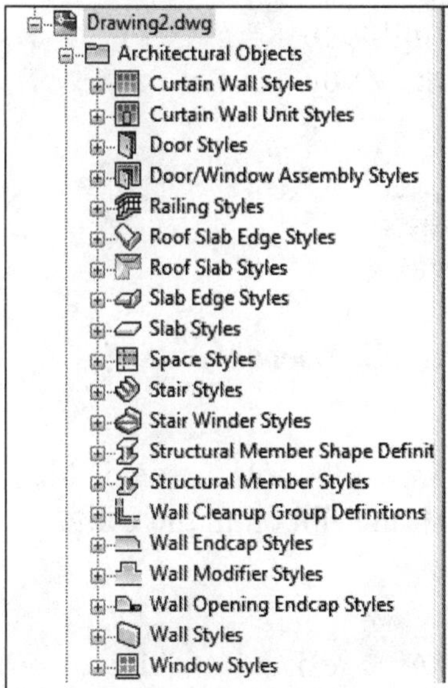

Most of the objects in Autodesk AutoCAD Architecture have a default Standard style. In addition, Autodesk AutoCAD Architecture includes a starter set of styles that you can use with your drawings. The Autodesk AutoCAD Architecture templates contain some of these styles. Any drawing that you start from one of the templates includes these styles.

You can also access the styles for doors, end caps, spaces, stairs, walls, and windows from drawings located in *Documents and Settings\All Users\ Application Data\Autodesk\... \Styles\Imperial or Metric.* Property set definitions and schedule tables are located in the *Documents and Settings\All Users\Application Data\ Autodesk...\AEC Content\ Imperial\ Documentation\Schedule Tags* folder.

TIP: I do not recommend modifying AutoCAD Architecture's standard styles as this may affect drawings you bring in from outside sources. Instead, copy the existing style to a NEW style and modify it using the desired properties.

Exercise 1-3:

Creating a New Geometric Profile

Drawing Name: New
Estimated Time: 15 minutes

This exercise reinforces the following skills:

- Use of AEC Design Content
- Use of Mass Elements
- Use of Views
- Visual Styles
- Modify using Properties

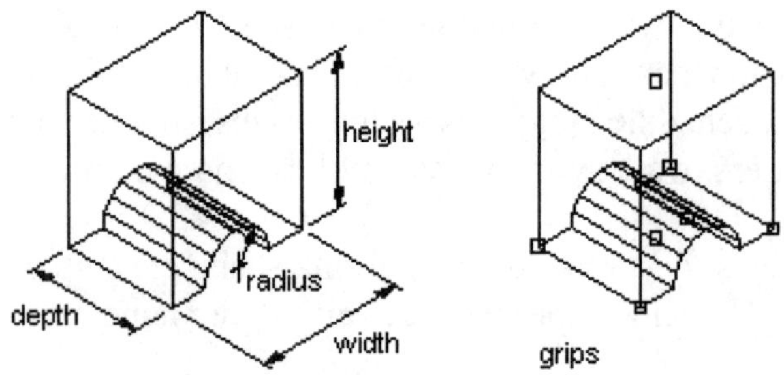

Creating an arch mass element

1. Start a New Drawing.

2.  Select the QNEW tool from the Standard toolbar.

   Because we assigned a template in Exercise 1-2, a drawing file opens without prompting us to select a template.

3. 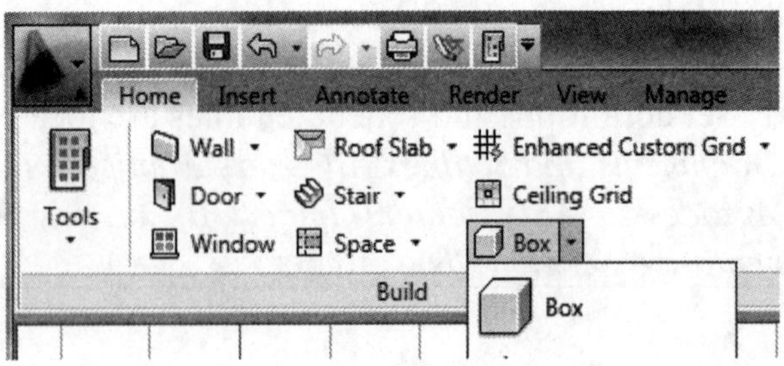

   All the massing tools are available on the **Home** ribbon in the Build section.

4. 

Select the **Arch** tool from the Massing drop down list.

5. 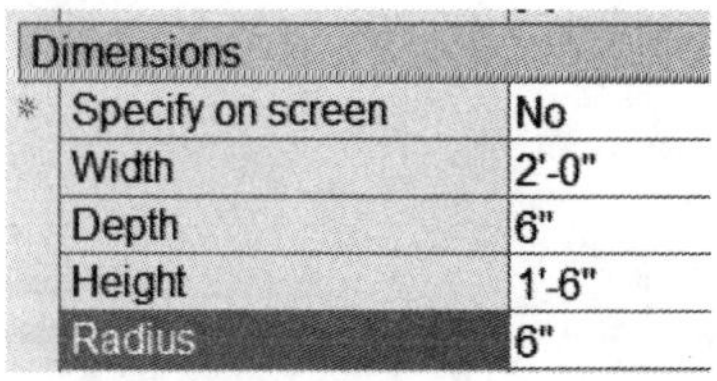

Expand the **Dimensions** section on the Properties dialog.

Set Specify on screen to **No.**
Set the Width to **2′** [**600**].
Set the Depth to **6″** [**200**].
Set the Height to **1′ 6″** [**500**].
Set the Radius to **6″** [**200**].

6. 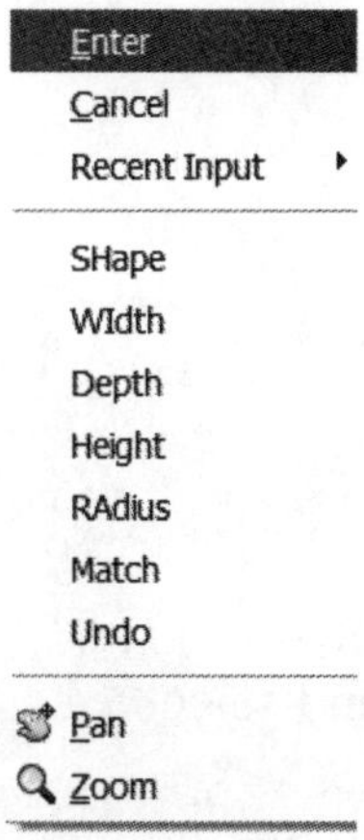

Pick a point anywhere in the drawing area.

Press ENTER to accept a Rotation Angle of 0 or right click and select **ENTER.**

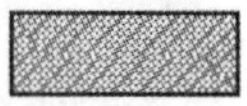

Press **ENTER** to exit the command.

7. 
Switch to an isometric view.

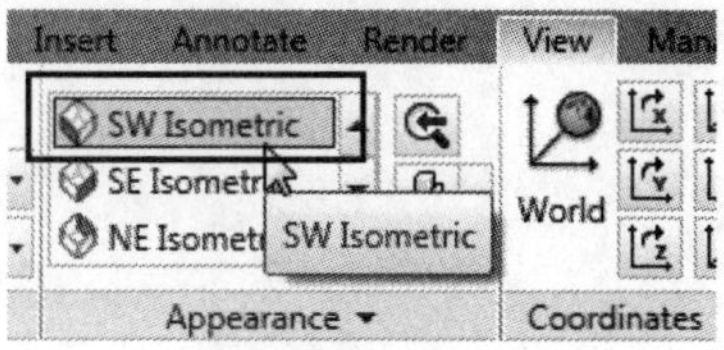

To switch to an isometric view, simply go to **View** Ribbon. Under the Views list, select **SW Isometric**.

Our model so far.

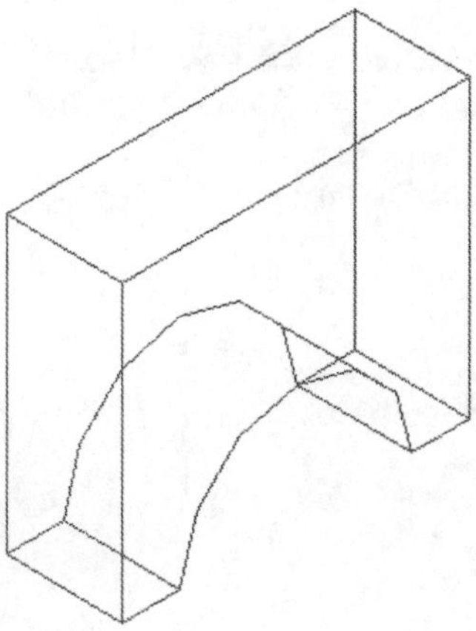

8. 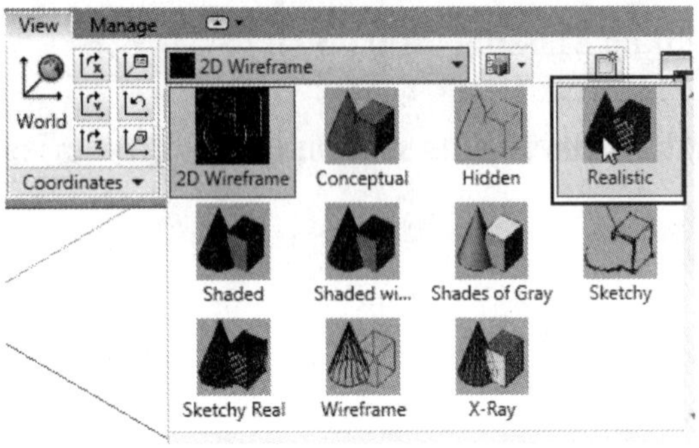

Select **Realistic** on the View ribbon under Face Effects to shade the model.

You can also type **SHA** on the command line, then **R** for Realistic.

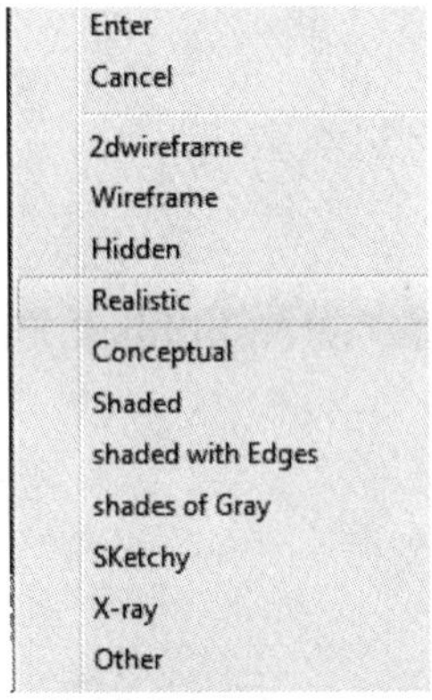

9. To change the arch properties, select the arch so that it is highlighted. If the properties dialog doesn't pop up automatically, right click and select **Properties**.

10. 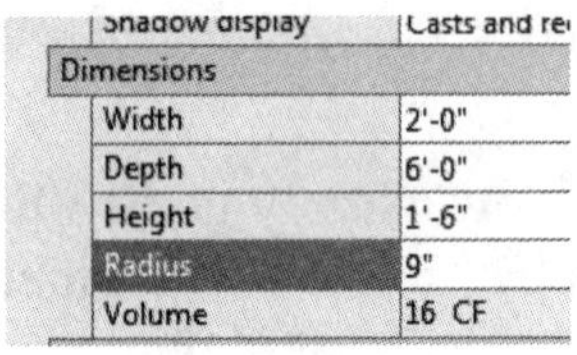

Change the Radius to **9″** [**250**].

Pick into the graphics window and the arch will update.

11. Press **ESC** to release the grips on the arc.

12. Save the drawing as *ex1-3.dwg*.

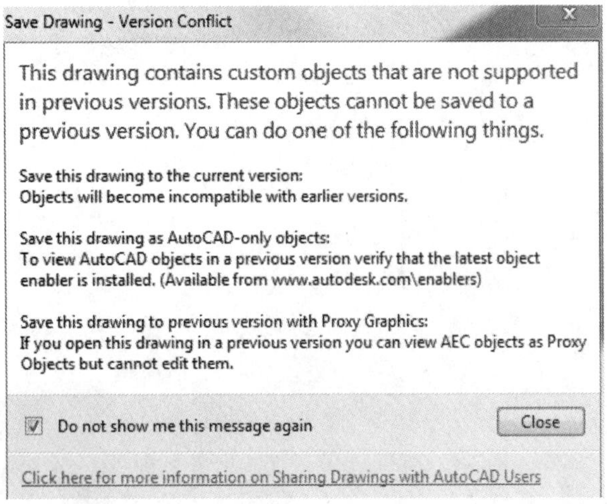

If you see this dialog, you can just ignore it and close it.

Exercise 1-4:

Creating a New Visual Style

Drawing Name: ex1-3.dwg
Estimated Time: 15 minutes

This exercise reinforces the following skills:d

- Workspaces
- Use of Visual Styles
- Controlling the Display of Objects

1. Open *ex1-3.dwg*.

2. 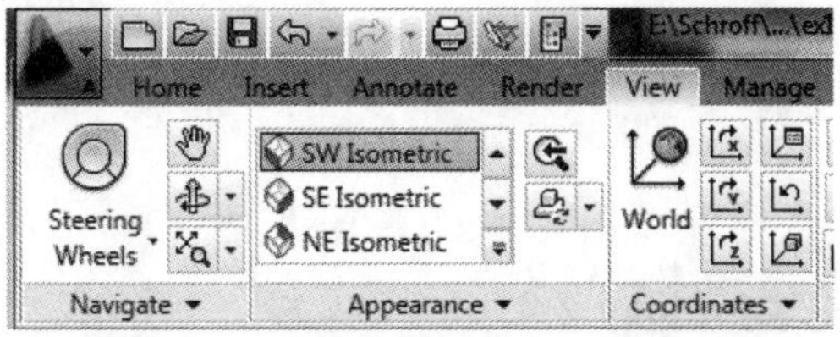

Activate the **View** ribbon.

3. 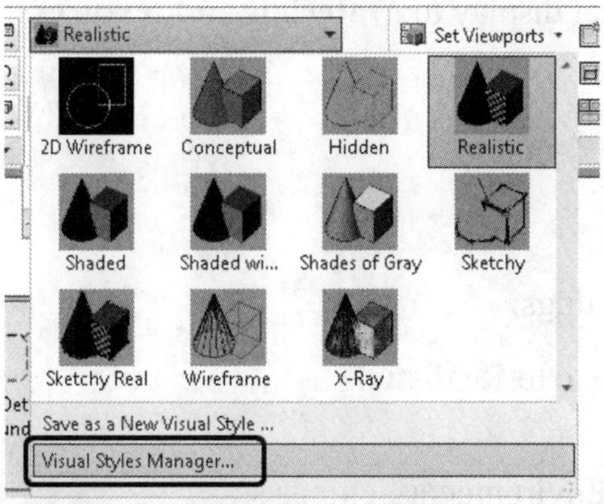

Launch the Visual Styles Manager.

To launch, select the drop-down next to the Visual Styles tool, then select **Visual Styles Manager**.

4. 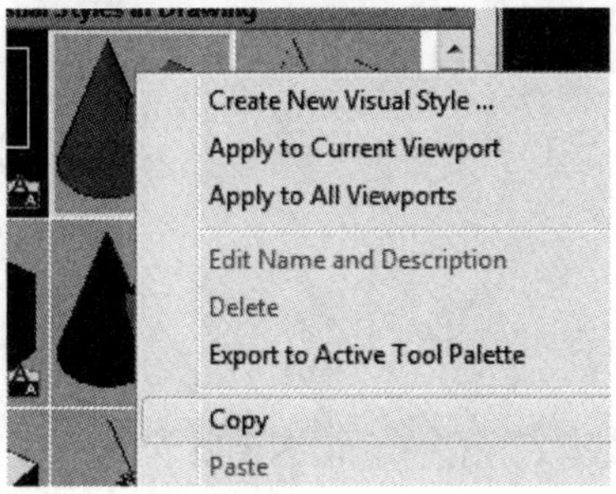

Highlight the **Conceptual** tool.

Right click and select **Copy**.

5. 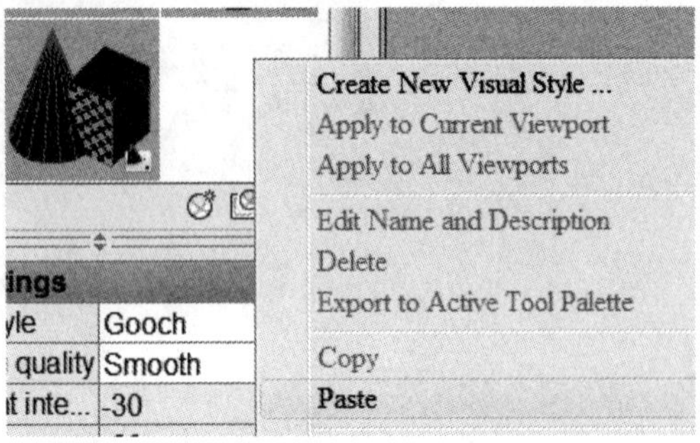

Right click and select **Paste**.

6. 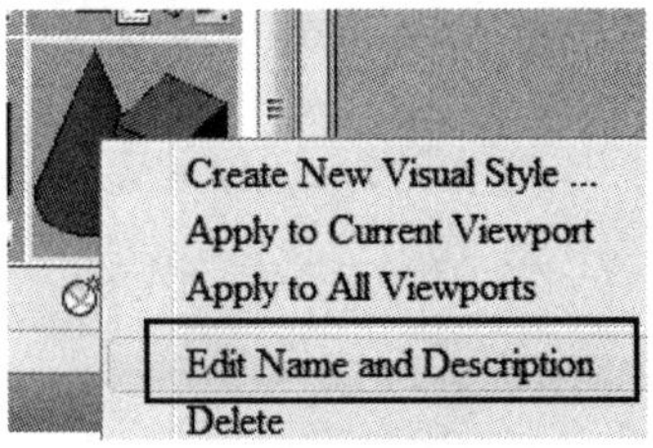

Highlight the copied tool.
Right click and select **Edit Name and Description**.

7. 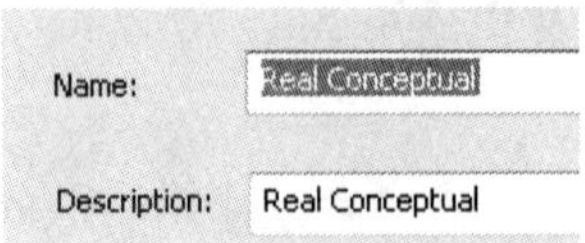

Change the name and description to **Real Conceptual**.

Press **OK**.

8. 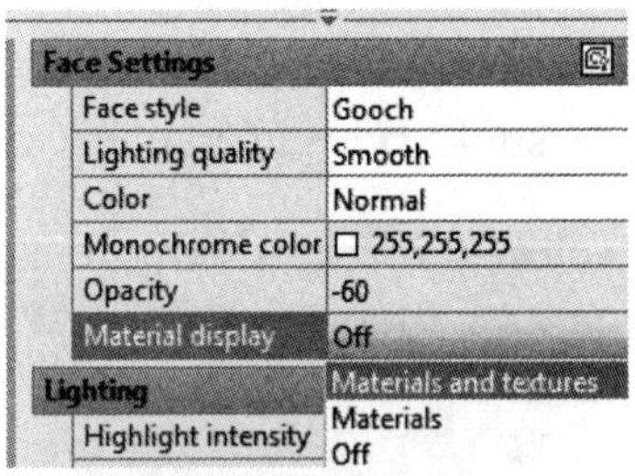

Under Face Settings:
Set Material display to **Materials and textures**.

9. 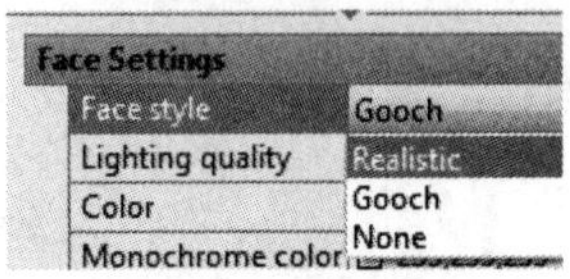

Under Face Settings:

Set the Face Style to **Realistic**.

10. 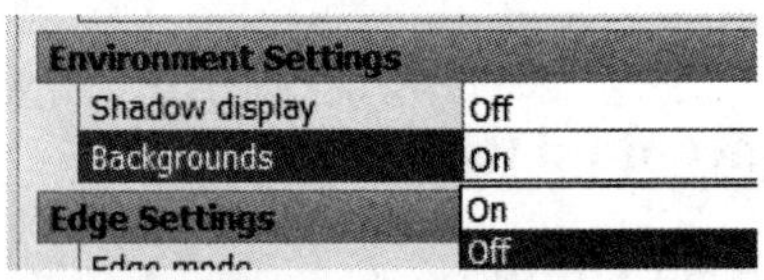

Under Environment Settings:

Set the Backgrounds to **Off**.

11. 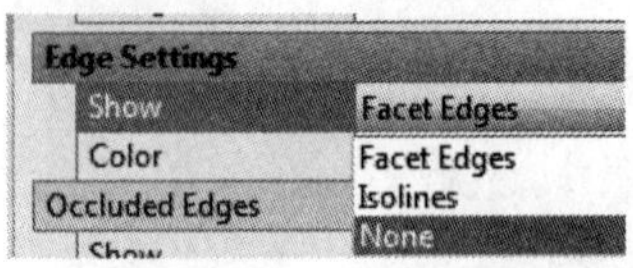

Under Edge Settings:

Set the Show to **None**.

12. 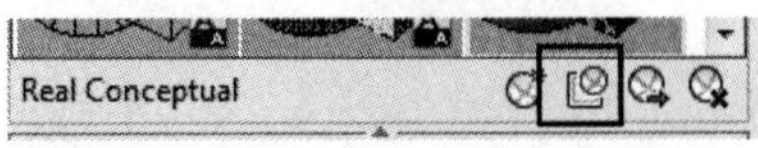

Verify that the Real Conceptual Style is highlighted/ selected.

Select the **Apply Visual Style to Current Viewport** tool.

13. Save the drawing as *ex1-4.dwg*.

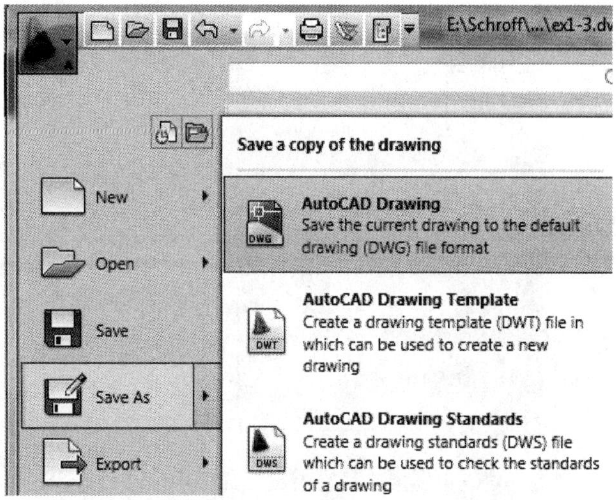

Exercise 1-5:

Creating a New Wall Style

Drawing Name: New using Imperial [Metric] (ctb).dwt
Estimated Time: 30 minutes

This exercise reinforces the following skills:

- Use of AEC Design Content
- Use of Wall Styles
- Workspaces

1.  Select the **QNEW** tool from the Standard toolbar.

2. 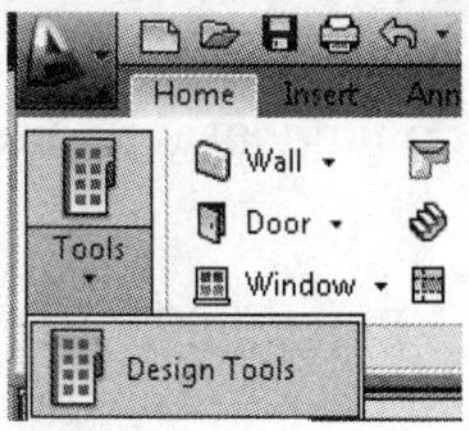

Activate the **Home** ribbon.

Select **Tools→Design Tools** from the drop down.

3. 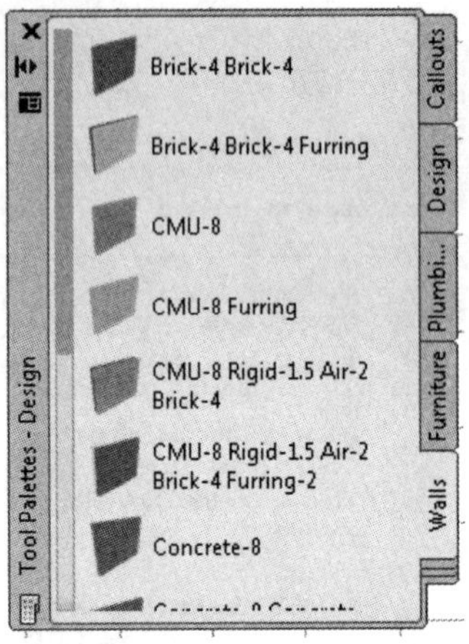

Select the **Walls** tab of the palette.

4. 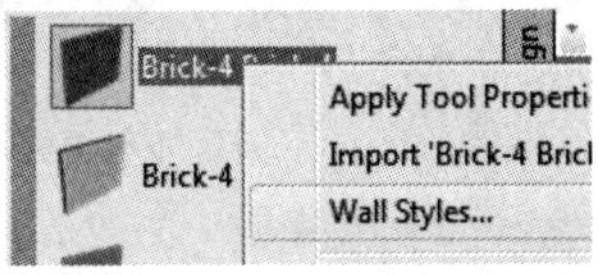

Highlight the first wall icon.

Right click and select **Wall Styles**.

5. The Style Manager is displayed, with the current drawing expanded in the tree view. The wall styles in the current drawing are displayed under the wall style type. All other style and definition types are filtered out in the tree view.

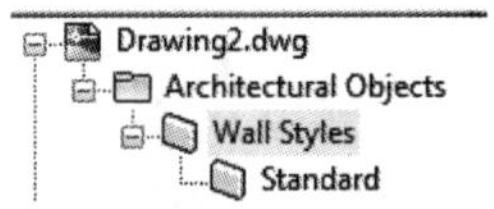

6. 

Select the **New Style** tool.

7. Change the name of the new style by typing **Brick_Block**.

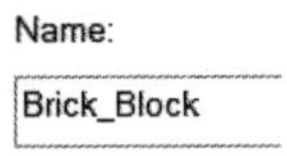

8. In the General tab, type in the description **8″ CMU and 3-1/2″ [200 mm CMU and 90 mm] Brick Wall** in the Description field as shown.

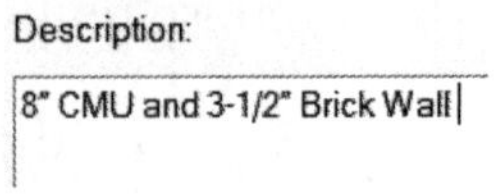

9. Select the Components tab.
Change the Name to **CMU** by typing in the Name field indicated.

Press the dropdown arrow next to the Edge Offset Button.
Set the Edge Offset to 0.

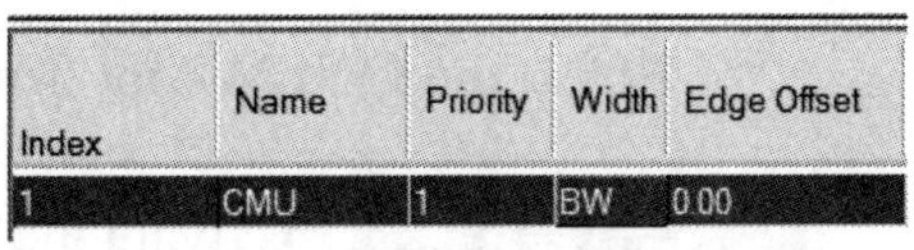

10. A 0 edge offset specifies that the outside edge of the CMU is coincident with the wall baseline.

11. 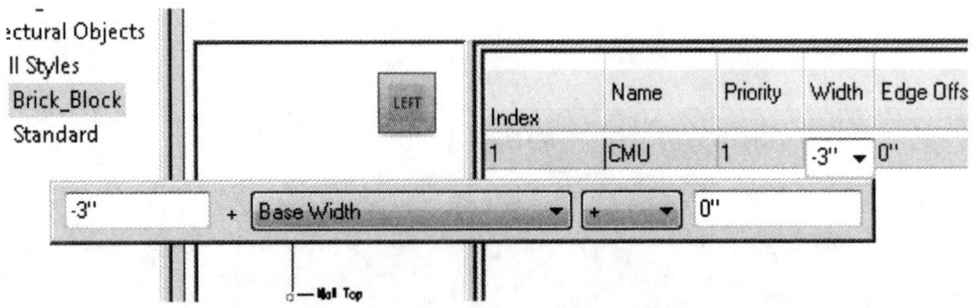

Press the **Width** down arrow button.

Set the value to **-3″ [-80]**.

This specifies that the CMU has a fixed width of 3 inches [80 mm] in the negative direction from the wall baseline (to the inside).

You now have one component defined for your wall named CMU with the properties shown.

12.  Press the **Add** Component button on the right side of the dialog box. Next, we'll add wall insulation.

13. In the Name field, type **Insulation**.

    Set the Priority to 1. (The lower the priority number, the higher the priority when creating intersections.)

    Set the Edge Offset with a value of **0**.

    Set the Component Width as shown, with a value of **1.5″** [**38**] and the Base Width set to 0.

    This specifies that the insulation has a fixed width of 1.5″ [38 mm] offset in a positive direction from the wall baseline (to the outside).

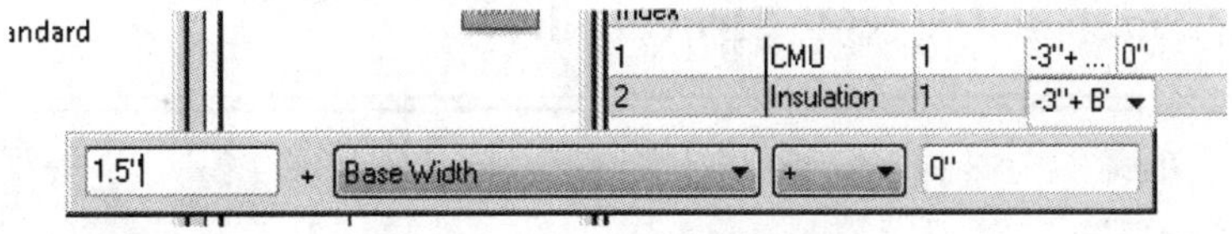

14. 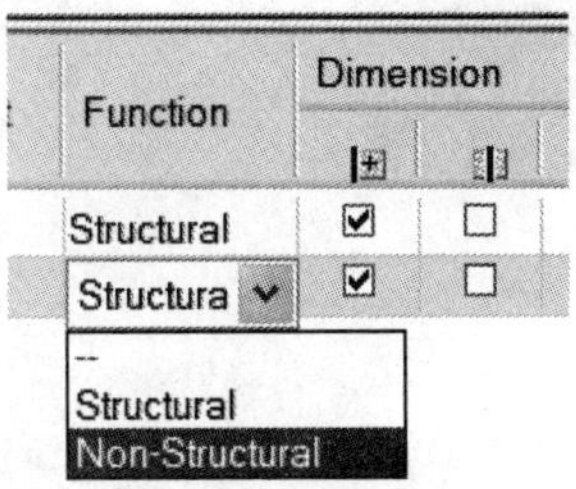

Set the Function to **Non-Structural**.

15. 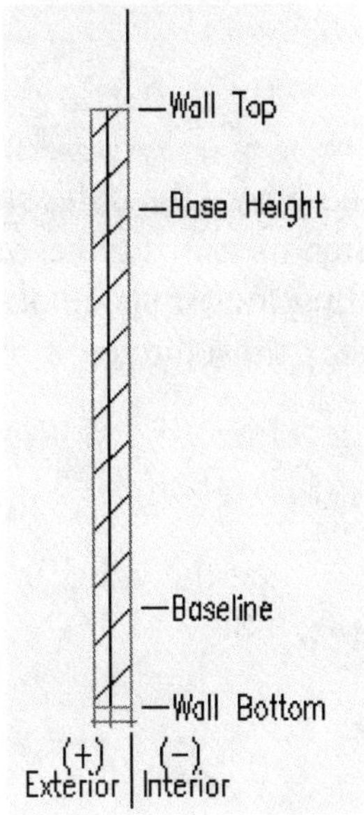

Note that the preview changes to show the insulation component.

16. Now, we add an air space component to our wall. Press the **Add Component** button.

17. Rename the new component **Air Space**. Set the Edge Offset to **0**.

    This specifies that the inside edge of the air space is coincident with the outside edge of the insulation.

Index	Name	Priority	Width	Edge Offset	Function
1	CMU	1	3"	0"	Structural
2	INSULATI...	1	1 1/2"	0"	Non-Struct...
3	AIR SPACE	1	1"	0"	Non-Struct...

    The width should be set to 1″ [25.4].

    This specifies that the air gap will have a fixed width of 1 inch [25.4 mm] offset in the positive direction from the wall baseline (to the outside).

18. Use the **Add Component** tool to add the fourth component.

    The Name should be **Brick**.
    The Priority set to **1**.
    The Edge Offset set to **2.5″** [**63.5**].
    The Width set to **3.5″** [**90**].

    The Function should be set to **Structural**.

Index	Name	Priority	Width	Edge Offset	Function	Dimension	
1	CMU	1	-3"+ BW	0"	Structural	☑	☐
2	Insulation	1	1 1/2"+ BW	0"	Non-Struct...	☑	☐
3	Air Space	1	1"+ BW	0"	Non-Struct...	☑	☐
4	Brick	1	3 1/2"+ BW	2 1/2"	Structural	☑	☐

Index	Name	Priority	Width	Edge Offset	Function
1	CMU	1	-80.0...	0.00	Structural
2	INSULATION	1	38.00...	0.00	Non-Structural
3	AIR SPACE	1	25.40...	0.00	Non-Structural
4	BRICK	1	90.00...	63.50	Structural

19.

Dimension		
☑	☐	☑
☐	☐	☐
☐	☐	☐
☑	☐	☑

The Dimension section allows you to define where the extension lines for your dimension will be placed when measuring the wall. In this case, we are not interested in including the air space or insulation in our linear dimensions. Uncheck those boxes.

20. 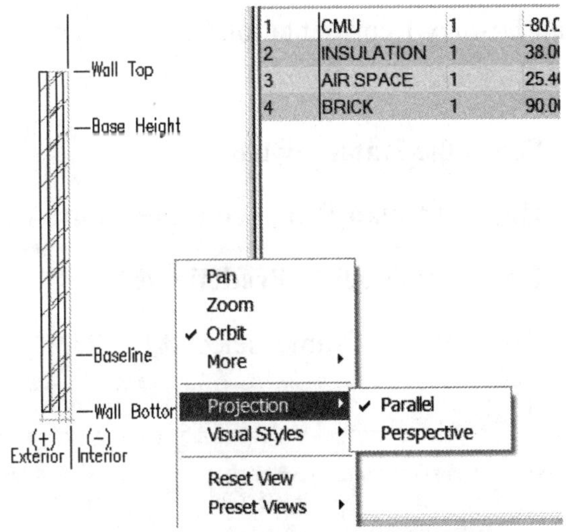

Note how your wall style previews.

If you right click in the preview pane, you can change the preview window by zooming, panning, or assigning a Preset View.

The preview pane uses a DWF-style interface.

21. Select the **Materials** tab.

Highlight the **CMU** component.

 Select the **Add New Material** tool.

22. 

Enter **CMU** in the New Name field and press **OK**.

23. Use the **Add New Material** tool to assign new materials to each component.

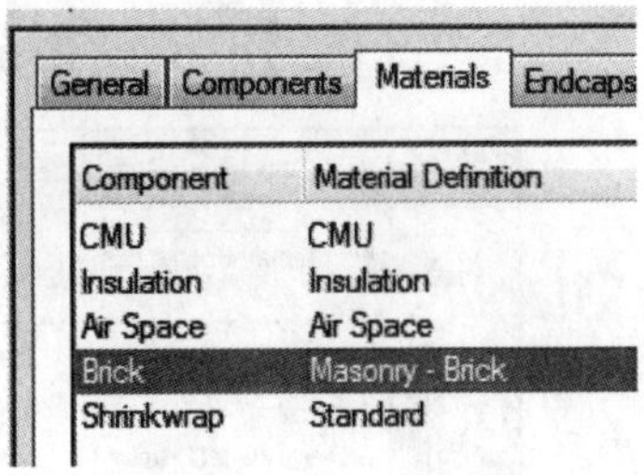

24. Highlight the **CMU** Component.

 Select the **Edit Material** tool.

25. Select the **Display Properties** tab.

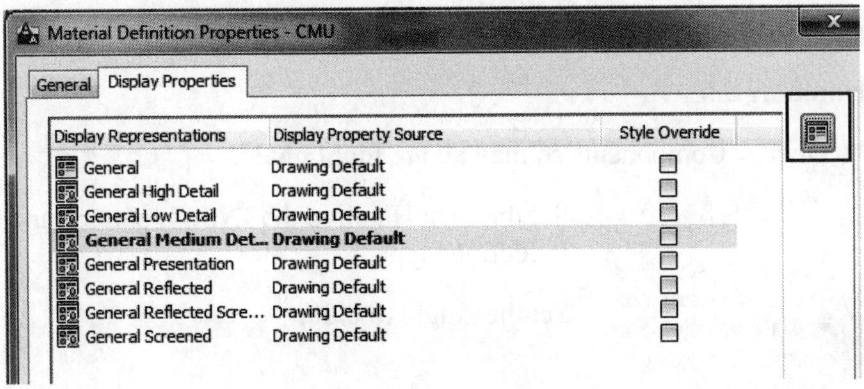

Highlight the **General Medium Detail** Display Representation.

Click on the **Style Override** button.

26. 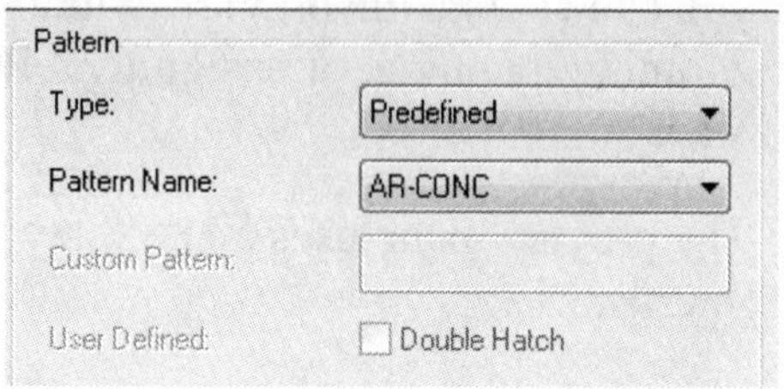

Select the **Hatching** tab.

Highlight **Plan Hatch** and select **Pattern**.

Under Type, select **Predefined**.

Under Pattern Name, select **AR-CONC**.

27. Assign the **AR-B88** Pattern to all the Display Components.

Set the Angles to **0**.

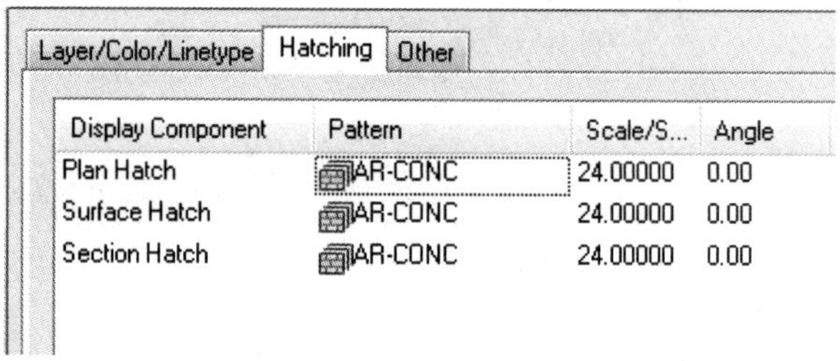

28. Press **OK** twice to return to the Materials tab of the Wall Properties dialog.

29.  Highlight **Insulation** and select the **Edit Material** tool.

30.

Select the **Display Properties** tab.

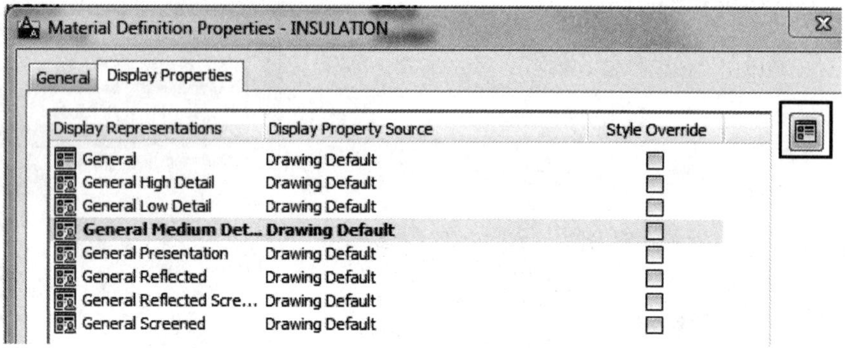

Highlight the **General Medium Detail** Display Property

Click on the **Style Override** button.

31. Select the **Hatching** tab.

Select all the Display Components so they all are highlighted.

32. 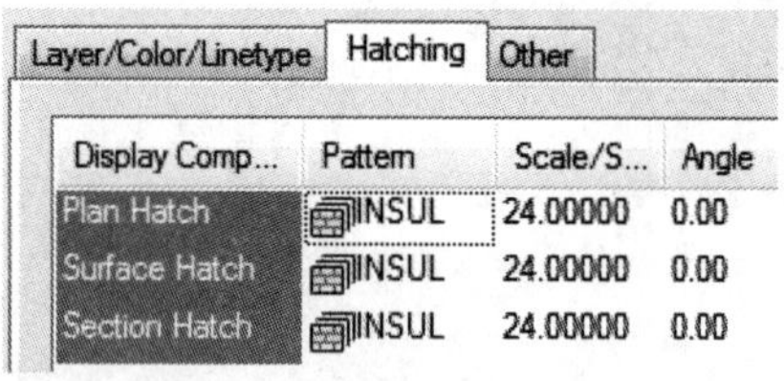

Set the Plan Hatch to the **INSUL** pattern under Predefined type.

Set the Angle to **0.00**.

33. 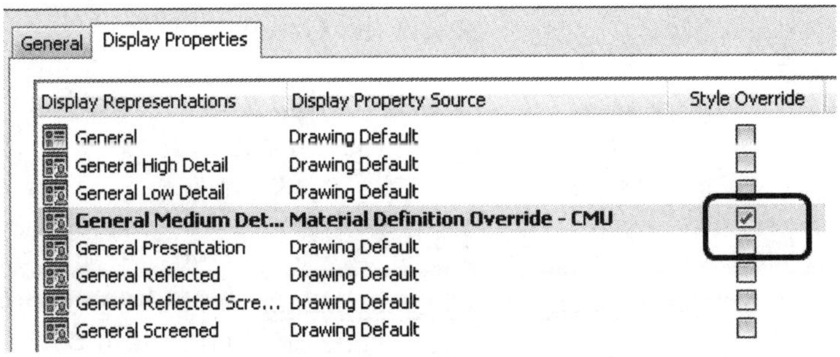

Verify that a check is placed in the Style Override button.

34. Press **OK** twice to return to the previous dialog.

35.  Highlight **Brick** and select the **Edit Material** tool.

36. 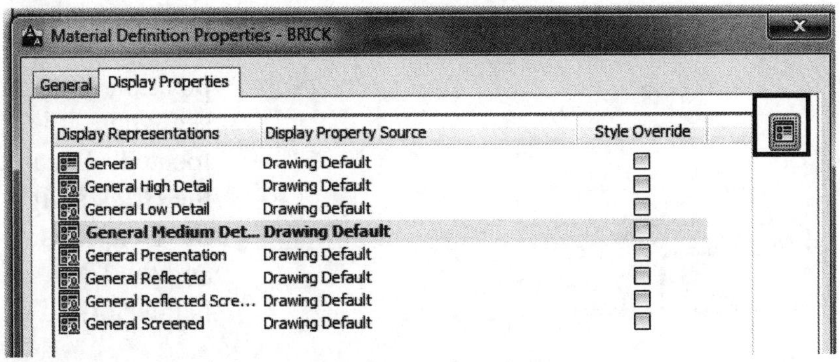

Select the **Display Properties** tab.

Highlight the **General Medium Detail** Display Representation.

Click on the **Style Override** button.

37. 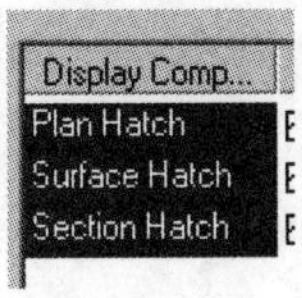

Select the **Hatching** tab.

Highlight the three display components.

Select the first pattern.

38. Set the Type to **Predefined**.

39. Select the **Browse** button.

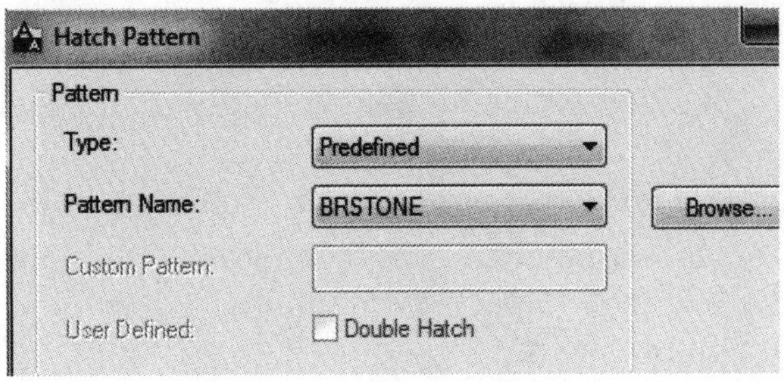

40. 

Select the **BRSTONE** pattern.

41. 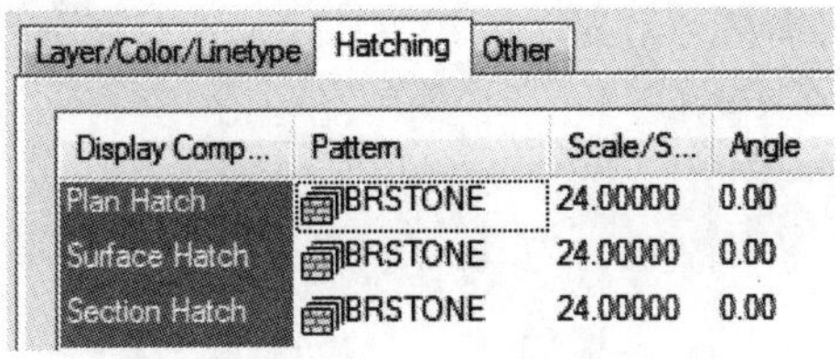

Set the Angle to 0 for all hatches.

Press **OK** twice.

42. 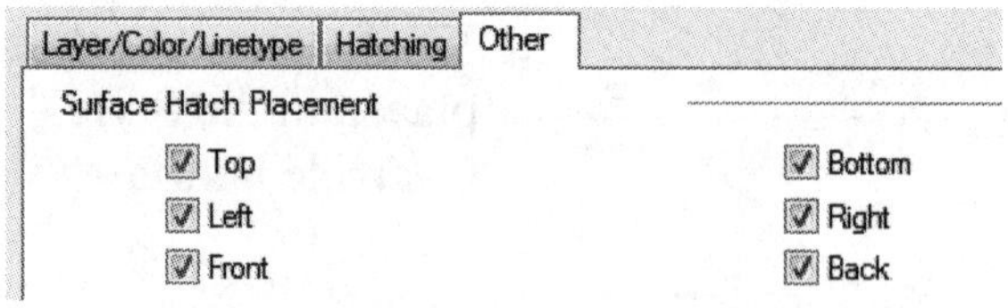

Select the **Other** tab.

Enable the top view for the Surface Hatch Placement.

43. 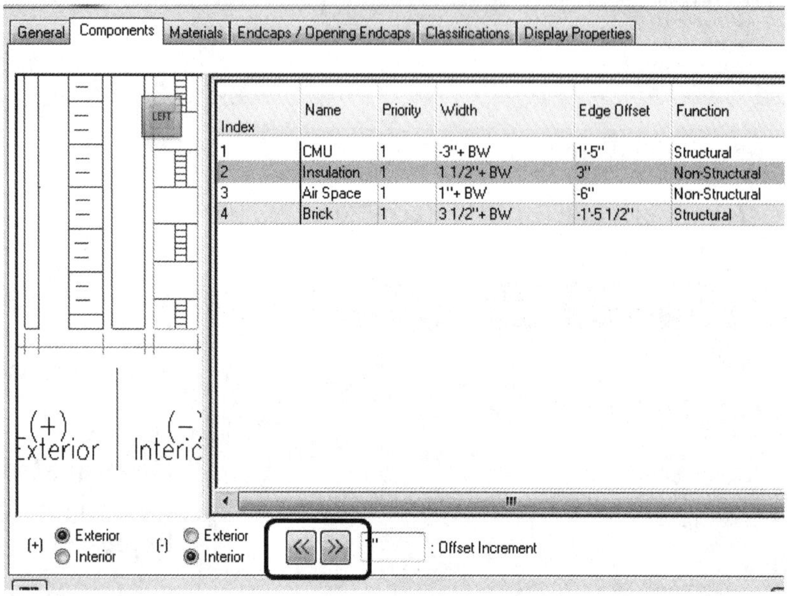

Activate the Components tab. Highlight each component and use the << >> arrows to position the component. By shifting each component position, you can see where it is located. Located the Brick so it is on the Exterior side and the CMU so it is interior.

44. 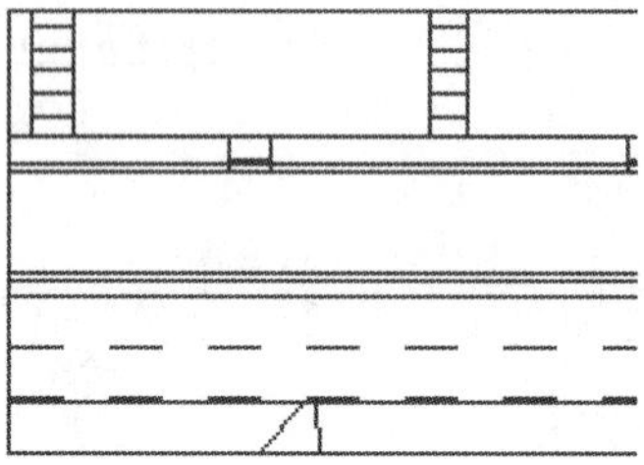

Close the Style Manager.

Press **OK** to exit the Edit dialog.
You can preview how the changes you made to the material display will appear when you create your wall.

45. Save as *ex1-5.dwg.*

Exercise 1-6:

Creating a Tool

Drawing Name: ex1-5.dwg
Estimated Time: 30 minutes

This exercise reinforces the following skills:

- Use of AEC Design Content
- Use of Wall Styles

1. Open or continue working in ***ex1-5.dwg***.

2. 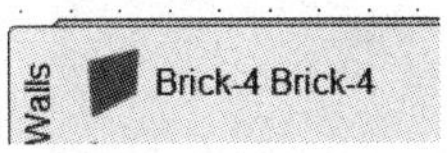

Verify that the tool palette is open with the Walls palette active.

3. 

Activate the **Manage** ribbon.

   Select the **Style Manager** tool.

4. 

Locate the Brick-Block wall style you created.

5. 

Drag and drop the wall style onto your Walls palette.

   Press **OK** to close the Style Manager.

6. 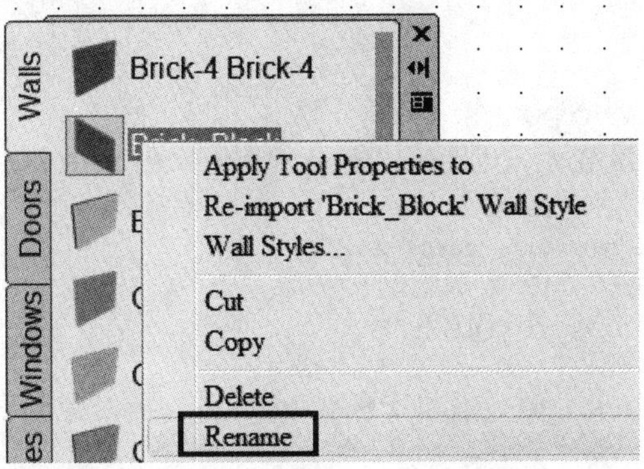

Highlight the Brick_Block tool.
Right click and select **Rename**.

7. 

Change the name to **8″ CMU- 3.5″ Brick [200 mm CMU – 90 mm]**.

8. 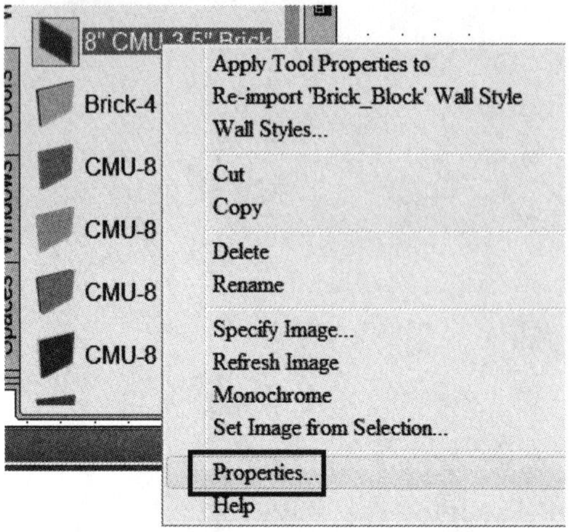

Highlight **8″ CMU- 3.5″ Brick** tool.

Right click and select **Properties**.

9. 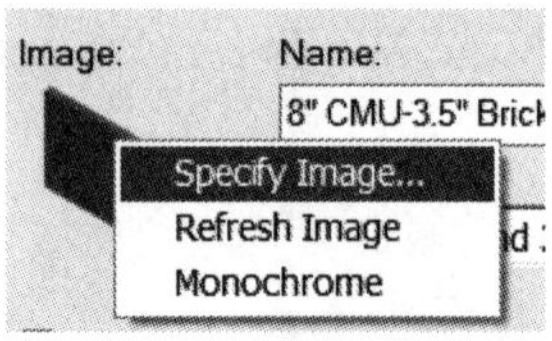

Highlight the image icon in the dialog.
Right click and select **Specify Image**.

10. Locate the file called **aecwall-CMU-8-Rigid-1.5 Air Brick-4.png**.

Press **Open**.

11. 

The image is reset.

Press **OK**.

12. Select the new tool and draw a wall.
You may draw a wall simply by picking two points.
If you enable the ORTHO button on the bottom of the screen, your wall will be straight.

13. 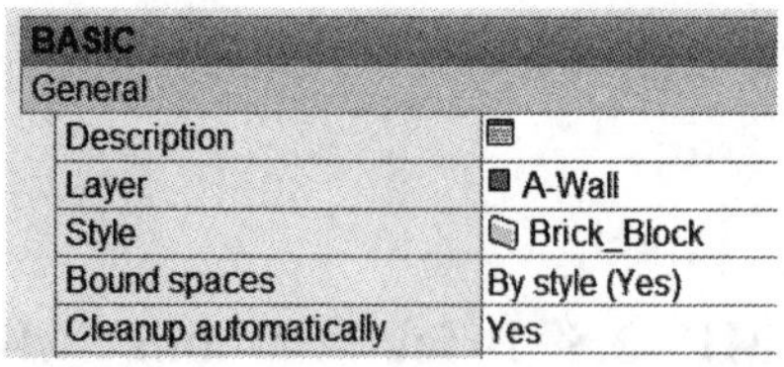

Select the wall you drew.

Right click and select **Properties**.

Note that the wall is placed on the A-Wall Layer and uses the Brick-Block Style you defined.

14. Save your file as ***Styles.dwg***.

TIP: The wall style you created will not be available in any new drawings unless you copy it over to the default template.

Exercise 1-7:

Copying a Style to a Template

Drawing Name: Styles1.dwg, Imperial (Metric).ctb.dwt
Estimated Time: 20 minutes

This exercise reinforces the following skills:

- Style Manager
- Use of Templates
- Properties dialog

1. 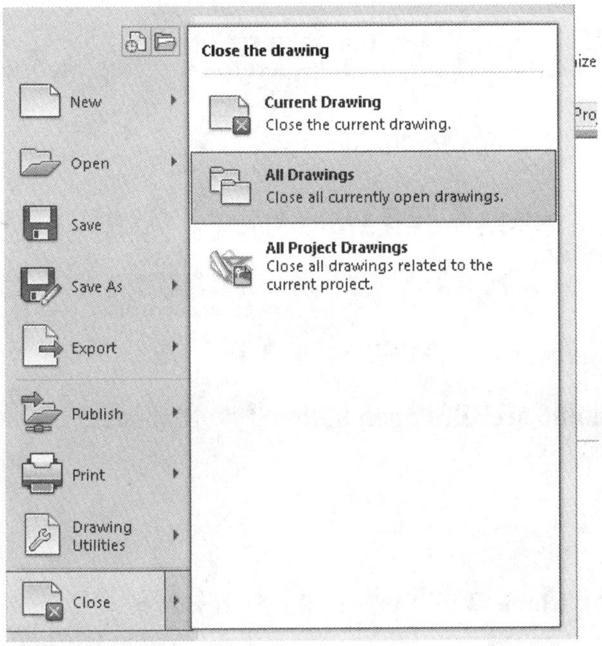

Close any open drawings.

2. 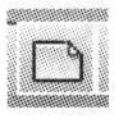

Open a New Drawing.

3. 

Activate the **Manage** ribbon.

Select the **Style Manager** tool.

4. 

Select the **File Open** tool.

5. 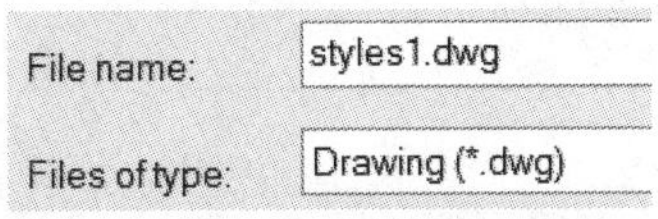

Locate the *styles.dwg* you created.
Select **Open**.

Note: Make sure the Files of type is set to dwg or you will not see your files.

6. 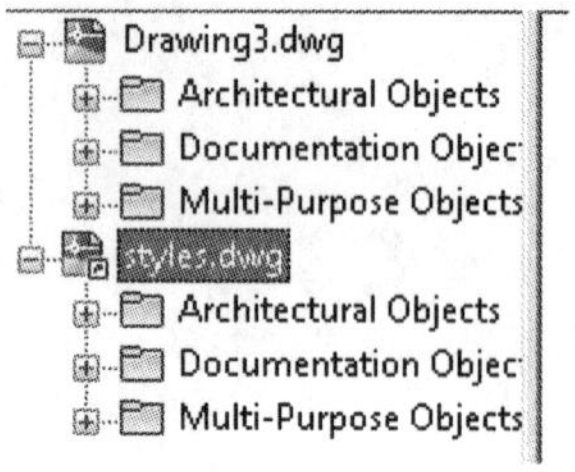

Styles is now listed in the Style Manager.

7. 

Select the **File Open** tool.

8. 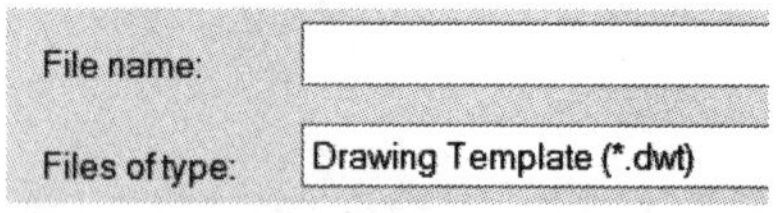

Set the Files of type to ***Drawing Template (*.dwt)***.

9. 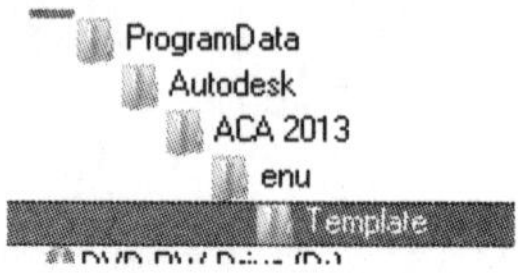

You should automatically be directed to the Template folder.

Browse to the *Template* folder.

10. 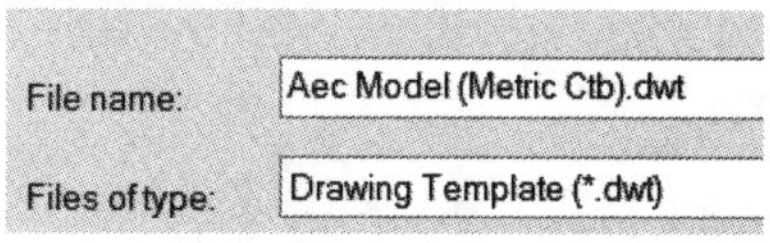

Locate the *AEC Model Imperial (Metric) Ctb.dwt* file.
Press **Open**.

This is the default template we selected for QNEW.

11. 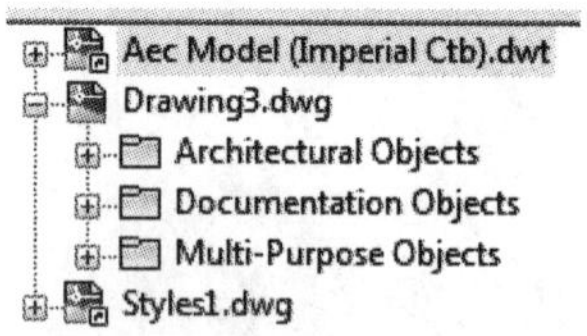

You should see files open in the Style Manager.

12. 

Locate the **Brick_Block** Wall Style in the *Styles.dwg*.

13. 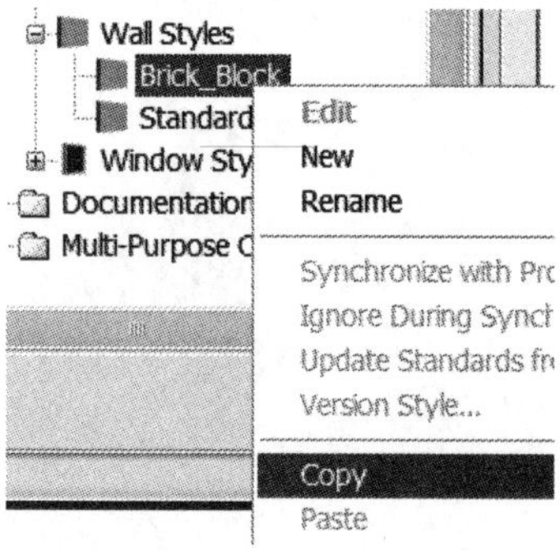

Right click and select **Copy**.

14. 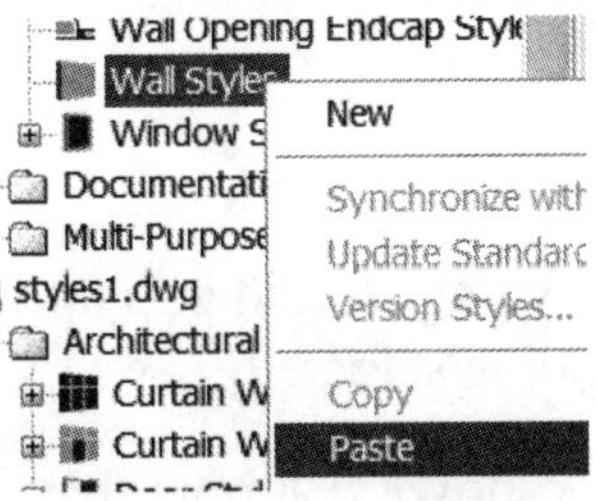

Locate Wall Styles under the template drawing.

Highlight, right click and select **Paste**.

15. 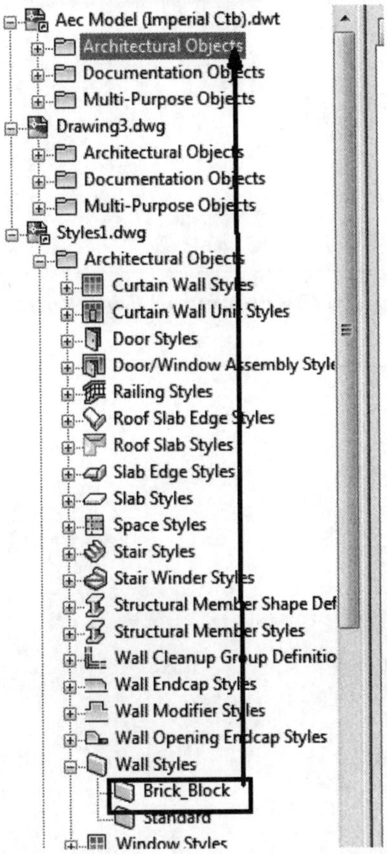

You could also just drag and drop the Brick_block style from the Styles file to the template.

16. 

Press **Apply**.

17. 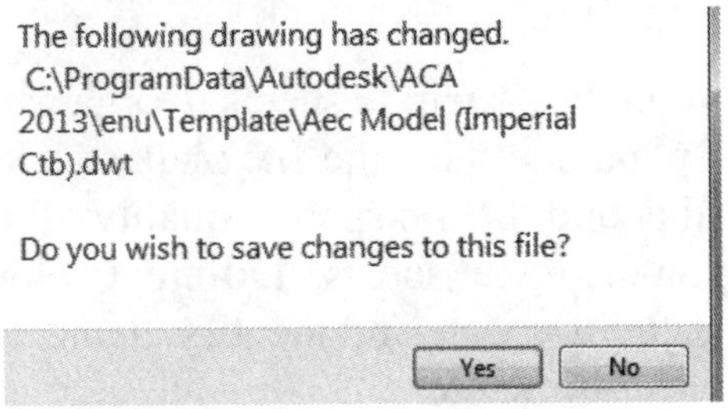

Press **Yes**.

18. Close the Style Manager.

19. 

If you go to Windows and look to see what drawings are open, you won't see Styles.dwg or the template drawing listed. These are only open in the Style Manager.

20. 

Select the **QNEW** tool.

21. 

Activate the Home ribbon.
Select the **Wall** tool.

22. 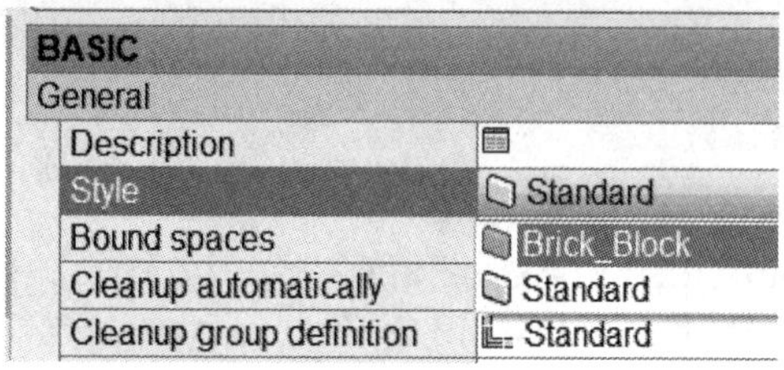

The Properties dialog should pop up when the WallAdd tool is selected.

In the Style drop-down list, note that Brick_Block is available.

23. Escape to end the WallAdd command.

24. Close all drawing files without saving.

A fast way to close all open files is to type CLOSEALL on the command line. You will be prompted to save any unsaved files.

Layer Manager

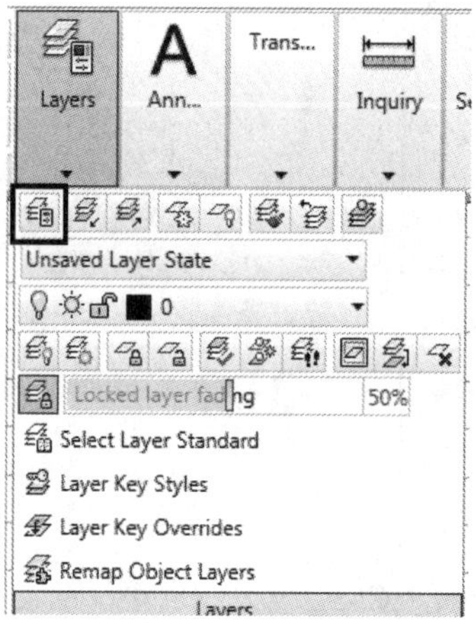

Back in the days of vellum and pencil, drafters would use separate sheets to organize their drawings, so one sheet might have the floor plan, one sheet the site plan, etc. The layers of paper would be placed on top of each other and the transparent quality of the vellum would allow the drafter to see the details on the lower sheets. Different colored pencils would be used to make it easier for the drafter to locate and identify elements of a drawing, such as dimensions, electrical outlets, water lines, etc.

When drafting moved to Computer Aided Design, the concept of sheets was transferred to the use of Layers. Drafters could assign a Layer Name, color, linetype, etc. and then place different elements on the appropriate layer.

AutoCAD Architecture has a Layer Management system to allow the user to implement AIA standards easily.

Layer Manager

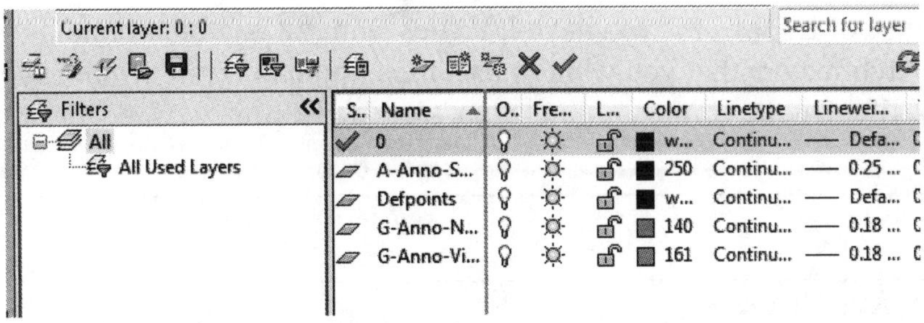

The Layer Manager helps you organize, sort, and group layers, as well as save and coordinate layering schemes. You can also use layering standards with the Layer Manager to better organize the layers in your drawings.

When you open the Layer Manager, all the layers in the current drawing are displayed in the right panel. You can work with individual layers to:

- Change layer properties by selecting the property icons
- Make a layer the current layer
- Create, rename, and delete layers

If you are working with drawings that contain large numbers of layers, you can improve the speed at which the Layer Manager loads layers when you open it by selecting the Layer Manager/Optimize for Speed option in your AEC Editor options.

The Layer Manager has a tool bar as shown.

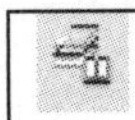	*Layer Standards* You can import Layer Standards from an existing drawing or Export Layer Standards using the current drawing. 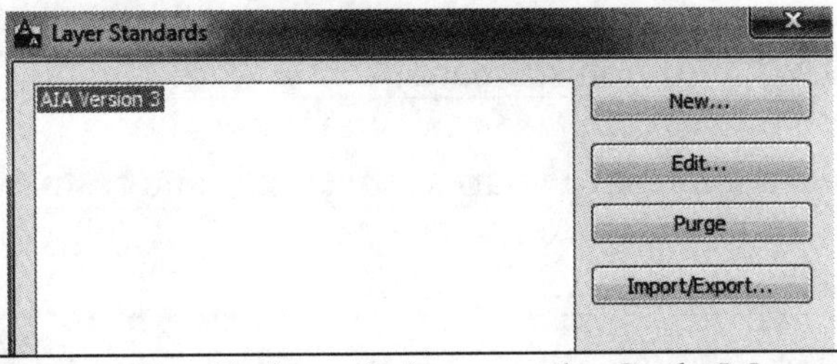
	*Layer Key Styles* – Brings up the Style Manager. A layer key is a map between the AEC object that you draw on screen and a defined layer. When you create an object, the layer key that is associated with the object automatically places that object on the layer to which the layer key is mapped. Using layer keys to automatically place objects on predefined layers is called *layer keying*.

TIP: The layer key styles in Autodesk AutoCAD Architecture, Release 3 and above replace the use of LY files. If you have LY files from S8 or Release 1 of AutoCAD AutoCAD Architecture that you want to use, then you can create a new layer key style from an LY file. On the command line enter **-AecLYImport** to import legacy LY files.

	Layer Key Overrides You can apply overrides to any layer keys within a layer key style that is based on a layer standard. The structure of the layer name of each layer that each layer key maps an object to is determined by the descriptive fields in the layer standard definition. You can override the information in each field according to the values set in the layer standard definition. You can allow overrides on all the layer keys within a layer key style, or you can select individual layer keys that you want to override. You can also choose to allow all of the descriptive fields that make up the layer name to be overridden, or you can specify which descriptive fields you want to override.
	Load Filter Groups This tool allows you to load a saved filter group.
	Save Filter Groups This tool allows you to save a defined filter group, so that you can use it in other drawings.
	New Property Filter A Property Filter displays only layers that meet a certain criteria, such as color, color, frozen/thawed, or names. You can specify more than one type of property for a filter.
	New Group Filter A Group Filter allows you to combine a set of layers together into a group. You can then turn on and off several layers by controlling the status of the group.
	New Standards Filter A Layer Standards filter contains layers that are assigned to a particular standard. For example, you can create a layer standards filter to only show layers associated with the AIA 2nd Edition standard.
	Layer States Manager The Layer States Manager allows you save your layer settings and restore them.
	New Layer Creates a new layer.
	New Layer from Standard Creates a new layer based on an existing layer standard.

	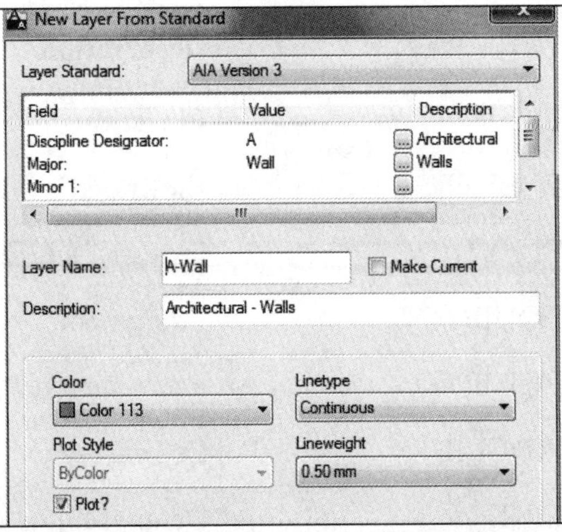
	*New Layer VP Frozen in All Viewports* Creates a new layer and automatically freezes it (makes it invisible).
	*Delete Layer* Highlight the layer(s) you wish to delete and select this tool.
	*Make selected layer current* Highlight a layer name in the list and press this button to set current.

The following are the default layer keys used by Autodesk AutoCAD Architecture when you create AEC objects.

Default layer keys for creating AEC objects			
Layer Key	**Description**	**Layer Key**	**Description**
ANNDTOBJ	Detail marks	COMMUN	Communication
ANNELKEY	Elevation Marks	CONTROL	Control systems
ANNELOBJ	Elevation objects	CWLAYOUT	Curtain walls
ANNMASK	Masking objects	CWUNIT	Curtain wall units
ANNMATCH	Match Lines	DIMLINE	Dimensions
ANNOBJ	Notes, leaders, etc.	DIMMAN	Dimensions (AutoCAD points)
ANNREV	Revisions	DOOR	Doors
ANNSXKEY	Section marks	DOORNO	Door tags
ANNSXOBJ	Section marks	DRAINAGE	Drainage
ANNSYMOBJ	Annotation marks	ELEC	Electric
APPL	Appliances	ELECNO	Electrical tags

Layer Key	Description	Layer Key	Description
AREA	Areas	ELEV	Elevations
AREAGRP	Area groups	ELEVAT	Elevators
AREAGRPNO	Area group tags	ELEVHIDE	Elevations (2D)
AREANO	Area tags	EQUIP	Equipment
CAMERA	Cameras	EQUIPNO	Equipment tags
CASE	Casework	FINCEIL	Ceiling tags
CASENO	Casework tags	FINE	Details- Fine lines
CEILGRID	Ceiling grids	FINFLOOR	Finish tags
CEILOBJ	Ceiling objects	FIRE	Fire system equip.
CHASE	Chases	FURN	Furniture
COGO	Control Points	FURNNO	Furniture tags
COLUMN	Columns	GRIDBUB	Plan grid bubbles
GRIDLINE	Column grids	SITE	Site
HATCH	Detail-Hatch lines	SLAB	Slabs
HIDDEN	Hidden Lines	SPACEBDRY	Space boundaries
LAYGRID	Layout grids	SPACENO	Space tags
LIGHTCLG	Ceiling lighting	SPACEOBJ	Space objects
LIGHTW	Wall lighting	STAIR	Stairs
MASSELEM	Massing elements	STAIRH	Stair handrails
MASSGRPS	Massing groups	STRUCTBEAM	Structural beams
MASSSLCE	Massing slices	STRUCTBEAMIDEN	Structural beam tags
MED	Medium Lines	STRUCTBRACE	Structural braces
OPENING	Wall openings	STRUCTBRACEIDEN	Structural brace tags
PEOPLE	People	STRUCTCOLS	Structural columns
PFIXT	Plumbing fixtures	STRUCTCOLSIDEN	Structural column tags
PLANTS	Plants - outdoor	SWITCH	Electrical switches
PLANTSI	Plants - indoor	TITTEXT	Border and title block

Layer Key	Description	Layer Key	Description
POLYGON	AEC Polygons	TOILACC	Arch. specialties
POWER	Electrical power	TOILNO	Toilet tags
PRCL	Property Line	UTIL	Site utilities
PRK-SYM	Parking symbols	VEHICLES	Vehicles
ROOF	Rooflines	WALL	Walls
ROOFSLAB	Roof slabs	WALLFIRE	Fire wall patterning
ROOMNO	Room tags	WALLNO	Wall tags
SCHEDOBJ	Schedule tables	WIND	Windows
SEATNO	Seating tags	WINDASSEM	Window assemblies
SECT	Miscellaneous sections	WINDNO	Window tags
SECTHIDE	Sections (2D)		

Desktop Display Manager

Exercise 1-8:

Exploring the Display Manager

Drawing Name: ex1-5.dwg
Estimated Time: 15 minutes

This exercise reinforces the following skills:

- ❑ Display Manager

1. Open *ex1-5.dwg*.

2. 

Access the **Display Manager** from the Manage ribbon.

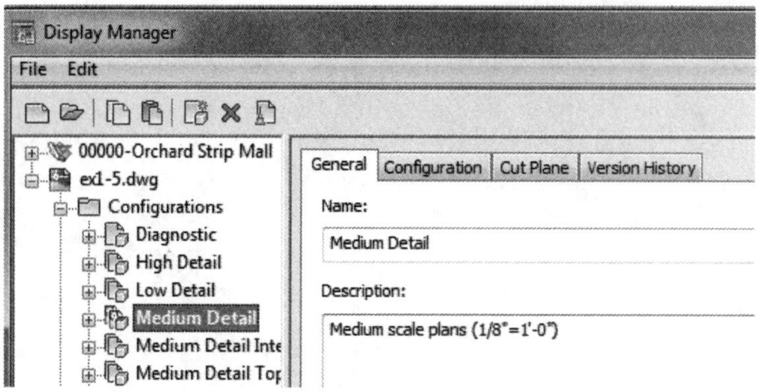

3. The display system in Autodesk® AutoCAD Architecture controls how AEC objects are displayed in a designated viewport. By specifying the AEC objects you want to display in a viewport and the direction from which you want to view them, you can produce different architectural displays, such as floor plans, reflected plans, elevations, 3D models, or schematic displays.

4. 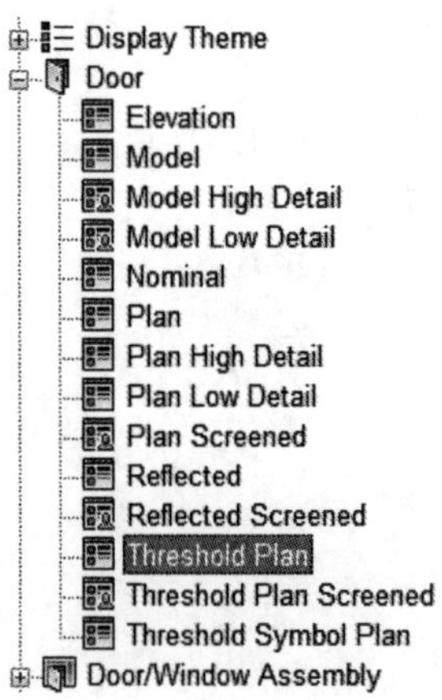

Expand the *Representations by Object* folder.

Locate Door.

You see that there are different ways a door will appear depending on the display configuration selected.

Highlight **Threshold Plan**.

5. 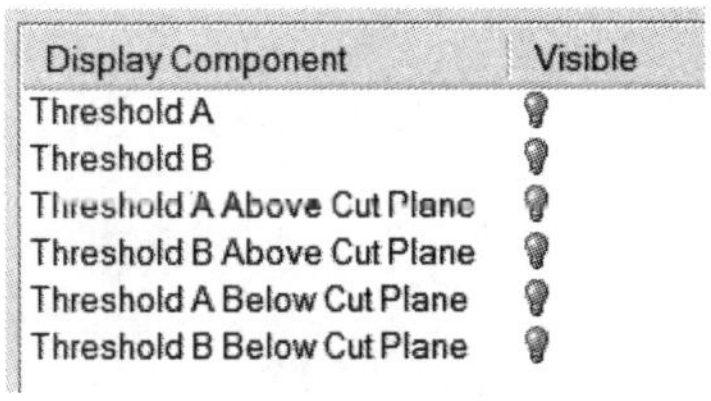

You see that the Threshold visibilities are turned off.

6. 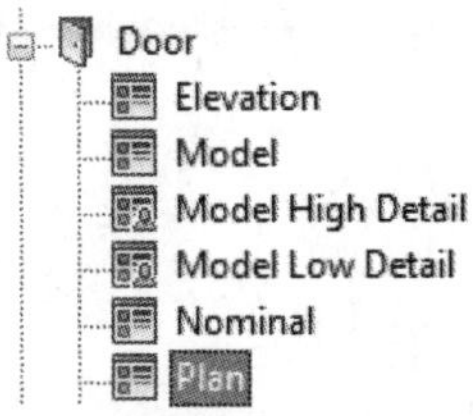

Highlight the **Plan** configuration.

7. 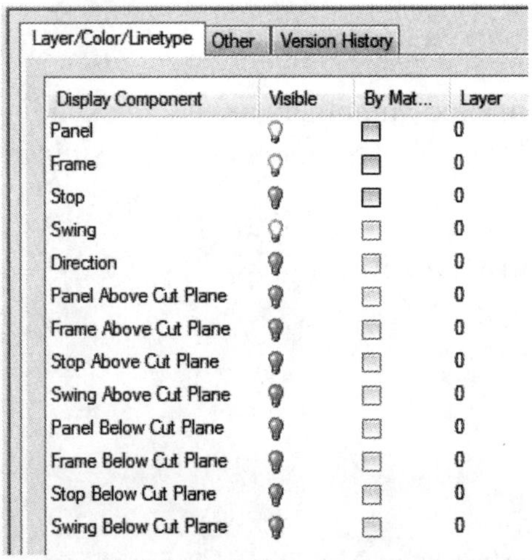

You see that some door components are turned on and others are turned off.

8. 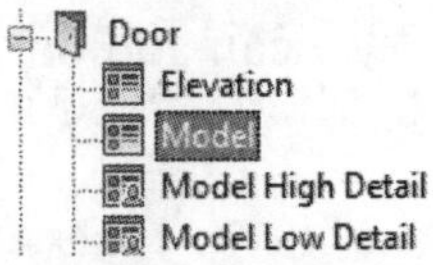

Highlight the Model configuration.

9. 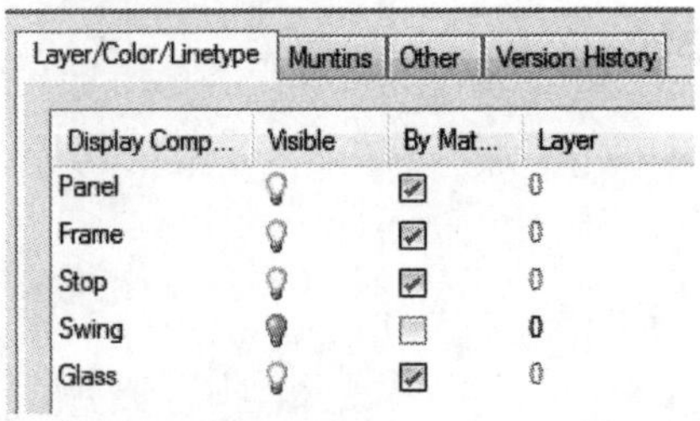

You see that some door components are turned on and others are turned off.

10. 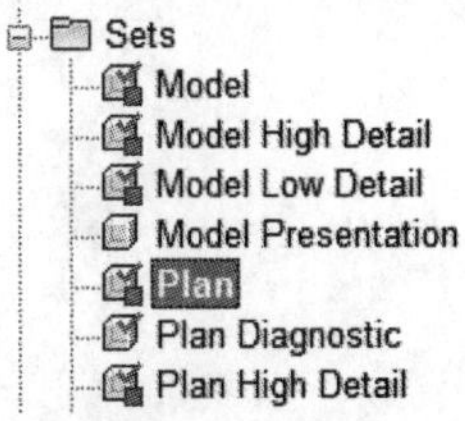

Go to the Sets folder. The Set highlighted in bold is the active Display Representation.

Highlight **Plan**.

11. 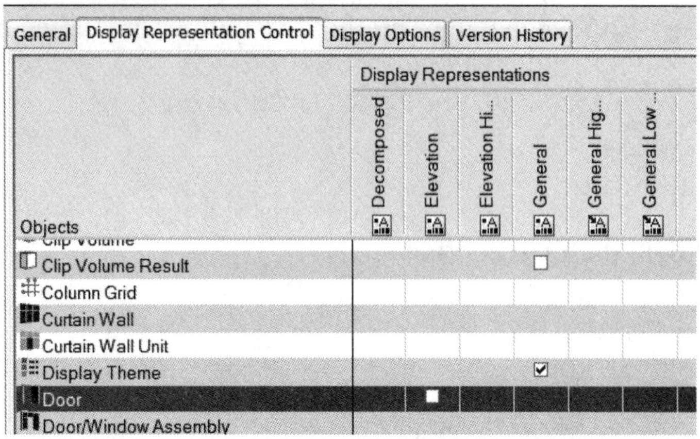

Select the Display Representation Control tab.
Locate **Door** under Objects.
Note that some display representations are checked and others are unchecked.
A check indicates that the door is visible. Which door components are visible is controlled under Representations by Object.

12. 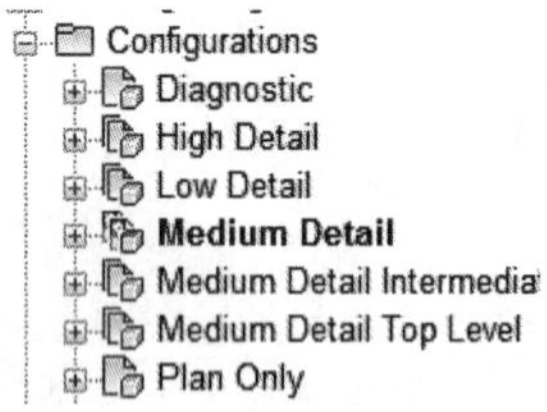

Expand the **Configurations** folder.

13. 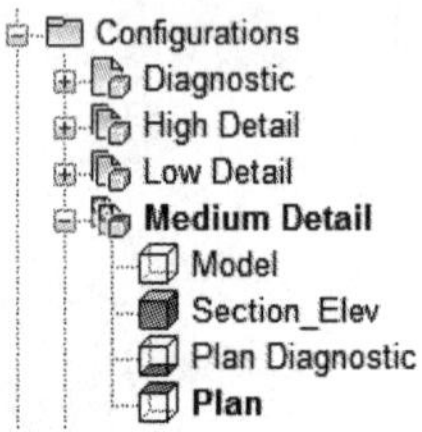

Expand Medium Detail.
You see the different display sets. Note that Medium Detail does not hold all the different display sets. You can add or remove display sets.
Close the Display Manager.

14. Close the drawing without saving.

Exercise 1-9:
Adding a Ribbon Tab

Drawing Name: new
Estimated Time: 15 minutes

This exercise reinforces the following skills:

- CUI – Custom User Interface
- Ribbon
- Panel
- Tab

1.  Start a new drawing.

2. 

Activate the **Manage** ribbon.

   Select the **User Interface** tool.

3. 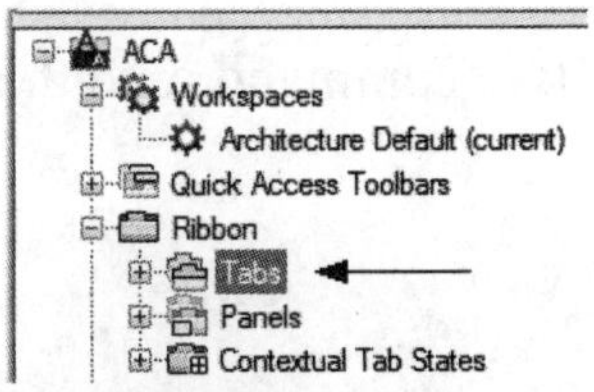

Locate the **Tabs** category under Ribbon.

4. 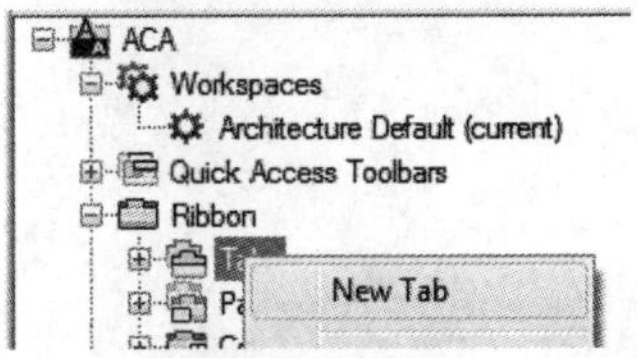

Highlight Tab.
Right click and select **New Tab**.

5. 

Rename it **Format – ACA**.

6. 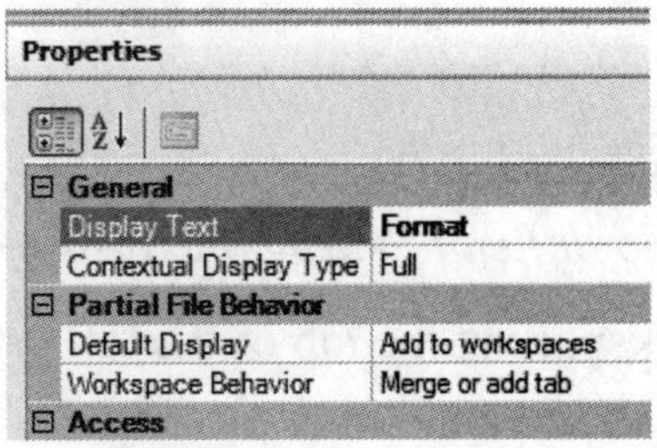

Under Properties, have the Display Text show only Format.

7. 

Highlight Panel.
Right click and select **New Panel**.

8. 

Rename the New Panel **Styles**.

9. 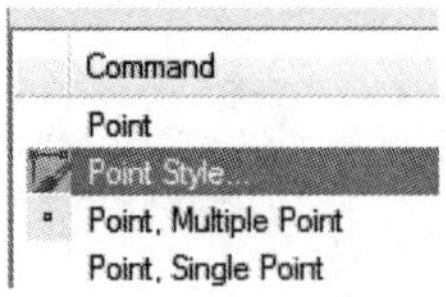

Locate the Point Style Command in the lower left pane.

10. 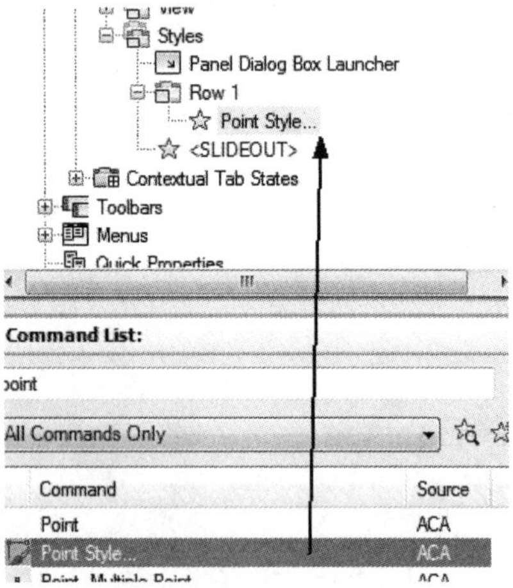

Drag and drop it into the Styles Panel you created.

11. 

Locate the **Text Style** command.

12. 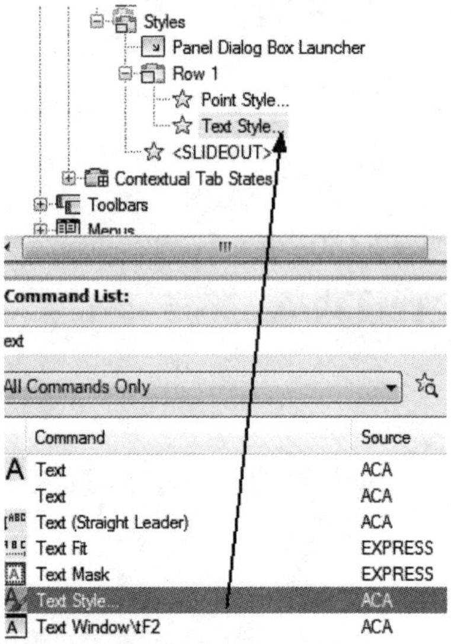

Drag and drop the Text Style command onto the new Styles Panel.

13. 

Drag and drop the Styles panel onto the Format tab.
You can also Copy and Paste if it is too difficult to drag and drop.

14. 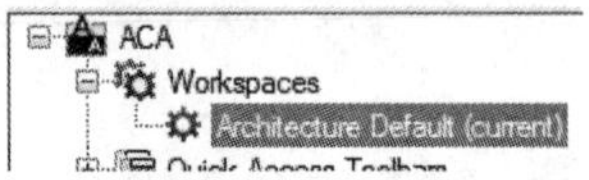

Highlight the current workspace at the top of the left pane.

15. 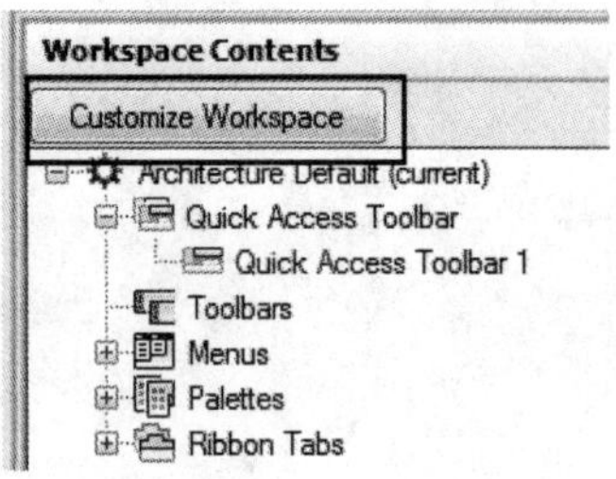

Select **Customize Workspace** on the upper right pane.

16. 

Place a check next to the Format tab you just created in the upper left pane.

17. 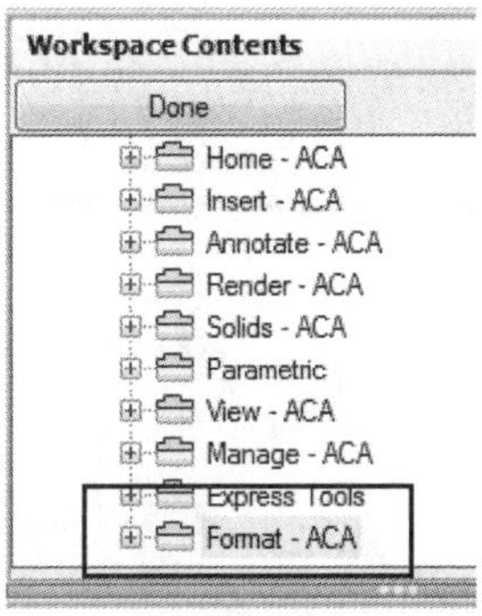

The Format tab will now appear in the Workspace on the upper right pane.

18. 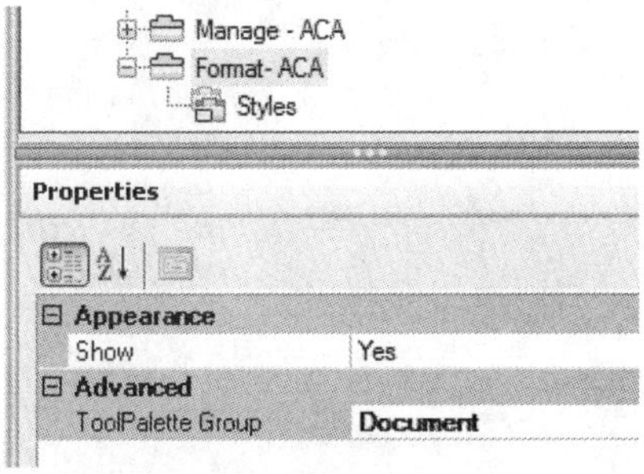

Highlight the **Format** tab.
Verify that Show is set to **Yes**.

Assign the Format tab to the **Document** ToolPalette group.

19. 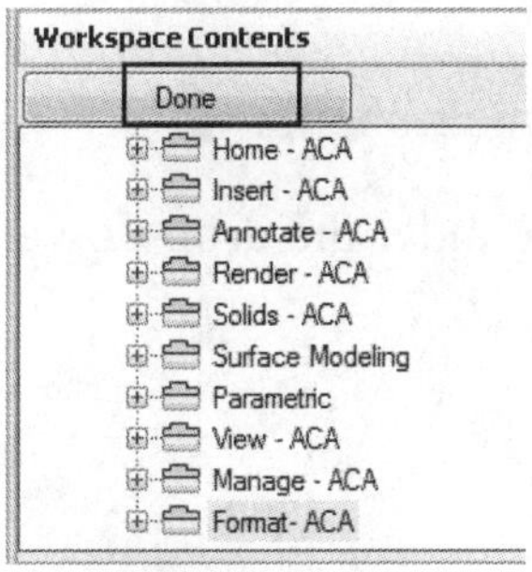

Press the **Done** button on the right pane.

20. 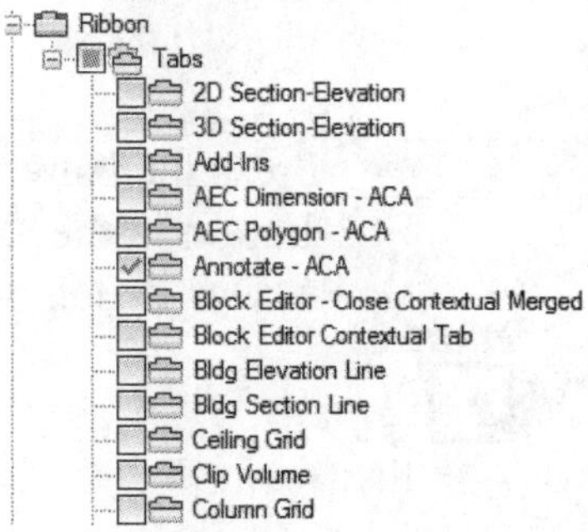

Checks indicate what is currently available in the workspace.

You can create different workspaces with different ribbon configurations.

21. 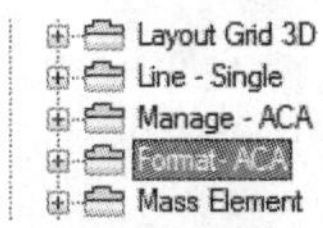

Move the new Format Tab so it is positioned below the Manage. This is done simply by dragging it into position.

22. Press **Apply** and **OK** to close the dialog.

The Format tab now appears on the ribbon.

23. 

If you select the Format tab, you see the tools that were added.

As you find tools you need, you can add them to this ribbon.

24. Close the drawing without saving.

Exercise 1-10:

Creating a Text Style

Drawing Name: new
Estimated Time: 15 minutes

This exercise reinforces the following skills:

- CUI – Custom User Interface
- Ribbon
- Panel
- Tab

1. 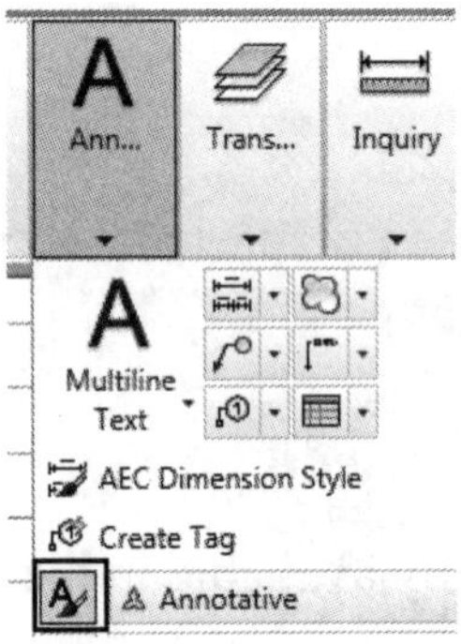

Select the Text Style tool on the Home ribbon.

It is located on the Annotation panel under the drop-down.

2. 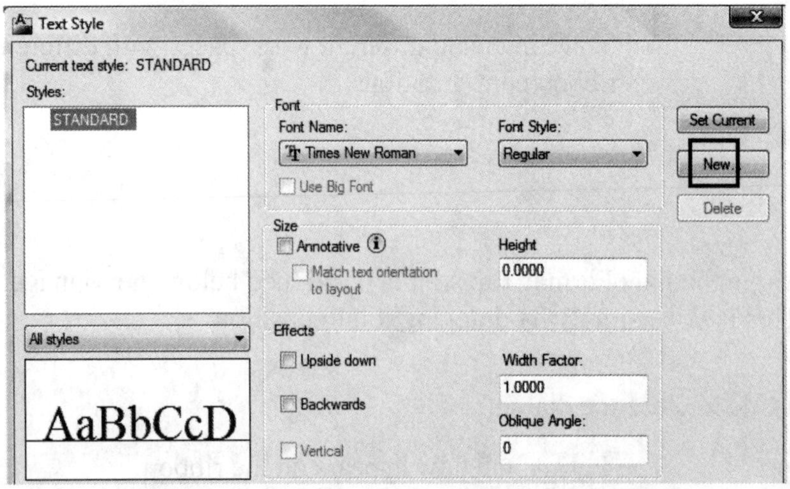

Press the **New** button in the Text Styles dialog box.

3. 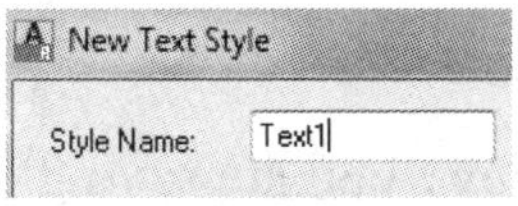

In the New Text Style dialog box, enter **TEXT1** for the name of the new text style and press **OK**.

4. 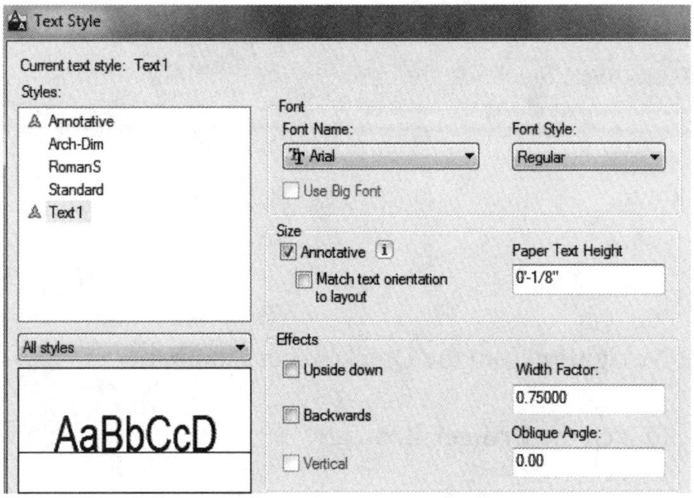

Fill in the remaining information in the Text Style dialog box as shown.
Set the Font Name to **Arial**.
Set the Font Style to **Regular**.
Set the Paper Text Height to **1/8″**.

5. Press the Apply button first and then the Close button to apply the changes to TEXT1 and then close the dialog box.

6. Save as *fonts.dwg*.

- You can use PURGE to eliminate any unused text styles from your drawing.
- You can import text styles from one drawing to another using the Design Center.
- You can store text styles in your template for easier access.

Exercise 1-11

Project Settings

Drawing Name: new
Estimated Time: 5 minutes

This exercise reinforces the following skills:

- Project Navigator
- Project Path Options

In order for tags on windows, doors, etc. to work properly, you must assign your building model to a project.

1. Start a new drawing.

2. 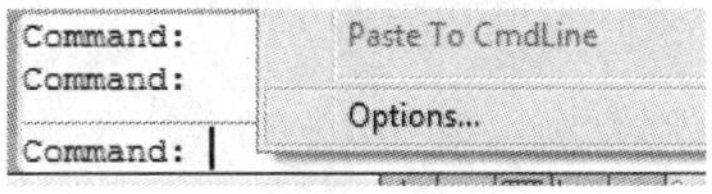

Right click in the command window and select **Options**.

3. 

Select the **AEC Project Defaults** tab.

4. Set the AEC Project Location Search Path to the location where you are saving your files.

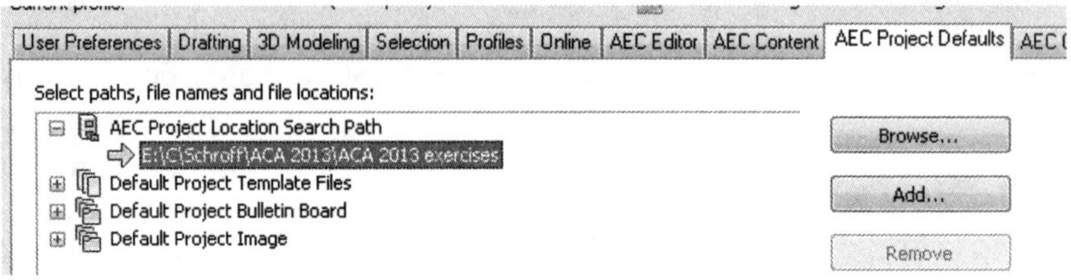

Close the dialog.

5.  Launch the **Project Navigator** from the Quick Access toolbar.

6.  Launch the **Project Browser**.

7.  Select the **New Project** tool.

8. 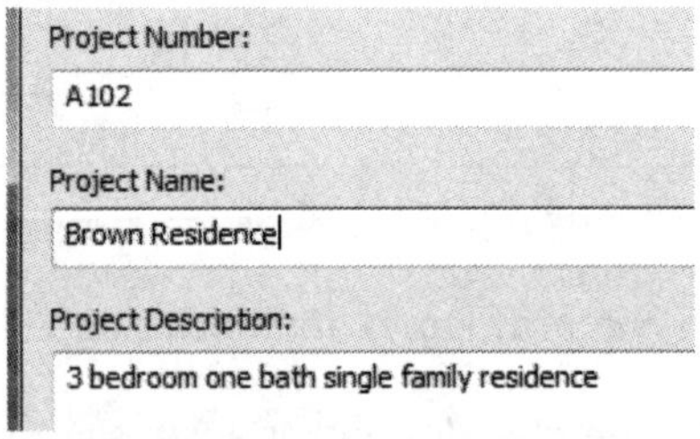

Type **A102** for the Project Number.

Type **Brown Residence** for the Project Name.

Enter a project description.

Press **OK**.

9. 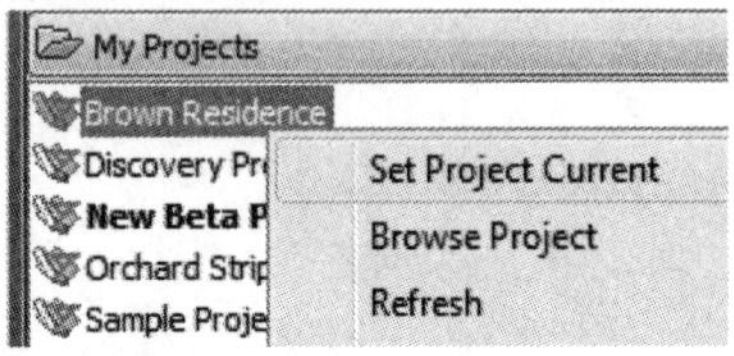

Highlight the **Brown Residence** project.

Right click and select **Set Project Current**.

10. Close the Project Browser.

11. Save as *ex1-11.dwg.*

Lesson 2:
Site Plans

Most architectural projects start with a site plan. The site plan indicates the property lines, the house location, a North symbol, any streets surrounding the property, topographical features, location of sewer, gas, and/or electrical lines (assuming they are below ground – above ground connections are not shown), and topographical features.

When laying out the floor plan for the house, many architects take into consideration the path of sun (to optimize natural light), street access (to locate the driveway), and any noise factors. AutoCAD Architecture includes the ability to perform sun studies on your models.

AutoCAD Architecture allows the user to simulate the natural path of the sun based on the longitude and latitude coordinates of the site, so you can test how natural light will affect various house orientations.

A plot plan must include the following features:

- ❑ Length and bearing of each property line
- ❑ Location, outline, and size of buildings on the site
- ❑ Contour of the land
- ❑ Elevation of property corners and contour lines
- ❑ North symbol
- ❑ Trees, shrubs, streams, and other topological items
- ❑ Streets, sidewalks, driveways, and patios
- ❑ Location of utilities
- ❑ Easements and drainages (if any)
- ❑ Well, septic, sewage line, and underground cables
- ❑ Fences and retaining walls
- ❑ Lot number and/or address of the site
- ❑ Scale of the drawing

The plot plan is drawn using information provided by the county/city and/or a licensed surveyor.

When drafting with pencil and vellum. you would draw to a scale, such as ⅛″ = 1′, but with AutoCAD Architecture, you draw full-size and then set up your layout to the proper scale. This insures that all items you draw will fit together properly. This also is important if you collaborate with outside firms. For example, if you want to send your files to a firm that does HVAC, you want their equipment to fit properly in your design. If everyone drafts 1:1 or full-size, then you can ensure there are no interferences or conflicts.

Exercise 2-1:
Installing the Express Tools

Drawing Name: None
Estimated Time: 15 minutes

This exercise reinforces the following skills:

- Modifying the Software Installation
- Customization
- Express Tools

The Express Tools are not installed using the default installation. If you did not install the Express Tools during your first installation, you can add them later. You will need your installation CD to complete the installation. To check if the Express Tools have been installed, type EXPRESSTOOLS in the command window.

1. Close all applications, including AutoCAD Architecture. Turn off any virus checking software, such as Norton.

2. Go to the **Control Panel→Programs and Features.**

3. 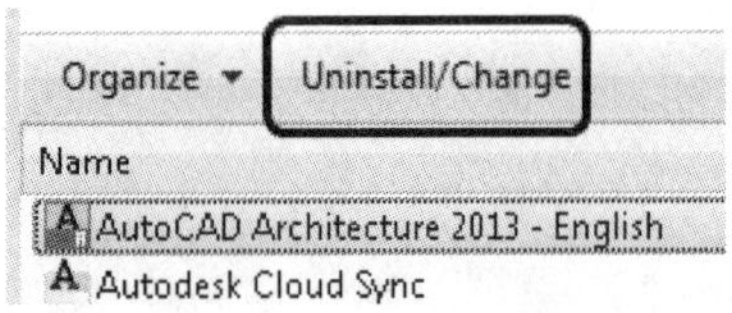

Locate the installation of Autodesk AutoCAD Architecture. Select **Uninstall/Change**.

4. 

Select **Add or Remove Features**.

5. 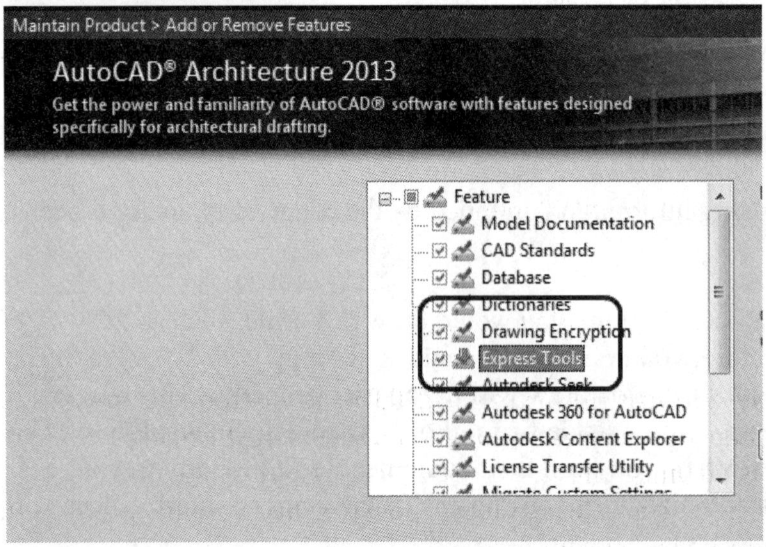

Press **Next**.

   Locate the *Express Tools* and enable.

   Press **Update**.

6. Press **Finish** to conclude the update.

Exercise 2-2:

Creating Custom Line Types

Drawing Name: New
Estimated Time: 15 minutes

This exercise reinforces the following skills:

- Creation of linetypes
- Customization

Architectural drafting requires a variety of custom linetypes in order to display specific features. The standard linetypes provided with AutoCAD Architecture are insufficient from an architectural point of view. You may find custom linetypes on Autodesk's website, www.cadalog.com, or any number of websites on the Internet. However, the ability to create linetypes as needed is an excellent skill for an architectural drafter.

It's a good idea to store any custom linetypes in a separate file. The standard file for storing linetypes is acad.lin. If you store any custom linetypes in acad.lin file, you will lose them the next time you upgrade your software.

1. Once the Express Tools are installed, you can start this exercise.

To verify that the Express Tools are installed, simply look at your ribbon headings.

2. Start a new drawing using **QNEW**.

3. Draw a property line.
This property line was created as follows:
Set ORTHO ON.
Draw a horizontal line 100 units long.

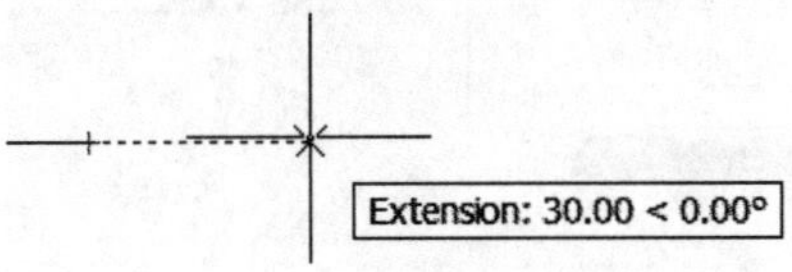

Use SNAP FROM to start the next line @30,0 distance from the previous line.
You can also simply use object tracking to locate the next line.
The short line is 60 units long.
Use SNAP FROM to start the next line @30,0 distance from the previous line.
The second short line is 60 units long.
Use SNAP FROM to start the next line @30,0 distance from the previous line.
Draw a second horizontal line 100 units long.

4. 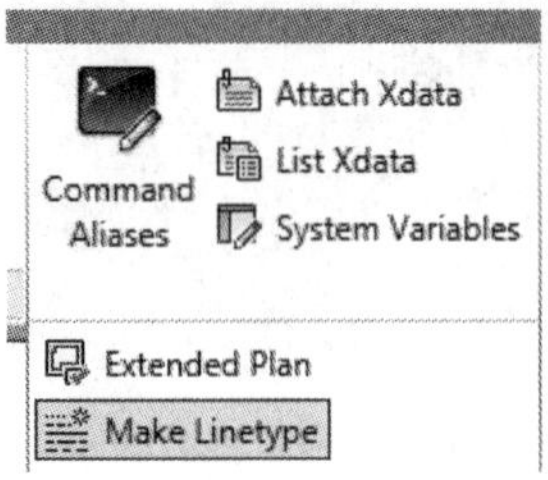

Activate the Express Tools ribbon.

Select the **Tools** drop-down.

Go to **Express→Tools→Make Linetype**.

5. Browse to the folder where you are storing your work.

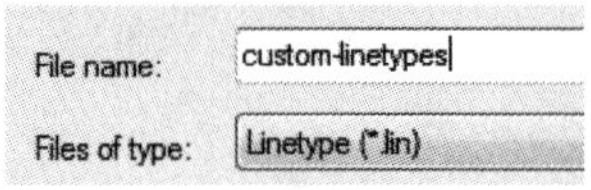

Create a file name called *custom-linetypes.lin* and press **Save**.

TIP: Place all your custom linetypes in a single drawing file and then use the AutoCAD Design Center to help you locate and load the desired linetype.

6. When prompted for the linetype name, type: property-line.
When prompted for the linetype description, type: property-line.
Specify starting point for line definition; select the far left point of the line type.
Specify ending point for line definition; select the far right point of the line type.
When prompted to select the objects, start at the long line on the left and pick the line segments in order.

7. Type **linetype** to launch the Linetype Manager.

8. 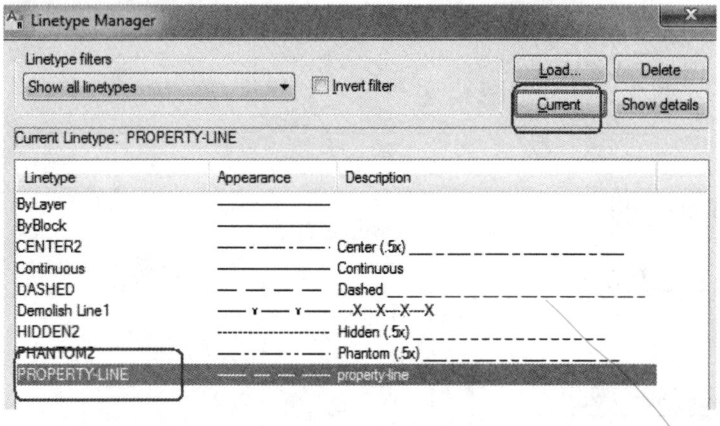

The linetype you created is listed.

Highlight the PROPERTY-LINE linetype and select CURRENT.

Press **OK**.

9. Draw some lines to see if they look OK. Make sure you make them long enough to see the dashes. If you don't see the dashes, adjust the linetype scale using Properties. Set the scale to 0.0125.

10. 

Locate the *custom-linetypes.lin* file you created.

Open it using NotePad.

11. 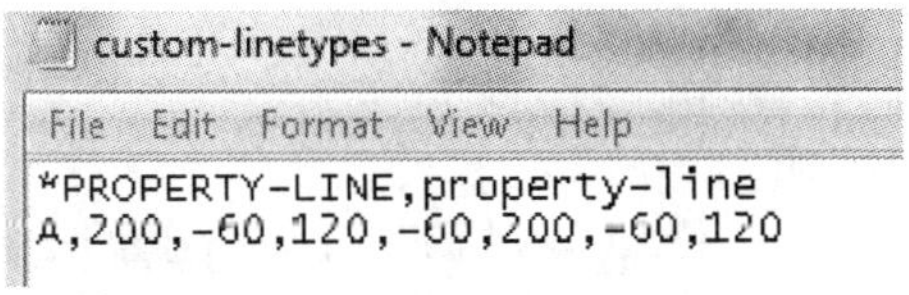

You see a description of the property-line.

12. Save as *ex2-2.dwg*.

Exercise 2-3:

Creating New Layers

Drawing Name: New, ex2-2.dwg
Estimated Time: 20 minutes

This exercise reinforces the following skills:

- ❑ Design Center
- ❑ Layer Manager
- ❑ Creating New Layers
- ❑ Loading Linetypes

1.  Start a new drawing using QNEW.

   Open Ex2-2.dwg.

2. Launch the Design Center.
   The Design Center is on the Insert ribbon in the Content section. It is located in the drop-down under the Content Browser. You can also launch using Ctl+2.

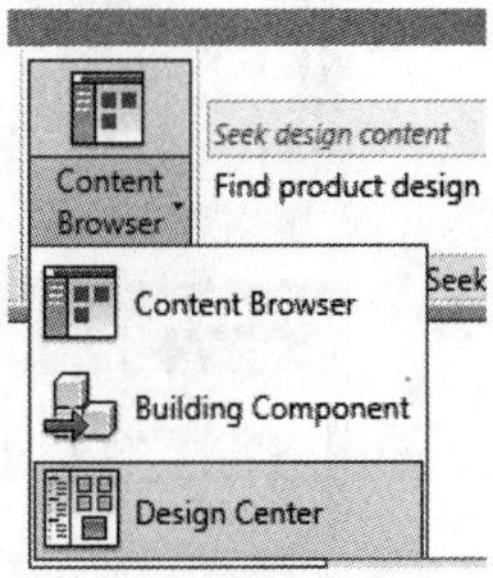

3. 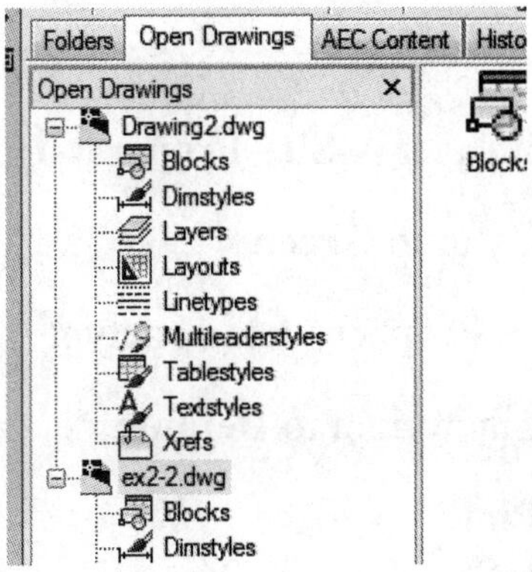

Select the **Open Drawings** tab.

Browse to the *Ex2-2.dwg* file.

Open the Linetypes folder.

Scroll to the **Property-line** linetype definition.

4. 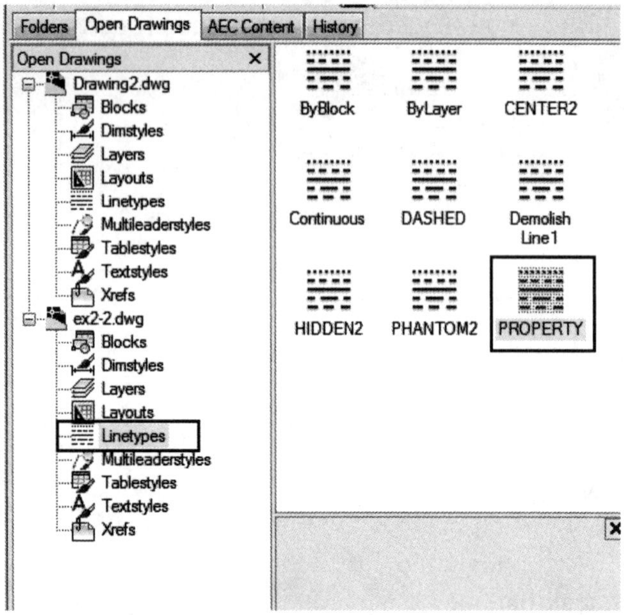

Highlight the PROPERTY-LINE linetype.

Drag and drop into your active window or simply drag it onto the open drawing listed.

5. Close the Design Center.

6. 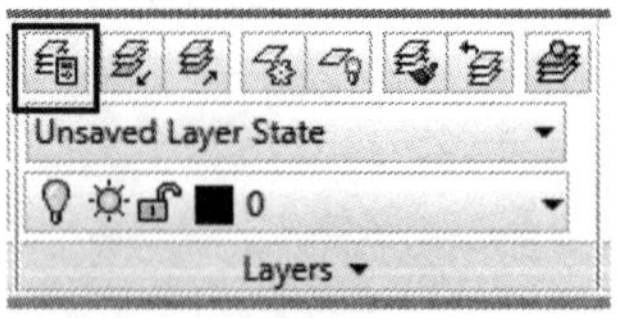

Activate the **Layer Manager** on the Home ribbon.

7. 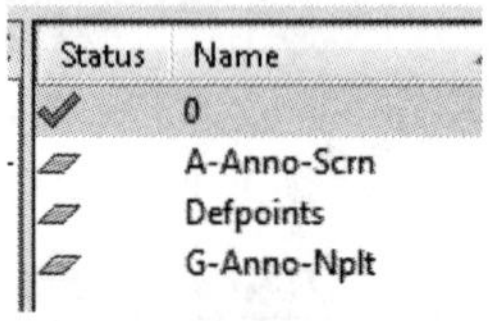

Note that several layers have already been created. The template automatically sets your Layer Standards to AIA.

8.  Select the New Layer from Standard tool.

9. 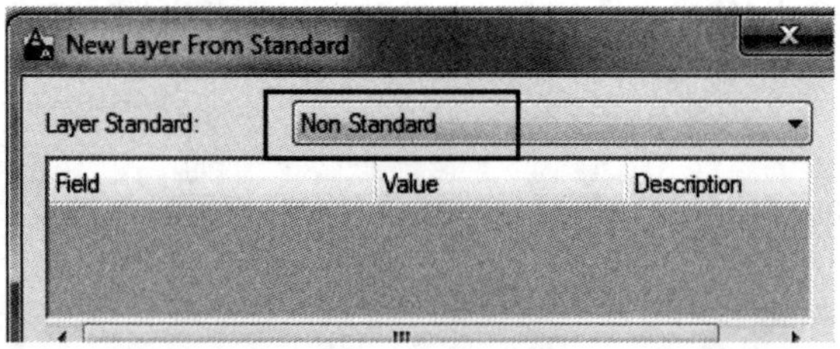

Under Layer Standard, select **Non Standard**.

10. 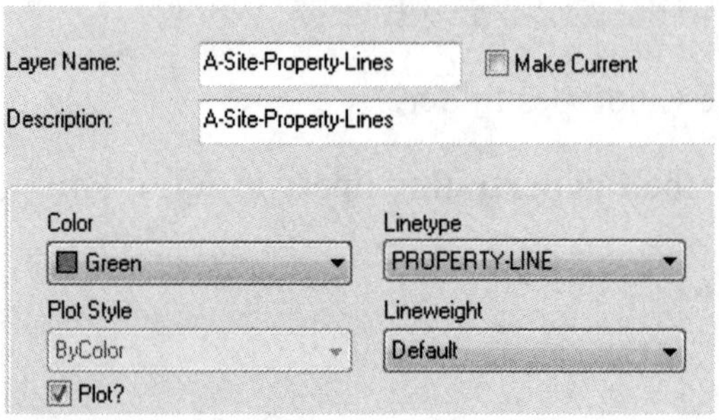

Name the layer **A-Site-Property-Lines**.

Set the Color to **Green**.

Select the **Property-Line** linetype.

Set the Lineweight to **Default**.

Enable **Plot**.
Press **Apply**.

11. 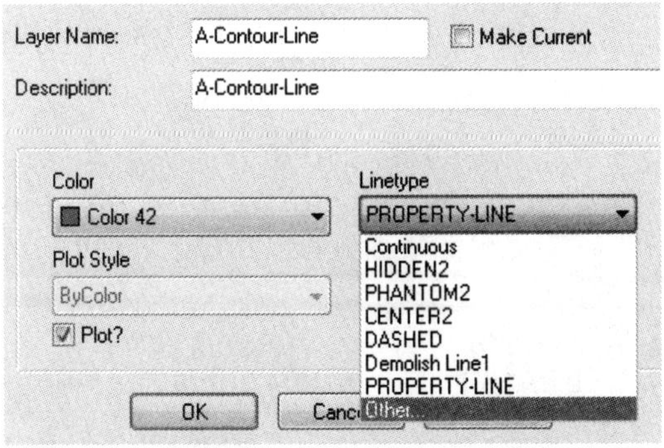

Create another layer.

Name the layer **A-Contour-Line**.

Set the color to **42**.

Select the linetype pane for the new linetype.

Press **Other**.

12. 

Enable **Show Linetypes in File.**

Highlight **DASHEDX2** and press **OK** to assign it to the selected layer name.

13. 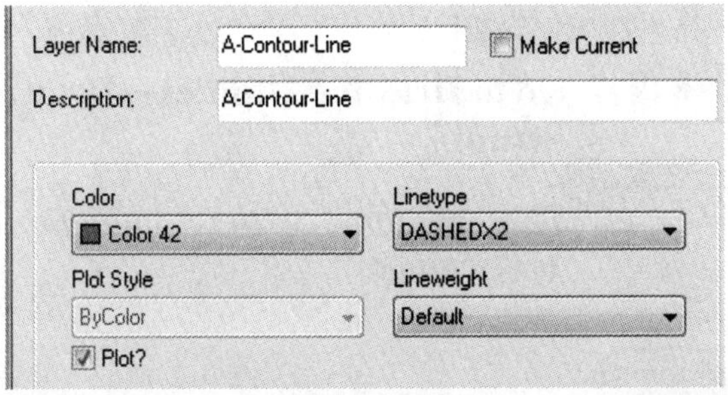

Note that the linetype was assigned properly.

Press **OK**.

14. 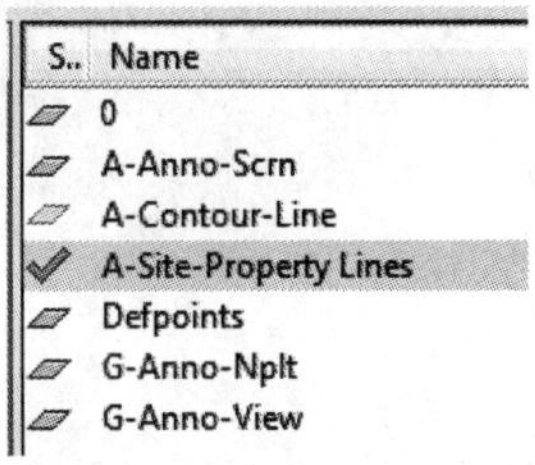

Set the A-Site-Property-Lines layer current.

Highlight the layer name then select the green check mark to set current.

You can also double left click to set the layer current.

15. Right click on the header bar and select **Maximize all columns** to see all the properties for each layer.

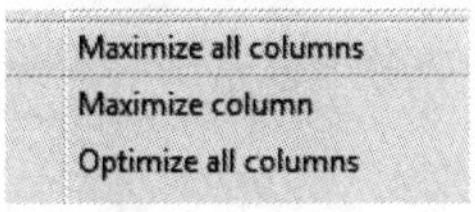

16. Use the X in the upper corner to close the Layer Manager.

17. Save as *Ex2-3.dwg*.

Exercise 2-4:

Creating a Site Plan

Drawing Name: Ex2-3.dwg
Estimated Time: 30 minutes

This exercise reinforces the following skills:

- Use of ribbons
- Documentation Tools
- Elevation Marks
- Surveyors' Angles

1.  Open or continue working in *ex-2-3.dwg*.

2. 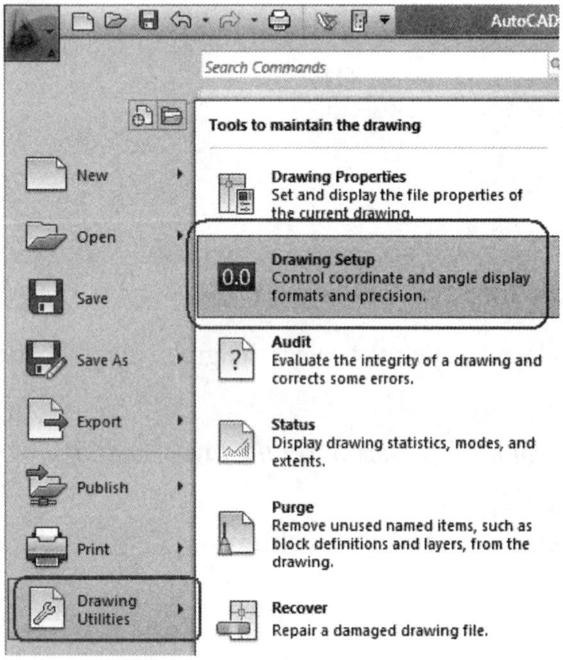

Go to **Drawing Utilities→Drawing Setup**.

This is located on the Applications Menu panel.

3. 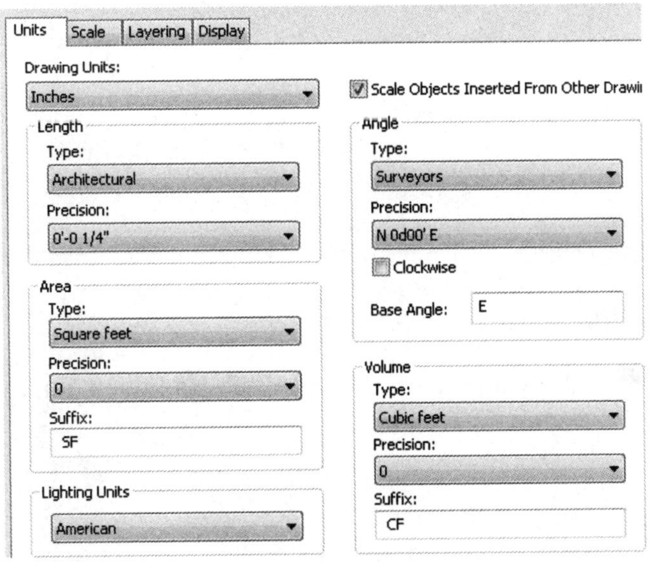

Select the **Units** tab.
Set the Drawing Units to **Inches**.
Set up the Length Type to **Architectural**.
Set the Precision to ¼″.
Set the Angle Type to **Surveyors**.
Set the Precision to **N 0d00′ E**.
Press **Apply** and **OK**.

TIP: You can set your units as desired and then enable **Save As Default** 

. Then, all future drawings will use your unit settings.

4. Draw the property line shown on the **A-Site-Property-Lines** layer.

Specify first point: 1′,5′
Specify next point: @186′ 11″ < s80de
Specify next point: @75′<n30de
Specify next point: @125′11″<n
Specify next point: @250′<180

Metric data entry using centimeters:

```
Specify first point: 12,60
Specify next point or [Undo]: @2243<s80de
Specify next point or [Undo]: @900<n30de
Specify next point or [Close/Undo]: @1511<n
Specify next point or [Close/Undo]: @3000<180
Specify next point or [Close/Undo]:
```

This command sequence uses Surveyor's Units.

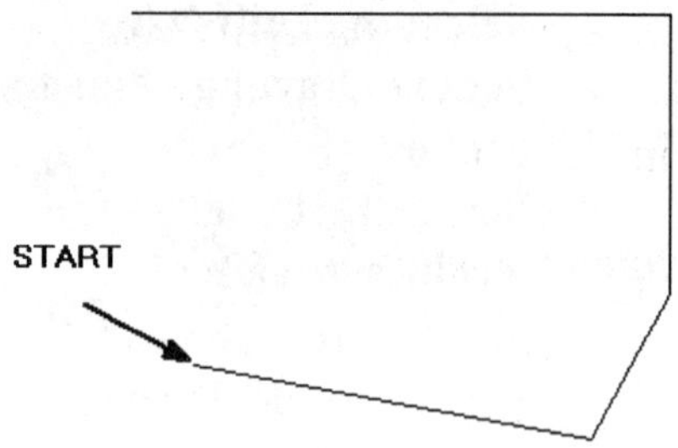

Turn ORTHO off before creating the arc.

5. 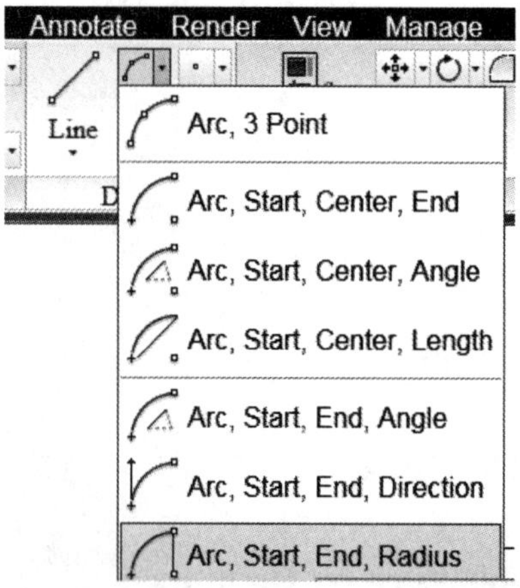

Draw an arc using Start, End, Radius to close the figure.

6. 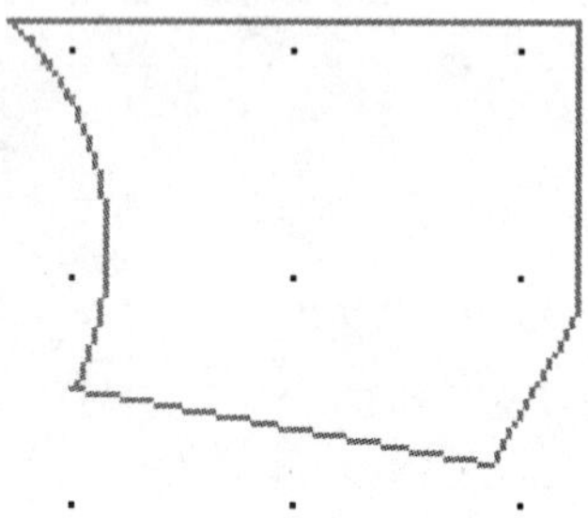

Select the bottom point as the Start point.
Right click and select the End option.
Select the top point at the End point.
Right click and select the Radius option.
The radius is 1584″ [4023.36 cm].

7. Set the **A-Contour-Line layer** current.

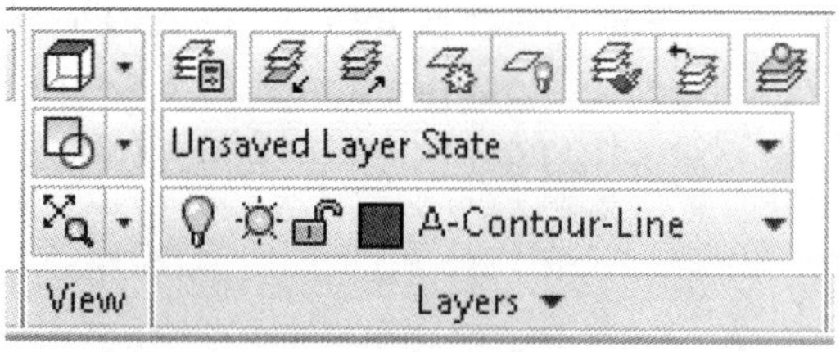

8. 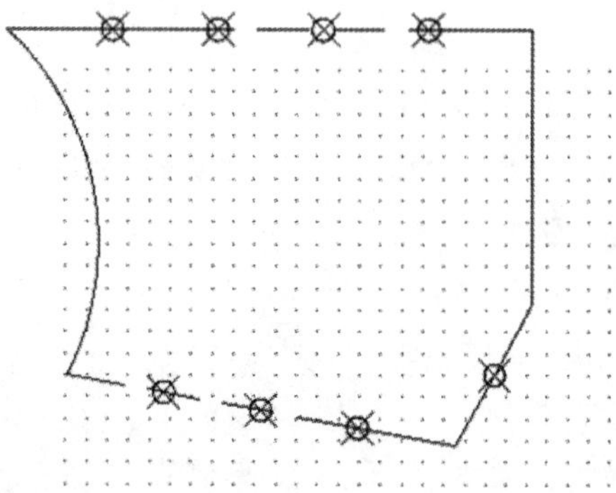

Use the **DIVIDE** command to place points as shown.
The top line is divided into five equal segments.
The bottom-angled line is divided into four equal segments.
The small angled line is divided into two equal segments.

9. 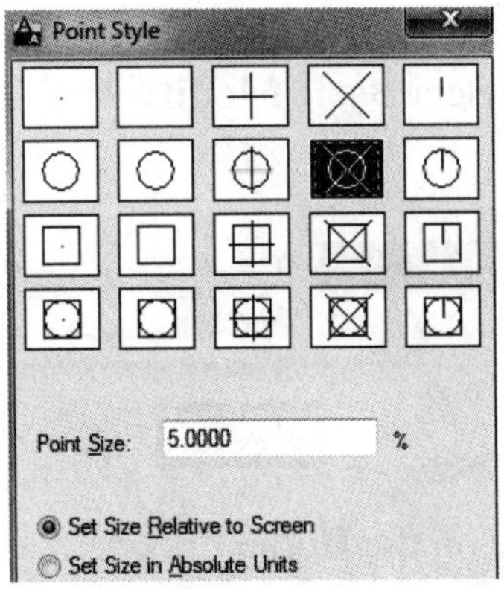

Type **DDPTYPE** to access the Point Style dialog or use the Point Style tool that was added to the Format tab on the ribbon in Lesson 1.

Go to **Format→Point Style** to set the points so they are visible.

Select the Point Style indicated.

Press **OK**.

10. Draw contour lines using **Pline** and **NODE** Osnaps as shown.

Be sure to put the contour lines on the contour line layer.

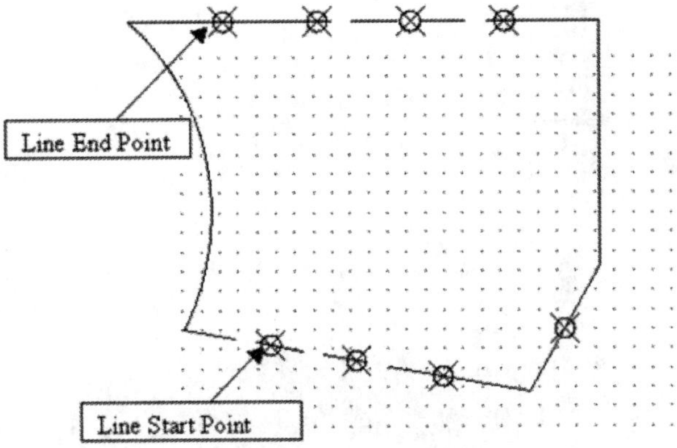

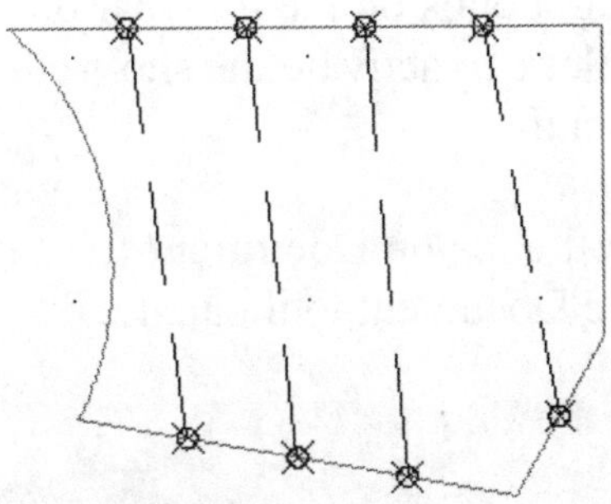

11. Type **qselect** on the *Command* line.

12. 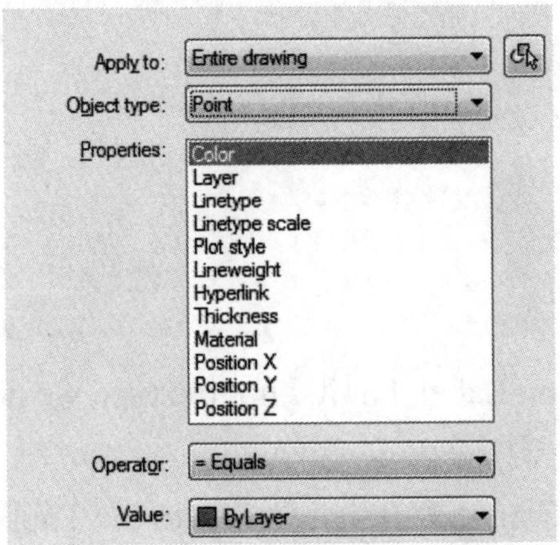

Set the Object Type to **Point**.
Set the Color = Equals **ByLayer**.

Press **OK**.

13. 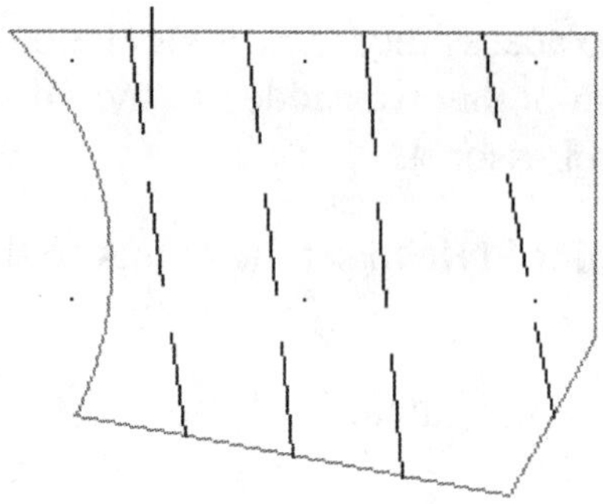

All the points are selected.
Right click and select **Basic Modify Tools→ Delete.**

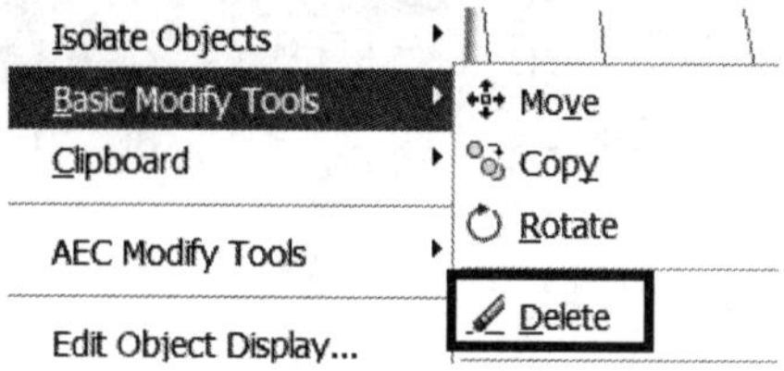

14. 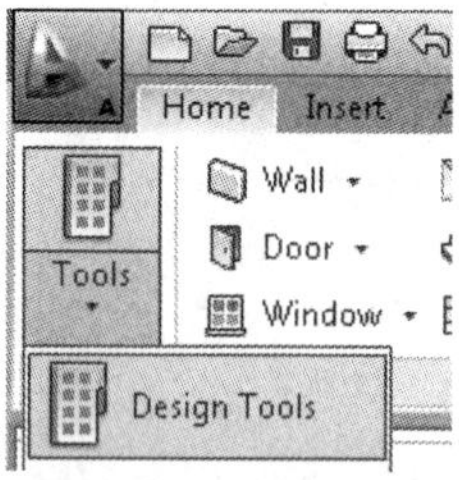

Activate the Design Tools palette on the Home ribbon.

15. 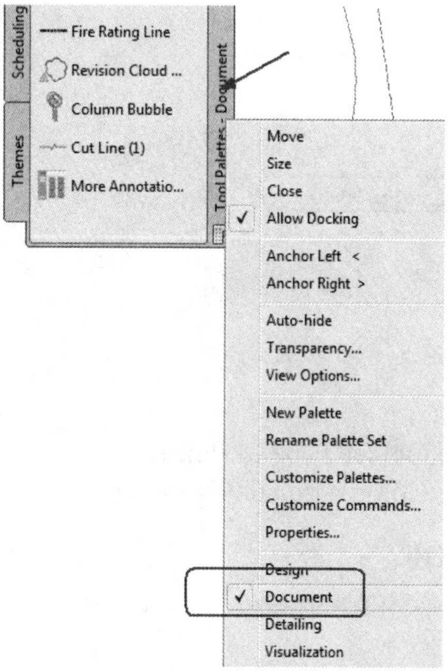

Right click on the gray bar on the palette to activate the short-cut menu.

Left click on **Document** to enable the Document tool palette.

16. Activate the Annotation tab on the palette.

Locate the Plan Elevation Label, but it's not the type we need for a site plan.

17. Instead we'll have to add an elevation label from the Design Center to the Tool Palette.

18. 

Type **Ctl+2** to launch the Design Center.
Or:
Activate the **Insert** ribbon.
Select the **Design Center** tool under Content
Or:
Type **ADC**.

19. 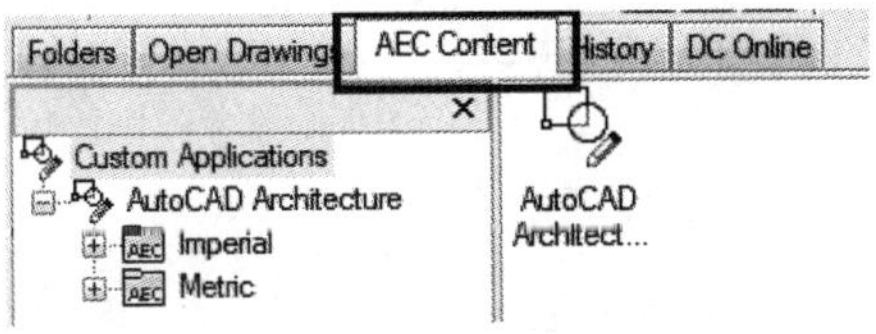

Select the **AEC Content** tab.

20. Browse to

Imperial/Documentation/Elevation Labels/ 2D Section.

[Metric/Documentation/Elevation Labels/2D Section].

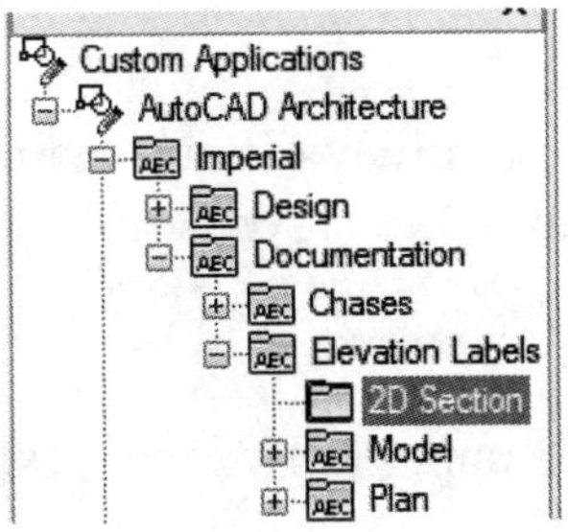

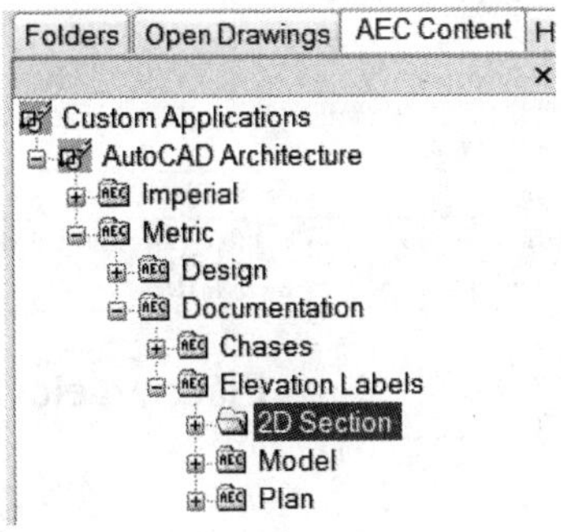

21. 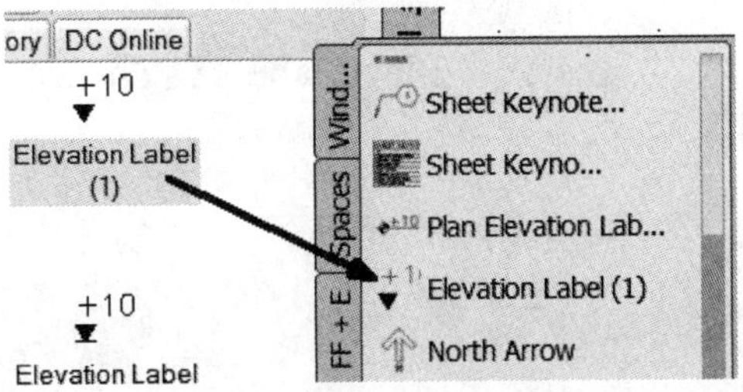

Locate the Elevation Label (1) file.

Highlight the elevation label.

Drag and drop onto the Tool Palette.

Close the Design Center.

22. 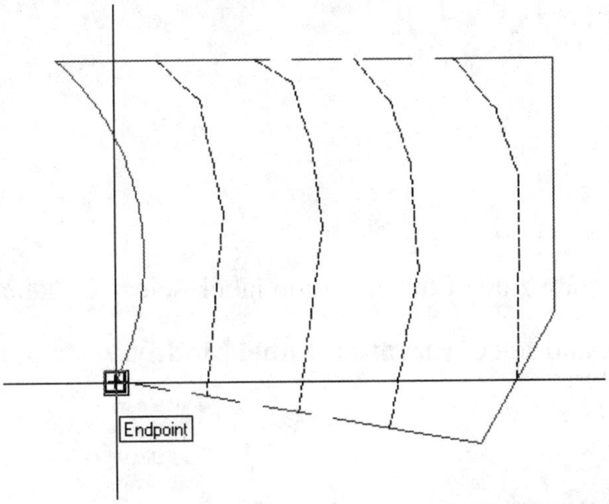

Select the Elevation Label on the Tool Palette.

Select the Endpoint shown.

23. Set the Elevation to **0″ [0.00]**.
Set the Prefix to **EL**.
Press **OK**.

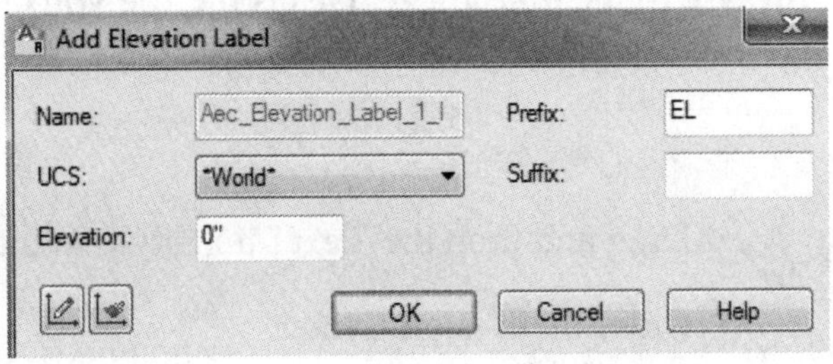

24. 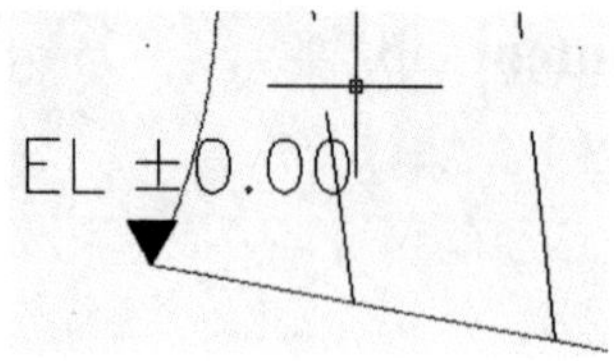

Zoom in to see the elevation label.

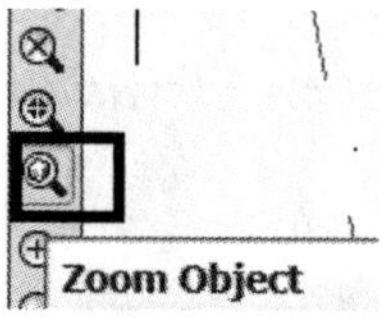

You can use the **Zoom Object** tool to zoom in quickly.

General	
Description	
Layer	A-Anno-Dims
Definition	Aec_Elevation_Label_1_I
Bound spaces	By style (No)

The Elevation Label is automatically placed on the A-Anno-Dims layer.

25. 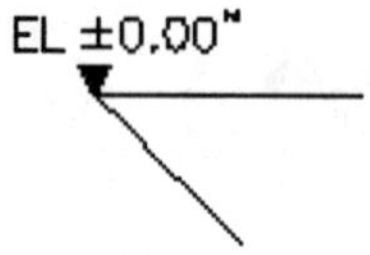

Place an elevation label on the upper left vertex as shown.

26. 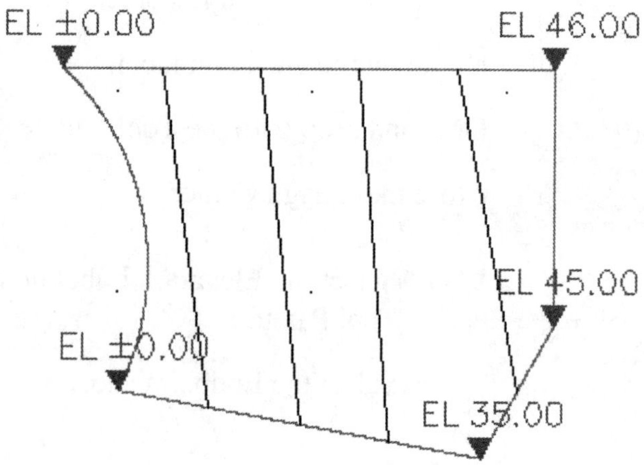

Place labels as shown.

27. 

To modify the value of the elevation label, select the label.

Right click and select **Elevation Label Modify**.

28. Type **Ctl+2** to launch the Design Center.

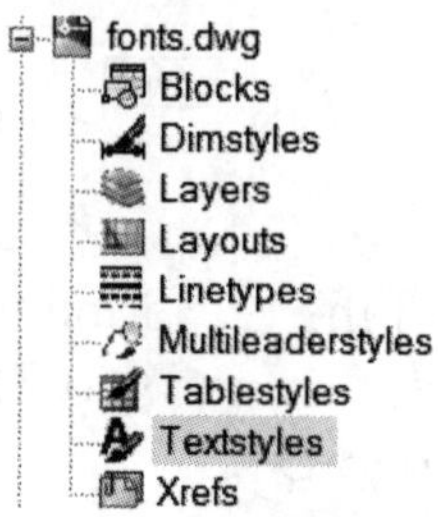

Select the Folders tab.
Browse to the *fonts.dwg*. This is the file you created in a previous exercise.

29. 

Drag and drop the **Text1** text style into the drawing.

Close the Design Center.

30. 

Use the **TEXT** command to create the text.

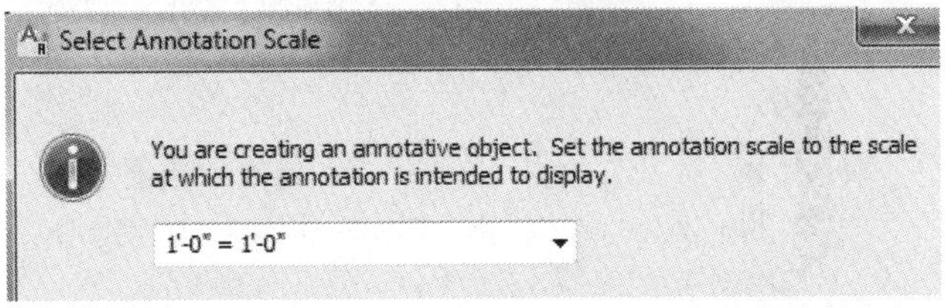

If this dialog appears, set the scale to the same scale as the current view.

Select the midpoint of the line as the insertion point.
Right click and select **Style**.
Set the current style to **Text1**.
Right click and select **Justify**.
Set the Justification to **Center**.
Set the rotation angle to **–10** degrees
Use %%d to create the degree symbol.

31. 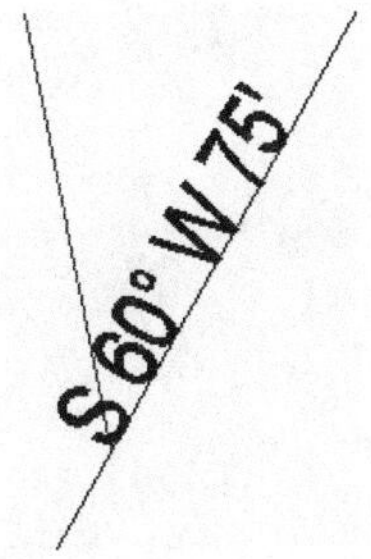

To create the S60… note, use the **TEXT** command.

Use a rotation angle of 60 degrees.

When you are creating the text, it will preview horizontally. However, once you left click or hit ESCAPE to place it, it will automatically rotate to the correct position.

32. 

Create the **Due South 125′ 11″ [Due South 3840.48]**, with a rotation angle of 90 degrees.

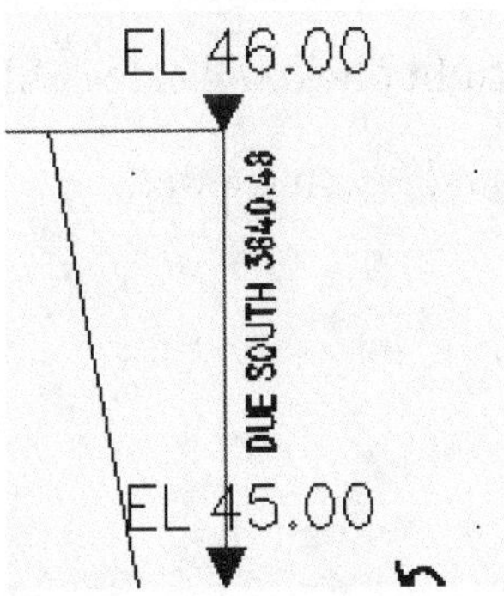

Add the text shown on the top horizontal property line.

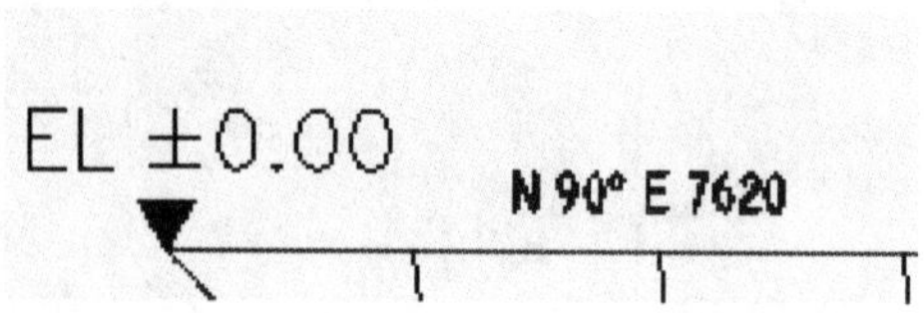

33. Add the Chord note shown. Rotation angle is 90 degrees.

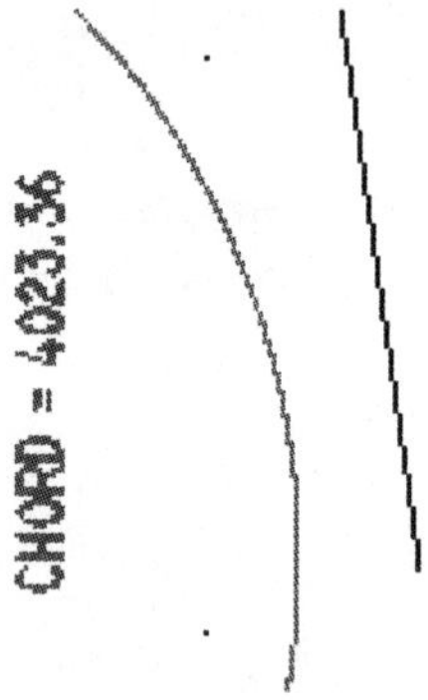

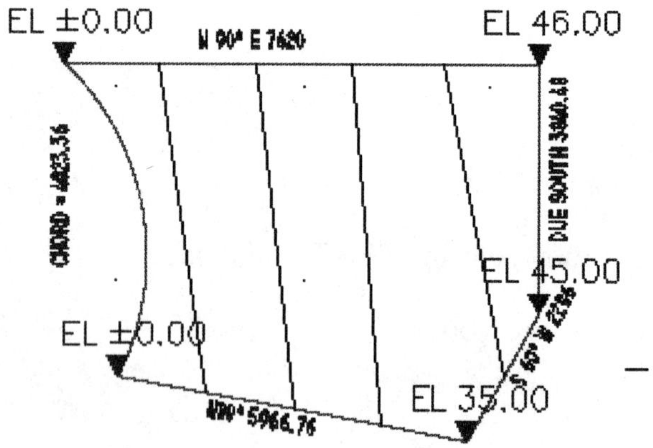

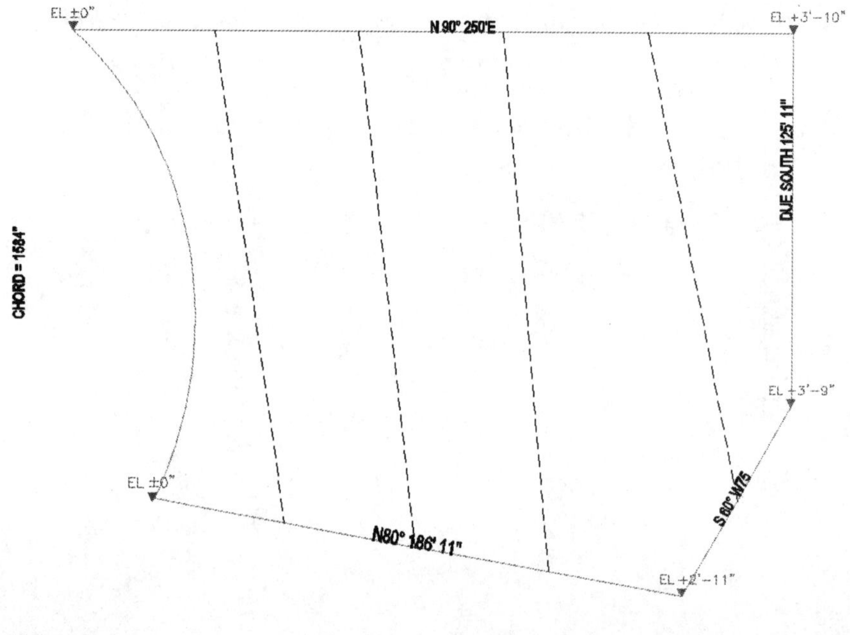

34. Save the file as *ex2-4.dwg.*

Exercise 2-5:
Creating a Layer User Group

Drawing Name: Ex 2-4.dwg
Estimated Time: 15 minutes

This exercise reinforces the following skills:

- Use of toolbars
- Layer Manager
- Layer User Group

A Layer User Group allows you to group your layers, so you can quickly freeze/thaw them, turn them ON/OFF, etc.

> **TIP:** The difference between FREEZING a Layer and turning it OFF is that entities on FROZEN Layers are not included in REGENS. Speed up your processing time by FREEZING layers.

We can create a group of layers that are just used for the site plan and then freeze them when we don't need to see them.

1.  Open *ex2-4.dwg*.

2.  Select the **Layer Manager** tool.

3. 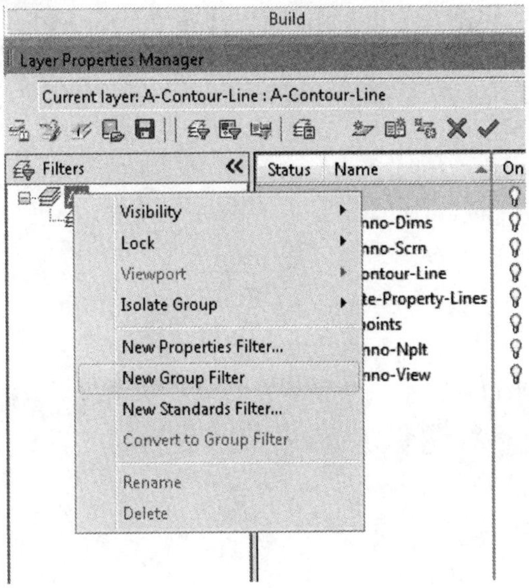

Highlight the word **All** in the Filters pane.

Right click and select the **New Group Filter**.

4. 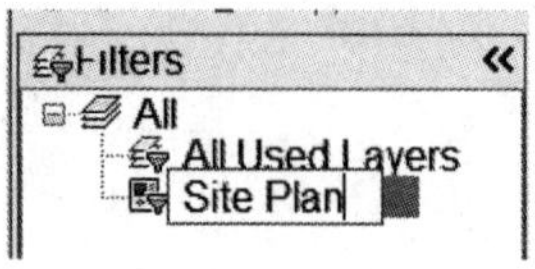

Name the group **Site Plan**.

5. 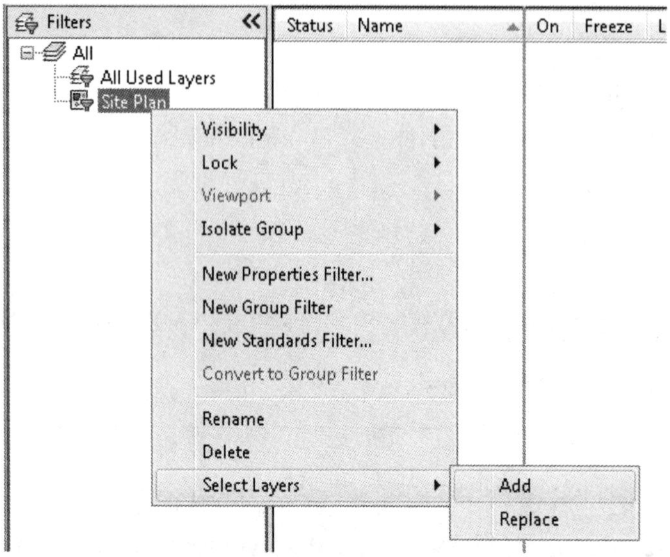

Highlight the Site Plan group.
Right click and select **Select Layers→Add**.

6. Type **ALL** on the command line.
This selects all the items in the drawing.
Press **ENTER** to finish the selection.
The layers are now listed in the Layer Manager under the Site Plan group.

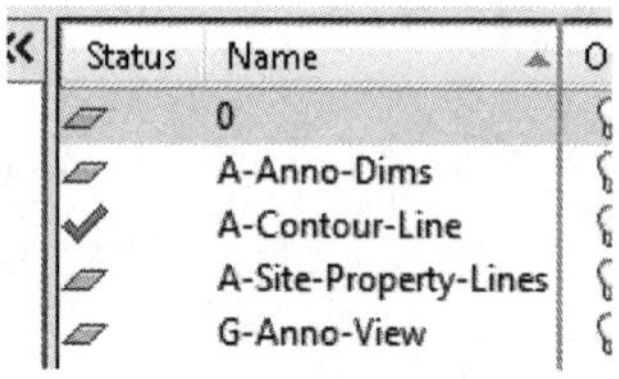

Close the Layer Manager.

7. We can use this group to quickly freeze, turn off, etc. the layers in the Site Plan group.

Save the drawing as *ex2-5.dwg* and close.

QUIZ 1

True or False

1. Doors, windows, and walls are inserted into the drawing as objects.
2. The Architectural Toolbars are loaded from the ACA Menu Group.
3. To set the template used by the QNEW tool, use Options.

4. If you start a New Drawing using the 'QNew' tool shown above, the Start-Up dialog will appear unless you assign a template.
5. Mass elements are used to create Mass Models.
6. The Layer Manager is used to organize, sort, and group layers.
7. Layer Standards are set using the Layer Manager.
8. You must load a custom linetype before you can assign it to a layer.

Multiple Choice
Select the best answer.

9. If you start a drawing using one of the standard templates, AutoCAD Architecture will automatically create __________ layouts.
   A. A work layout plus Model Space
   B. Four layouts, plus Model Space
   C. Ten layouts, plus Model Space
   D. Eleven layouts, plus Model Space

10. Options are set through:
   A. Options
   B. Desktop
   C. User Settings
   D. Template

11. The Display Manager controls:
   A. How AEC objects are displayed in the graphics window
   B. The number of viewports
   C. The number of layout tabs
   D. Layers

12. Mass Elements are created using the _____ Tool Palette.

    A. Massing
    B. Concept
    C. General Drafting
    D. Documentation

13. Wall Styles are created by:

    A. Highlighting a Wall on the Wall tab of the Tool Palette, right click and select Wall Styles
    B. Type **WallStyle** on the command line
    C. Go to **Format→Style Manager**
    D. All of the above

14. To create a New Layer, use:

    A. Type **LayerManager** at the command line
    B. Type **Layer** at the command line
    C. Use **Format→Layer Management→Layer Manager**
    D. All of the above

15. You can change the way AEC objects are displayed by using:

    A. Edit Object Display
    B. Edit Display Properties
    C. Edit Entity Properties
    D. Edit AEC Properties

ANSWERS:

1) T; 2) T; 3) T; 4) F; 5) T; 6) T; 7) T; 8) T; 9) A; 10) A; 11) A; 12) A; 13) D; 14) D; 15) A

Lesson 3
Floor Plans

The floor plan is central to any architectural drawing. We start by placing the exterior walls, then the interior walls, then doors, and finally windows.

Exercise 3-1:
Creating Walls

Drawing Name: New
Estimated Time: 10 minutes

This exercise reinforces the following skills:

- Create Walls
- Wall Properties
- Wall Styles
- Model and Work space

1.  Start a new drawing using QNEW.

2. 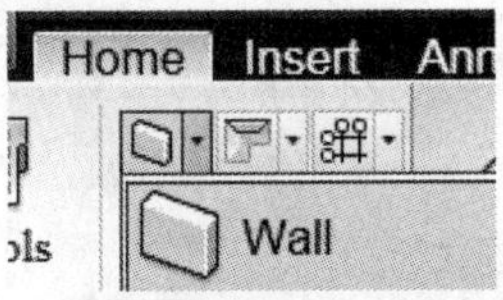

Select the **Wall** tool from the Home ribbon.

3. 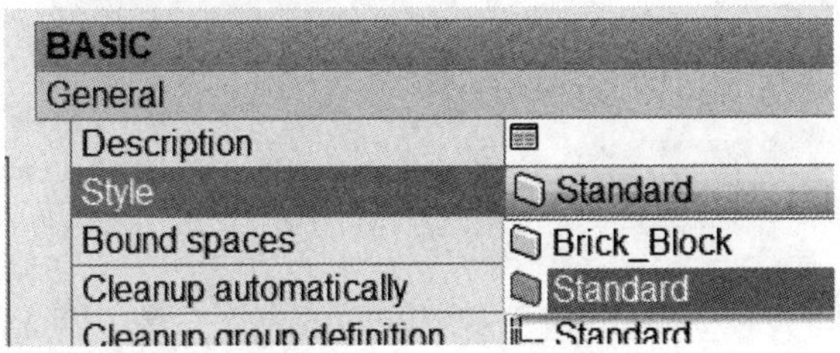

In the Properties dialog, check under the Style drop-down list.

   Only the Brick_Block and Standard styles are available.

   These are the wall styles that are loaded in the template.

4. Exit out of the command by pressing ESC.

5. 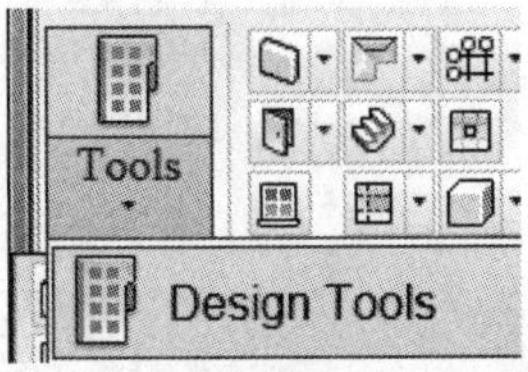

Launch the Design Tools palette from the Home ribbon.

6. 

Activate the Walls tab on the palette.
Select the CMU-8 Rigid-1.5 Air 2 Brick-4

   [CMU 190 Rigid-038 Air – 050 Brick -090].

7. 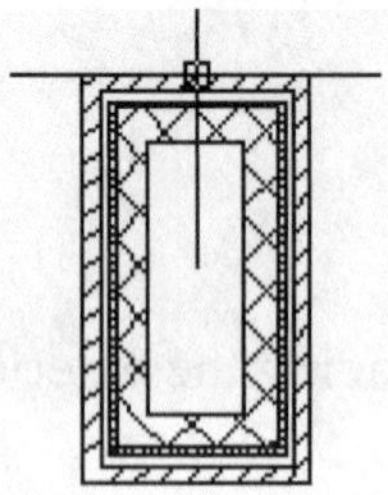

Toggle **ORTHO** ON.

Start the wall at 0,0.
Create a rectangle 72 inches [1830 mm] tall and 36 inches [914 mm] wide.

8. Select the **Work** tab.

9. 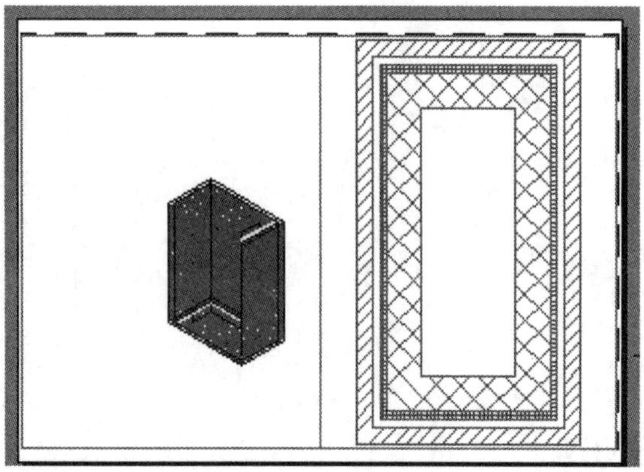

You see that the walls you placed are really 3-dimensional.

10. 

Switch back to the Model space tab.

11. 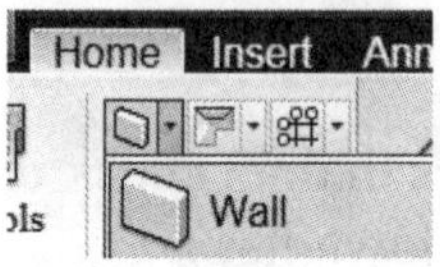

Select the **Wall** tool from the Home ribbon.

12. 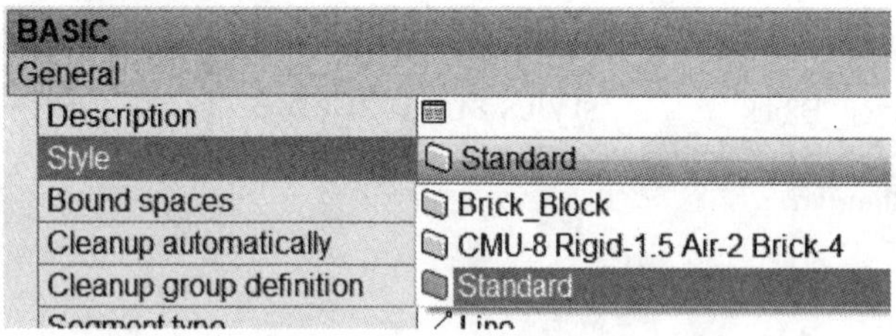

In the Properties dialog, check under the Style drop-down list.

Note that the CMU wall style is now available under the drop-down list.

13. Exit out of the command by pressing ESC.

14. Save your drawing as *Ex3-1.dwg.*

TIP: If you draw a wall and the materials composing the wall are on the wrong side, you can reverse the direction of the wall. Simply select the wall, right click and select the Reverse option from the menu.

Exercise 3-2:

Inserting a Drawing Reference

Drawing Name: new
Estimated Time: 60 minutes

This exercise reinforces the following skills:

- Drawing references (previously known as external references or Xrefs)

1.  Start a new drawing using **QNEW**.

2. 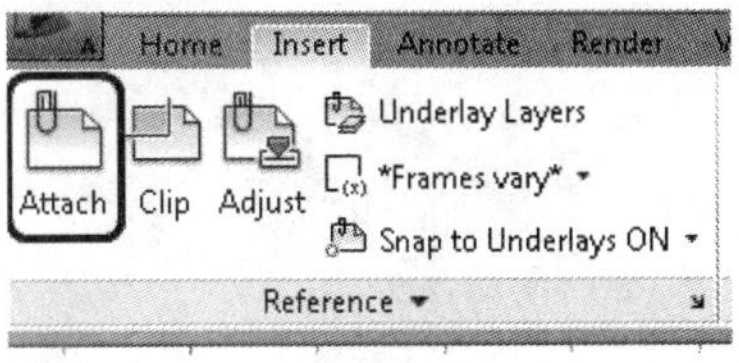

   Activate the Insert ribbon.

   Select **Attach** on the Reference panel.

3. 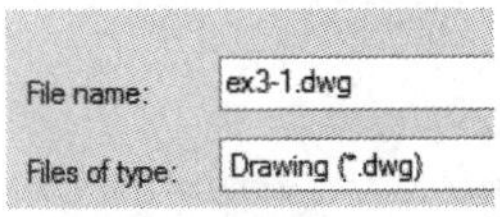

   Set the Files of type to **.dwg*.

   Locate *ex3-1.dwg*.

   Press **Open**.

> **TIP:** Many architects use external drawing references to organize their projects. That way teams of architects can concentrate just on their portions of a building. External references also use less system resources.

4. 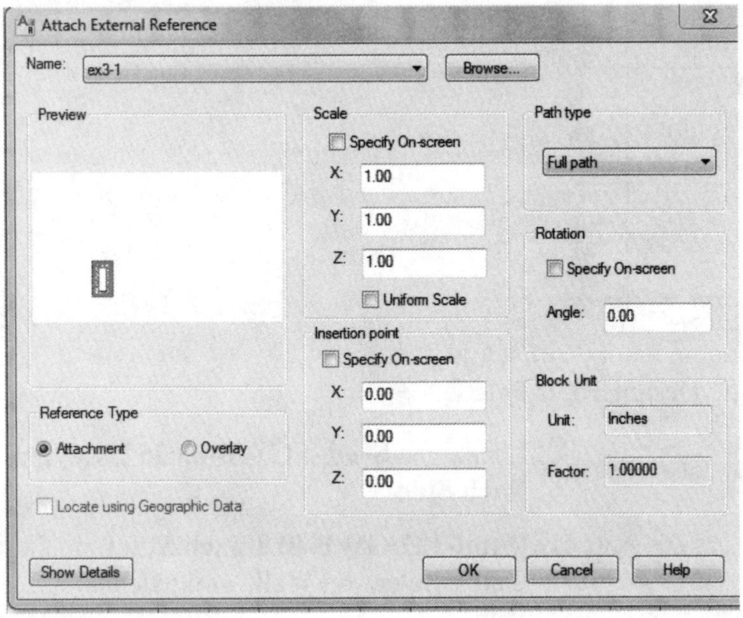

   Uncheck **Specify On-Screen** under Insertion point, scale, and rotation.

   Press **OK**.
   This will insert the file as an external reference at 0,0,0.

5. Save the file as *ex3-2*.

> **TIP:** You can convert lines, arcs, circles, or polylines to walls. If you have created a floor plan in AutoCAD and want to convert it to 3D, open the floor plan drawing inside of AutoCAD Architecture. Use the Convert to Walls tool to transform your floor plan into walls.

Exercise 3-3

Convert to Walls

Drawing Name: floor plan.dwg
Estimated Time: 10 minutes

This exercise reinforces the following skills:

- ❑ Convert to Walls

1. 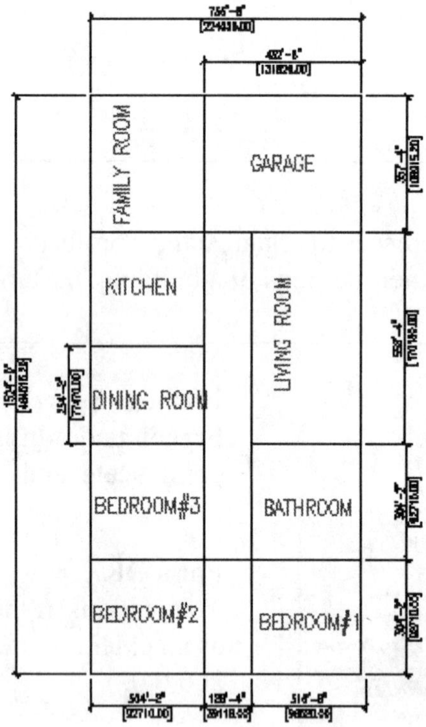

Open *floor plan.dwg*.
This file can be downloaded from the book's detail page on www.SDCpublications.com.

This floor plan has both architectural and metric units shown.

2. On the Walls tab of the Design Tools Palette:

Locate the **Stud-4 GWB-0.625 2 Layers Each Side**

[Stud-102 GWB-018 Each Side]
wall style on the Walls tool palette.

3. Highlight the wall tool.

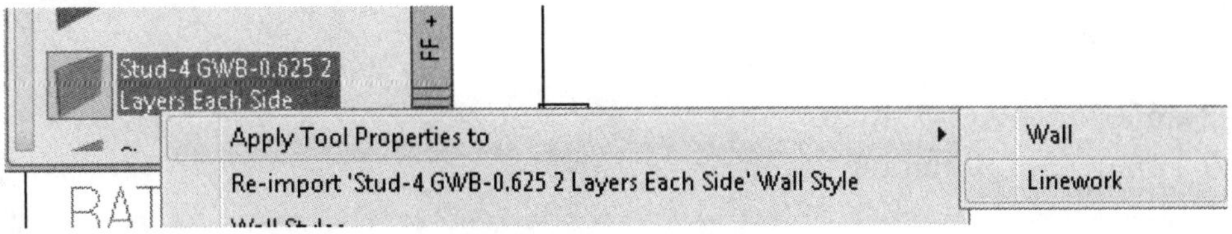

Right click and select
Apply Tool Properties to →Linework.

4. Select all the interior lines.

Press **ENTER** when you are done selecting.

You are prompted if you want to erase the layout geometry. Type **Y** for Yes.

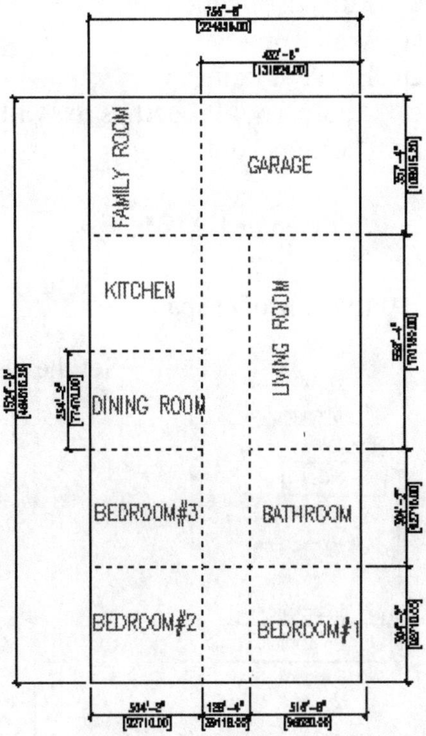

5. Switch to the Work tab so you can see how your house looks in 3D.

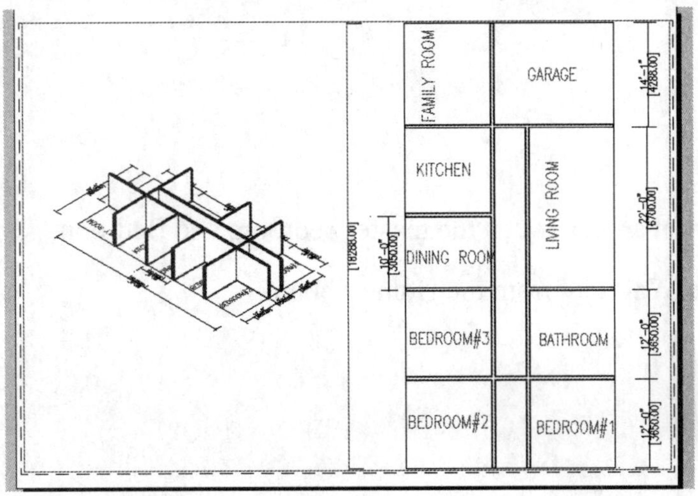

6. Save the file as *ex3-3.dwg*.

Exercise 3-4:
Wall Cleanup

Drawing Name: ex3-3.dwg
Estimated Time: 30 minutes

This exercise reinforces the following skills:

- Modifying Walls
- Edit Justification
- Wall Tools
- Break at Point
- Apply Tool Properties to Wall
- Cleanup Tools

1.  Open *ex3-3.dwg.*

2. Activate Model space.

3. 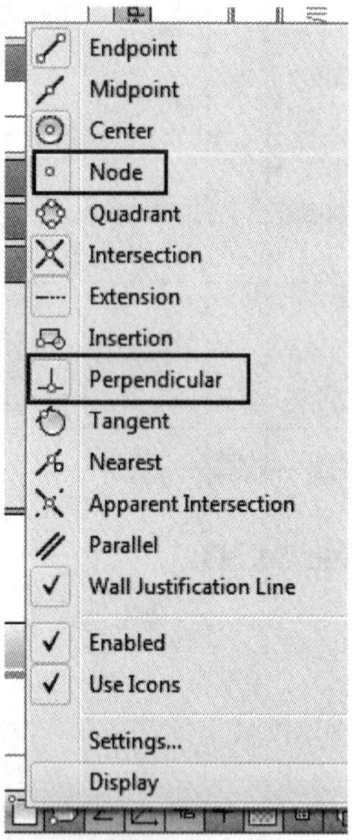

Set the Osnaps so that Node and Perpendicular are enabled.

4. 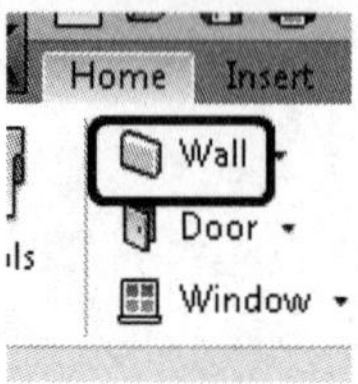

Add a closet area between the master bedroom and Bedroom #1.

Select the **Wall** tool from the Home ribbon.

5. 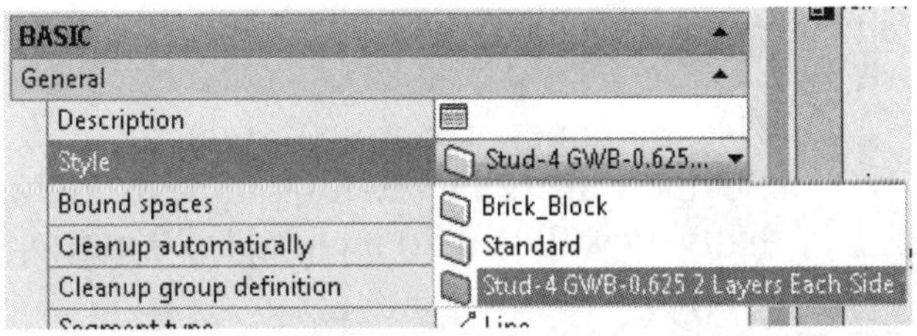

Verify that the Stud-4GWB is the selected as the active style.

6. 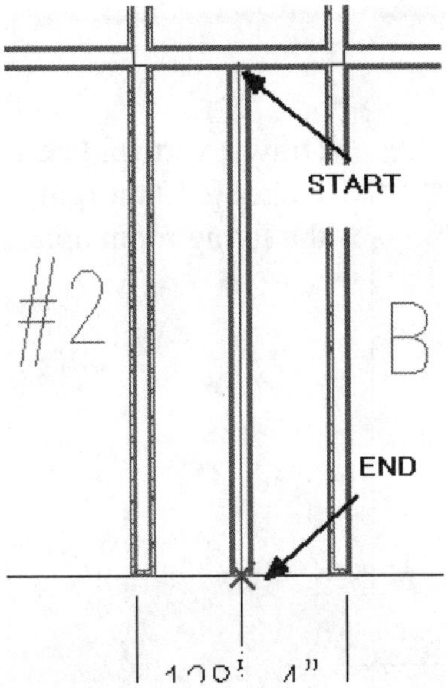

Pick the start point as shown.

You should see a node snap at the start point.

Select the endpoint shown using a perpendicular osnap.

7. 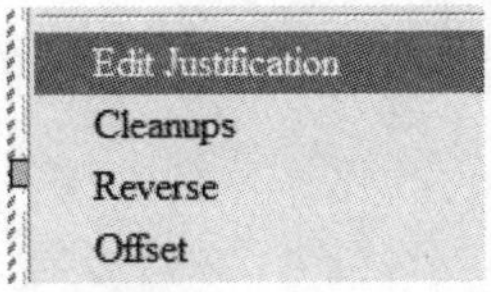

Select the wall just placed.

Right click and select **Edit Justification**.

8. 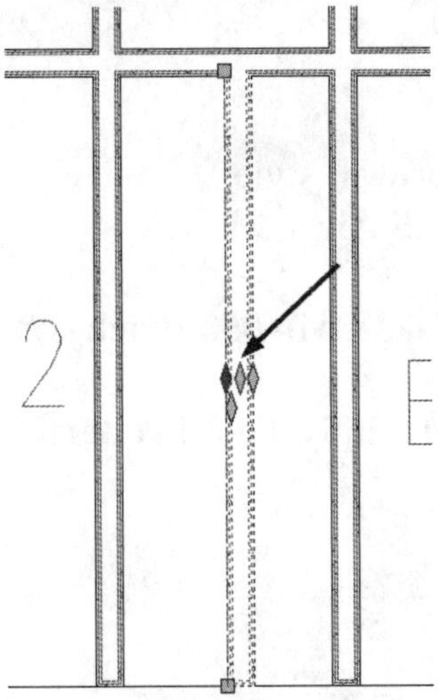

Diamond grips will appear to indicate different wall justification methods (Left/Right/Center).

The diamond on the top indicates the current justification.

Select the Center Diamond.

This will justify the wall to the center.

9. 

If you mouse over a diamond, you will see a tool tip to tell you what type of justification will be selected.

10. 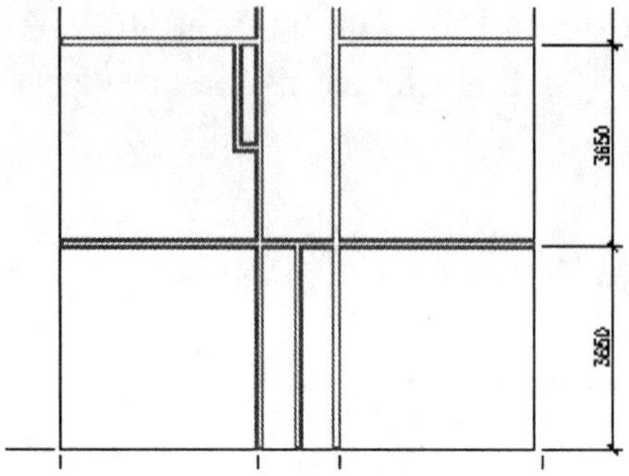

Draw a closet in Bedroom #2.

– Use the same interior wall style.
Set the wall 12 inches [304 mm] from the hallway wall and 70 inches [1820 mm] in length.

11. 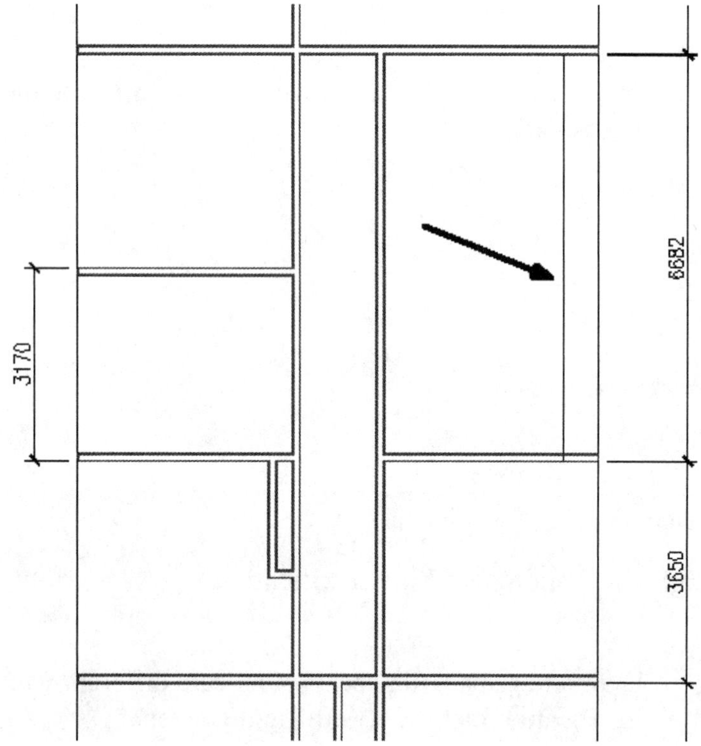

Draw a vertical line 24 inches [610 mm] inside the living room area.

12. 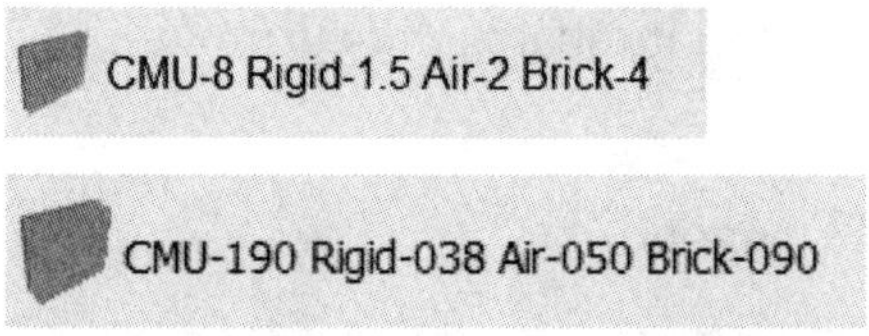

Locate the exterior wall style:
CMU-8 Rigid – 1.5 Air – 2 Brick -4

[CMU-190 Rigid-038 Air-050 Brick-090].

13. Convert the outside lines to the exterior wall style using **Apply Tool Properties to Linework**.

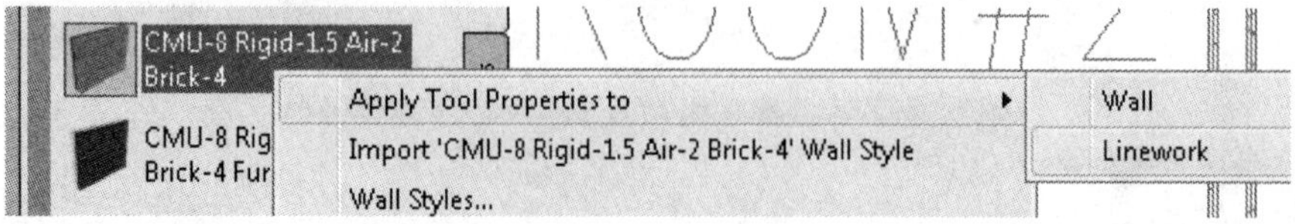

14. 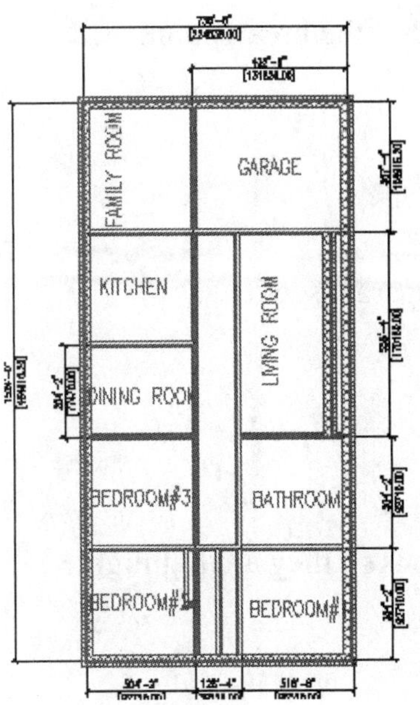

Our floor plan so far.

15. When prompted to erase layout geometry, enter **Yes**.

16. 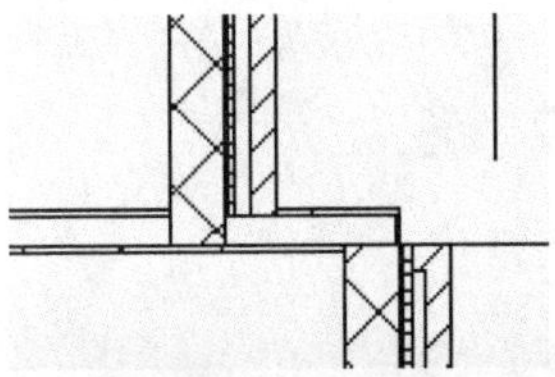

We have a small section of wall on the upper and lower right corners of the living room area that should be split so that it can be assigned the exterior wall style.

17. 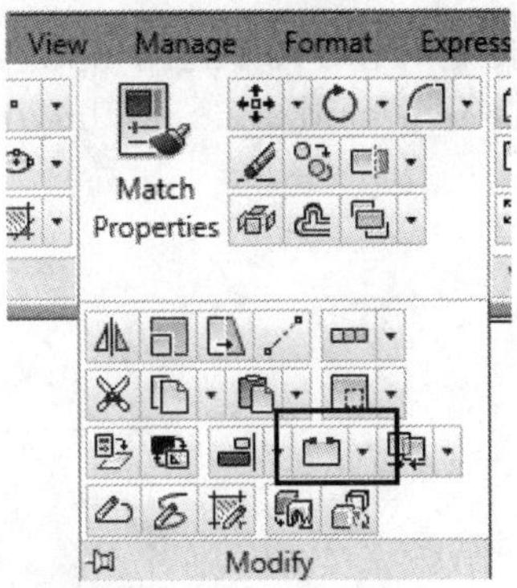

Locate the **Break** tool located on the Modify panel of the Home ribbon.

18. 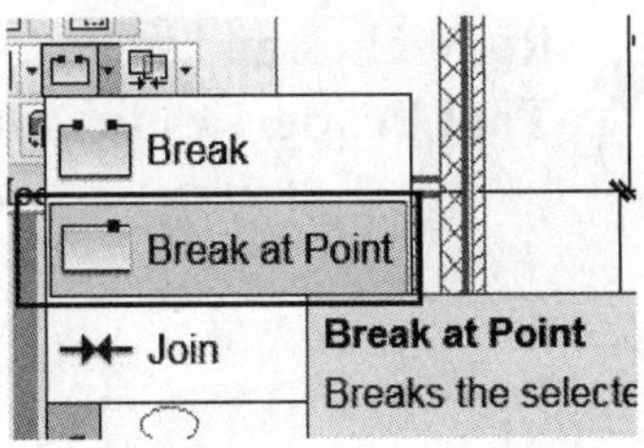

Select the **Break at Point** tool on the Break tool drop-down list to split the wall into two sections.

19. 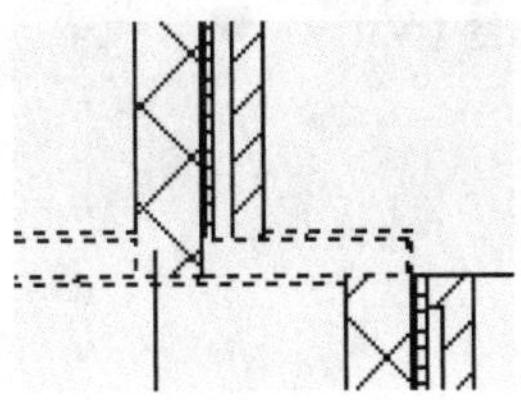

Select the wall.

It will highlight.

20. 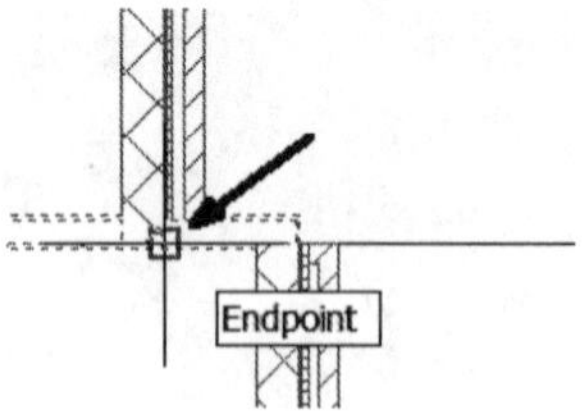

Select the point indicated as the break point.

21. 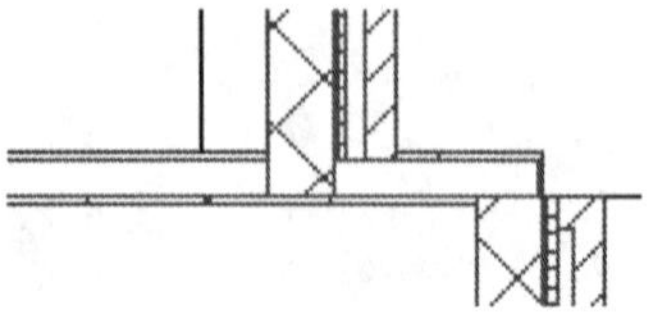
The wall is now two separate sections.

22. Repeat for the other side of the wall.

23. 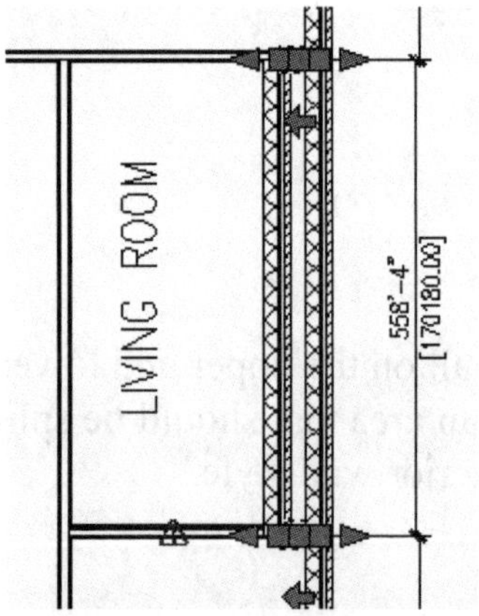

Select both wall sections so they are highlighted.

24. 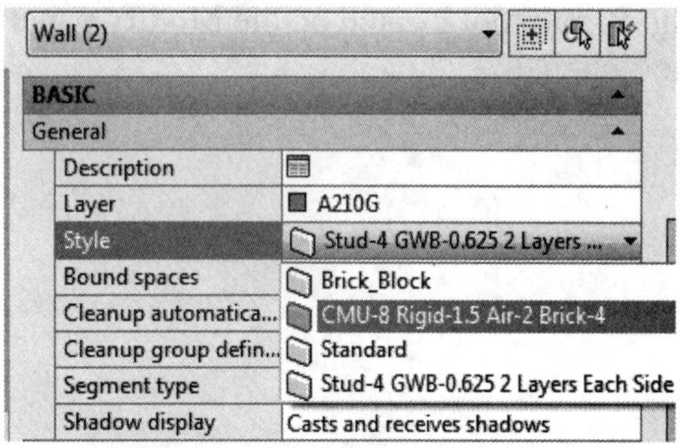

Locate the **CMU-190 Rigid-038 Air-050 Brick-090** wall style on the tool palette.

25. 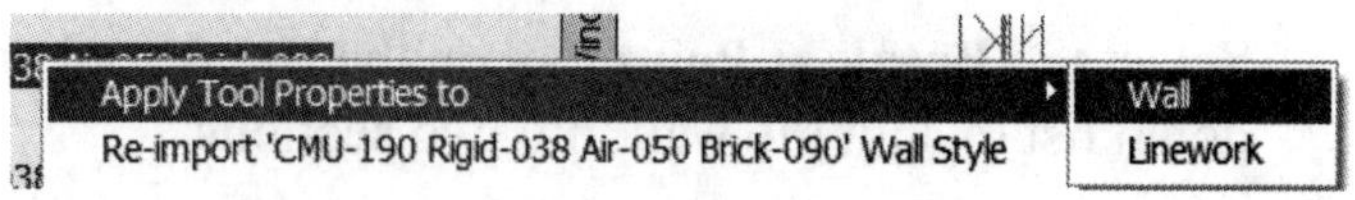

Right click and select **Apply Tool Properties to→Wall.**

The walls will be converted to the correct wall style.

26. Press ESC to deselect the walls.

27. 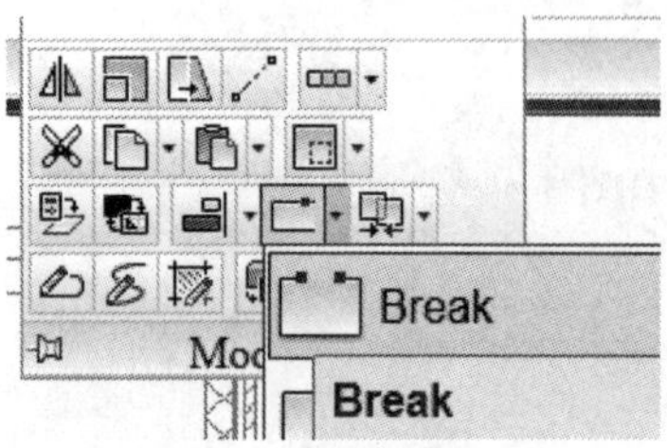

Select the **Break at two points** tool.

28. 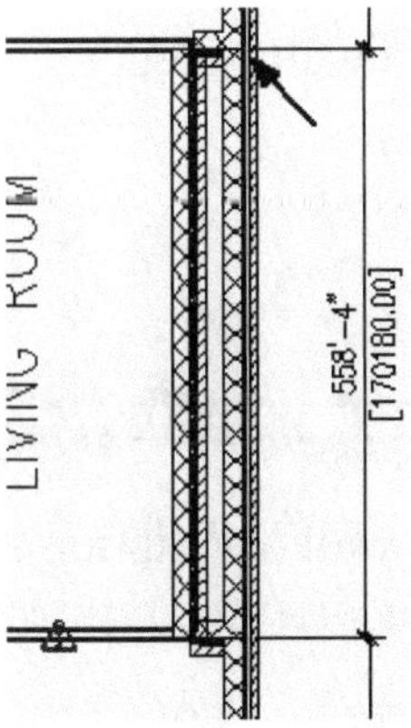

Select the point indicated to break the wall.

29. 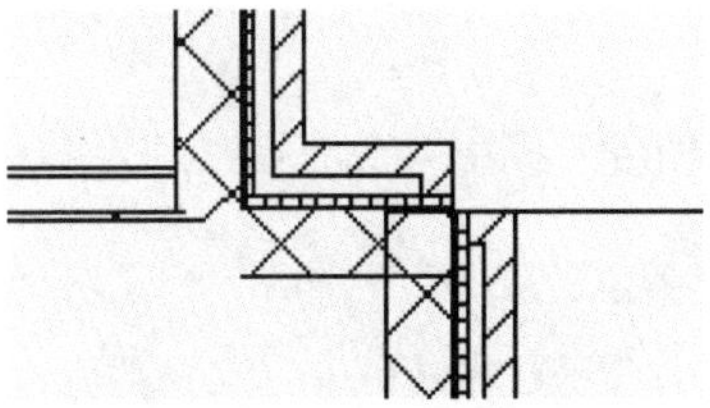

Select the small section of wall.

30. 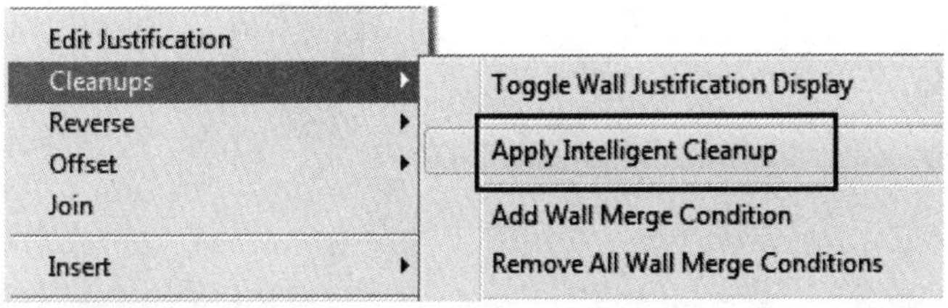

Right click and select **Cleanups→Apply Intelligent Cleanup**.

31. 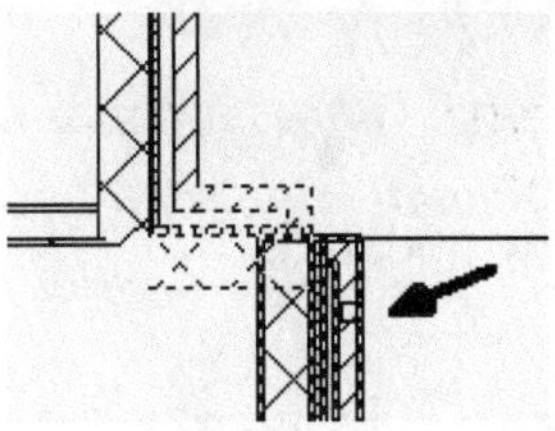

You'll be prompted to select the wall to cleanup with.

Select the wall indicated.

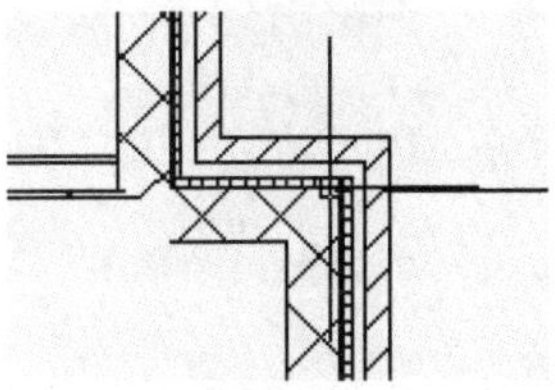

The corner is cleaned up.

32. 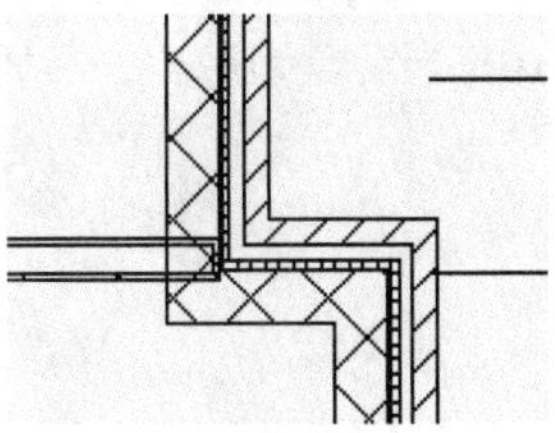

Repeat on the other corner.

33. 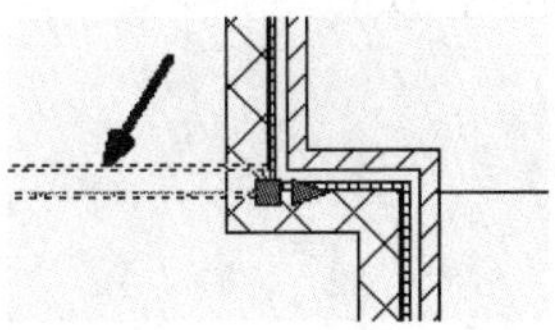

Select the interior wall.
Right click and select **Cleanups→Apply Intelligent Cleanup**.

34. 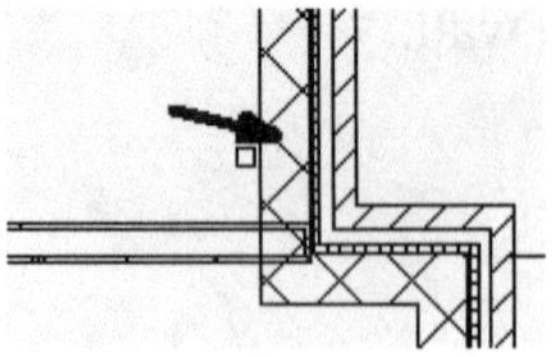
When prompted to select the boundary wall, select the wall indicated.

35. 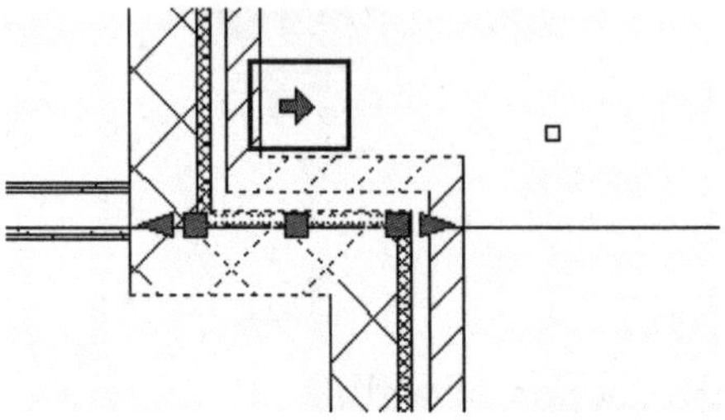
If the wall does not clean up properly, select the wall.
Use the arrow to flip the wall orientation so the exterior side of the wall is oriented properly.

Then try the Cleanup again.

36. 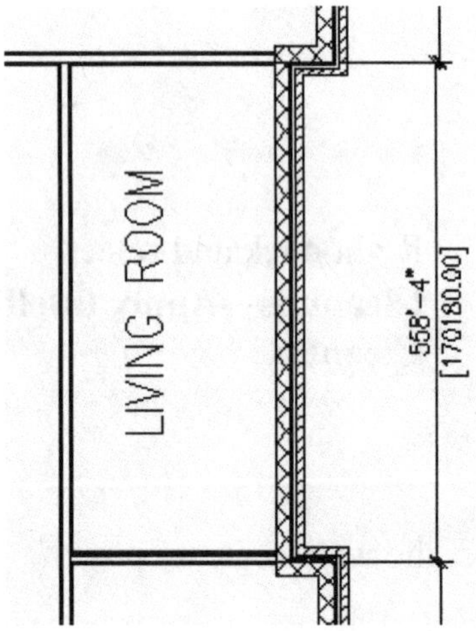

The walls appear cleaner.

37. 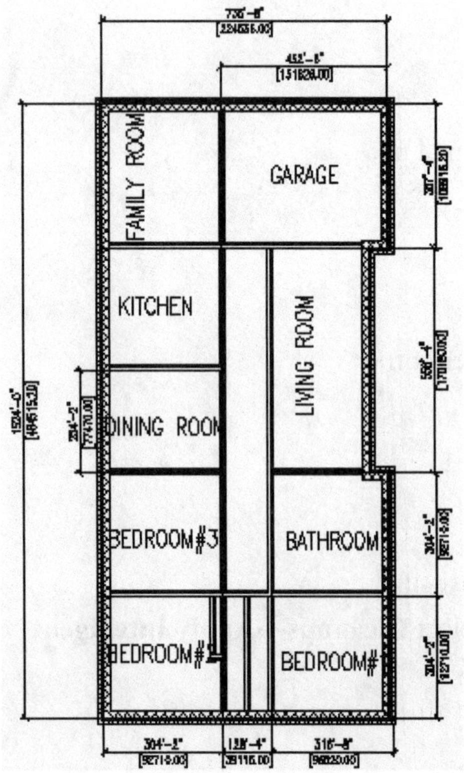

The drawing is now updated.

Save as *ex3-4.dwg.*

TIP: To create a freestanding door, press the ENTER key when prompted to pick a wall. You can then use the grips on the door entity to move and place the door wherever you like.

To move a door along a wall, use Door→Reposition→Along Wall. Use the OSNAP From option to locate a door a specific distance from an adjoining wall.

Exercise 3-5:

Adding Closet Doors

Drawing Name: Ex3-4.dwg
Estimated Time: 10 minutes

This exercise reinforces the following skills:

- Adding Doors
- Door Properties

1.  Open *ex3-4.dwg.*

2. 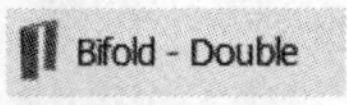

Locate the **Bifold-Double** door on the Doors tab of the Tool Palette.

3. 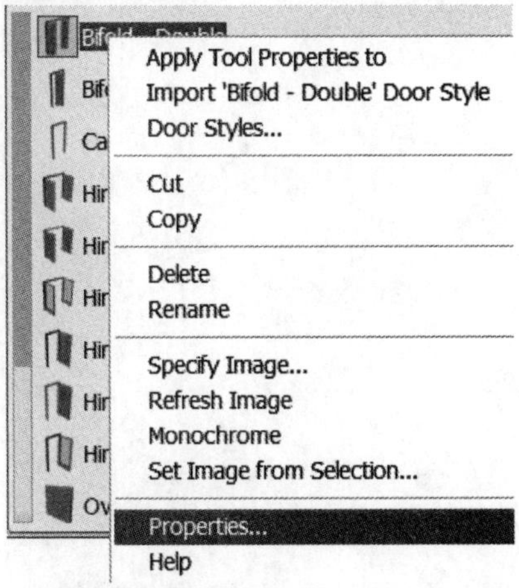

Highlight the **Bifold-Double** door.
Right click and select **Properties**.

4. 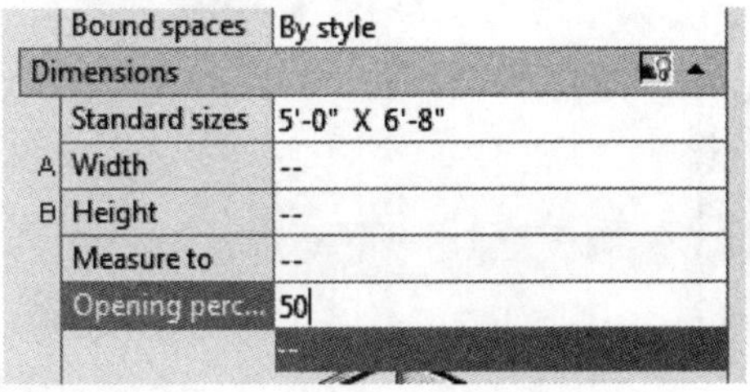

Expand the **Dimensions** section.
Set the Standard sizes to **5′-0″ x 6′-8″ [1500.00 x 2100.00]**.

Set the Opening percent to **50**.

TIP: If you left click in the field, a down arrow will appear…select the down arrow and you will get a list of standard sizes. Then, select the size you want.

A 25% opening will show a door swing at a 45-degree angle.
The value of the Opening percentage determines the angle of the arc swing.
A 50% value indicates the door will appear half-open at a 90-degree angle.

5. 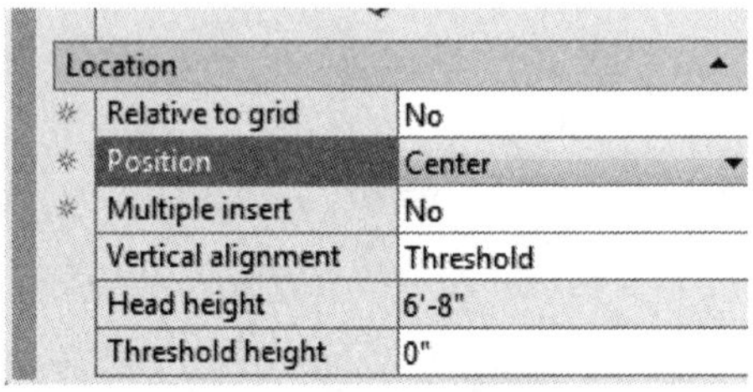

Expand the **Location** section.

Set Position along wall to **Center**.
This will center the closet doors along the wall.

6. Place the Bifold Double doors at the two closets.

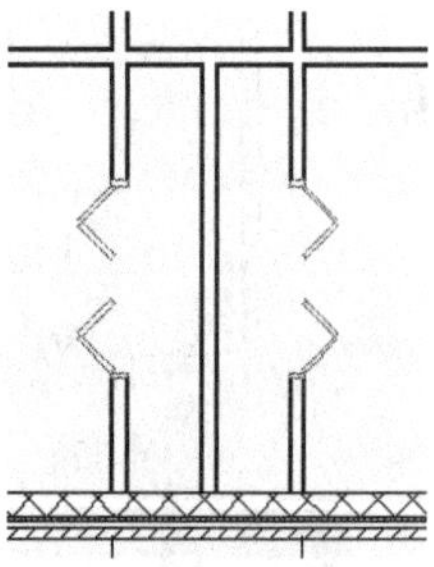

The orientation of the door swing is determined by the wall side selected.

In both cases, you want to select the outside face of the wall.

7. 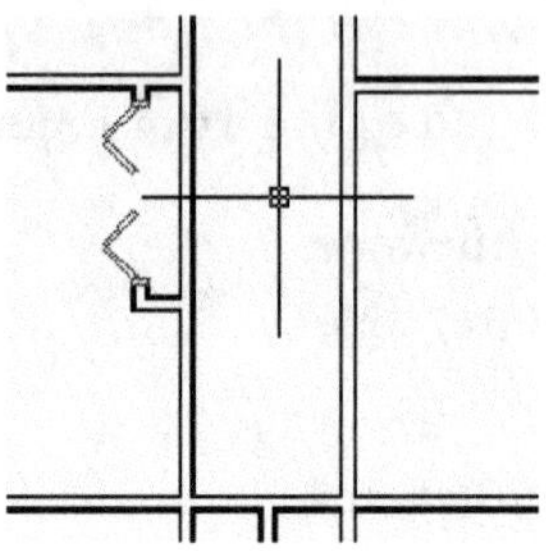

Place a Bi-fold Double door in the wall shown.

Right click and select ENTER to exit the command.

8. Save as *ex3-5.dwg*.

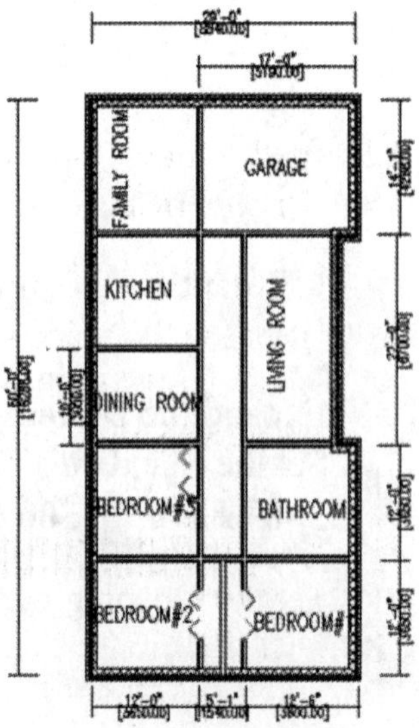

Exercise 3-6:

Adding Interior Doors

Drawing Name: ex3-5.dwg
Estimated Time: 10 minutes

This exercise reinforces the following skills:

- Adding Doors
- Door Properties

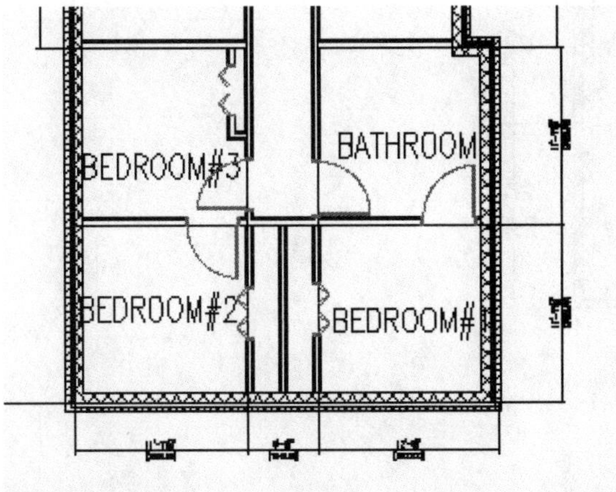

We will add single hinge doors in the areas shown.

You may need to do some wall cleanup to get the rooms to look proper.

Use AddWall, Extend, and Trim as needed.

Try to keep the walls so they line up to keep the floor plan looking clean.

1.  Open *ex3-5.dwg.*

2. Hinged - Single — Locate the **Single Hinged** door on the Doors tab of the Tool Palette. Right click and select **Properties**.

3. Expand the **Dimensions** section. Set the Standard sizes to **3′6″ x 6′8″ [1000.00 X 2100.00]**. Set the Swing angle to **90**.

Dimensions	
Standard sizes	3'-6" X 6'-8"
A Width	3'-6"
B Height	6'-8"
Measure to	Inside of frame
Swing angle	90

Dimensions	
Standard sizes	1000.00 X 2100.00
A Width	1000.00
B Height	2100.00
Measure to	Inside of frame
Swing angle	90

4. 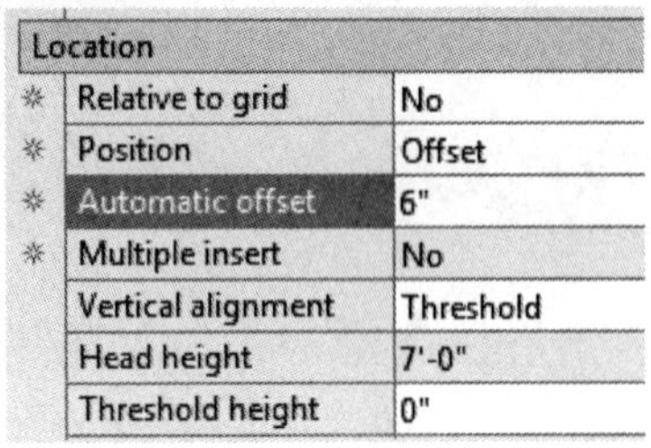

Location	
Relative to grid	No
Position	Offset
Automatic offset	6"
Multiple insert	No
Vertical alignment	Threshold
Head height	7'-0"
Threshold height	0"

Set the Position along wall to **Offset**.
Set the Automatic offset to **6″ [150]**.

Press **OK**.

5. Place the doors as indicated.

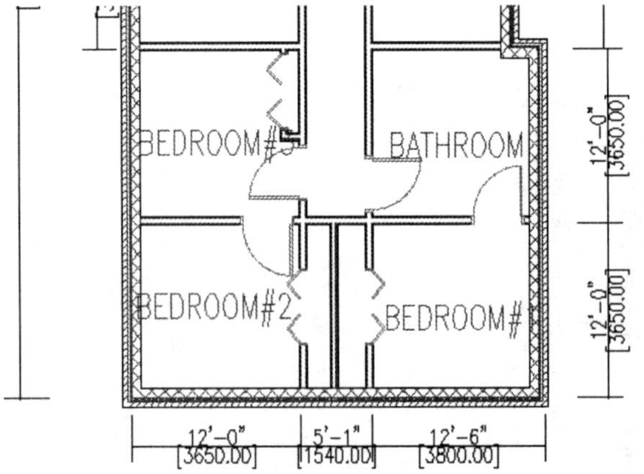

6. Save the file *ex3-6.dwg*.

Exercise 3-7:

Create an Arched Opening Tool

Drawing Name: ex3-6.dwg
Estimated Time: 10 minutes

This exercise reinforces the following skills:

- Copying Tools
- Tool Properties

1.  Open *ex3-6.dwg*.

2. 

Locate the **Cased Opening** tool on the Doors tab of the Tool Palette.

3. 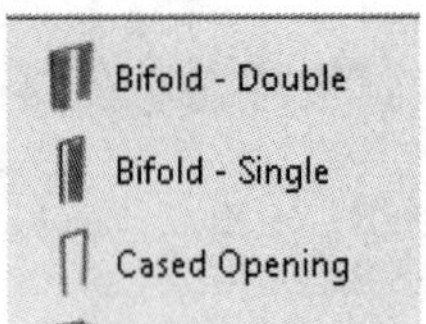

Right click and select **Copy**.

4. 

Select the **Doors** tab.
Right click and select **Paste**.

5. 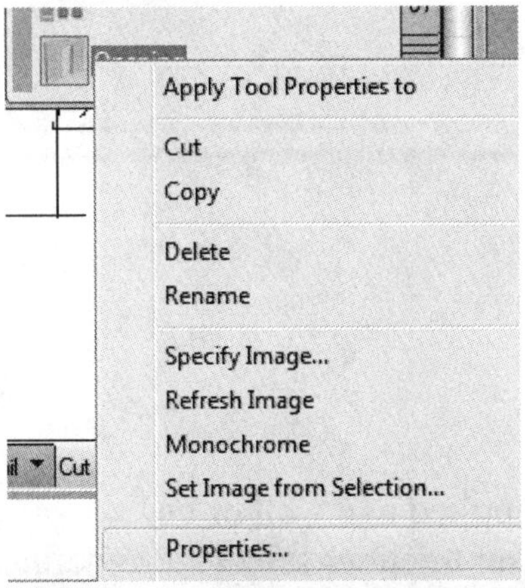

Highlight the copied tool.
Right click and select **Properties**.

6. 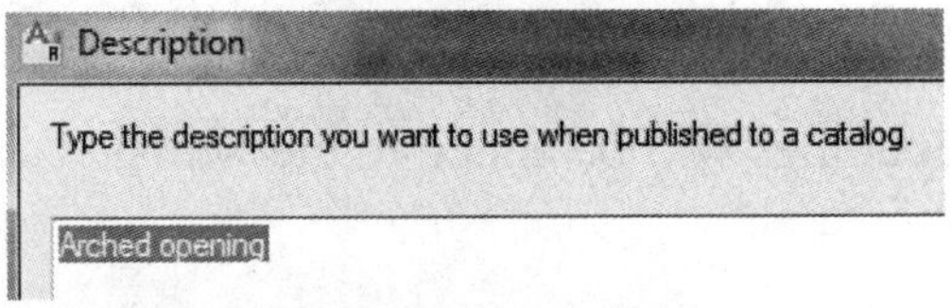

Change the Name to **Arched Opening**.
Change the Description to **Arched Opening**.
Press **OK**.

7. 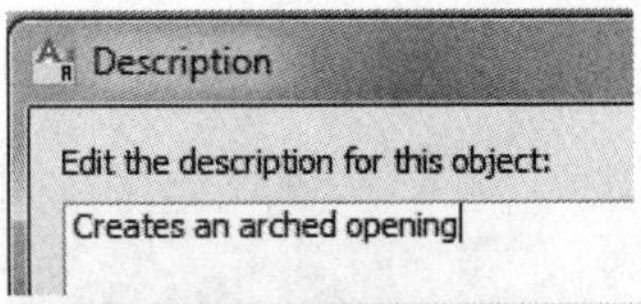

Expand the General section.
Set the Description to **Creates an Arched Opening.**

8. 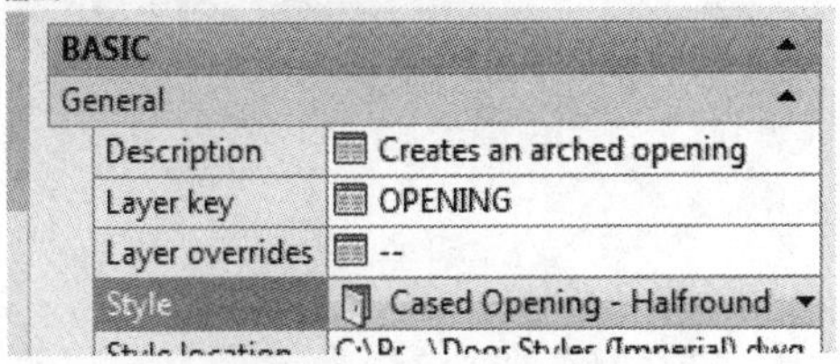

Set the Layer key to **OPENING**.
Set the Style to **Cased Opening-Half round**.

The tool is defined in the palette.

9. Save as *ex3-7.dwg*.

Exercise 3-8:

Adding an Opening

Drawing Name: ex3-7.dwg
Estimated Time: 10 minutes

This exercise reinforces the following skills:

- Adding Openings
- Opening Properties
- Copying Tools
- Set Image from Selection

Openings can be any size and elevation. They can be applied to a wall or be freestanding. The Add Opening Properties allow the user to either select a Pre-defined shape for the opening or use a custom shape.

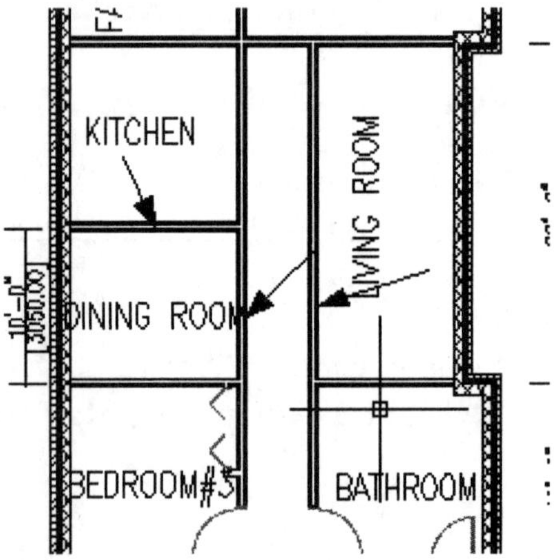

Openings will be added to the walls indicated.

1.  Open *ex3-7.dwg.*

2. 

Select the **Arched Opening** tool.

3. 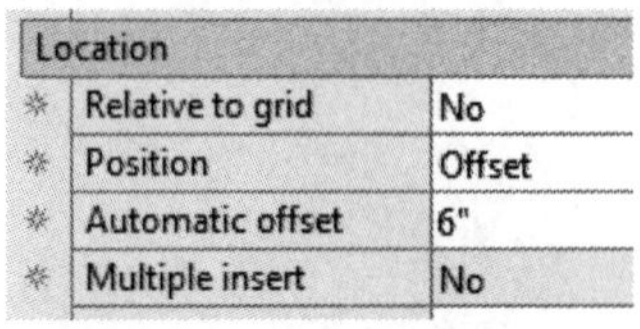

Expand the Location section.
Set the Position to **Offset**.
Set the Automatic offset to **6″ [300.00].**

4. 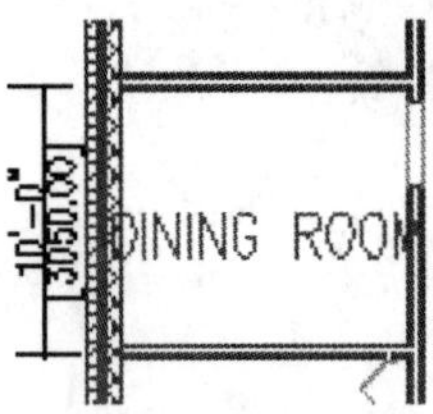

Place the arched opening in the dining room wall.

5. Use the View tools on the View ribbon **View→SW Isometric** and **3D orbit** to view the arched opening.

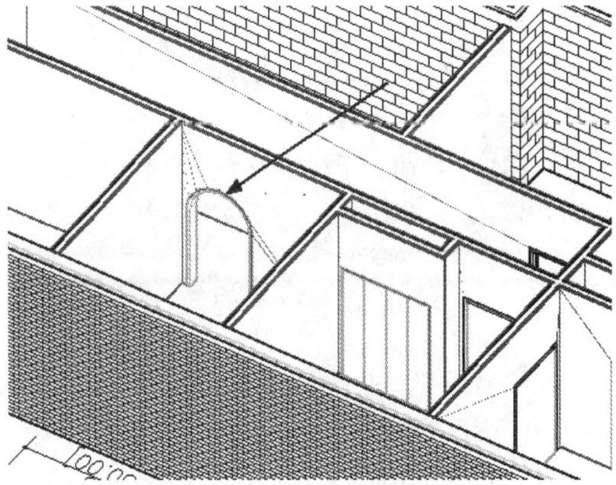

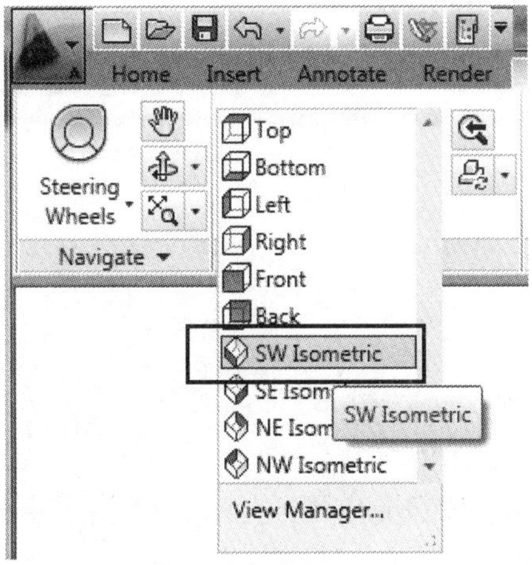

6. 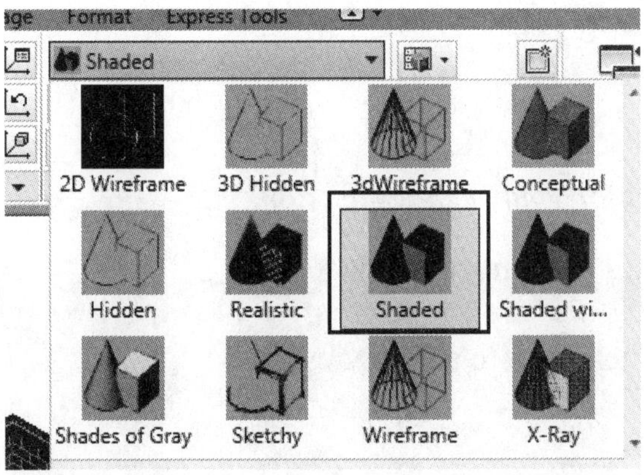

On the View ribbon:

Switch to a **Shaded** display.

If your walls are reversed, you can change the orientation in the plan/top view.

7. 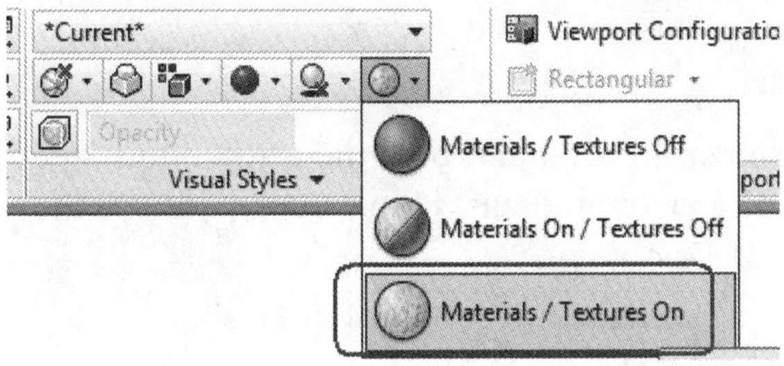

Set the **Materials/Textures On**.

8. 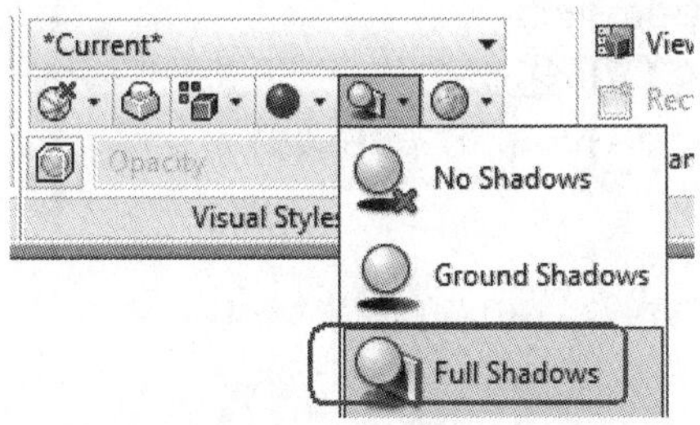

Set to **Full Shadows**.

Note how the display changes.

When materials, textures, and shadows are enabled, more memory resources are used.

9. 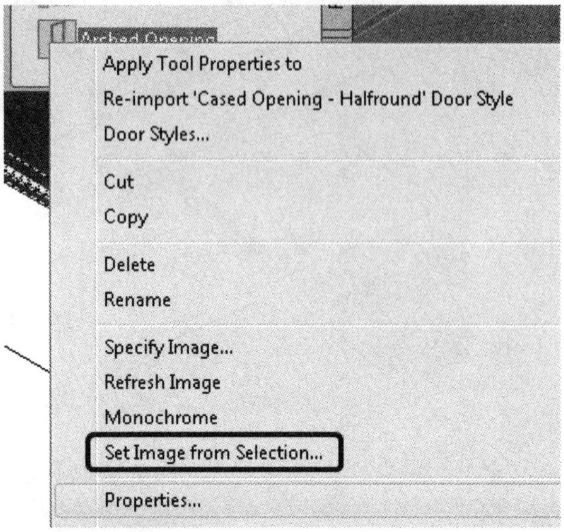

Select the **Arched Opening** icon on the tool palette.
Right click and select **Set Image from Selection…**
Pick the arched opening you created.

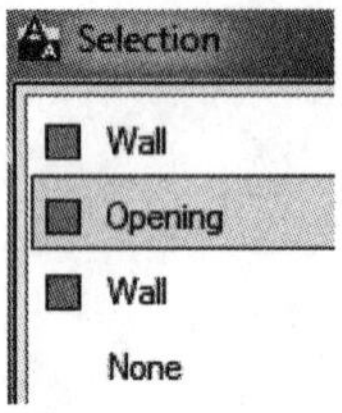

A dialog box allows you to choose which object to use for the image selection.

Select **Opening**.

Press **Enter**.

You can select more than one object for your image selection.

10. 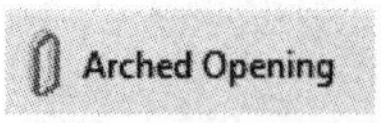

The tool icon updates with the new image.

11. 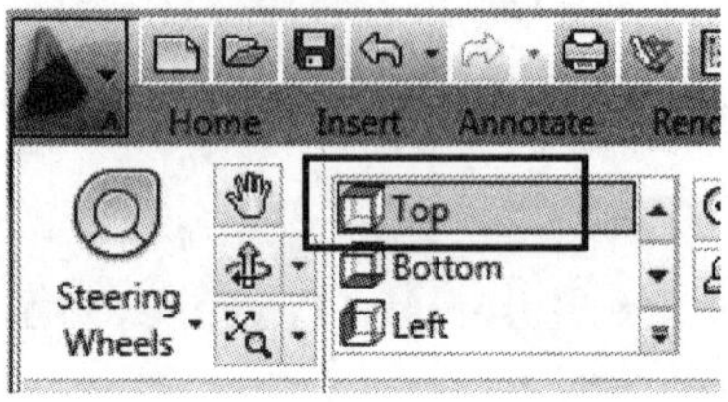

Switch back to a **Top** view.

To flip a wall orientation, simply select the wall and pick the arrow icon that appears in the center of the door. The arrow indicates the exterior side of the wall.

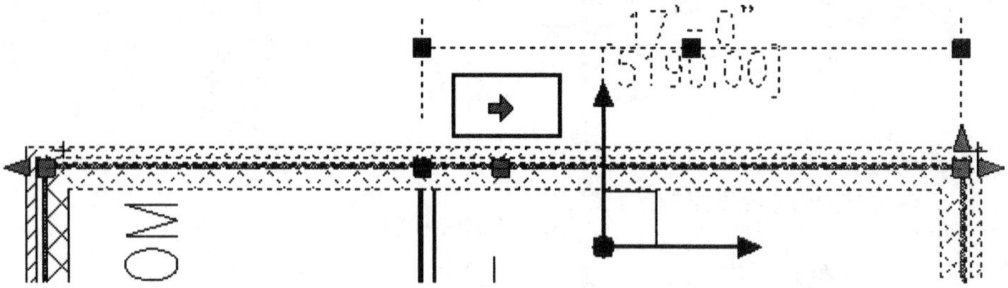

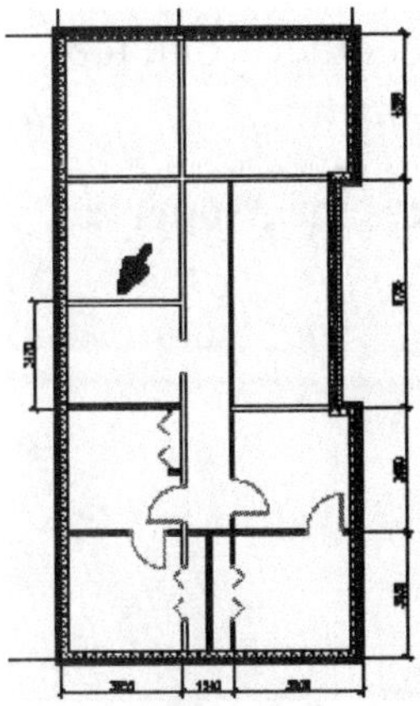

Next we place a rectangular opening in the location indicated.

12. 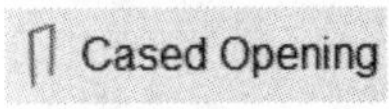

Select the **Cased Opening** tool from the Doors tool palette.

13.

Dimensions		
	Standard sizes	3'-6" X 6'-8"
A	Width	3'-6"
B	Height	6'-8"
	Measure to	Inside of frame
	Opening percent	50

Expand the Dimensions section.
Select the Standard sizes of **3′6″ x 6′8″**

Dimensions		
	Standard sizes	1000.00 X 2200.00
A	Width	1000.00
B	Height	2200.00
	Measure to	Inside of frame
	Opening percent	50

[1000.00 X 2200.00].

14.

Location		
*	Relative to grid	No
*	Position	Center
*	Multiple insert	No
	Vertical alignment	Threshold
	Head height	7'-0"
	Threshold height	0"
	Rotation	0.00

Expand the Location section.
Set the Position to **Center**.

15. 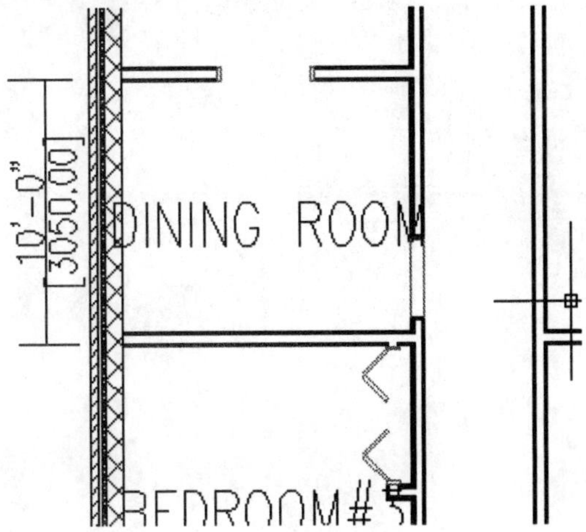

Place the opening in the wall between the kitchen and the dining room.

16.

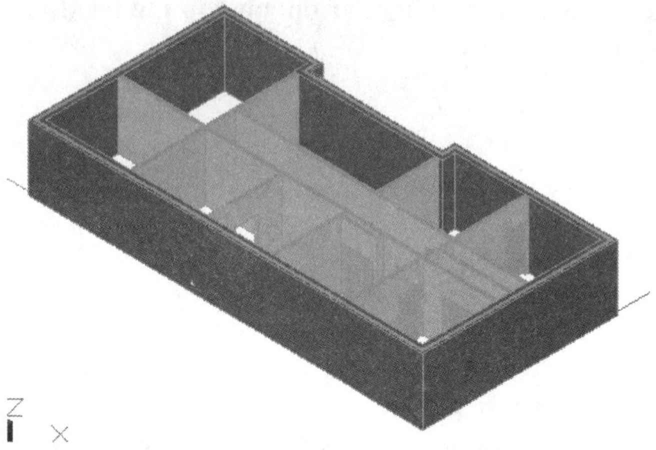

Select the **Work** tab to view the openings.

Select the **Model** tab.

17.

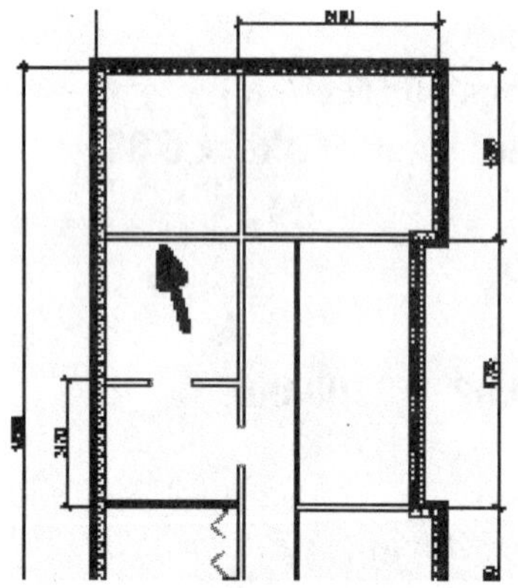

Place a rectangular opening between the kitchen and the family room.

18.

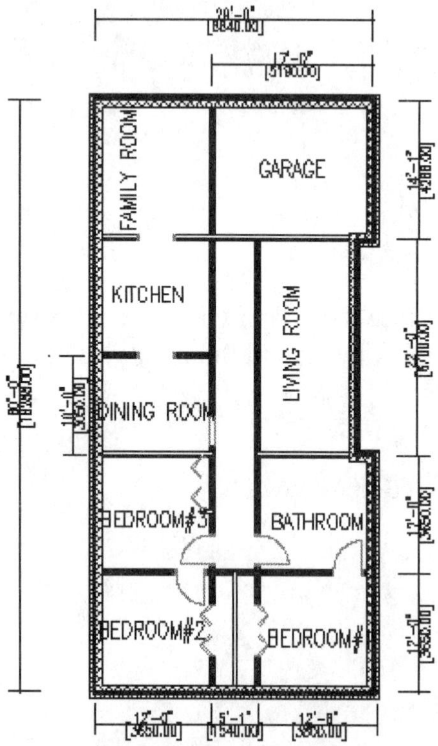

This is our floor plan so far.

Save the file as *ex3-8.dwg.*

Exercise 3-9:

Adding Doors

Drawing Name: ex3-8.dwg
Estimated Time: 20 minutes

This exercise reinforces the following skills:

- Adding Doors

1.  Open *ex3-8.dwg.*

2. 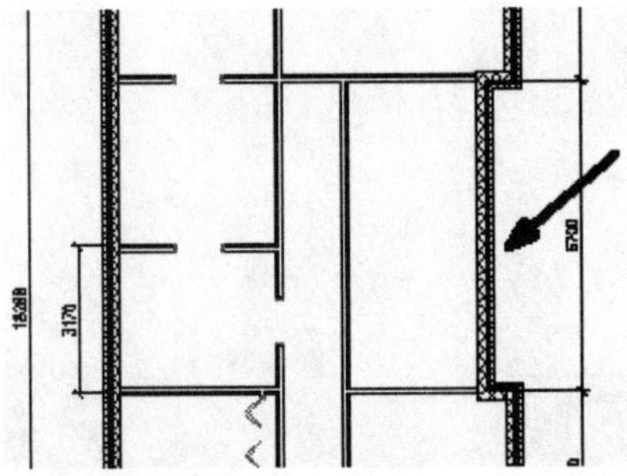 We will add an entry door on the wall indicated.

3. 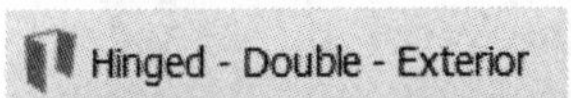

Select the **Hinged-Double-Exterior** door.

4. 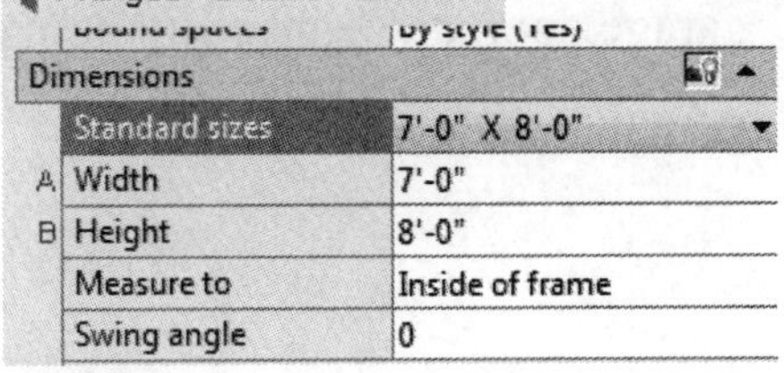

Expand the Dimensions section.
Set the Standard size to **7′-0" x 8′-0" [1800.00 x 2200.00]**.
Set the Swing angle to **0**.

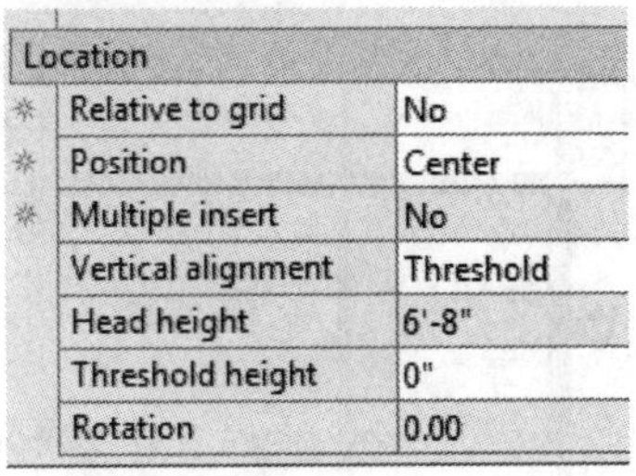

Expand the Location section.
Set the Position to **Center**.

5. 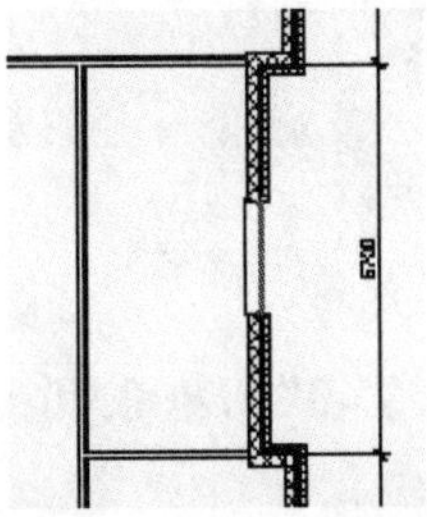 Place the door so it is centered in the wall.

6. 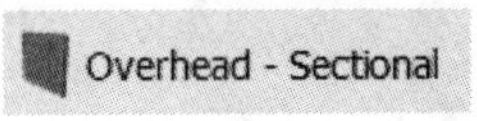

Select the **Overhead - Sectional** door.

7.

Dimensions		
	Standard sizes	8'-0" X 7'-0"
A	Width	8'-0"
B	Height	7'-0"
	Measure to	Inside of frame
	Opening percent	0

Expand the Dimensions section.
Set the Standard size to **8′ 0″ x 7′-0″ [2440.00 x 2134.00]**.
Set the Swing angle to **0**.

8.

Location		
*	Relative to grid	No
*	Position	Center
*	Multiple insert	No
	Vertical alignment	Threshold
	Head height	8'-0"
	Threshold height	0"
	Rotation	0.00

Set the Position along wall to **Center**.

9. 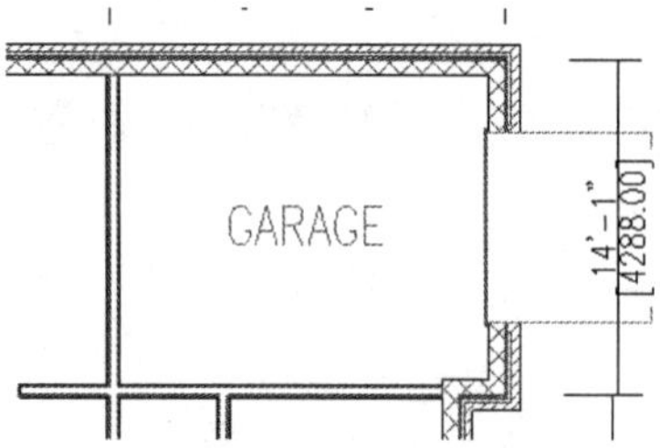

Place the door in the garage wall.

10. 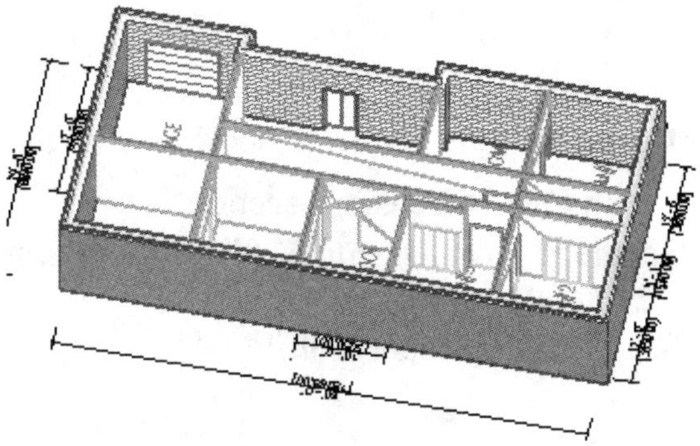

Switch to the Work tab to view the garage door and front entry door.

Switch back to the Model tab.

11. Next we add a sliding door to the family room wall indicated.

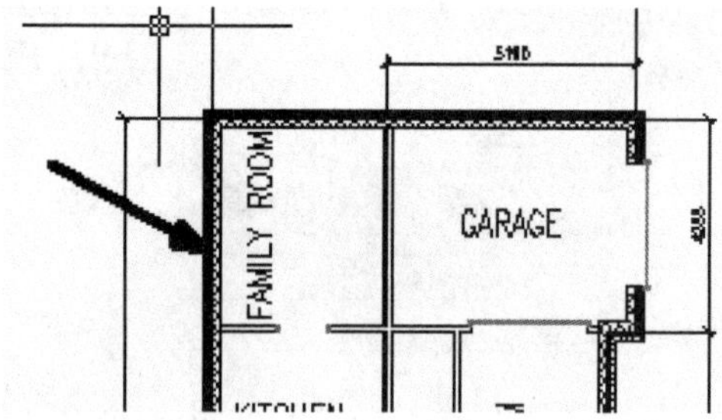

12. Select a **Sliding Door - Double - Full Lite** to add to the family room.

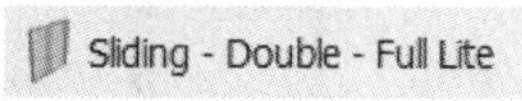

13.

Dimensions		
	Standard sizes	6'-0" X 7'-0"
A	Width	6'-0"
B	Height	7'-0"
	Measure to	Inside of frame
	Opening percent	0

Expand the Dimensions section.
Set the Standard size to **6′-0″ x 7′-0″ [1800.00 x 2200.00]**.
Set the Swing angle to **0**.

14. 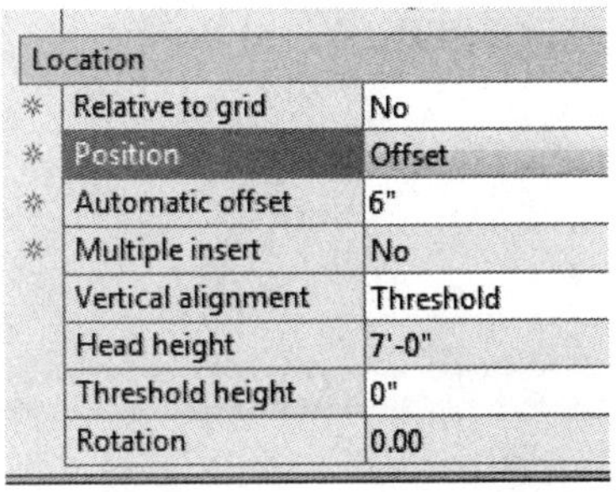

Expand the **Location** section.
Set the Position to **Offset**.
Set the Automatic offset to **6″ [300]**.

15. 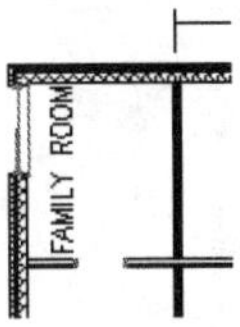

Place the sliding door.

16. 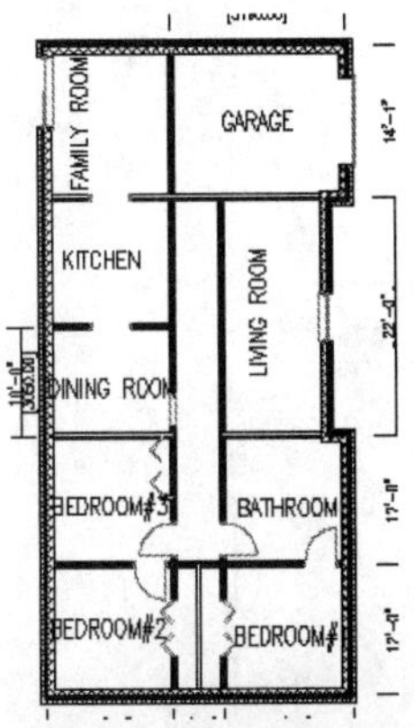

If your doors don't look proper, use the Display Manager to modify the appearance.

17. 

Activate the Manage ribbon.

Select **Display Manager**.

18. 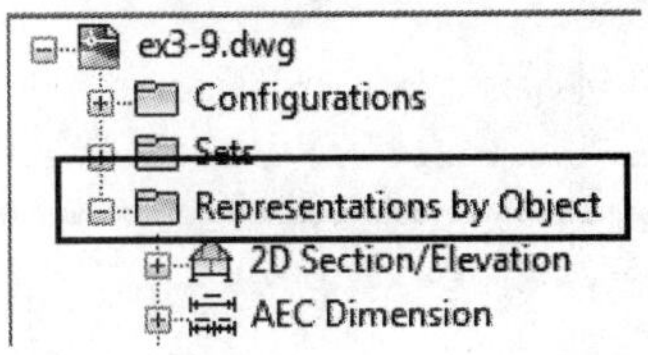

Expand the **Representations by Object** folder.

Scroll down to **Doors**.

19. 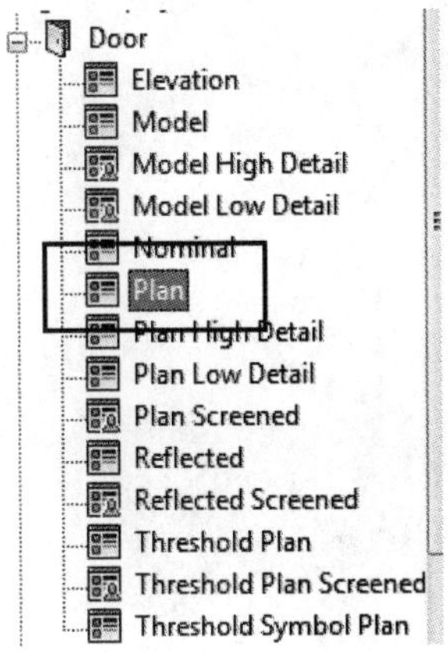

Highlight the **Plan** view.

Note you can control how doors appear in different views.

20. 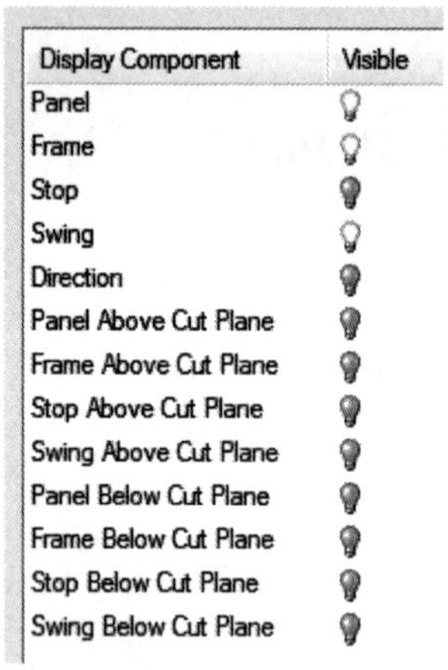

Note you can turn the visibility of different door components on or off.

21. Press **Apply** and **OK**.

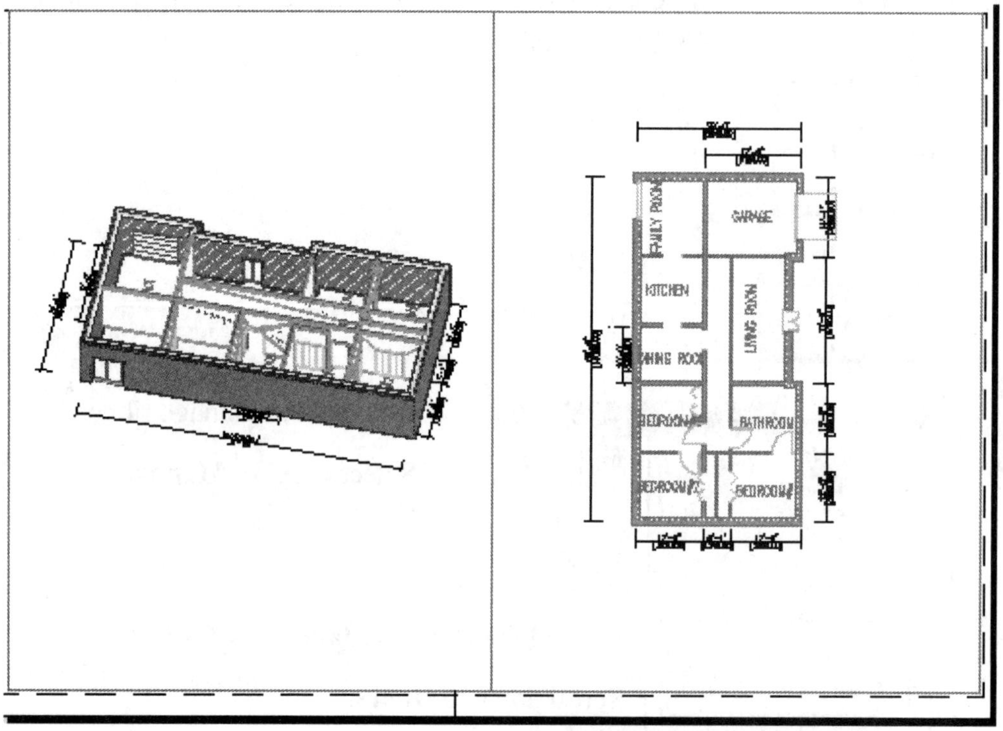

22. Select the Work tab to view your model. 

23. Save the file as *ex3-9.dwg.*

Exercise 3-10

Add Window Assemblies

Drawing Name: Lesson 3-9dwg
Estimated Time: 30 minutes

This exercise reinforces the following skills:

- Add Windows

1.  Open *ex3-9.dwg.*

2.  Select the Model tab.

3. 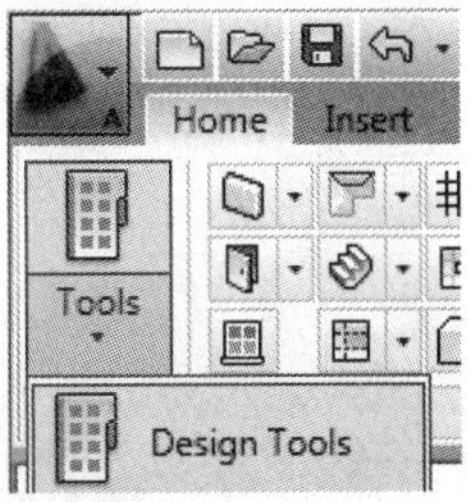

Activate the **Design Tools** from the Home ribbon, if they are not launched.

4. 

Select the Windows tab of the Tool Palette.

5. 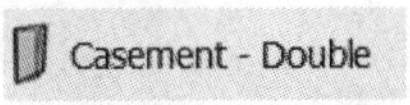

Select the **Casement-Double** window.

6. 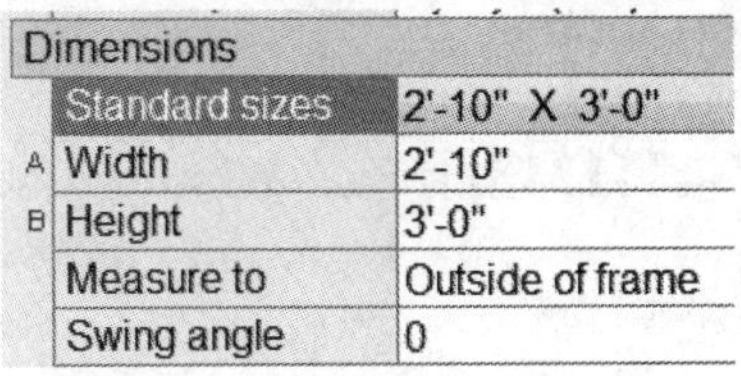

Expand the Dimensions section.
Set the size to **2′-10″ x 3′-0″ [600 x 900]**.

7. 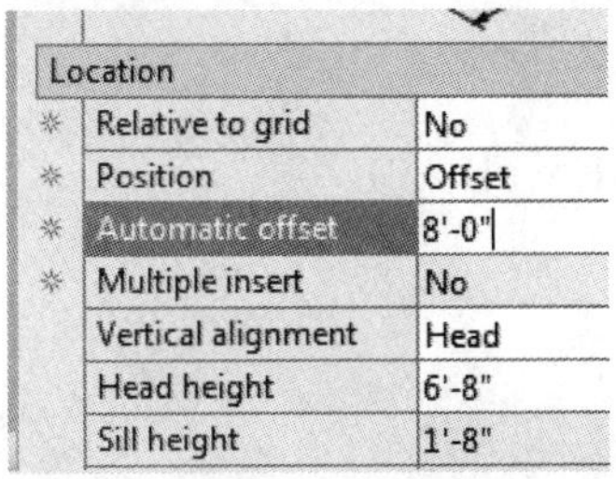

Expand the Location section.
Set the Position to **Offset**.
Set the Automatic Offset to **8′-0″ [2510.00]**.

8. 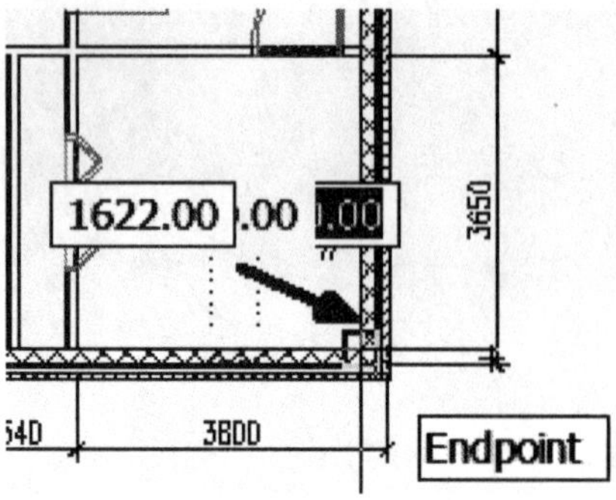

Select the wall shown and the endpoint indicated.

The endpoint is where the offset is calculated from.

9. Select the **Casement-Double** window again

10. 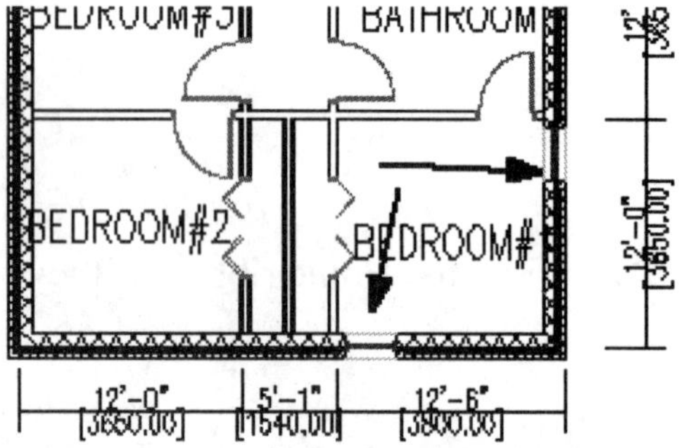

Place the window on the vertical bedroom wall.

Remember – if you don't like the position of any of the Windows, you can reposition them. Just select the window, right click, and select **Reposition Along Wall**.

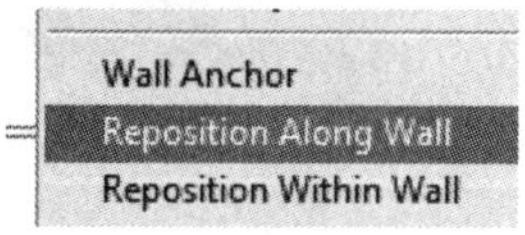

11. 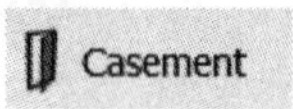

Select the **Casement** window from the Design Palette.

12. 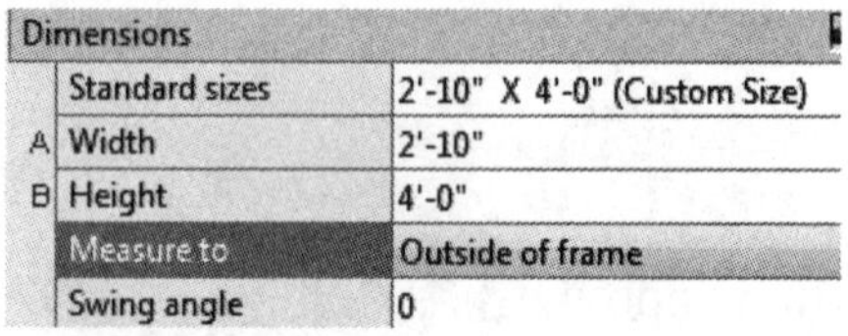

Expand the Dimensions section.
Set the size to **2′-10″ x 4′-0″ [600.00 x 1200.00]**.

13. 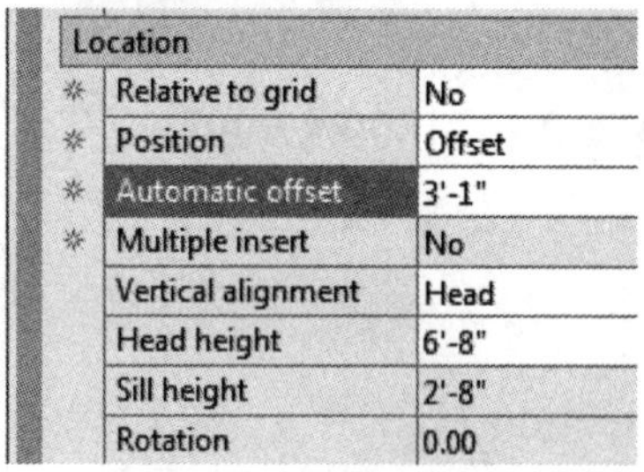

Expand the Location section.
Set the Position to **Offset**.
Set the Offset to **3′-1″ [1215]**.

14. 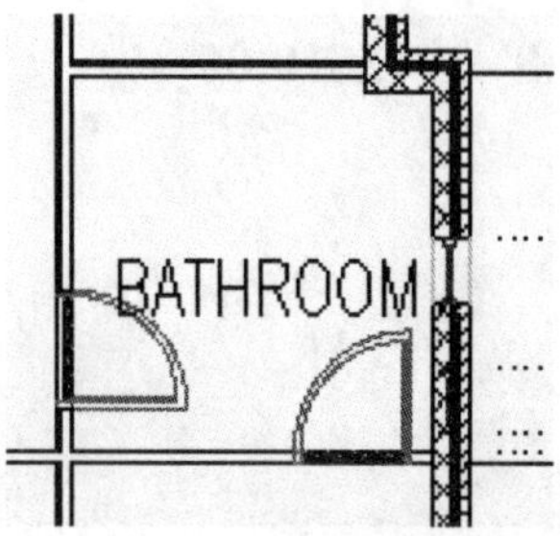

Place the window in the bath wall.

15. Place a Double Casement window in Bedroom #2.

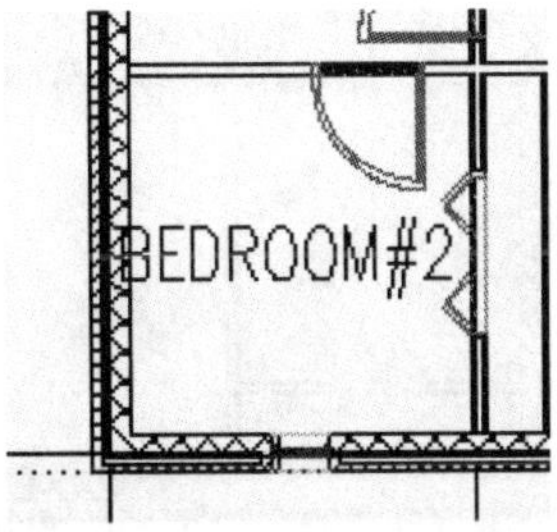

16. Place a Double Casement window in Bedroom #2 on the left vertical wall.

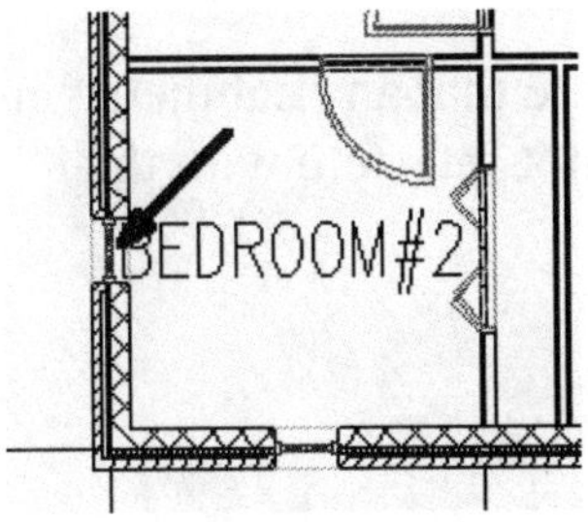

17. Place a Double Casement window in Bedroom #3 on the left vertical wall.

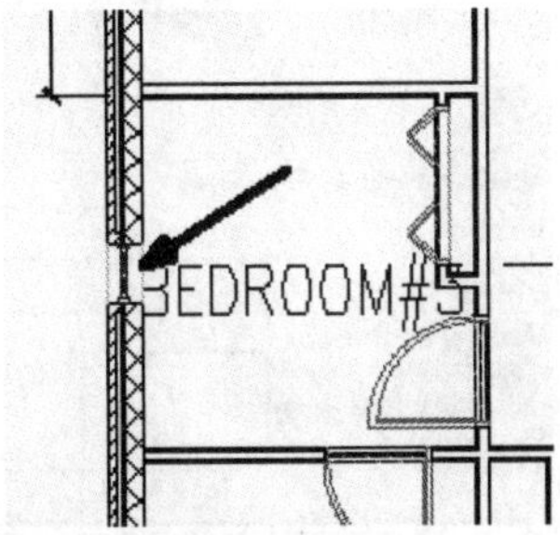

18. Picture - Arched — Locate the **Picture- Arched** to place in the left dining room wall.

19. Expand the Dimensions section.
Set the size to **3′-0″ x 4′10″ Rise: 5″ [600.00 x 1500.00 Rise 300.00]**.

Dimensions		
	Standard sizes	3'-0" X 4'-10" Rise: 5"
A	Width	3'-0"
B	Height	4'-10"
C	Rise	5"
	Measure to	Outside of frame
	Opening percent	0

20. Expand the Location section.
Set the Position to **Center**.
Set the Offset to **0″ [0.00]**.

Location	
Relative to grid	No
Position	Center
Multiple insert	No
Vertical alignment	Head
Head height	6'-8"
Sill height	2'-8"
Rotation	0.00

21. Place the window.

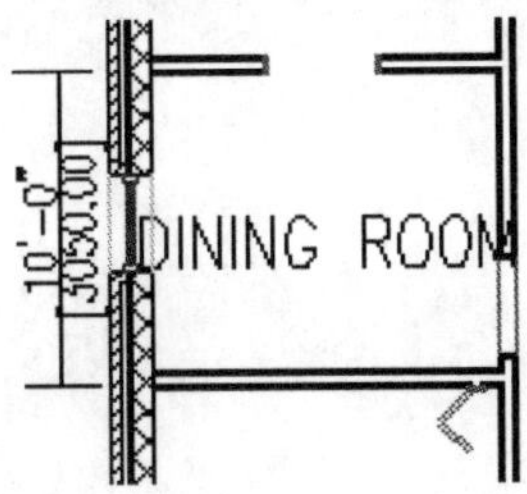

22. 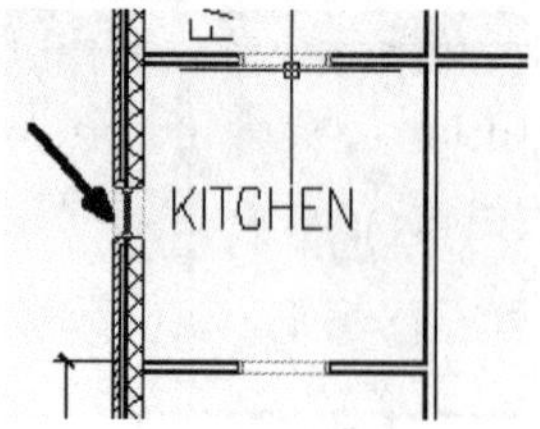

Add a **Casement: Single** window to the kitchen.

23. 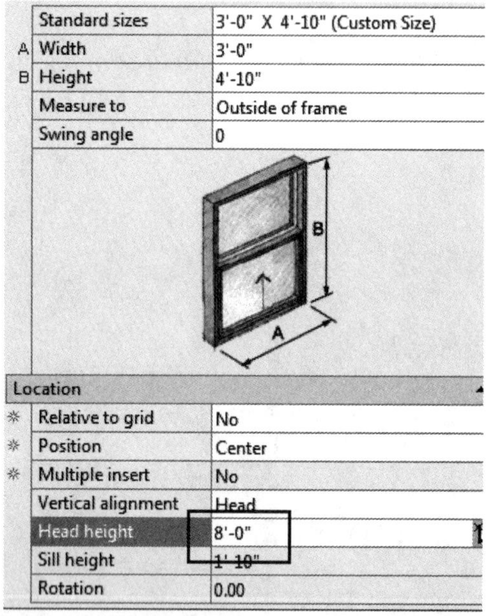

Set the Head height to **8′-0″ [2050]**.

This will ensure that any cabinetry in the kitchen does not interfere with the window.

24. 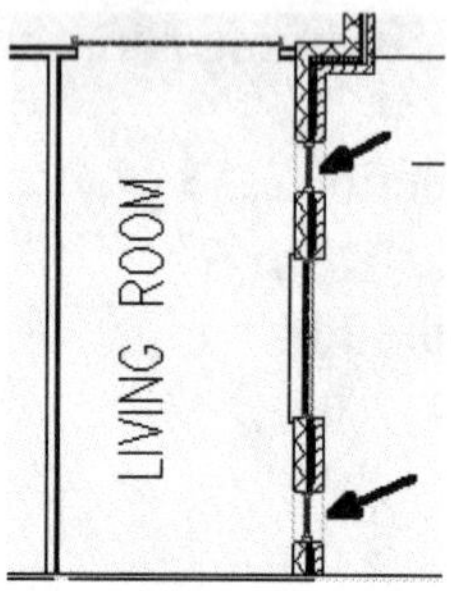

Place an **Arched Picture** window on each side of the entry door in the right living room wall.

25. 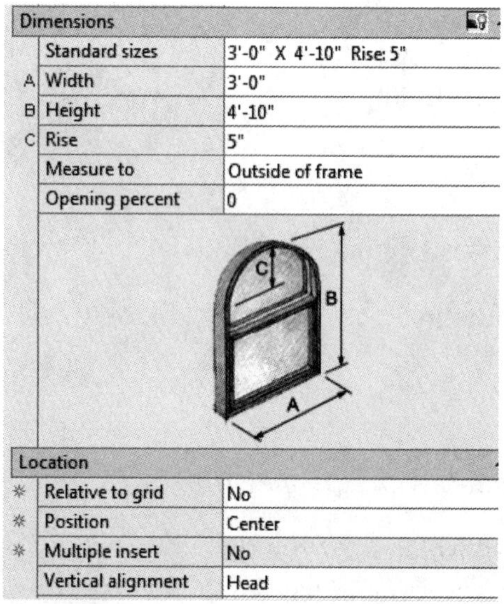

Use the previous settings to place the windows.

26. 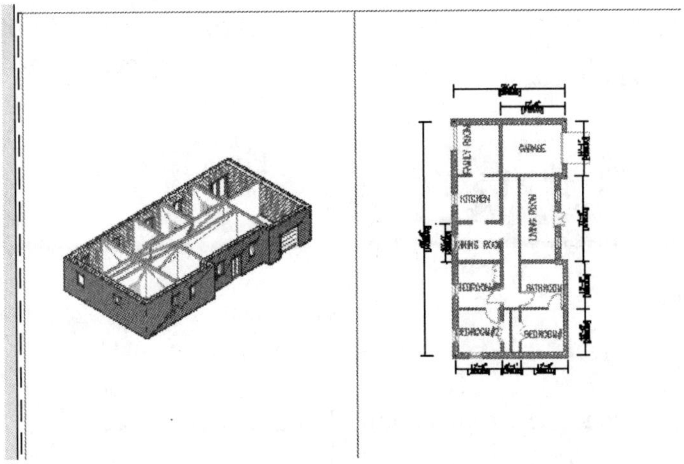

Your floor plan should look similar to the one shown here.

Save as *ex3-10.dwg*.

Exercise 3-11:

Adding a Fireplace

Drawing Name: ex3-10.dwg
Estimated Time: 20 minutes

This exercise reinforces the following skills:

- Using the Design Center
- Adding Openings

In this exercise, we add a fireplace to the family room. You can download the fireplace from the publisher's website.

1.  Open *ex3-10.dwg*.

Select the Model tab.

2. 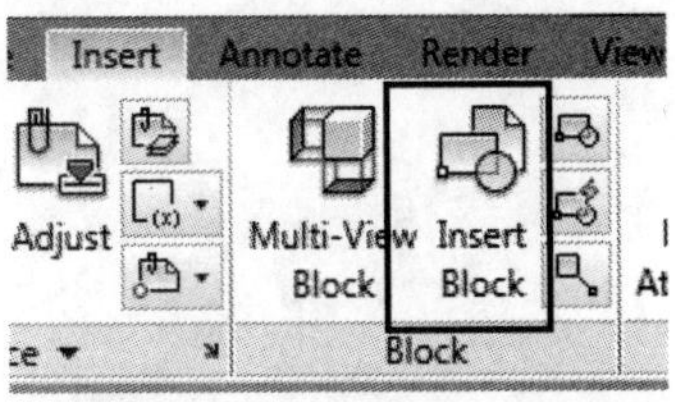

Activate the **Insert** ribbon.

Select **Insert Block**.

3. 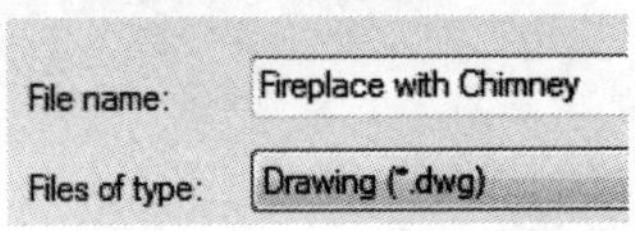

Locate the *Fireplace with Chimney* file.

This file can be downloaded from the book's detail page on the publisher's website at www.SDCpublications.com.

4. 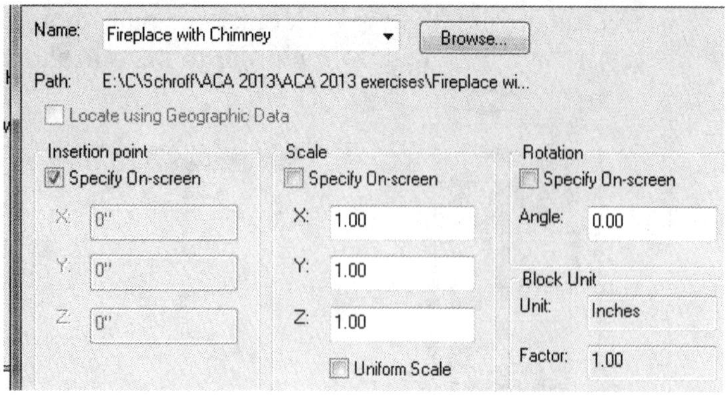

Under Insertion point: Enable **Specify On-Screen**.

Press **OK**.

5. 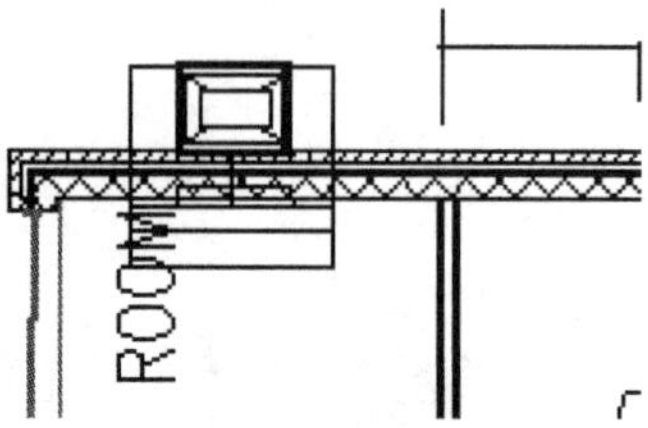

Place the fireplace into the family room wall.

Use a midpoint osnap to help place the fireplace. You can also Shift-right click to select a midpoint snap on the fly.

6. 

Set the display to **Shaded**.

7. 

Use the ViewCube tool to inspect your work so far.

8. 

Use the 3D Orbit tool to inspect how the fireplace appears.

We need to add an opening

Switch back to a plan view.

9. 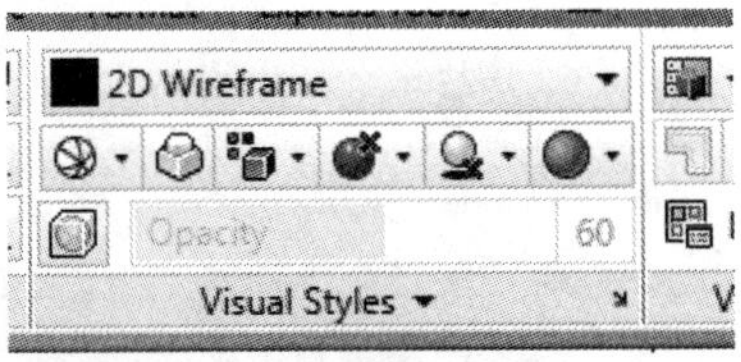

Set the display to **2D Wireframe**.

10. 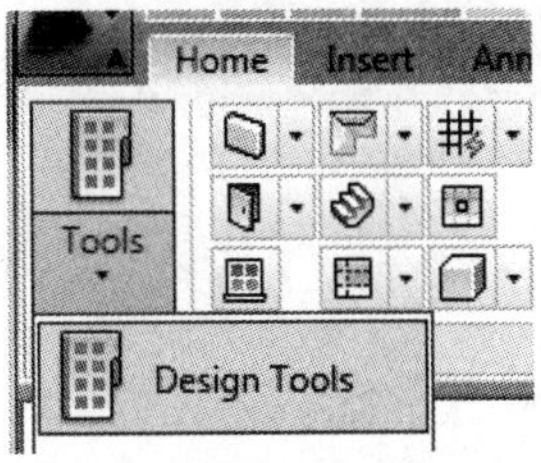

Activate the Home ribbon.

Launch the Design Tools palette.

11. 

Select the **Opening** tool from the Design Palette.

12. 

Change the Width to **3′-6″ [914.4]**.
Change the Height to **3′-0″ [862.6]**.

13. 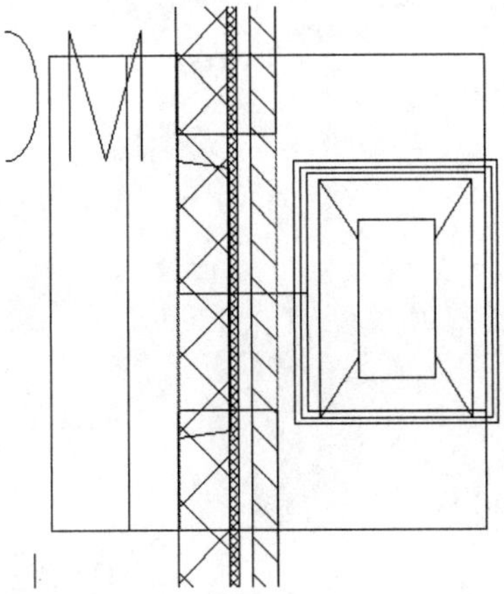

Place the opening in the wall.

14. 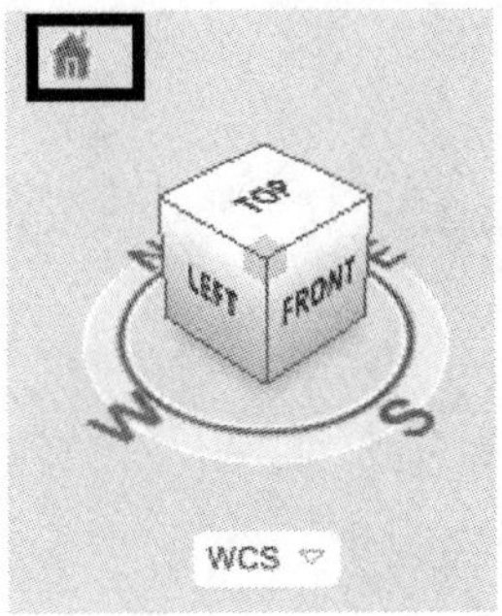

Select the Home icon to switch to a 3D view.
Then use the ViewCube to inspect the opening in the fireplace.

Your finished fireplace and chimney should look similar to this.

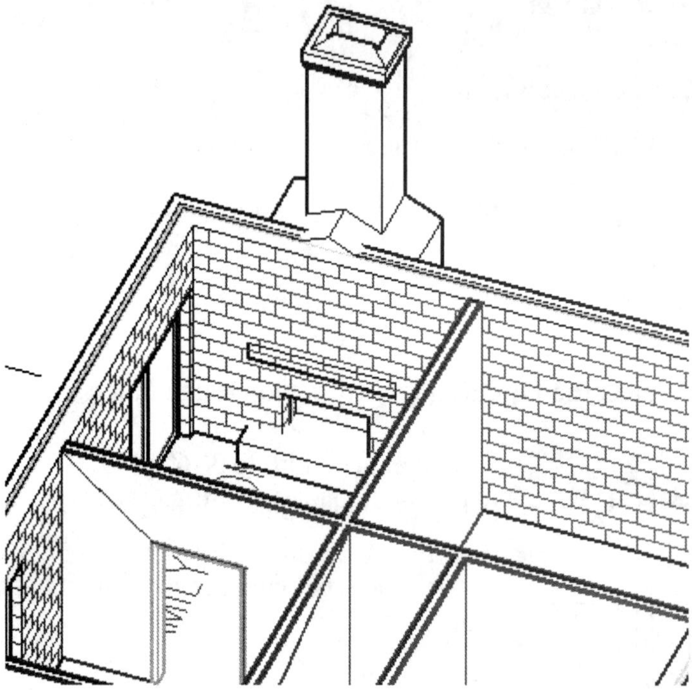

15. Save the file as *ex3-11.dwg*.

Close all open drawings.
You can do this by typing **CLOSEALL** on the command line.

Lesson 4
Space Planning

A residential structure is divided into three basic areas:

- Bedrooms: Used for Sleeping and Privacy
- Common Areas: Used for gathering and entertainment, such as family rooms and living rooms, and dining area
- Service Areas: Used to perform functions, such as the kitchen, laundry room, garage, and storage areas

When drawing your floor plan, you need to verify that enough space is provided to allow placement of items, such as beds, tables, entertainment equipment, cars, stoves, bathtubs, lavatories, etc.

AutoCAD Architecture comes with Design Content to allow designers to place furniture to test their space.

Exercise 4-1:
Creating AEC Content

Drawing Name: new
Estimated Time: 20 minutes

This lesson reinforces the following skills:

- Design Center
- AEC Content
- Customization

1. 
Start a new drawing using **QNEW**.

2. 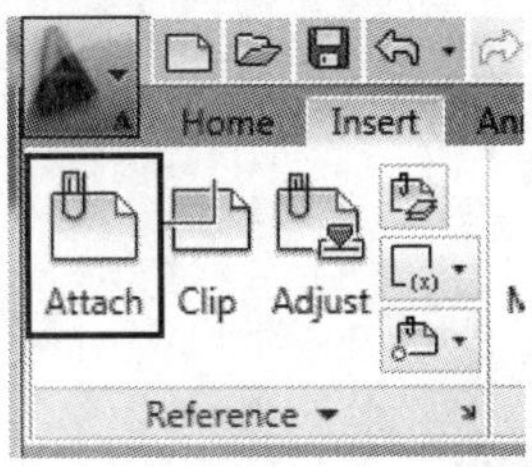

Activate the Insert ribbon.

Select **Attach**.

3. 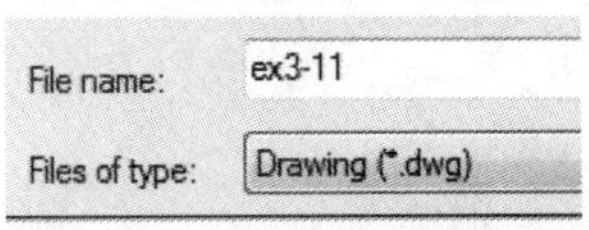

Browse for *ex3-11.dwg* and press **Open**.

4. 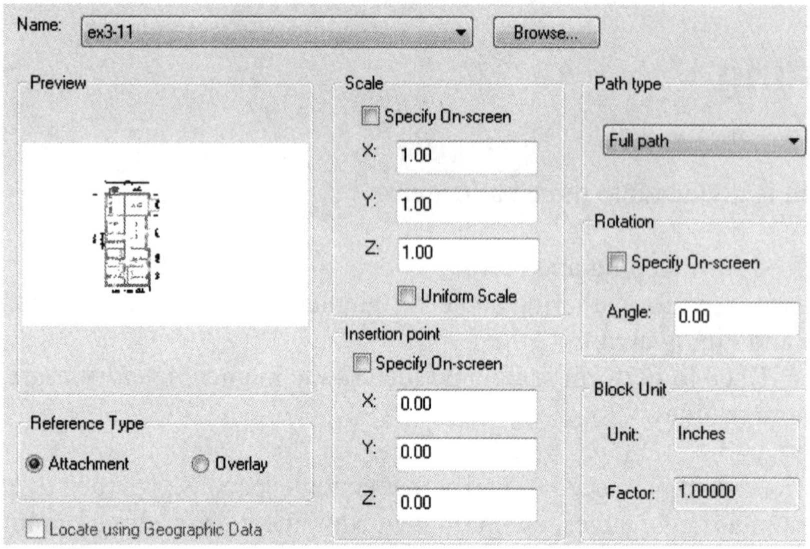

Accept the defaults.

Uncheck **Specify On-screen** for the insertion point.

Press **OK**.

5. 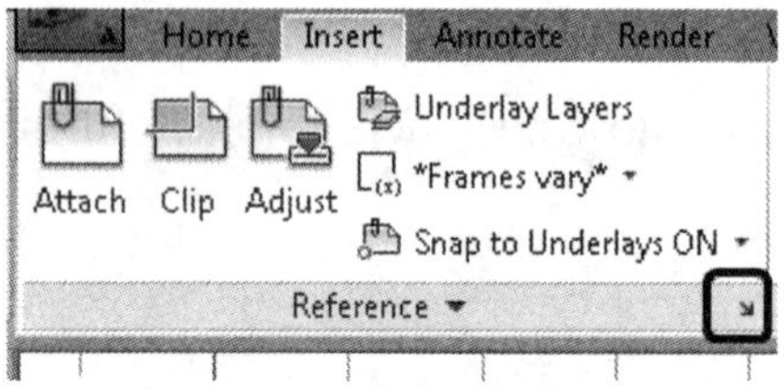

Launch the XREF Manager by selecting the small arrow in the Reference drop-down.

6. The palette lists the file references now loaded in the drawing.

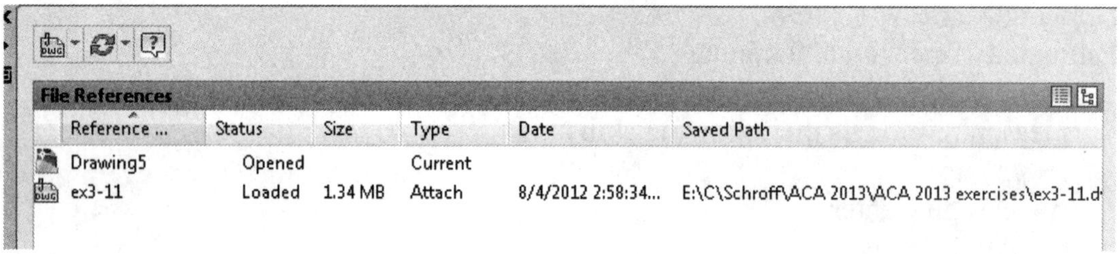

7. 

Zoom Extents

8. 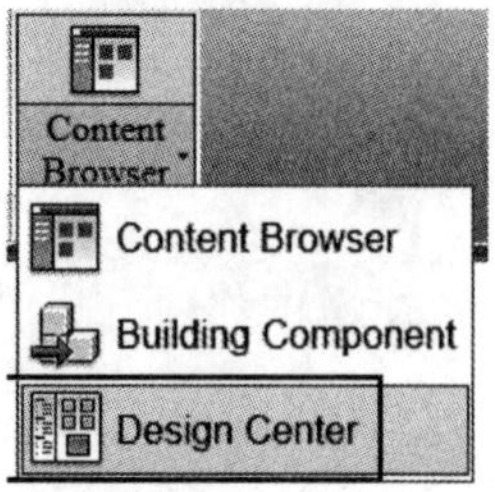

Launch the Design Center from the Insert ribbon or press Ctrl+2.

9. 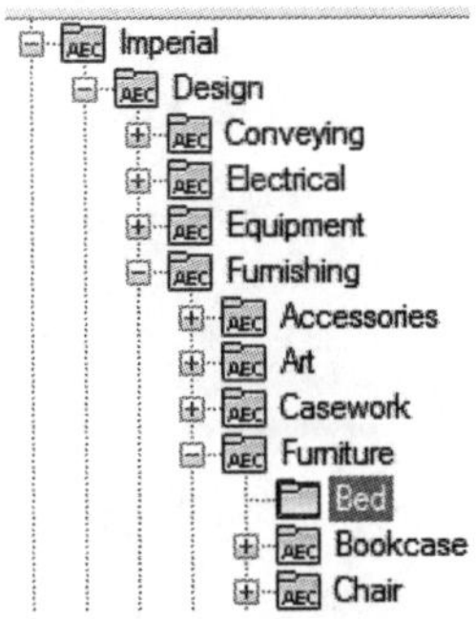

Select the AEC Content tab.

Browse to *AutoCAD Architecture/Imperial/Design/ Furnishing/ Furniture/Bed*

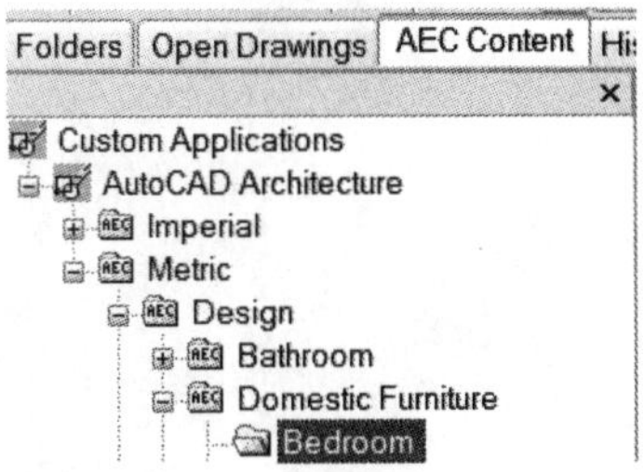

[AutoCAD Architecture/Metric/Design/Domestic Furniture/Bedroom].

10. 

Select the *Double* [*3D Double Bed*]*.dwg* file.
Right click and select **Insert**.

11. 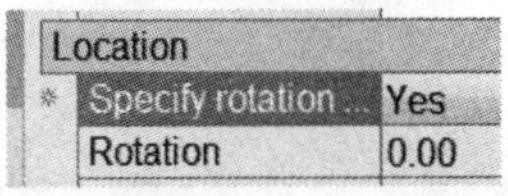

Set Specify rotation to **Yes** in the Properties dialog.

12. 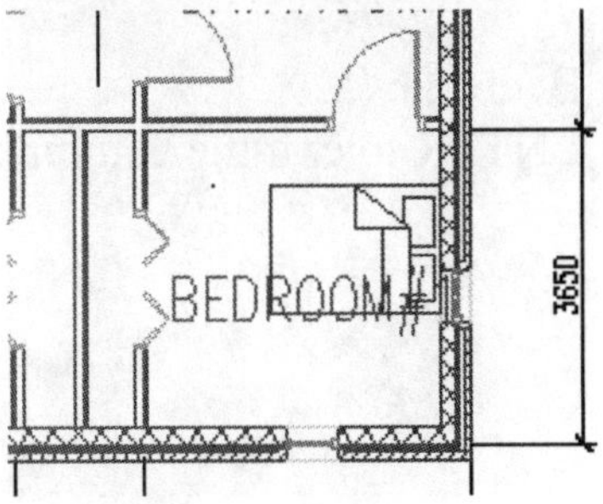

Place the bed in Bedroom #1.

Right click and select ENTER to exit the command.

13. 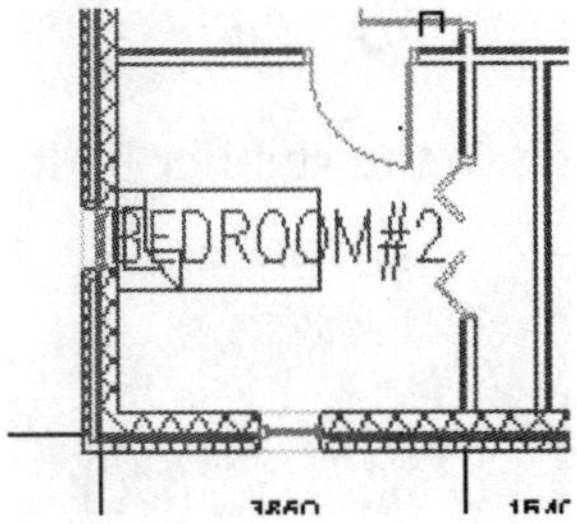

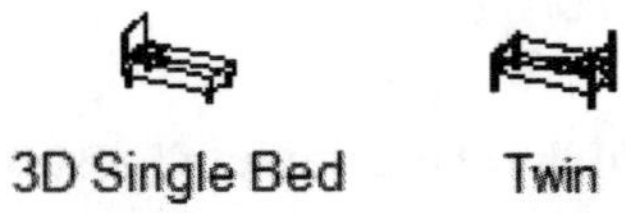

Locate the *Twin [3D Single Bed].dwg.*

Drag and drop it into Bedroom #2 as shown.

14. 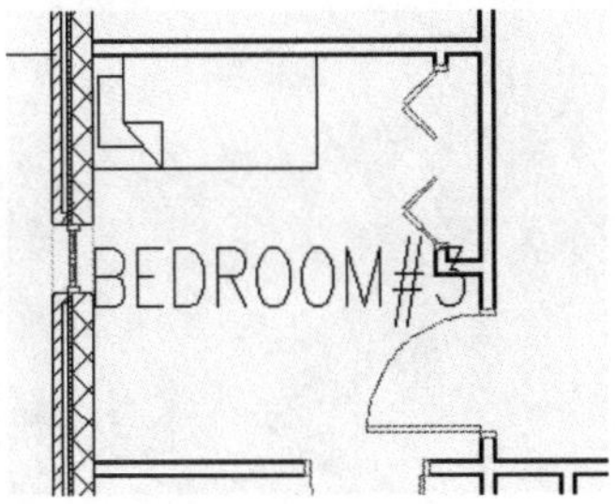

Place the *Twin* [*3D Single Bed.dwg]* in Bedroom#3.

Right click and select ENTER to exit the command.

15. 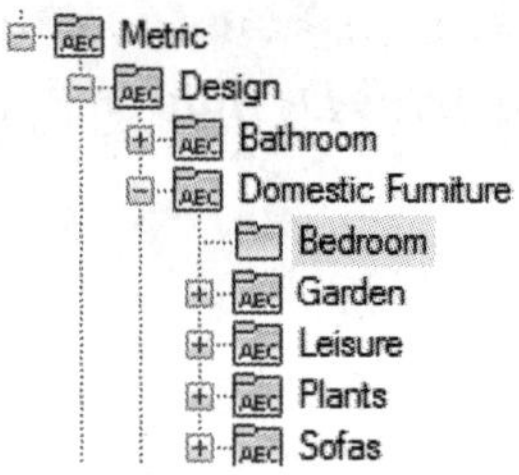

Browse to the *Bedroom* folder in the *Metric/Design/ Domestic Furniture* folder.

16. 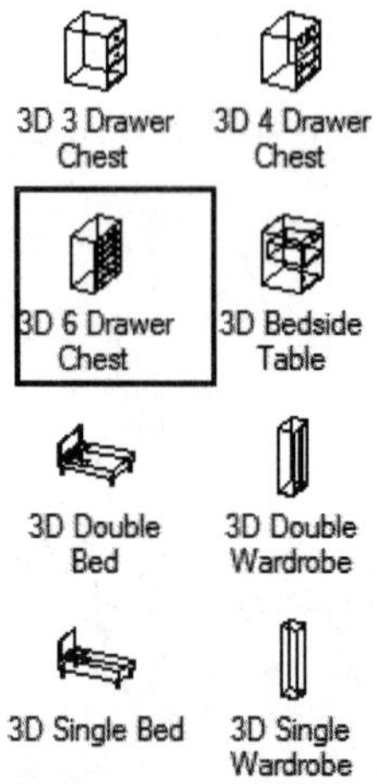

Locate the *3D 6 Drawer Chest*.

17. 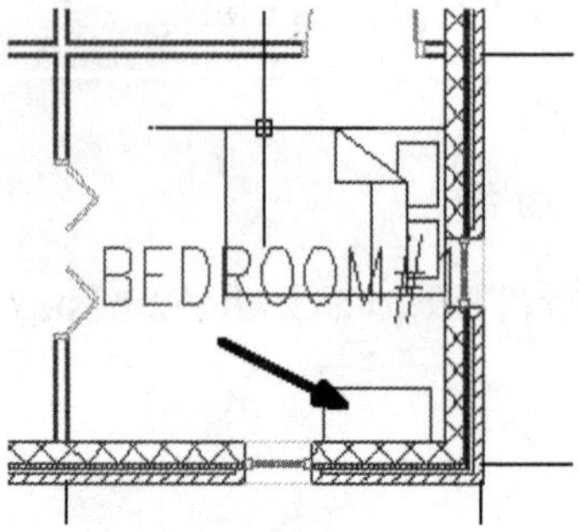

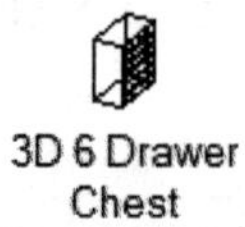

Place a Dresser in the Bedroom#1.
Right click and select ENTER to exit the command.

18. 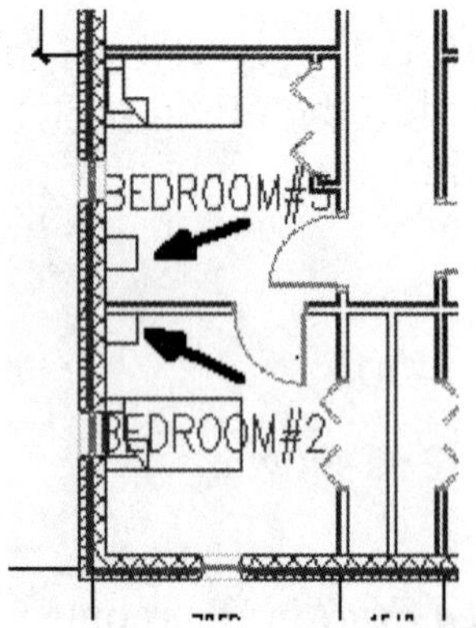

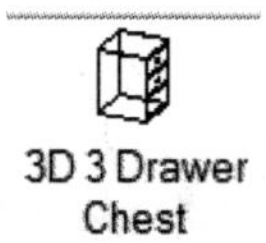

Add a 3D 3 Drawer Chest to each of the smaller bedrooms.

19. 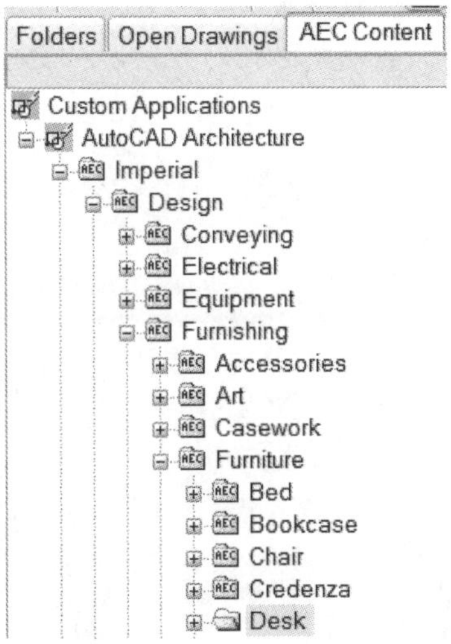

Browse to the *Desk* folder under *AutoCAD Architecture/Imperial/Design/Furnishing/Furniture/*.

20. 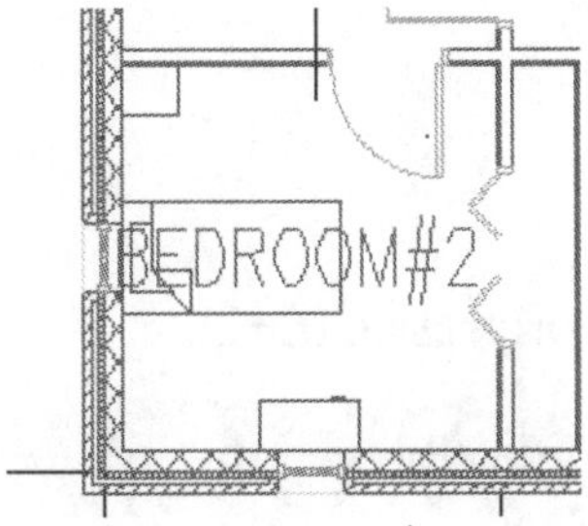

Locate the *36x18 Left.dwg* file under the *Desk* folder.
Place into Bedroom #2.

21. 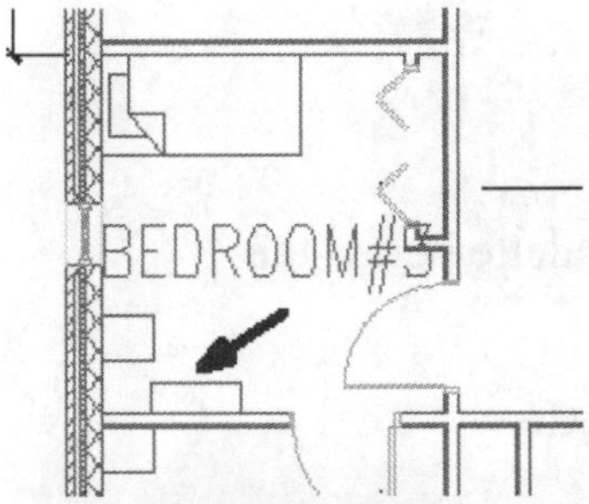

Locate the *6 Shelves.dwg* bookcase in the *Bookcase* folder.
Place in Bedroom #3.

22. 

Switch to a 3D view and use 3D Orbit to view the furniture placement.

23. Save as *ex4-1.dwg*.

Exercise 4-2:

Create a Tool Palette

Drawing Name: Ex4-1.dwg
Estimated Time: 30 minutes

This lesson reinforces the following skills:

- Design Center
- Tool Palette
- Customization

1.  Open *ex4-1.dwg.*

2. Select the Model tab.
Switch to a top view.

3.  Launch the **Design Center** from the Insert ribbon or press Ctrl+2.

4. 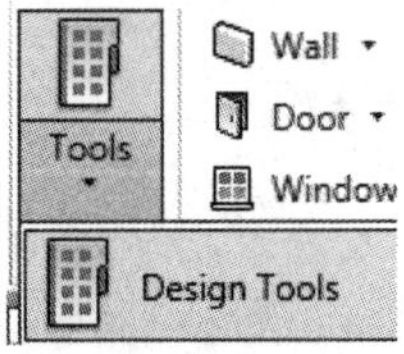

Launch the **Design Tools** from the Home ribbon.

5. 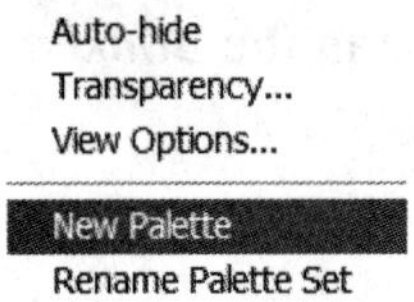

Select the title bar of the Tool Palette below the expand/contract arrows.

Right click and select **New Palette.**

6. 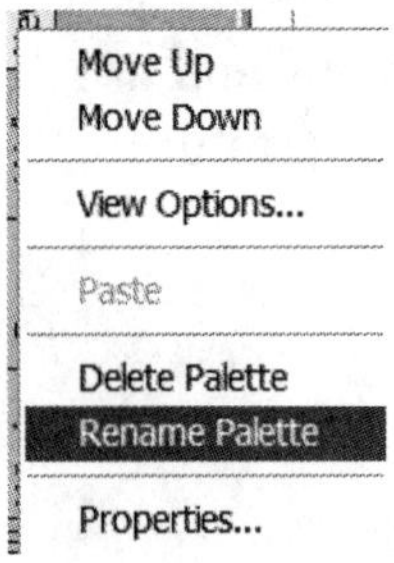

Pick the new palette tab.
Right click and select **Rename Palette.**

7. 

Type **Plumbing**.

8. 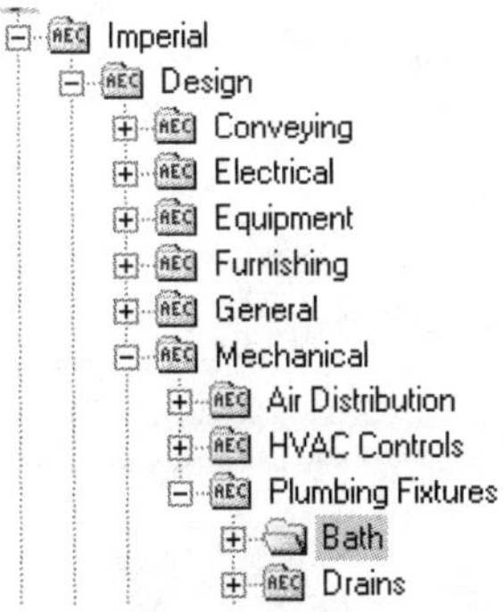

Locate the *Tub 32 x 66* file in the *Imperial/Design/ Mechanical/Plumbing Fixtures/Bath* folder.

9. 

Drag and drop the *Tub 32 x 66* onto the Plumbing Palette. You can release when you see the bar as shown.

10. 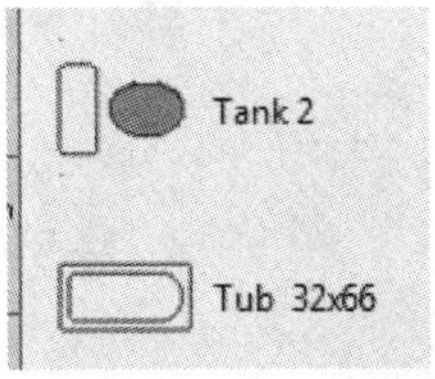

Locate *Tank 2* in the Toilet folder.
Drag and drop onto the Plumbing palette.

11. 

Locate the *32 x 34* shower in the shower folder.
Drag and drop onto the Plumbing palette.

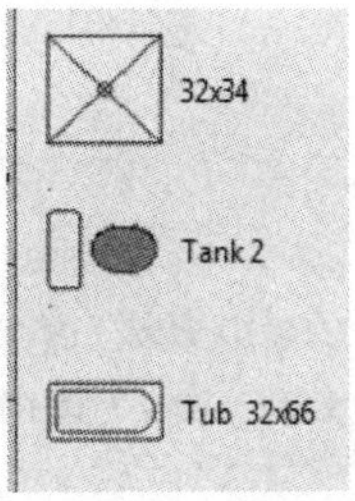

12. 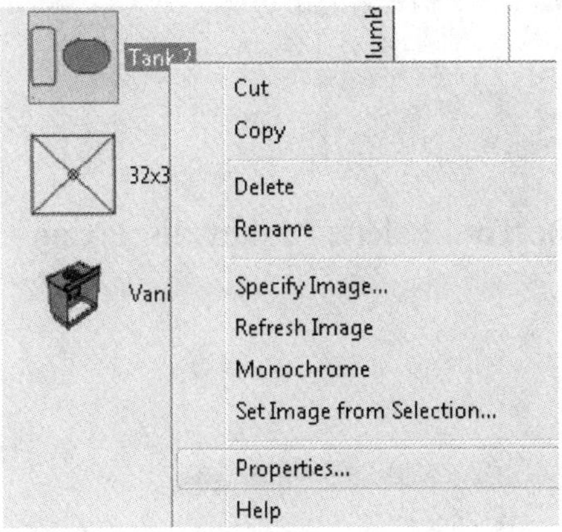

You change how icons appear on the tool palette by using the View options.

Highlight the icon for the Toilet.
Right click and select **Properties**.

13. 

In the Viewer, orient the toilet to the desired view.

Press **OK**.

14. 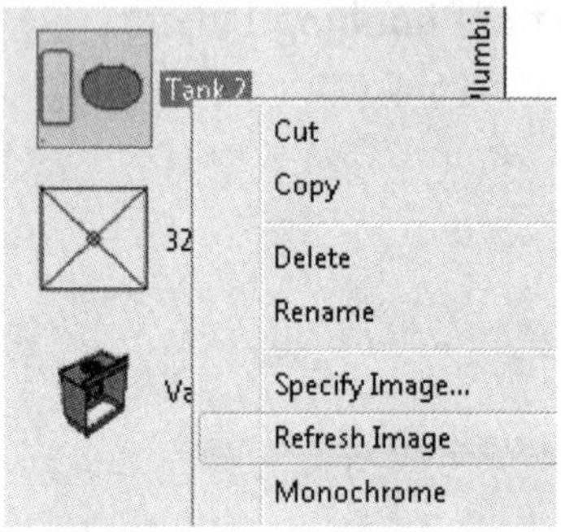

Highlight the toilet icon.

Right click and select **Refresh Image**.

15. 

The image will update.

16. 

Locate the *Vanity* in the *Lavatory* folder. Drag and drop onto the Plumbing palette.

Close the Design Center.

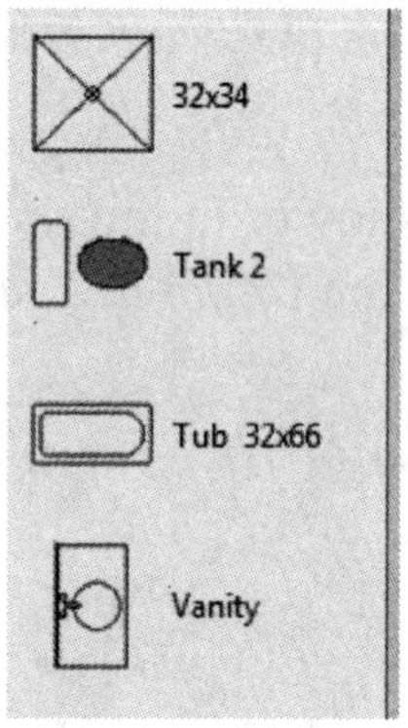

17. 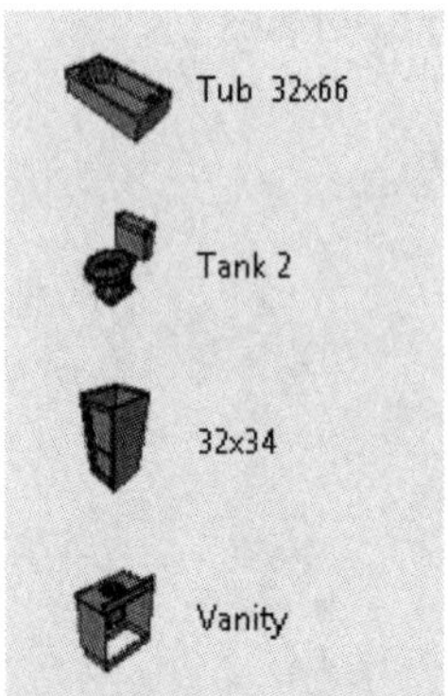

Adjust all the icons on the Tool Palette so they display an isometric view.

18. 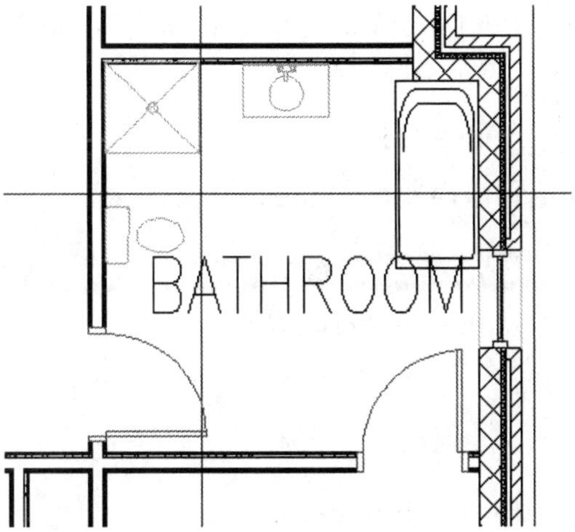

Using the tools on the new Plumbing Palette, equip the bathroom as shown.

19. Save as *ex4-2.dwg.*

TIP: The Space Planning process is not just to ensure that the rooms can hold the necessary equipment, but also requires the drafter to think about plumbing, wiring, and HVAC requirements based on where and how items are placed.

As an additional exercise, place towel bars, soap dishes and other items in the bathrooms.

Exercise 4-3:

Furnishing the Common Areas

Drawing Name: Ex4-2.dwg
Estimated Time: 30 minutes

Common areas are the Living Room, Dining Room, and Family Room.

This lesson reinforces the following skills:

- Design Center
- Tool Palette
- Customization

You will need Internet access in order to complete this exercise.

1.  Open *ex4-2.dwg.*
Select the Model tab.
Switch to a top view.

2.  Launch the Design Center.

3.  Launch the Tool Palette

4. 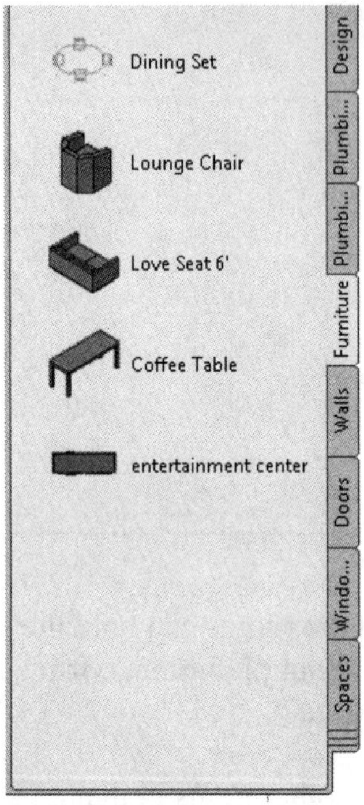

Activate the **Furniture tab** on the tool palette.

If you don't have a furniture tab, you can create one by using New Palette and renaming it.

5. 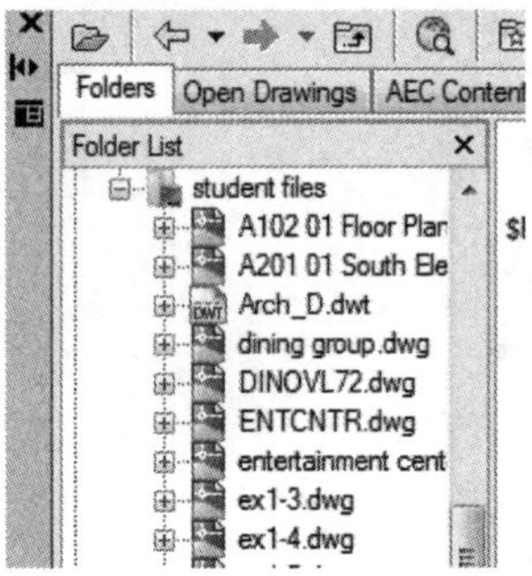

In the Design Center dialog, select the Folders tab.

Browse to the folder where you stored the files downloaded from the publisher.

6. 

Drag and drop the file called **dining group** onto the new palette.

7. Select the dining group tool.
Right click and select **Properties**.

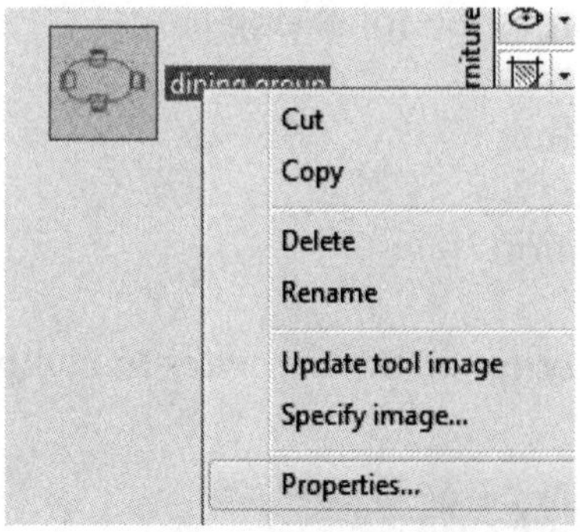

8. 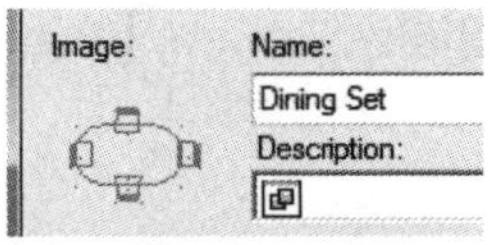

Change the name to **Dining Set**.

9. 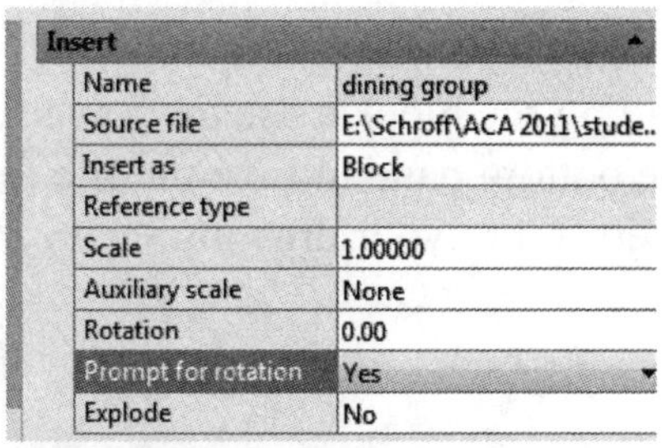

Set the Prompt for rotation to **Yes**.

10. 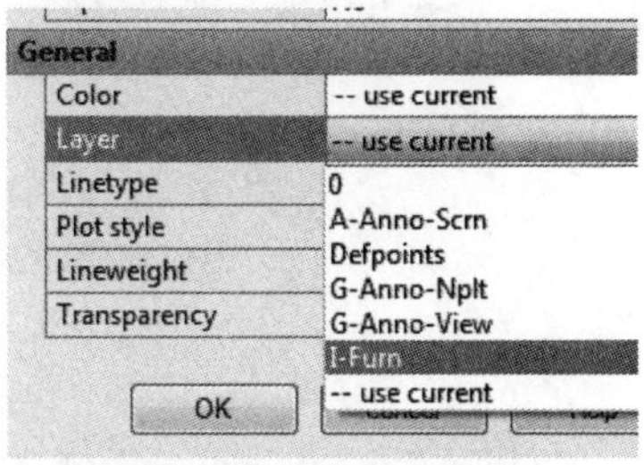

Set Layer **to I-Furn**.

This ensures that the block will be placed on the I-Furn layer regardless of what layer is current.

11. 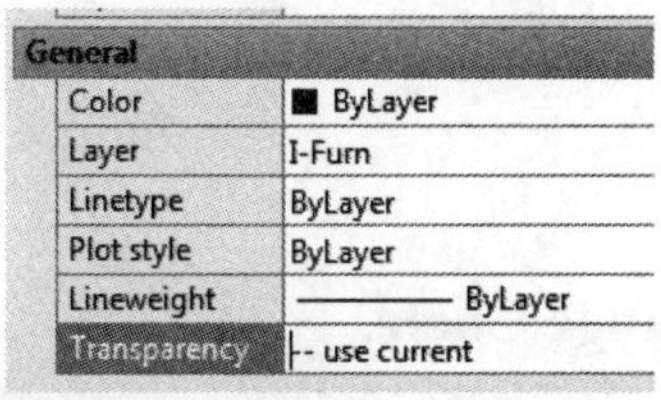

Set the Color, Linetype, Plot Style, and Lineweight to ByLayer.

This means that the I-Furn layer properties will control the display of color, linetype, plot style and lineweight.

Press **OK** to close the Properties dialog.

12. 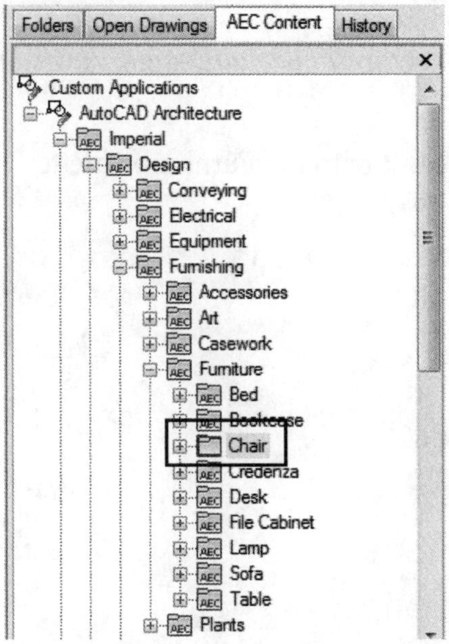

Activate the **AEC Content** tab on the Design Center.

Browse to *AutoCAD Architecture/Imperial/Design/Furnishing/ Furniture/Chair* folder.

13. 

Drag and drop the **Lounge Circular** chair onto the Furniture palette.

14. 

If you have problems downloading the blocks, use the **Save this symbol as...**link located in the bottom pane to save the file to your work folder. Then, simply insert it into your drawing.

15. 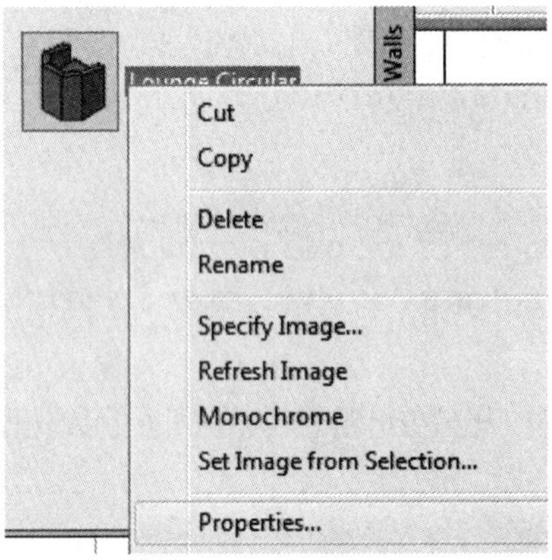

Select the **Lounge Circular** tool.

Right click and select **Properties**.

16. 

Change the name to **Lounge Chair**.

Press **OK** to close the Properties dialog.

18. 

Browse to *AutoCAD Architecture/Imperial/Design/Furnishing/Furniture/Sofa* folder.

Drag and drop the **Love Seat 2** onto the Furniture palette.

19. Select the **Love Seat 2** tool.
Right click and select **Properties**.

20. 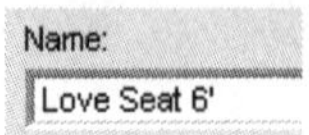

Change the Name to **Love Seat 6′**.

21. 

Browse to *AutoCAD Architecture/Imperial/Design/Furnishing/Furniture/Table* folder.

Drag and drop the **Coffee Table** onto the Furniture palette.

22. 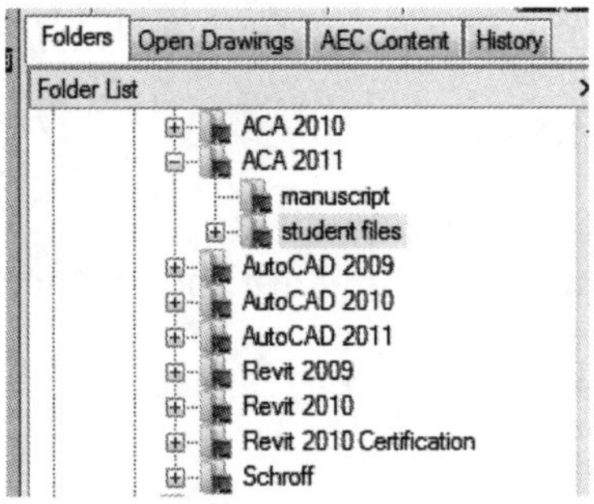

In the Design Center dialog, select the Folders tab.

Browse to the folder where you stored the files downloaded from the publisher.

23. 

Drag and drop the file called **entertainment center** onto the new palette.

24. Select the **entertainment center** tool. Right click and select **Properties**.

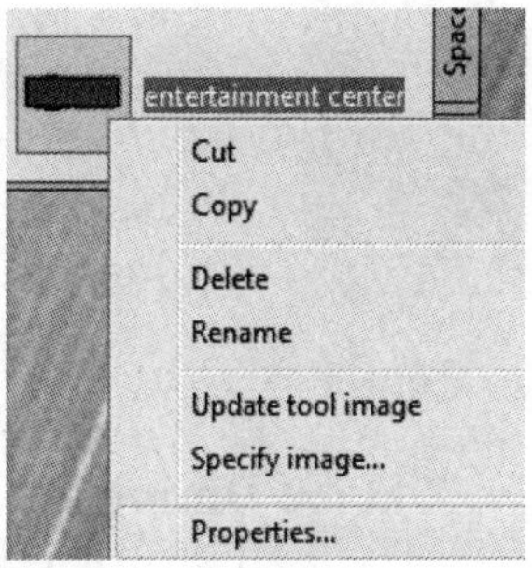

25. 

Change the name to **Entertainment Center**.

26. 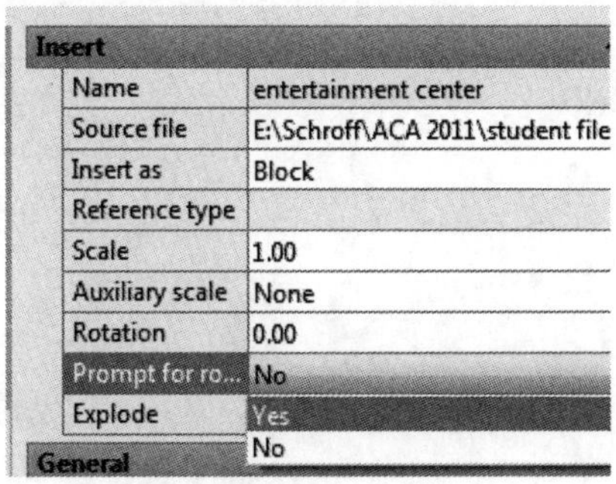

Set the Prompt for rotation to **Yes**.

27. 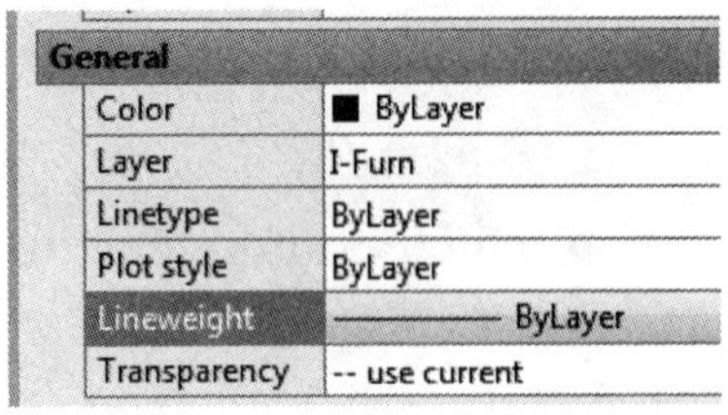

Set Layer **to I-Furn**.

This ensures that the block will be placed on the I-Furn layer regardless of what layer is current. The available layers are in the active drawing.

28. 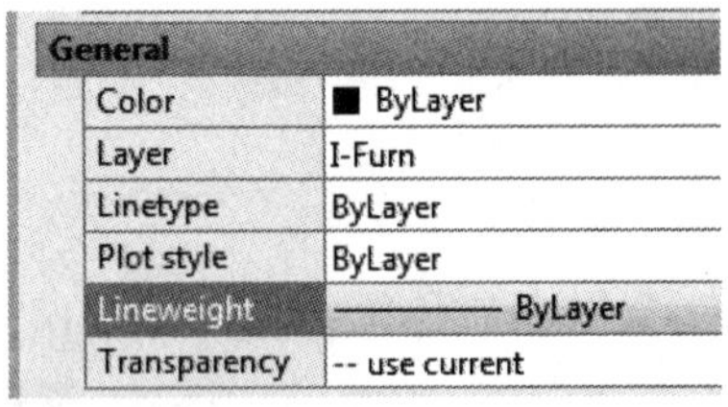

Set the Color, Linetype, Plot Style, and Lineweight to ByLayer.

This means that the I-Furn layer properties will control the display of color, linetype, plot style and lineweight.

Press **OK** to close the Properties dialog.

29. 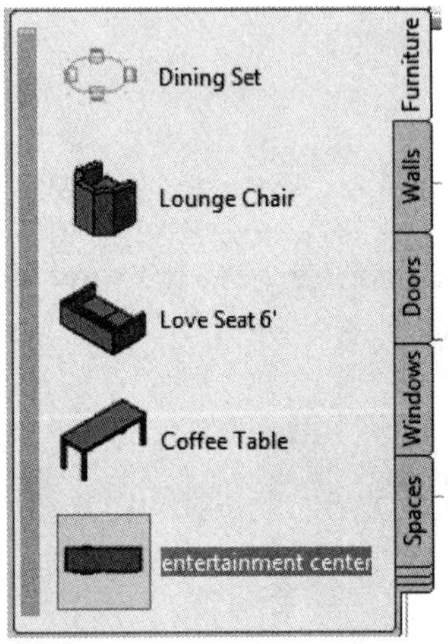

This is what your Furniture tool palette should look like.

30. Close the Design Center.

31. 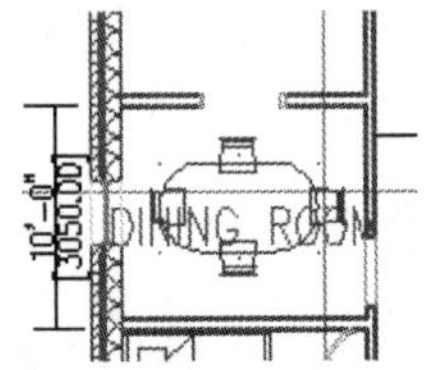

Add the **Dining Set** to the dining room.

32. 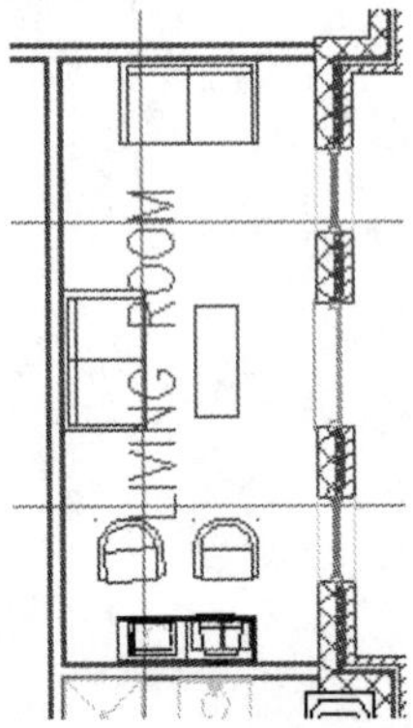

Furnish the living room with the lounge chair, sofa, coffee table, and entertainment center.

33. Add a sofa and coffee table to the family room.

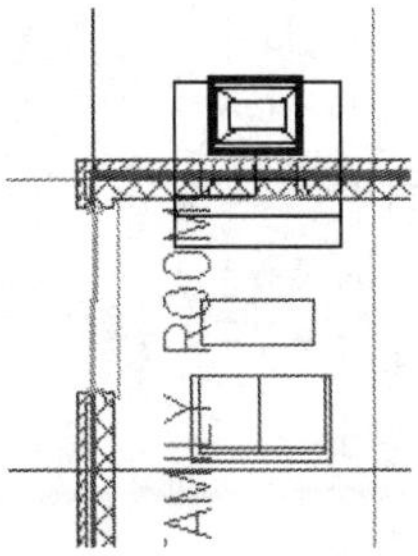

34. Save the file as *ex4-3.dwg.*

TIP: If the preview shown in the Design Center does not appear as a 3D object, then it is a 2D object. Don't select it for use in your model.

Exercise 4-4

Adding to the Service Areas

Drawing Name: Ex4-3.dwg
Estimated Time: 30 minutes

1.  Open *ex4-4.dwg.*
Select the Model tab.
Switch to a top view.

2.  Launch the Design Center.

3. 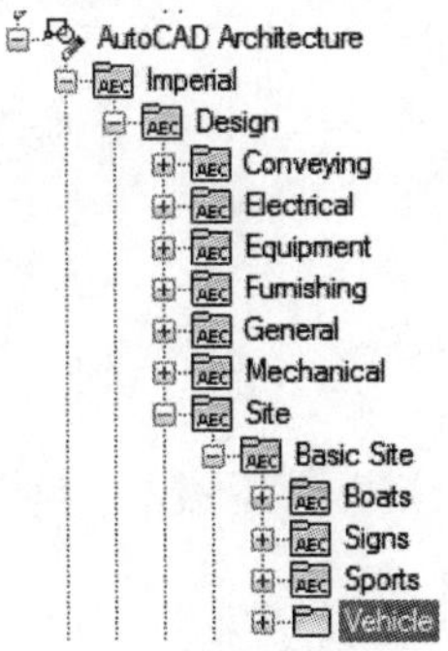

Select the AEC Content tab.
Browse to the *AutoCAD Architecture/Imperial/Design/Site/ Basic Site/Vehicles* folder.

4. 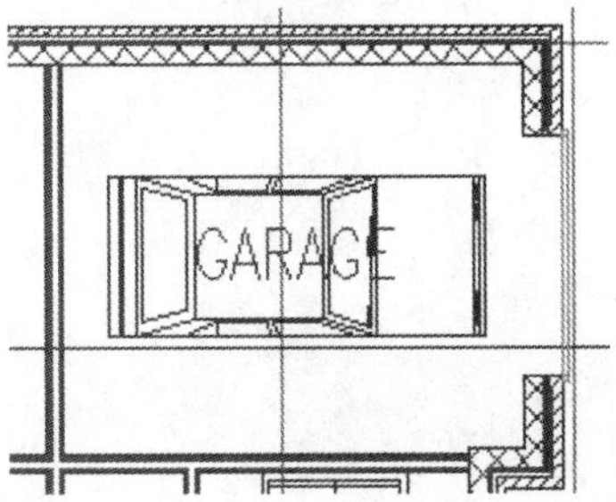

Sub-Compact

Drag and drop the *Sub-Compact* car into the garage.

All that remains is the kitchen area.

5. 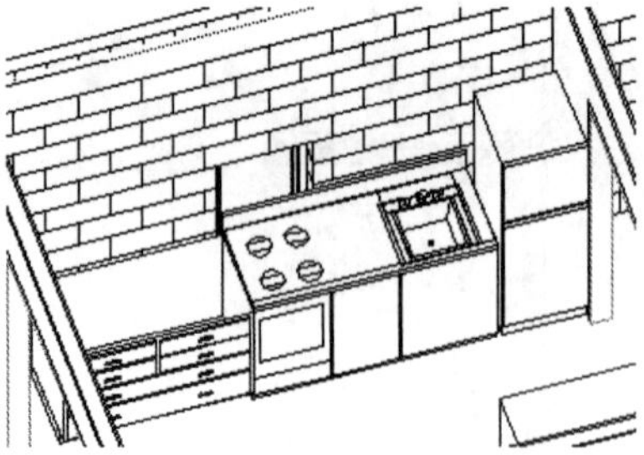

Use the Design Center to add casework, a kitchen sink, and an oven into the kitchen area.

We see now using our space planning that the window needs to be shifted up.

6. 

Add a refrigerator and additional cabinets to the other side of the kitchen.

Our completed floor plan.

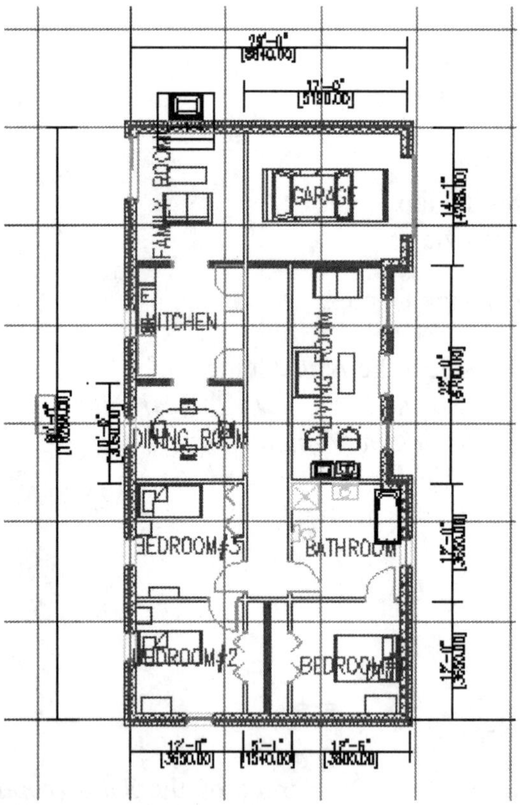

7. Save the file as *ex4-5.dwg*.

QUIZ 2

True or False

1. Once a door or window is placed, it can not be moved or modified.
2. Openings can be any size and any elevation.
3. The Offset value when placing a door/window/opening determines how far the door/window/opening is placed from a selected point.
4. Door, window and opening dimensions can be applied using the Design Center.

Multiple Choice

5. Select the entity type that can NOT be converted to a wall:
    A. Line
    B. Polyline
    C. Circle
    D. Spline

6. A HOT grip is indicated by this color:
    A. GREEN
    B. BLUE
    C. RED
    D. YELLOW

7. To assign an image to a tool on the tool palette using existing geometry, use
    A. Assign image
    B. Set Image from selection
    C. Insert
    D. Import

ANSWERS:

1) F; 2) T 3) T; 4) F; 5) C; 6) C; 7) A

Notes:

Lesson 5
Roofs

Roofs can be created with single or double slopes, with or without gable ends, and with or without overhangs. Once you input all your roof settings, you simply pick the points around the perimeter of the building to define your roof outline. If you make an error, you can easily modify or redefine your roof.

You need to pick three points before the roof will begin to preview in your graphics window. There is no limit to the number of points to select to define the perimeter.

To create a gable roof, uncheck the gable box in the Roof dialog. Pick the two end points for the sloped portion of the roof. Turn on the Gable box. Pick the end point for the gable side. Turn off the Gable box. Pick the end point for the sloped side. Turn the Gable box on. Pick the viewport and then press ENTER. A Gable cannot be defined with more than three consecutive edges.

Roofs can be created using two methods: ROOFADD places a roof based on points selected or ROOFCONVERT which converts a closed polyline or closed walls to develop a roof.

Tips & Tricks

- If you opt to use ROOFCONVERT and use existing closed walls, be sure that the walls are intersecting properly. If your walls are not properly cleaned up with each other, the roof conversion is unpredictable.
- The Plate Height of a roof should be set equal to the Wall Height.
- You can create a gable on a roof by gripping any ridgeline point and stretching it past the roof edge. You cannot make a gable into a hip using grips.

Shape – Select the Shape option on the command line by typing 'S.'	Single Slope – Extends a roof plane at an angle from the Plate Height.	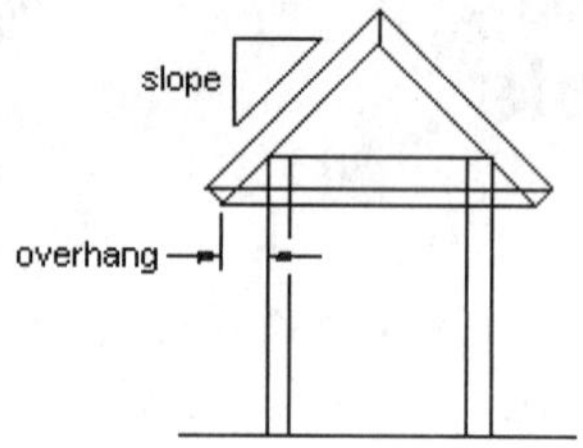 end elevation view
	Double Slope – Includes a single slope and adds another slope, which begins at the intersection of the first slope and the height specified for the first slope.	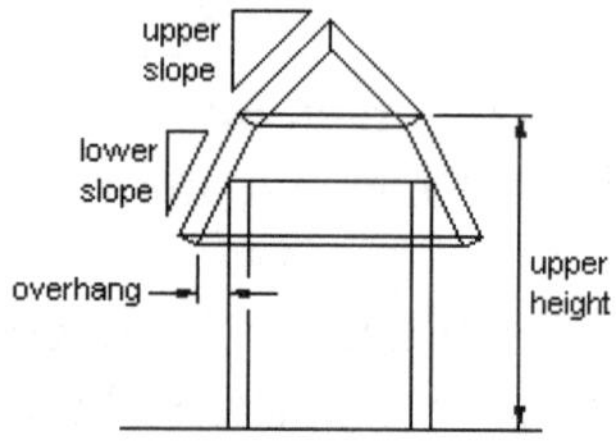 end elevation view
Gable – Select the Gable option on the command line by typing 'G.'	If this is enabled, turns off the slope of the roof place. To create a gable edge, select Gable prior to identifying the first corner of the gable end. Turn off gable to continue to create the roof.	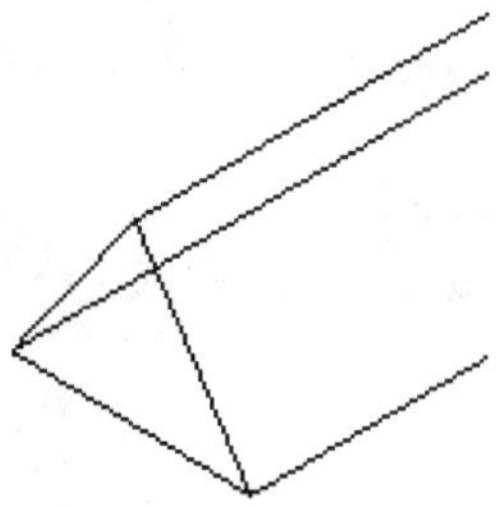 gable roof end
Plate Height – Set the Plate Height on the command line by typing 'PH.'	Specify the top plate from which the roof plane is projected. The height is relative to the XY plane with a Z coordinate of 0.	
Rise – Set the Rise on the command line by typing 'PR.'	Sets the angle of the roof based on a run value of 12.	A rise value of 5 creates a 5/12 roof, which forms a slope angle of 22.62 degrees.
Slope – Set the Slope on the command line by typing 'PS.'	Angle of the roof rise from the horizontal.	If slope angles are entered, then the rise will automatically be calculated.

Upper Height – Set the Upper Height on the command line by typing ‘UH.’	This is only available if a Double Slope roof is being created. This is the height where the second slope will start.	
Rise (upper) – Set the Upper Rise on the command line by typing ‘UR.’	This is only available if a Double Slope roof is being created. This is the slope angle for the second slope.	A rise value of 5 creates a 5/12 roof, which forms a slope angle of 22.62 degrees.
Slope (upper) – Set the Upper Slope on the command line by typing ‘US.’	This is only available if a Double Slope roof is being created. Defines the slope angle for the second slope.	If an upper rise value is set, this is automatically calculated.
Overhang – To enable on the command line, type ‘O.’ To set the value of the Overhang, type ‘V.’	If enabled, extends the roofline down from the plate height by the value set.	
	The Floating Viewer opens a viewer window displaying a preview of the roof.	
	The match button allows you to select an existing roof to match its properties.	
	The properties button opens the Roof Properties dialog.	
	The Undo button allows you to undo the last roof operation. You can step back as many operations as you like up to the start.	
?	Opens the Roof Help file.	

Exercise 5-1:

Creating a Roof using Existing Walls

Drawing Name: ex3-1.dwg
Estimated Time: 10 minutes

This exercise reinforces the following skills:

- ❑ Roof
- ❑ Roof Properties
- ❑ Visual Styles

1.  Open *ex3-1.dwg*.

2. 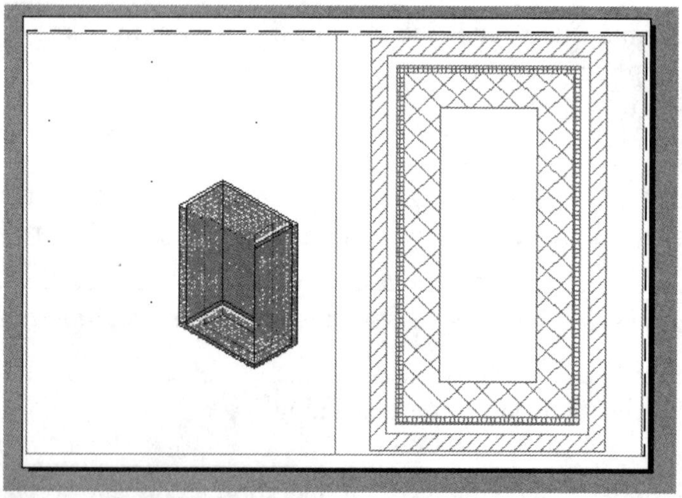

Select the Work icon.
Activate the right viewport that shows the top or plan view.

3. 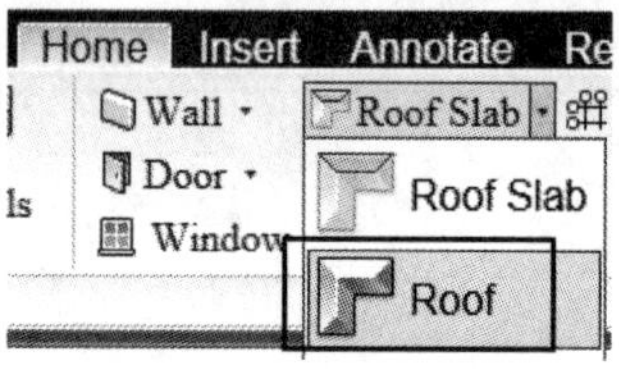

Select the **Roof** tool from the Home ribbon.

4. 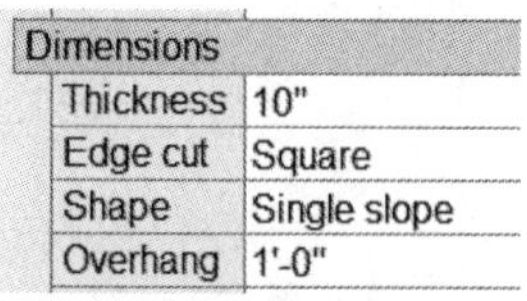

Expand the Dimensions section.
Set the Thickness to **10″** **[254.00 mm]**.
Set the Shape to **Single slope**.
Set the Overhang to **1′-0″** **[609.6 mm]**.

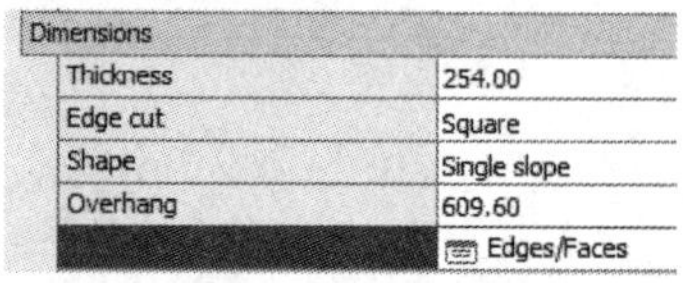

5. 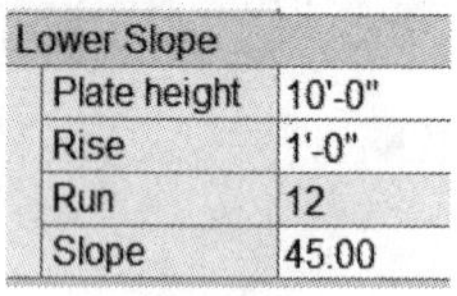

Expand the Lower Slope section.
Set the Plate height to **10′-0″** **[3000 mm]**.

The plate height determines the level where the roof rests.

6. 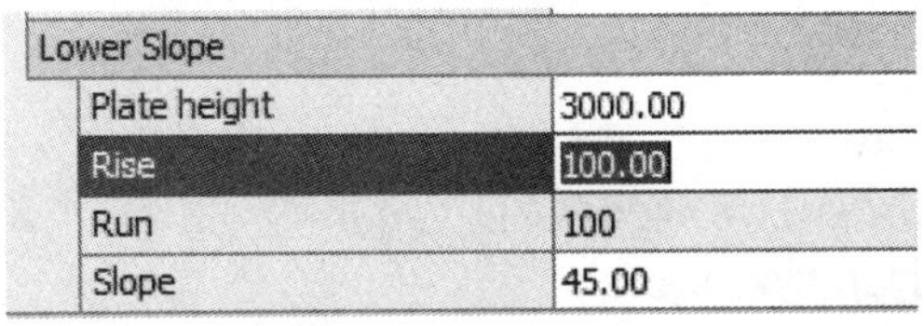

Set the Rise to **1′-0″ [100 mm]**.

7. 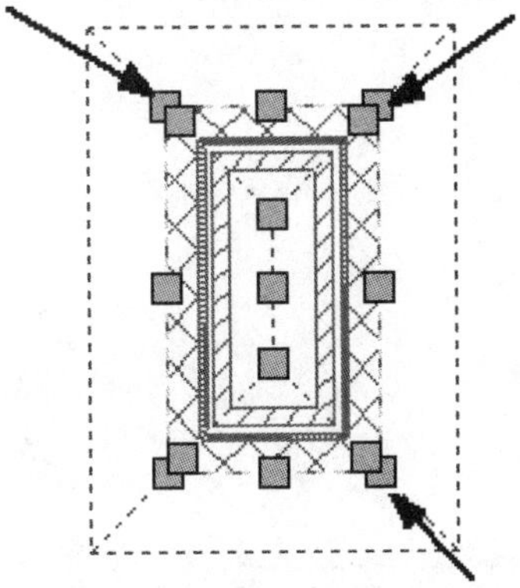
Pick the corners indicated to place the roof.

Press **Enter**.

8. 

Switch to the **Work** layout.

9. 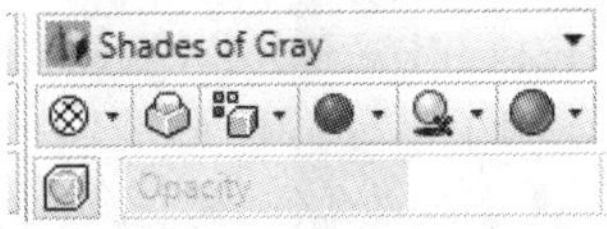

Activate the View ribbon.

Select the **Shades of Gray** under Visual Styles.

10. 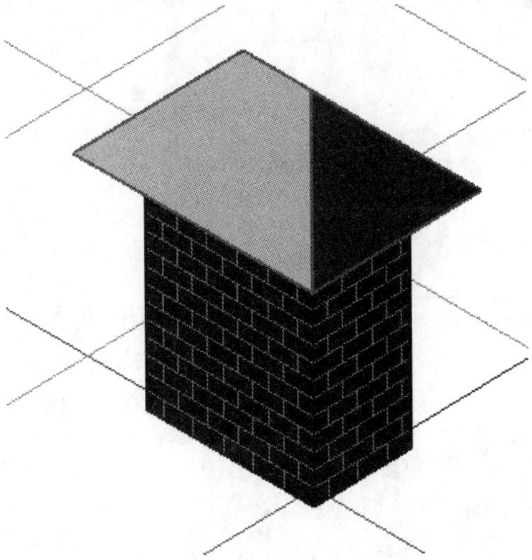
Save as *ex5-1.dwg*.

Our roof works, but strictly speaking we can make it better with a couple of changes around the chimney. AutoCAD Architecture allows us to cut holes through roofs (to allow for vents, chimneys and skylights), and to add other faces or subsidiary roofs such as dormers.

In order to edit a roof you have to convert it to Roof Slabs.

Exercise 5-2:
Roof Slabs

Drawing Name: i_ex5-2.dwg, m_ex5-2.dwg
(download from the publisher's website)
Use the i_ version for Imperial units.
Use the m_ version for Metric units.

Estimated Time: 15 minutes

This exercise reinforces the following skills:

- Convert to Roof
- Roof Slab Tools

1.  Open *i_ex5-2.dwg [m_ex5-2.dwg].*

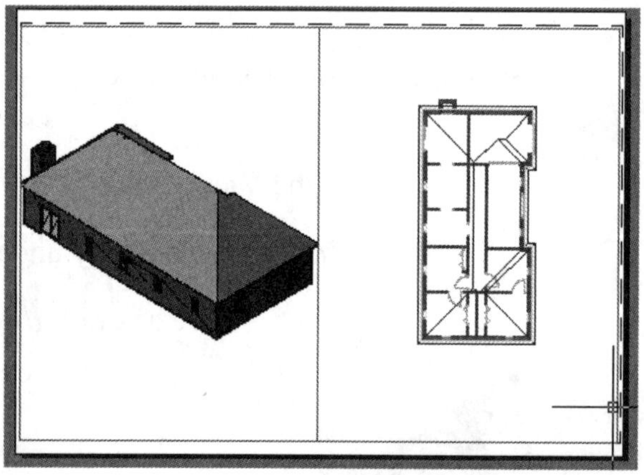

2. 

Select the Work icon.

3. 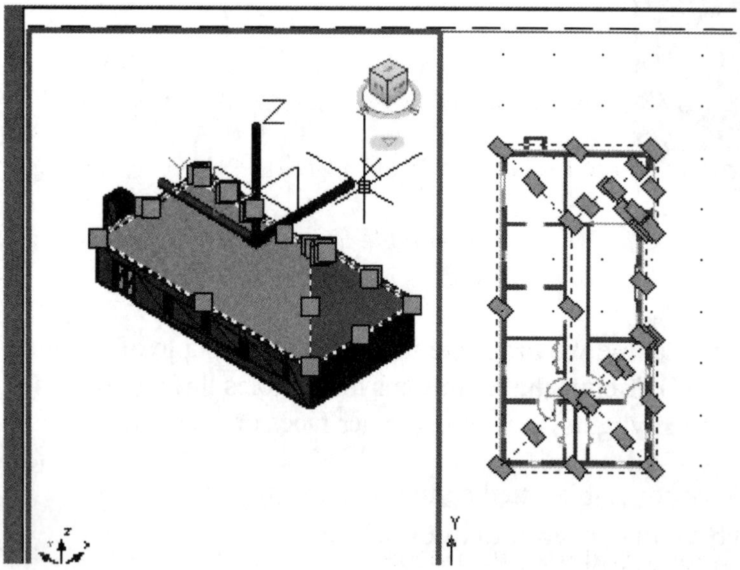

Activate the left viewport that shows the isometric view.

4. 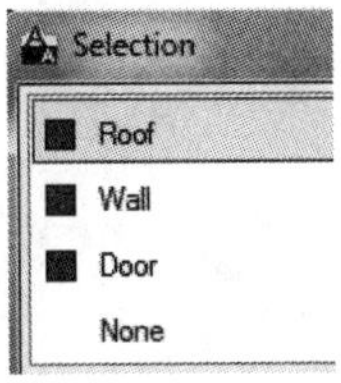

Select the **Roof** in the Selection dialog.

The roof will highlight.

5. 

Select **Convert** from the Roof ribbon.

6. 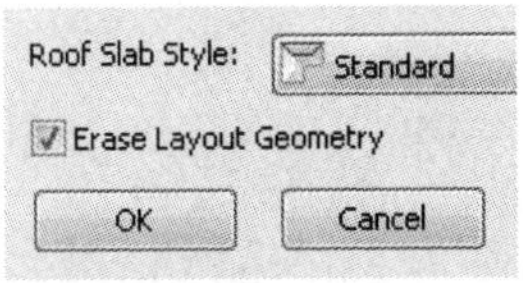

Enable the **Erase layout geometry** checkbox.

Press **OK**.

The Roof Slab Properties dialog appears.
Close it.

The roof will change appearance slightly. It now consists of individual slabs.

7. 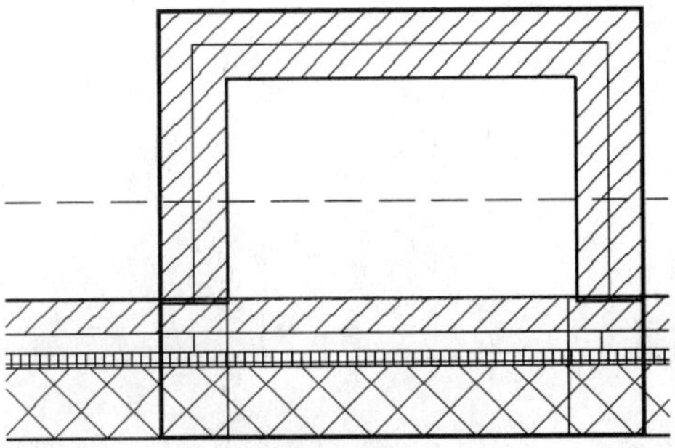

Activate the right viewport.
Zoom into the area where the chimney is located.

Activate the Home ribbon.
Draw a rectangle over the outline of the chimney. Make sure that the rectangle extends beyond the roof line.

8. 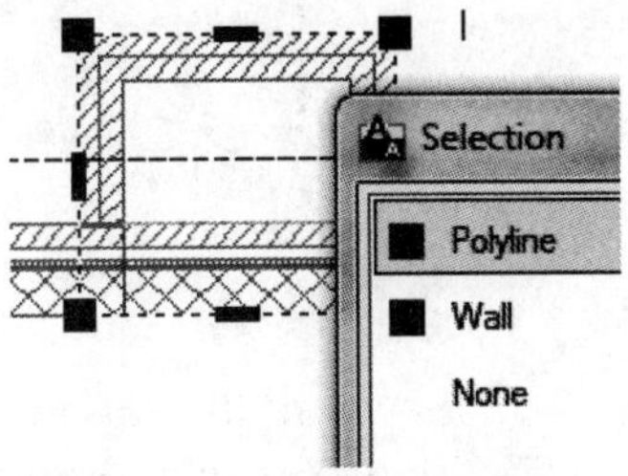

Select the rectangle.

Select the **Polyline** in the Selection dialog.

9. 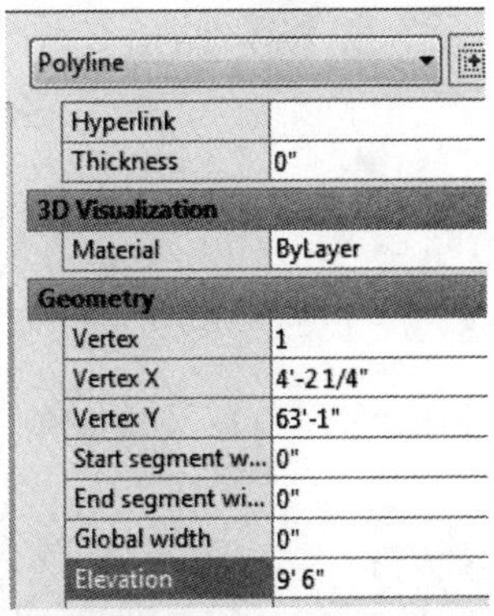

Right click and select **Properties**.

Set the Elevation to **9′-6″ [3000]**.

This moves the rectangle to the same elevation as where the roof is placed.

Close the Properties dialog.
Deselect the rectangle by hitting the ESC key.

10. 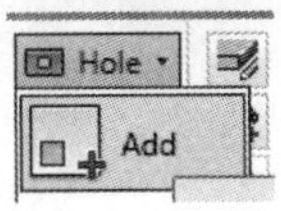

Select the roof slab located on top of the chimney.

Select **Hole→Add** from the ribbon.

11. 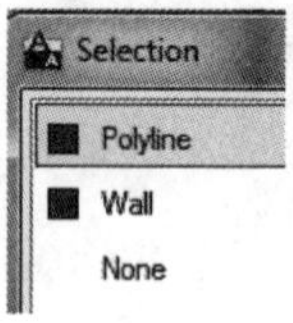

At the next prompt pick the rectangle.
Select the **Polyline** in the Selection dialog.

At the 'Erase Layout Geometry?' prompt hit, right click and select **Yes**.

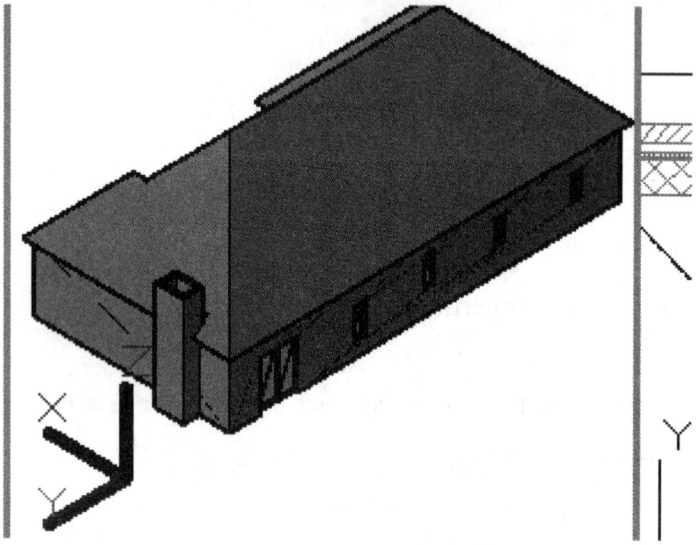

The hole will appear.

Use the Viewcube in the viewport to orient the view so you can see the chimney.

The chimney now appears OK.

12. Save as *i_ex5-2a.dwg*.

Lesson 6
Structural Members

Architectural documentation for residential construction will always include plans (top views) of each floor of a building, showing features and structural information of the floor platform itself. Walls are located on the plan but not shown in structural detail.

Wall sections and details are used to show:

- the elements within walls (exterior siding, sheathing, block, brick or wood studs, insulation, air cavities, interior sheathing, trim)
- how walls relate to floors, ceilings, roofs, eaves,
- openings within the walls (doors/windows with their associated sills and headers)
- how walls relate to openings in floors (stairs).

Stick-framed (stud) walls usually have their framing patterns determined by the carpenters on site. Once window and door openings are located on the plan, and stud spacing is specified by the designer (or the local building code), the specific arrangement of vertical members is usually left to the fabricators and not drafted, except where specific structural details require explanation.

The structural members in framed floors that have to hold themselves and/or other walls and floors up are usually drafted as framing plans. Designers must specify the size and spacing of joists or trusses, beams and columns. Plans show the orientation and relation of members, locate openings through the floor and show support information for openings and other specific conditions.

In the next exercises, we shall create a floor framing plan. Since the ground floor of our one-story lesson house has already been defined as a concrete slab, we'll assume that the ground level slopes down at the rear of the house and create a wood deck at the sliding door to the family room. The deck will need a railing for safety.

Autodesk AutoCAD Architecture includes a Structural Member Catalog that allows you to easily access industry-standard structural shapes. To create most standard column, brace, and beam styles, you can access the Structural Member Catalog, select a structural member shape, and create a style that contains the shape that you selected. The shape, similar to an AEC profile, is a 2D cross-section of a structural member. When you create a structural member with a style that you created from the Structural Member Catalog, you define the path to extrude the shape along.

You can create your own structural shapes that you can add to existing structural members, or use to create new structural members. The design rules in a structural member style allow you to add these custom shapes to a structural member, as well as create custom structural members from more than one shape.

All the columns, braces, and beams that you create are sub-types of a single Structural Member object type. The styles that you create for columns, braces, and beams have the same Structural Member Styles style type as well. When you change the display or style of a structural member, use the Structural Member object in the Display Manager and the Structural Member Styles style type in the Style Manager.

If you are operating with the AIA layering system as your current layer standard, when you create members or convert AutoCAD entities to structural members using the menu picks or toolbars, AutoCAD Architecture assigns the new members to layers: A-Cols, A-Cols-Brce or A-Beam, respectively. If Generic AutoCAD Architecture is your standard, the layers used are A_Columns, A_Beams and A_Braces. If your layer standard is Current Layer, new entities come in on the current layer, as in plain vanilla AutoCAD.

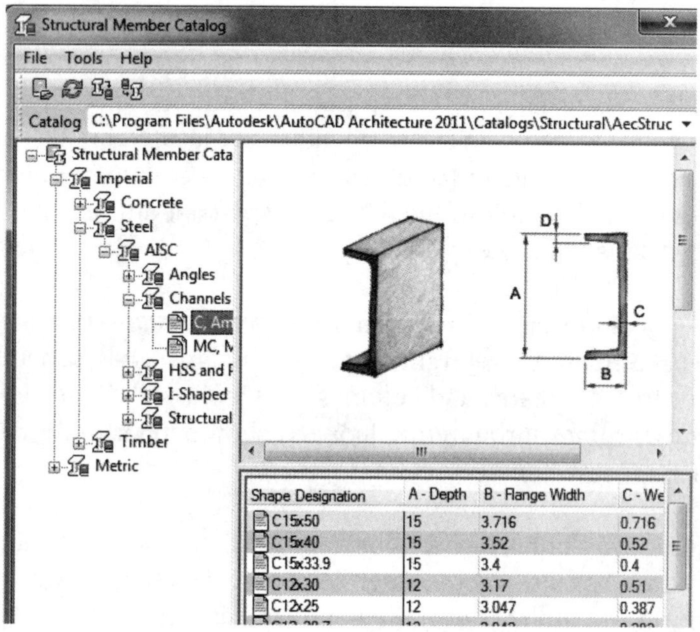

The Structural Member Catalog includes specifications for standard structural shapes. You can choose shapes from the Structural Member Catalog, and generate styles for structural members that you create in your drawings.

A style that contains the catalog shape that you selected is created. You can view the style in the Style Manager, create a new structural member from the style, or apply the style to an existing member.

When you add a structural member to your drawing, the shape inside the style that you created defines the shape of the member. You define the length, justification, roll or rise, and start and end offsets of the structural member when you draw it.

You cannot use the following special characters in your style names:

- less-than and greater-than symbols (< >)
- forward slashes and backslashes (/ \)
- quotation marks (")
- colons (:)
- semicolons (;)
- question marks (?)
- commas (,)
- asterisks (*)
- vertical bars (|)
- equal signs (=)
- backquotes (`)

The left pane of the Structural Member Catalog contains a hierarchical tree view. Several industry standard catalogs are organized in the tree, first by imperial or metric units, and then by material.

	Open a catalog file - The default is the catalog that comes with ADT, but you can create your own custom catalog. The default catalog is located in the following directory path: \\Program Files\Autodesk AutoCAD Architecture R3\Catalogs\catalogs.
	Refresh Data
	Locate Catalog item based on an existing member – allows you to select a member in a drawing and then locates it in your catalog.
	Generate Member Style – allows you to create a style to be used.

We will be adding a wood framed deck, 4000 mm x 2750 mm, to the back of the house. For purposes of this exercise we will assume that the ground level is 300 mm below the slab at the back of the house and falls away so that grade level below the edge of the deck away from the house is 2 meters below floor level: - 2 m a.f.f. (above finish floor) in architectural notation. We will place the top of the deck floorboards even with the top of the floor slab.

We will use support and rim joists as in standard wood floor framing, and they will all be at the same level, rather than joists crossing a support beam below. In practice this means the use of metal hangers, which will not be drawn. Once the floor system is drawn we will add support columns at the outside rim joist and braces at the columns.

Exercise 6-1:

Creating Member Styles

Drawing Name: i_ex6-1.dwg [m_ex6-1.dwg]
Estimated Time: 5 minutes

This exercise reinforces the following skills:

- ❑ Creating Member Styles
- ❑ Use of Structural Members tools

1.  Open *i_ex6-1.dwg [m_ex6-1.dwg].*

2. 

Activate the Manage ribbon.

Go to **Style & Display→Structural Member Catalog**.

3. 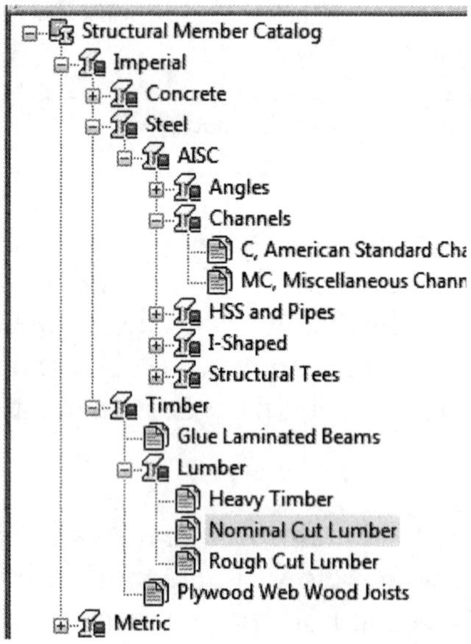

Browse to the **Imperial/Timber/Lumber/Nominal Cut Lumber [Metric/Timber/Lumber Metric]** folder.

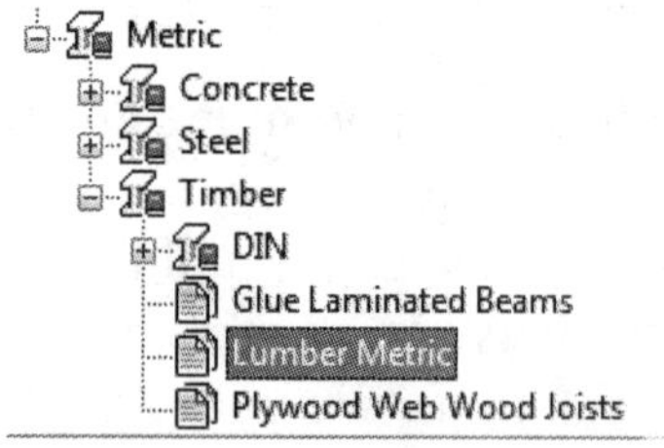

4. In the lower right pane:

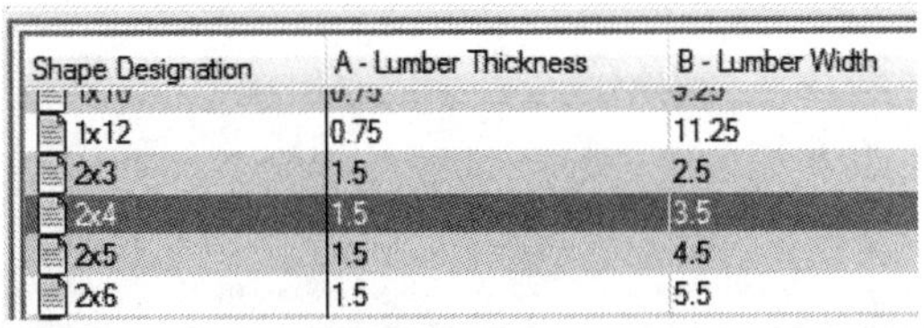

Locate the **2x4 [50mmx150mm]** shape designation.

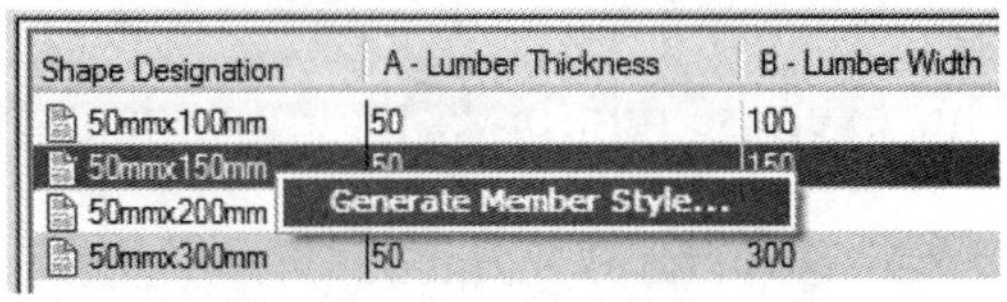

Right click and select **Generate Member Style**.

5. 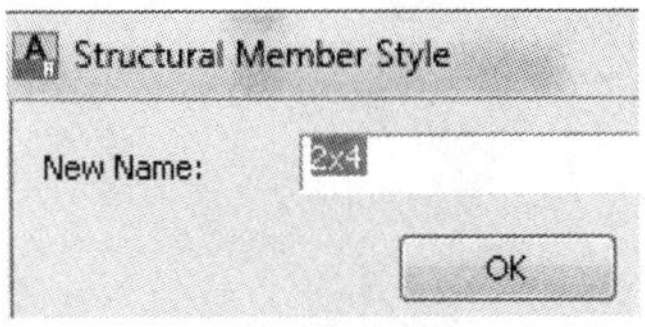

In the Structural Member Style dialog box, the name for your style automatically fills in.

Click **OK**.

6. In the lower right pane:

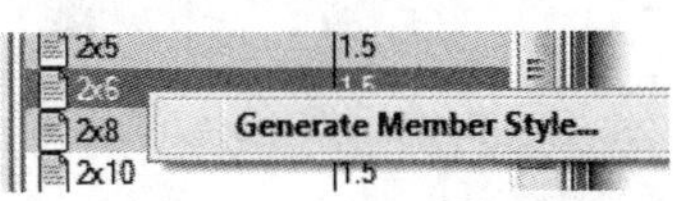

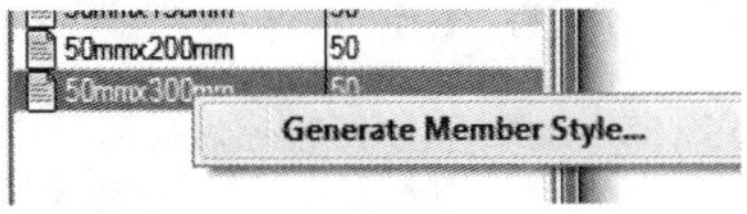

Locate the **2x6 [50mmx300mm]** shape designation.
Right click and select **Generate Member Style**.

7. 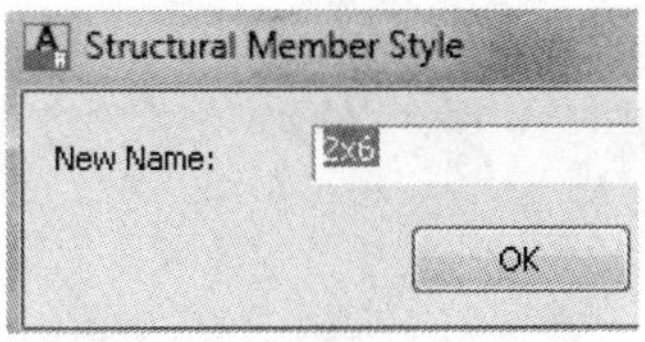

In the Structural Member Style dialog box, the name for your style is displayed.

Click **OK**.

8. Close the dialog.
Save as *i_ex6-1a.dwg*.

Exercise 6-2:
Creating Member Shapes

Drawing Name: i_ex6-1a.dwg
Estimated Time: 10 minutes

This exercise reinforces the following skills:

- Structural Member Wizard

1. 
Open *i_ex6-1a.dwg.*
Select the Work tab.
Activate the right viewport.

2. 

Activate the **Manage** ribbon.
Go to **Style & Display→Structural Member Wizard**.

3. 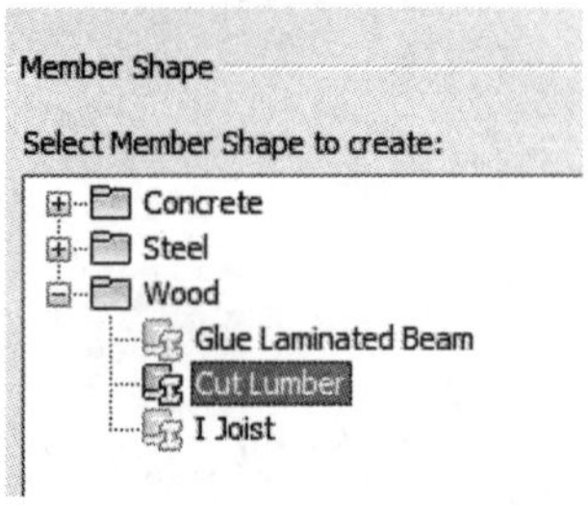

Select the **Cut Lumber** category under Wood.
Press **Next**.

4. 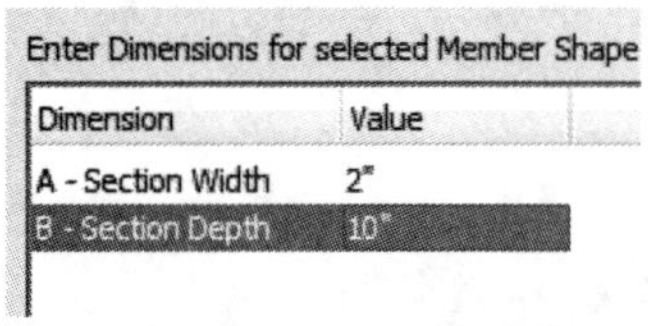

Set the Section Width to **2″ [50.00]**.
Set the Section Depth to **10″ [250.00]**.
Press **Next**.

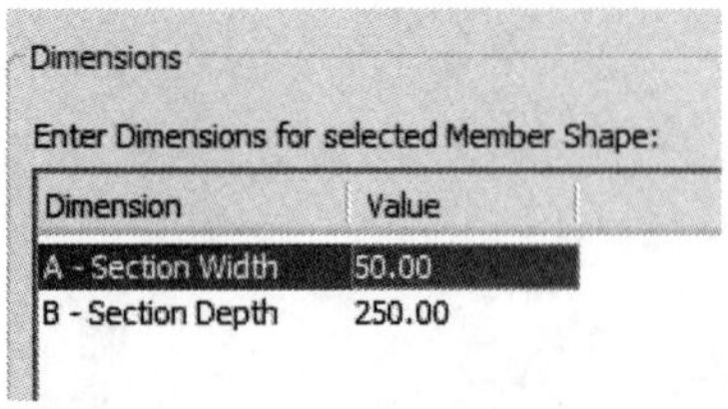

5. 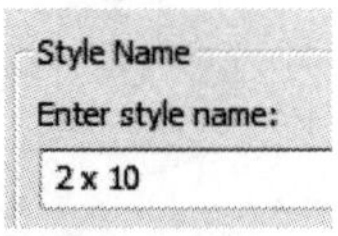

Enter the style name as **2 x 10 [50mmx250mm]**.

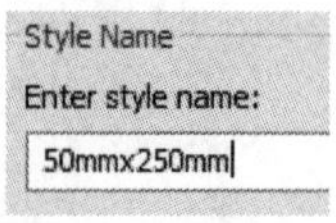

Press **Finish**.

6. 

Activate the **Manage** ribbon.

Go to **Style & Display→Structural Member Wizard**.

7. 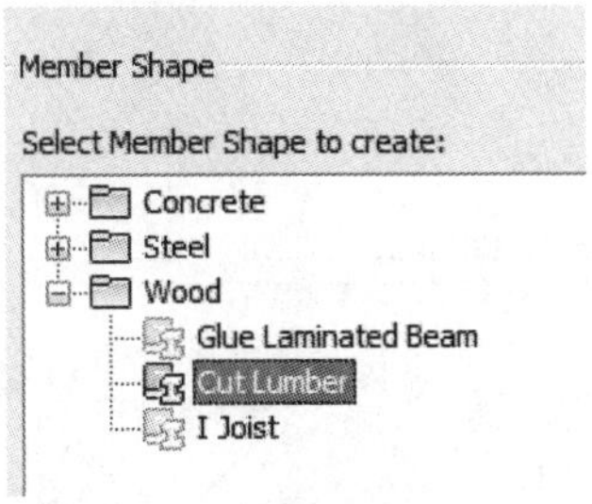

Select the **Cut Lumber** category under Wood.

Press **Next**.

8. 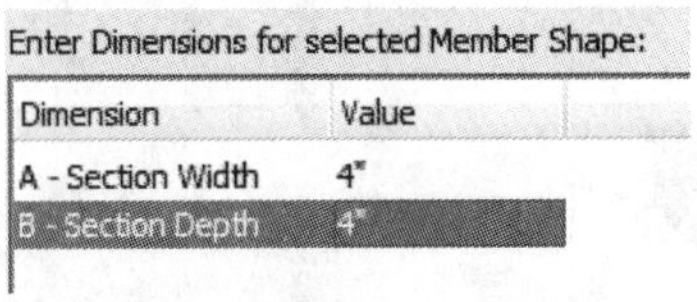

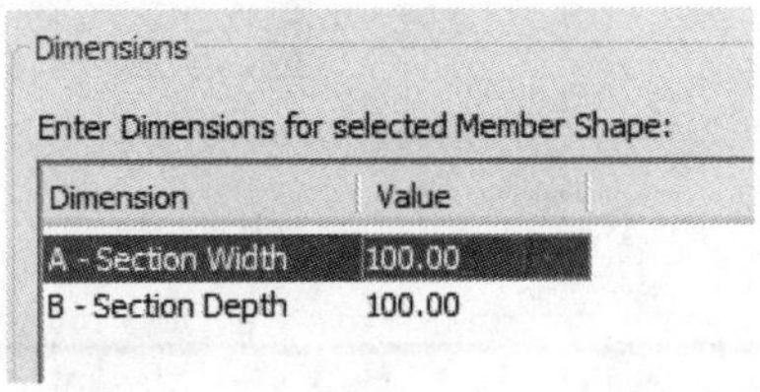

Set the Section Width to **4″ [100.00]**.

Set the Section Depth to **4″ [100.00]**.

Press **Next**.

9. 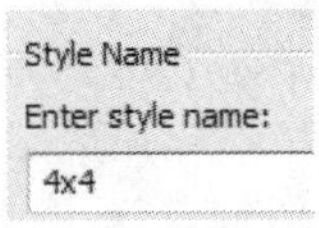

Enter the style name as **4x4 [100mmx100mm]**.

Press **Finish**.

10. Save as *ex6-2.dwg*.

Exercise 6-3:

Adding Structural Members

Drawing Name: ex6-2.dwg
Estimated Time: 25 minutes

This exercise reinforces the following skills:

- Creating Member Styles
- Use of Structural Members tools

1.  Open *ex6-2.dwg.*

2. Select the Work icon.
Activate the right viewport.

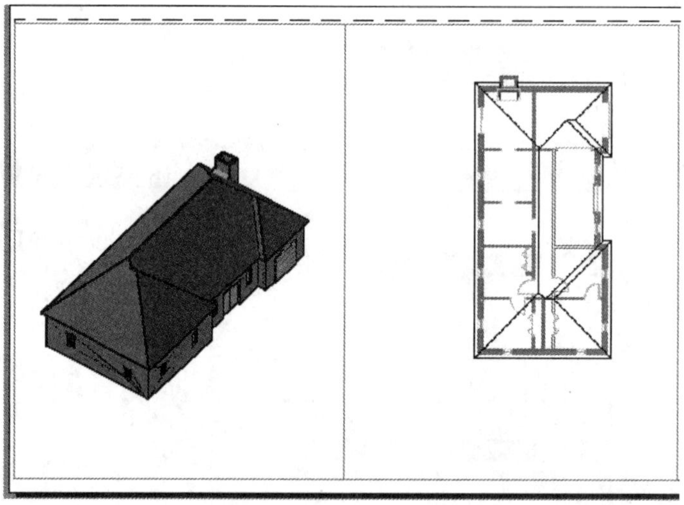

3. 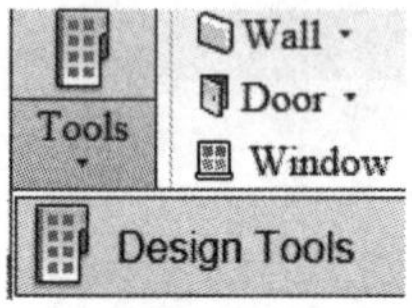

Activate the Tools palette if it is not available.

To activate, launch from the Home ribbon.

4. 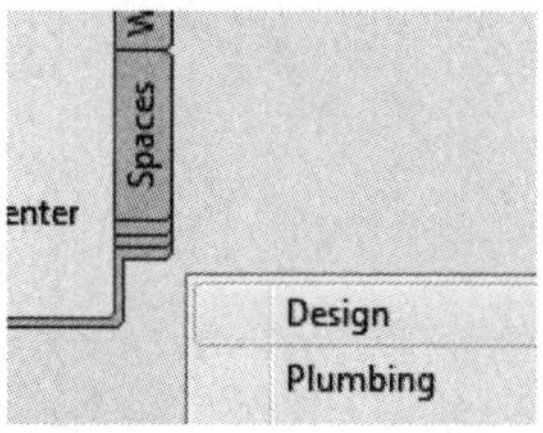

Activate the **Design** Palette.
To do this, right click on the palette and select **Design**.

5. 

Select the Structural **Beam** tool on the **Design** Tool Palette.

6. 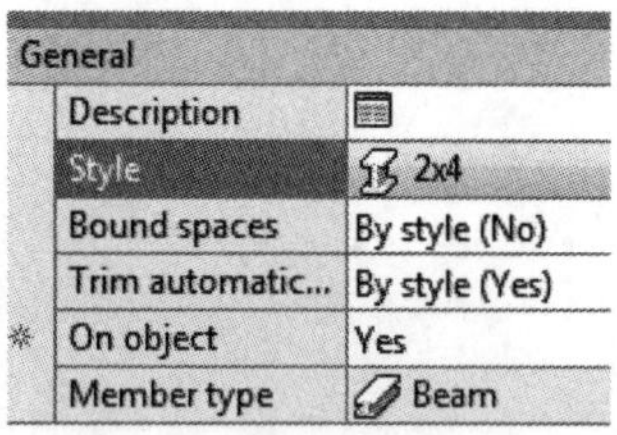

Select the **2x4 [50mmx250mm]** style from the Style drop-down on the Properties dialog.

7. 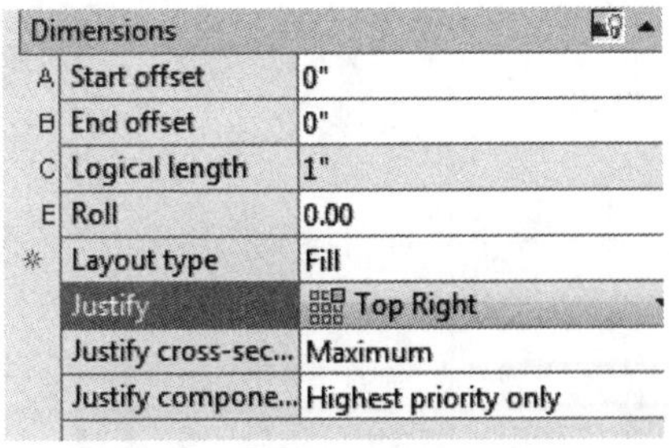

Set Justify to Top Right.
Set the Roll to 0.
Set the Start Offset to 0″.

8. Zoom into the family room area (the top left of the floor plan).

Use the From Osnap, pick the upper left corner of the house wall, and type **@14′-0″ <90 [@4250<90]** for the Offset; press ENTER. This shifts the first beam slightly below the wall.

Pull the cursor down at a 270° angle, and type in **14′-0″ [4250]** for the length. DO NOT EXIT THE COMMAND.

9. Change the Justification to Top Left.
Pull the cursor to the left (180°) and enter **9′-0″ [2750]** for the length.

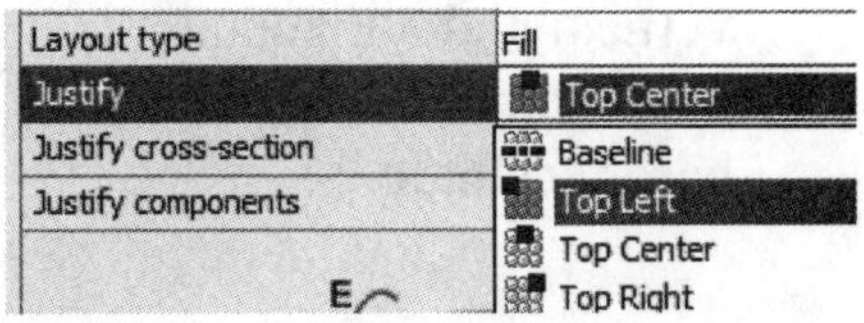

Hit ENTER to terminate the command.

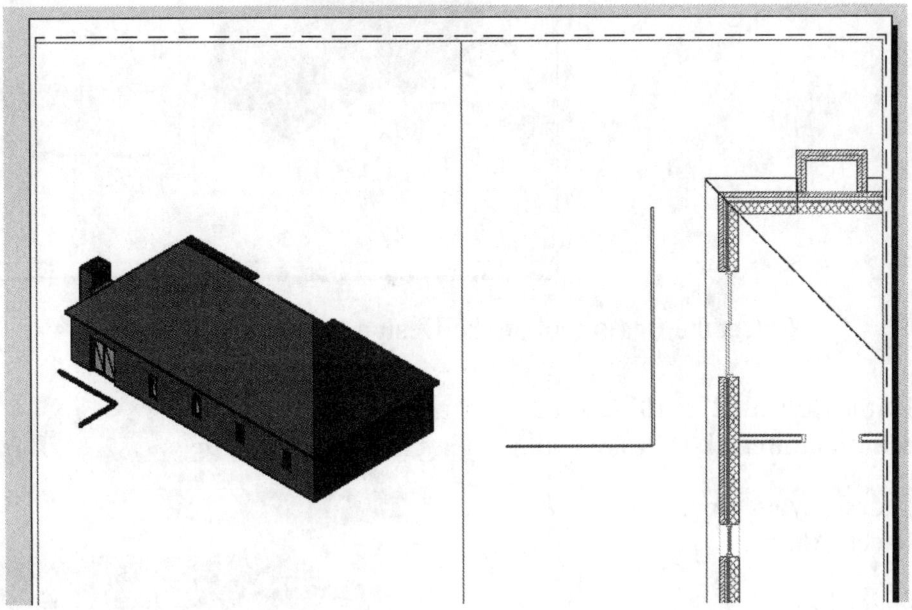

TIP: If you have difficulty starting the beam, draw the first two beams to the left of the building and then move them into position.

10. Select the first beam.
Right click and select **Basic Modify Tools→Mirror**.

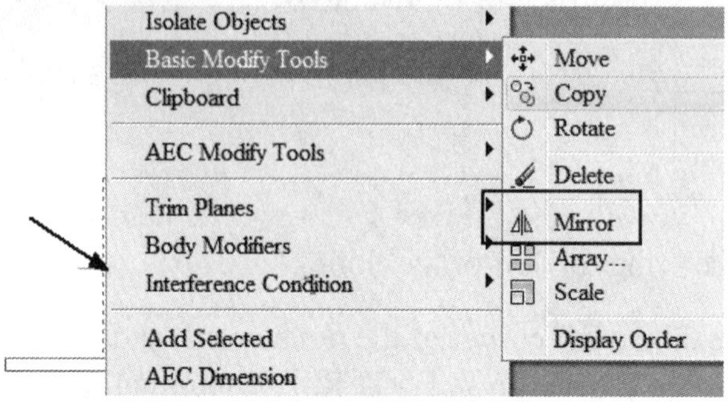

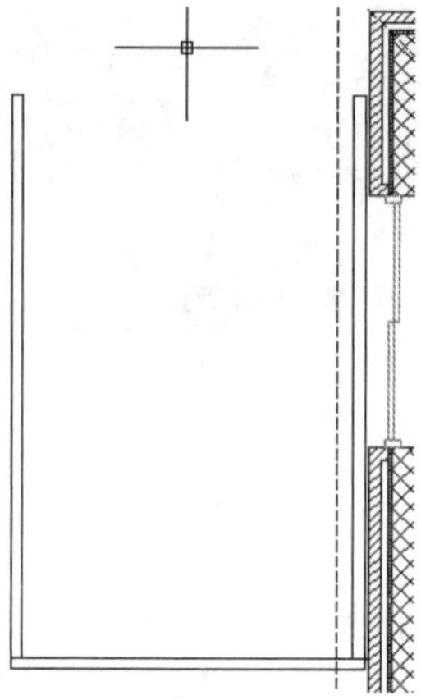

11. When prompted if you want to erase the source object, press ENTER to accept the default response of NO.

12. You should have the vertical and horizontal beam mirrored to create a base rectangle.

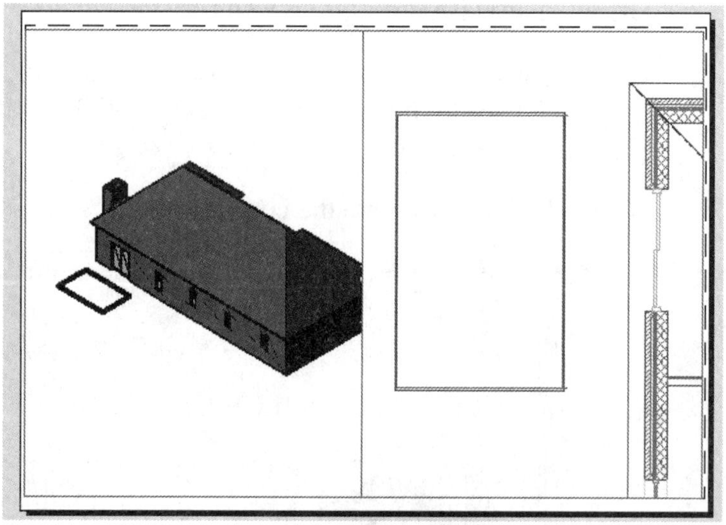

13. 

Select the **Beam** tool on the Design Palette.

14. Set the Style to **2″ x 10″ [50mmx250mm]**.

Under Layout type:
Select **Fill**.

Under Layout:
Set Array to **Yes**.
Set Layout Method to **Space evenly**.
Set Number of bays to **10**.

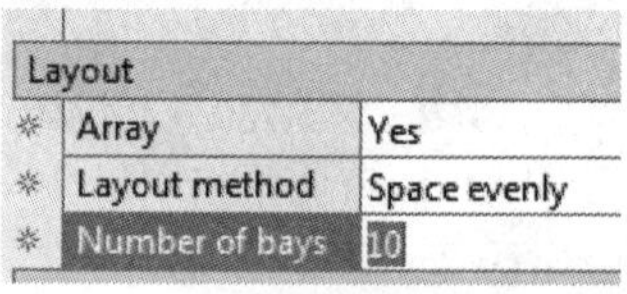

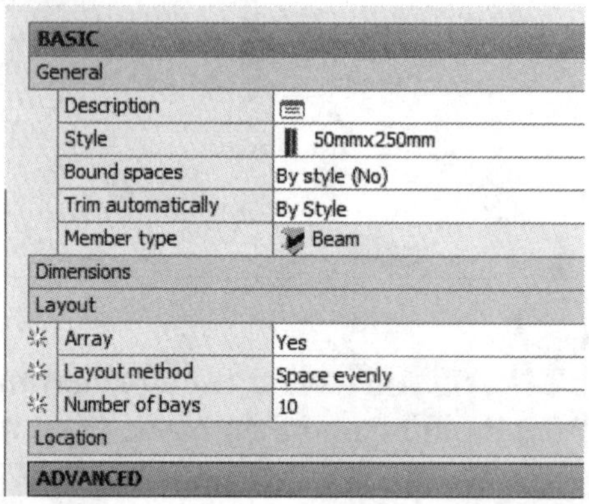

15. 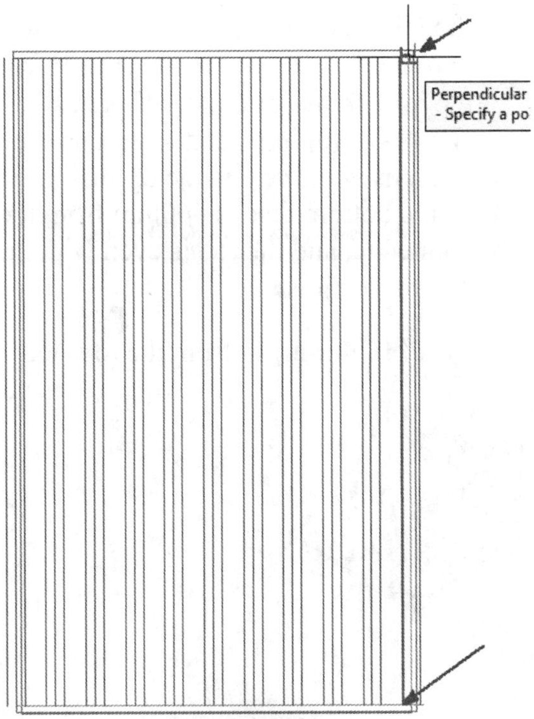

Select the start and end points for the beginning and end of the array.
Pick the bottom left side of the right vertical beam.
Pick the top left side of the right vertical beam.
You should see a preview image of the array that will be placed.

Press ENTER to accept the array placement.

16. 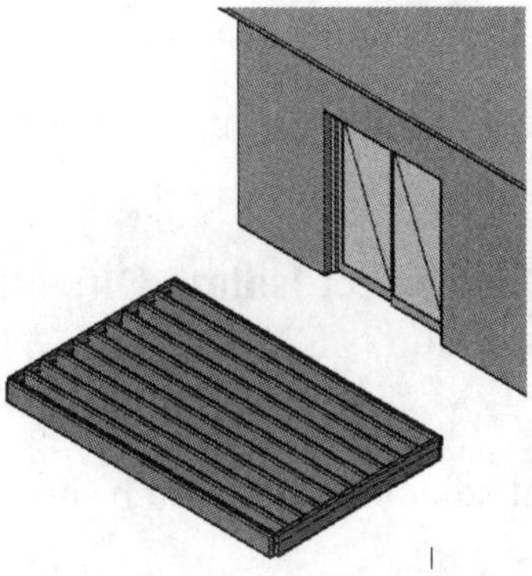

The array is placed.

If you are unable to create the array using the beam tool, verify that the UCS is set to view. Then, use the standard array command; select the horizontal beam and use a row spacing of 1′ 6″ [450 mm].

Some students may find it easier to construct this deck away from the house and then move it into position.

17. 

Select the **Column** tool from the Design Palette.

18. Set the Style to **4″ x 4″ [100mm x 100mm]**.
Set the Length to **5′ 9″ [1800]**.
Set Justify to **Bottom Left**.
Set the Roll to **0**.

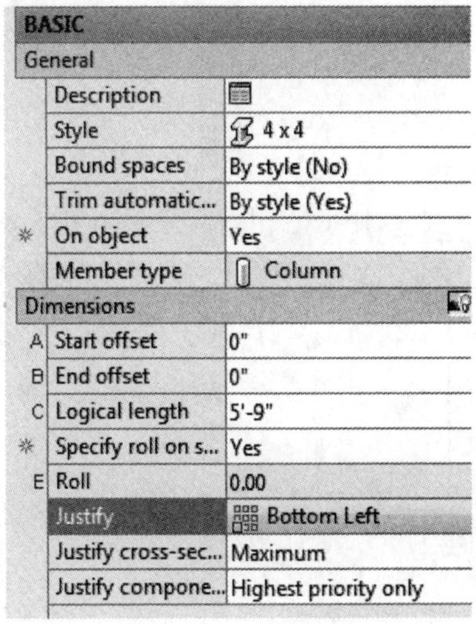

19. 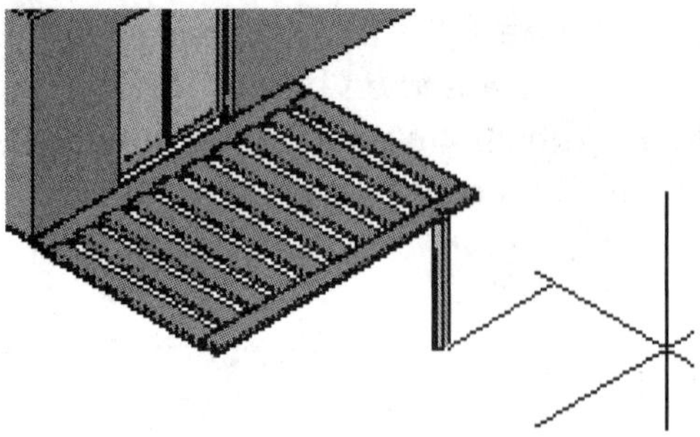

In the left viewport in the isometric view, use the From Osnap, pick the lower right corner of the joist frame, and enter **@0,2′,-6′ [@0,600,-1800]** to place the post so the left face aligns with the outside of the doubled joist, the bottom face is 600mm from the bottom edge, and the top is even with the bottom of the joists.

20.  Mirror the post to place another column **2′ [600mm]** in from the top (left side) of the frame.

21. Zoom in to the isometric view of the structure.

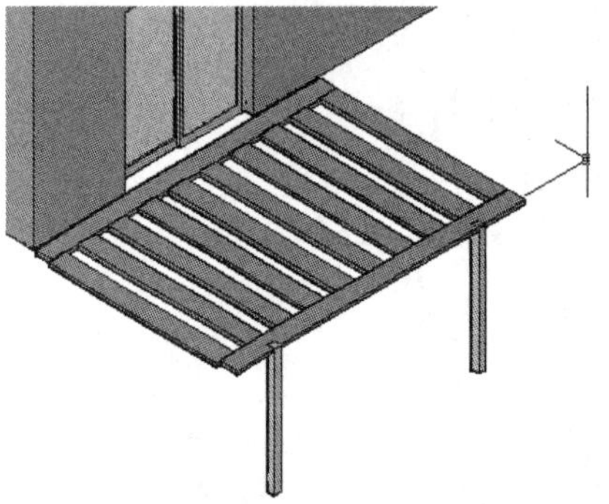

22. Select the front joist and the two posts. You may select using crossing, window, the control key, and de-select using the SHIFT key.

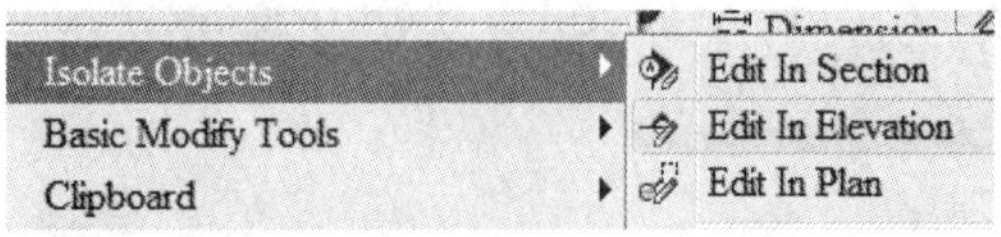

Right click and select **Isolate Objects→ Edit In Elevation**.

This will temporarily hide all the objects that were not selected and switch the display to an elevation view.

23. 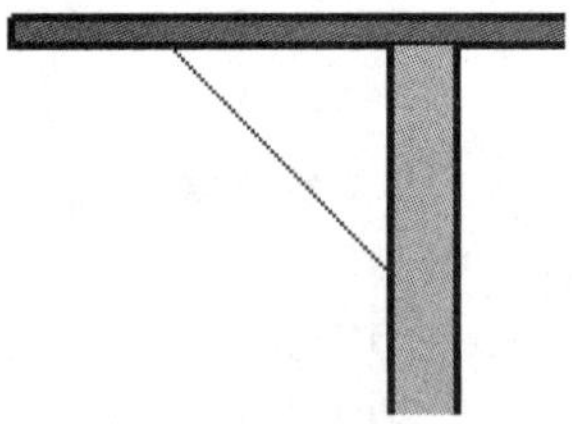

Draw a line to locate a brace in the elevation view.

24. 

In the plan view in the right viewport, adjust the line so it is straight and half-way into the front joist.

25. 

On the Design Palette:
Highlight the **Brace** tool.
Right click and **select Apply Tool Properties to→Linework.**

26. 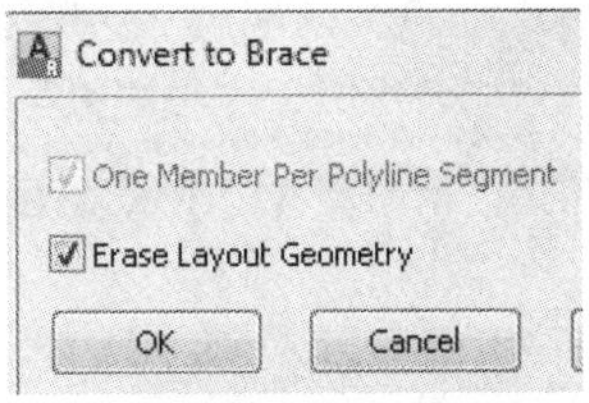

Select the line you just drew.

Place a check on **Erase Layout Geometry**.

Press **OK**.

27. 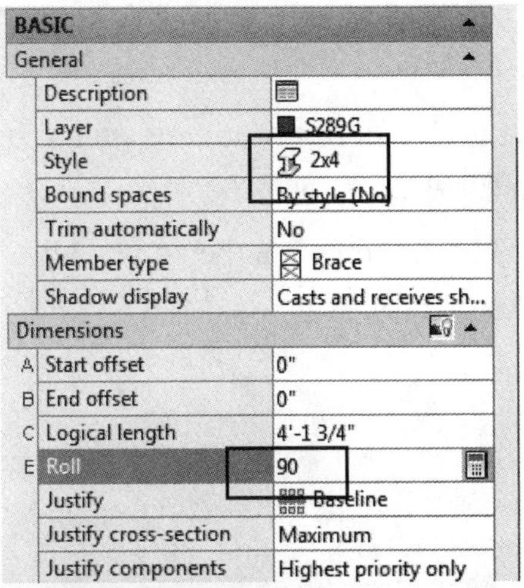

By default, the standard style brace is placed.

In the Properties dialog, select the **2 x 4** style.

Set the Roll to **90**.

28. 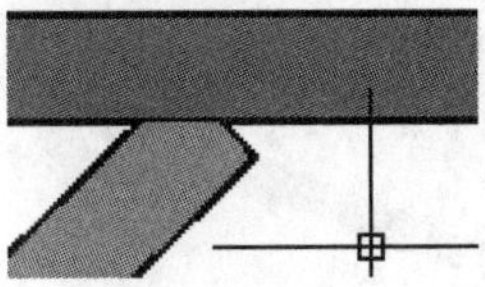

The brace needs to be trimmed.

29. 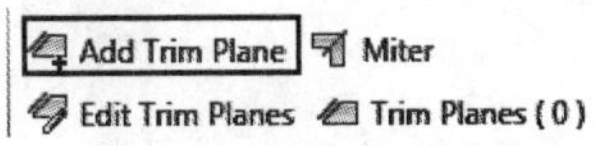

With the brace selected, select **Add Trim Plane** from the ribbon.

30. 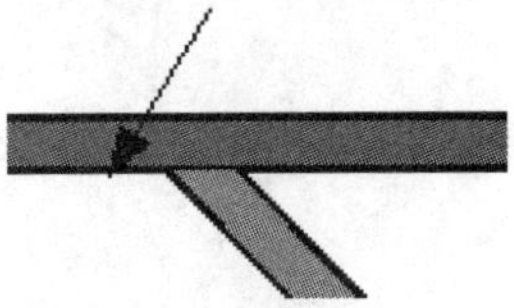

Select the bottom edge of the joist.

The brace will trim to the joist.

31. 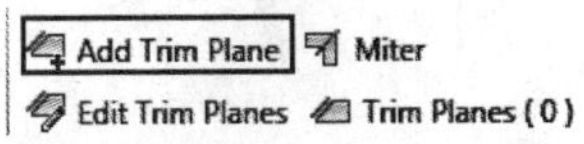

With the brace selected, select **Add Trim Plane**.

32. 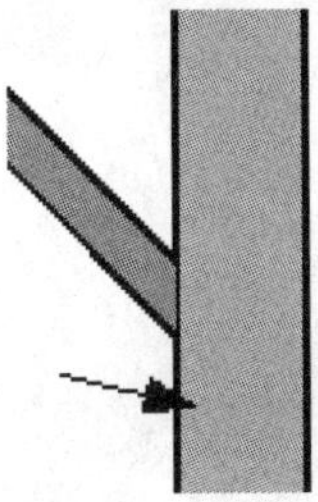

Select the side face of the joist.

The brace will trim to the joist.

Press ESC to release the selection.

33. 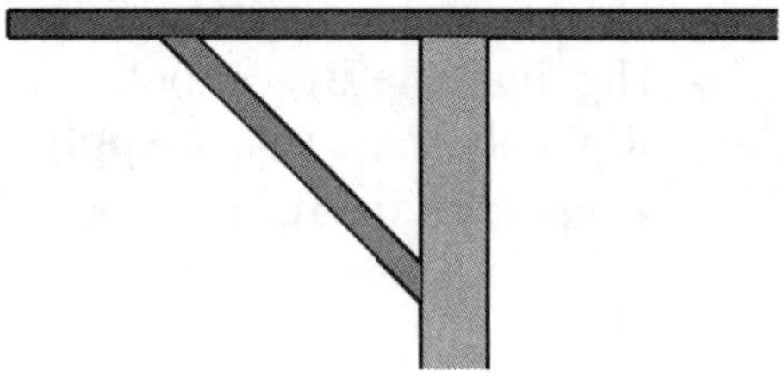

Select the brace and mirror it to the other side of the column.

34. 

The Mirror tool is on the Home ribbon in the Modify drop-down.

35. 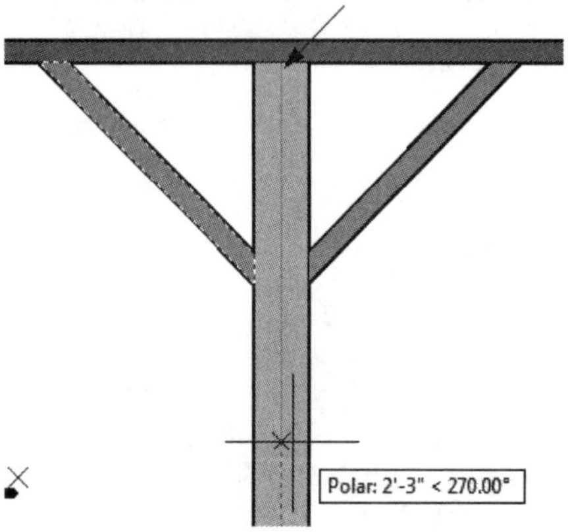

Select the midpoint of the column and move the cursor down at a 270° angle.

Press ENTER to complete the command.

36. Use Mirror to copy the brace to the other column.

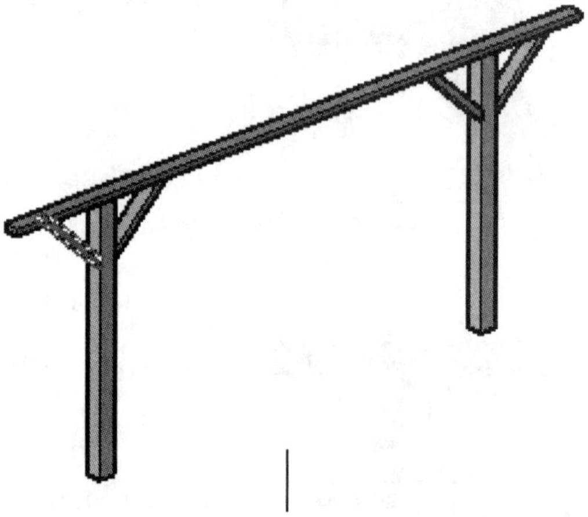

37. 

Locate the **Edit in View** window.

Click the X to end the isolate mode.

You may have to search for this window.

38. Save as *ex6-3.dwg*.

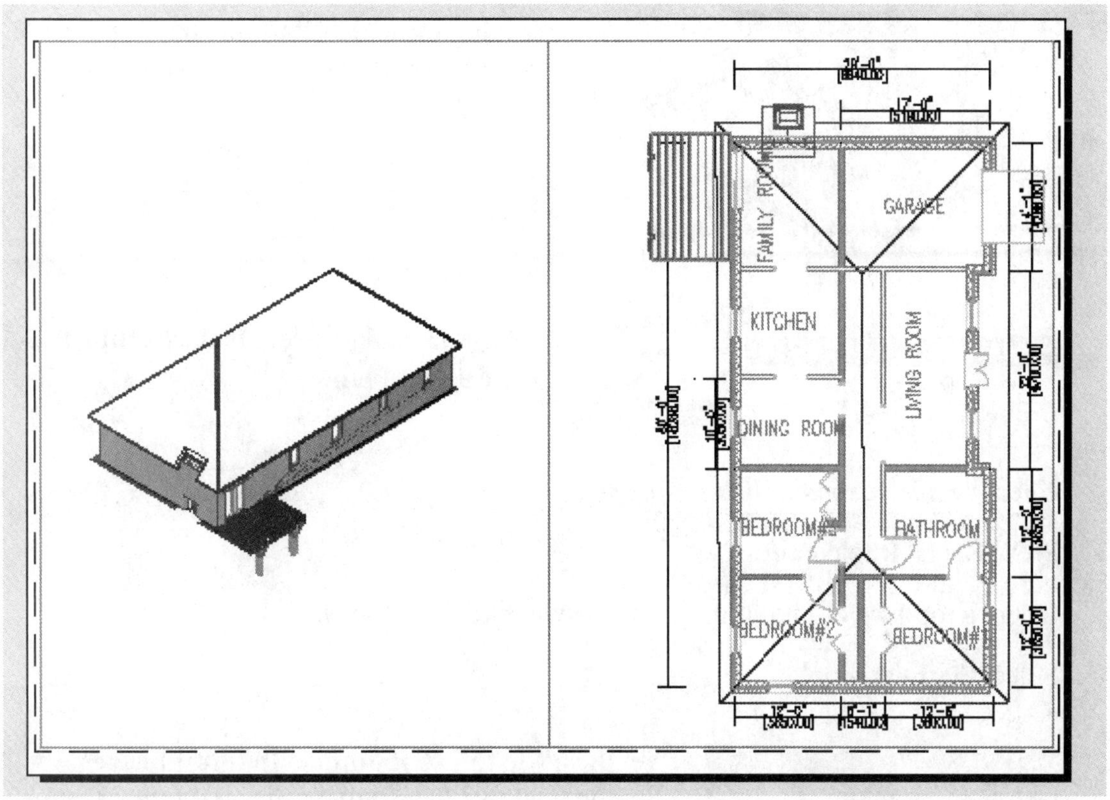

Exercise 6-4:

Add Floorboards

Drawing Name: ex6-3.dwg
Estimated Time: 20 minutes

This exercise reinforces the following skills:

- Structural Members
- Use of Structural Members tools

The top of the joist frame we created in the last exercise is sitting even with the top of the floor slab. It needs to be lowered to allow for nominal 2x6 deck boards.

1.  Open *ex6-3.dwg.*
Select the Work tab.
Activate the right viewport.

2. 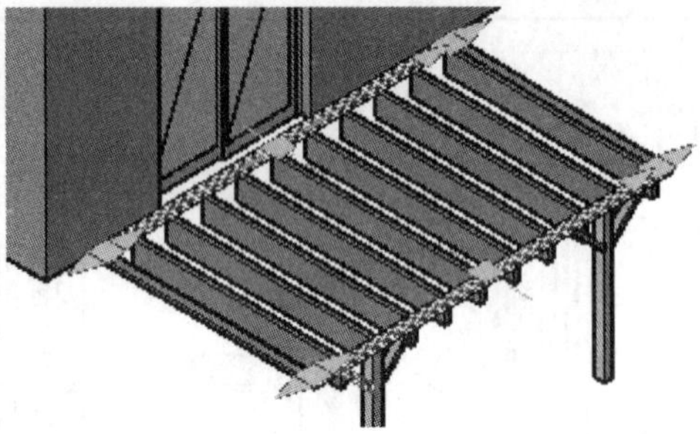

Select the joists that form the base of the deck. Do not select the braces or the posts.

3. 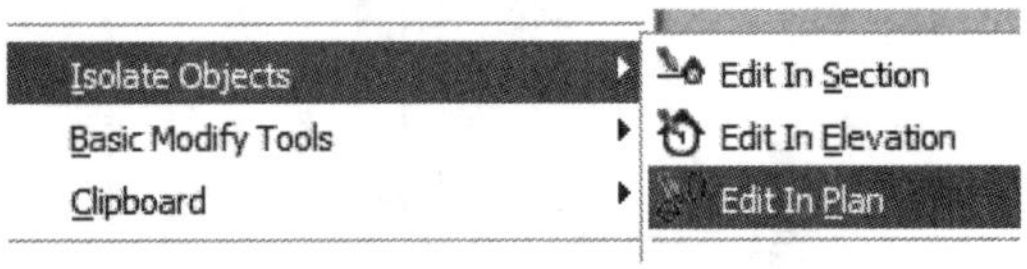

Right click and select **Isolate Objects →Edit In Plan**.

Check on the command line for prompts.

Press **ENTER** to continue.

4. Select a top face of one of the joists to switch to a plan view.

5. Select the **Beam** tool. 

6. 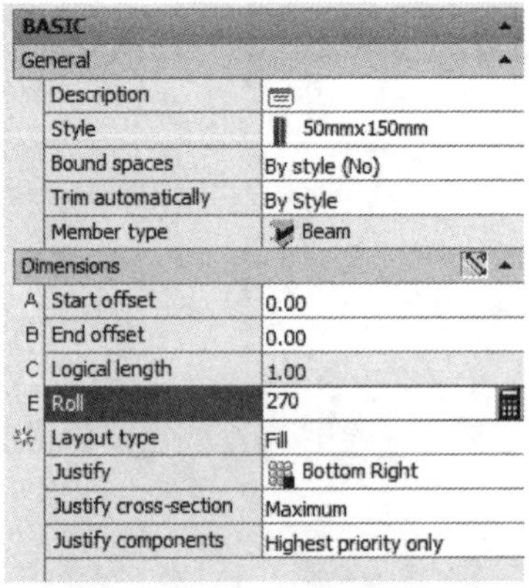

Set the Style to **2x6 [50mm x 150mm] brace**.
Set the Roll to **270°**, so that it lies flat rather than vertical.
Set the Justification to **Bottom Right**, so the board sits on top of the joists.

7. 

Pick the lower right corner of the joist at the house wall, drag the cursor up (90°), and give the board a length of 8′ [2430mm]. Drag the cursor up at 90° and add a second board of length 6′ [1820mm].

> **TIP:** If you have difficulty starting the beam, draw the first beam to the left of the building and then move them into position.

8. 

Enter twice to terminate and restart the command so you can pick a new starting point.

Pick the lower left corner of the first deck board you created, pull the cursor up at 90°, enter a distance of 4′ [1200mm], then pull the cursor up at 90° and enter a distance of 10′ [3050mm]. (Although not strictly necessary, we are providing suggested lengths of deck boards to minimize wastage.) Deck boards are laid with a nominal ⅜″ [10 mm] space between them to allow for drainage and board warping, so move the last two deck boards ⅜″ [10 mm] to the left.

9. 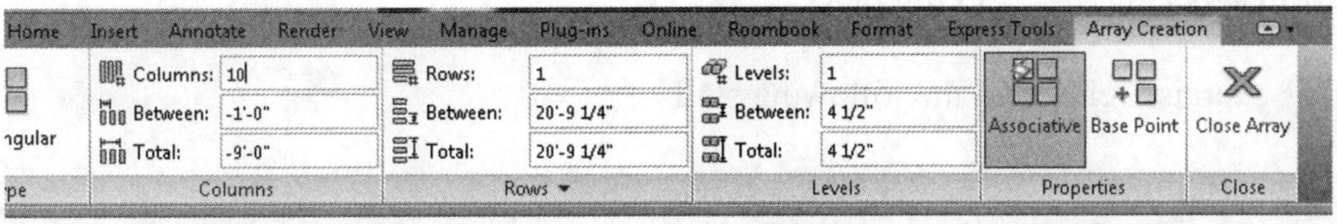

Array the 4 deck boards to fill the deck: 1 row, 10 columns with a column offset of **1′ [300mm]**.

10. 

Use the Preview option of the Array to check your array.

Right click the mouse to accept.

11. 

Select the **Exit Edit In View** button.

Note: You want a gap between the boards to allow for expansion and compression due to seasonal changes.

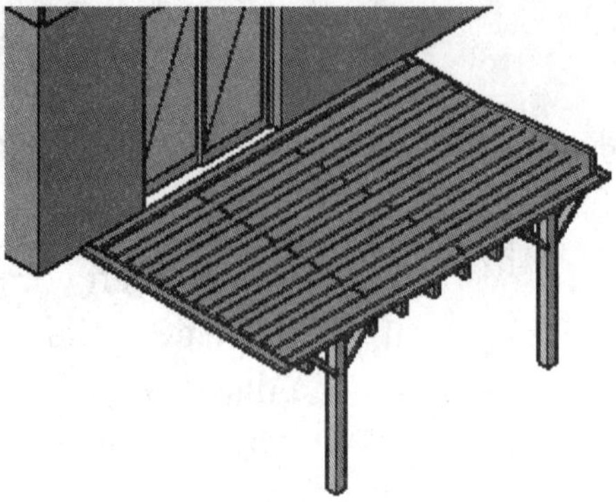

12. Save as *ex6-4.dwg*.

Exercise 6-5:

Add Railing

Drawing Name: Ex6-4.dwg
Estimated Time: 15 minutes

This exercise reinforces the following skills:

- Railings
- Railing Styles

1.  Open *ex6-4.dwg*.
Select the Work tab.
Activate the right viewport.

2. 

Select the **Railing** tool from the Design palette.

3. Create endpoints at 8′ 6″ [2620 mm] to the left (180°), then 13′ 6″ [4100 mm] up (90°), and 6′ 4″ [1900 mm] to the right (0°). This leaves an opening at the corner of the house.

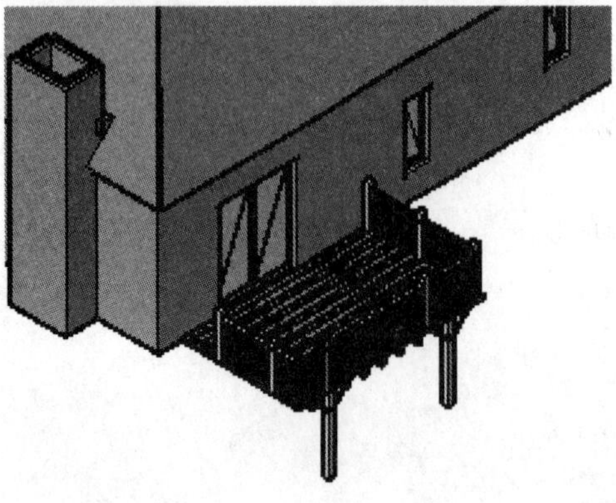

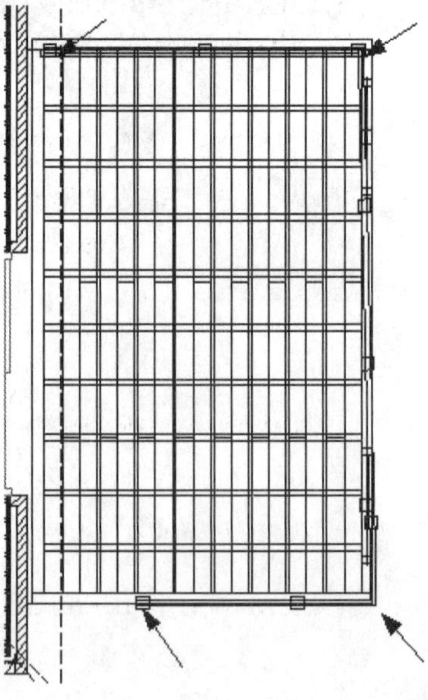

4. 

Select the **Railing** tool from the Design Palette. Right click and select **Railing Styles**.

5. 

Select **Standard** under Railing Styles. Right click and select **New**.

6. 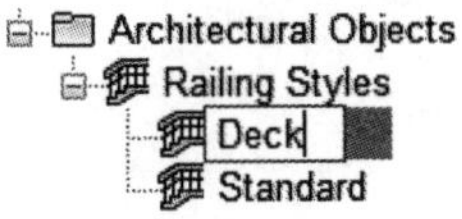

Name the new railing style **Deck**.

7. 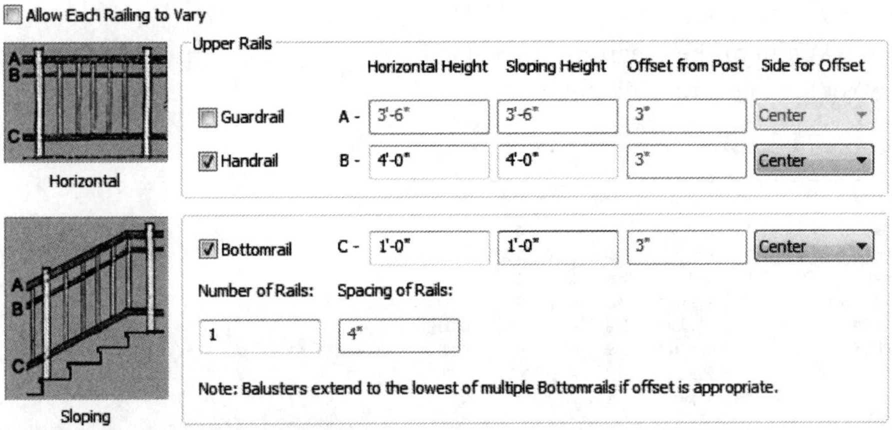

Select the **Rail Locations** tab.
Enable **Handrail** for the Upper Rails.
Set the Horizontal Height to **4′ [900]**.
Set the Sloping Height to **4′ [900]**.
Set the Side for Offset to **Center**.
Enable the **Bottom Rail**. (This adds a bottom rail)
Set the Horizontal Height to **1′-0″ [100]**.
Set the Sloping Height to **1′-0″ [150]**.
Set the Number of Rails to **1**.

8. 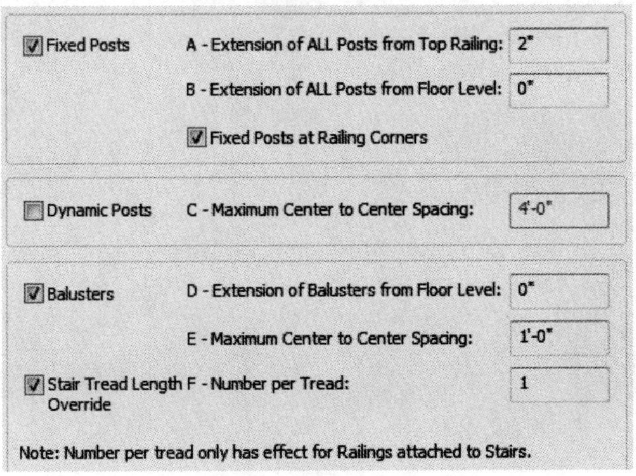

Select the **Post Locations** tab.
Enable **Fixed Posts.**
Enable **Fixed Posts at Railing Corners**. (This adds a post to each corner.)
Set the Extensions of ALL Posts from Top Railing to **2″ [50]**.
Enable **Dynamic Posts**.
Set the Maximum Center to Center Spacing to **4′ 0″ [1350]**.
Enable **Balusters**.
Set the Maximum Center to Center Spacing to **1′-0″ [100]**.
Enable the **Stair Tread Length Override**.
Set the Number per Tread to 1.

9. Select the **Components** tab.
Change the Width of the Guardrail to **3″ [75]**.
All the other settings are unchanged.

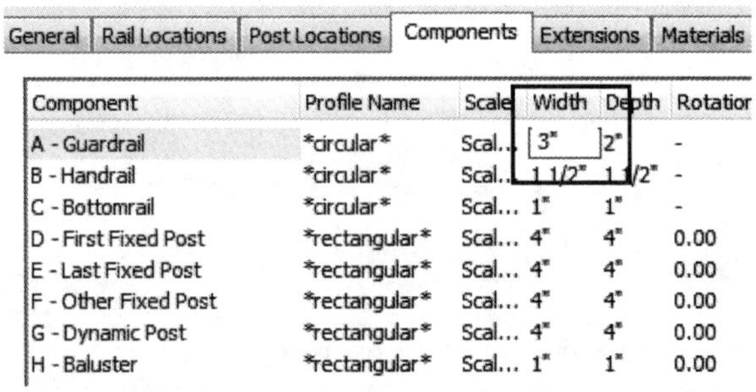

Press **OK** to close the dialog box.

10. 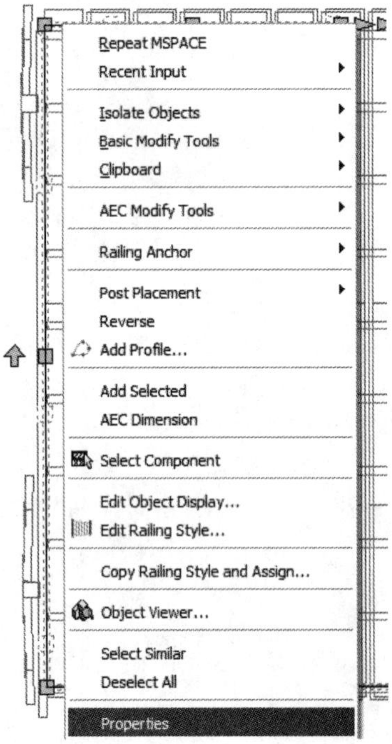

Select the Railing.
Right click and select **Properties**.

11. 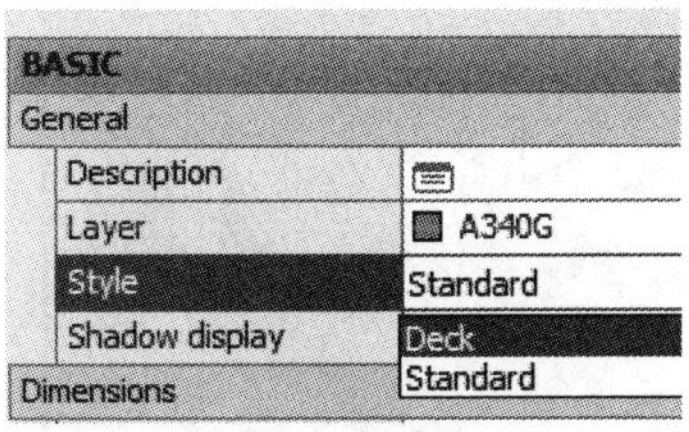

Change the Style to **Deck.**
Close the dialog.

12. Save as *ex6-5.dwg*.

Stairs

A house may have main stairs (from the first floor to the second floor) and/or a set of service stairs. Main stairs are usually constructed using pre-fabricated parts and are generally of better quality than service stairs. Service stairs are built on location. They are generally constructed of construction lumber.

There are six general types of stairs commonly used in residential construction. They are straight-run, L stairs, double-L stairs, U stairs, winder stairs and spiral stairs.

Straight run stairs are the most common. They are the least expensive to build, but they require a long open space.

Common terms associated with stairs include:

Balusters:	vertical members that support the handrail on open stairs
Enclosed stairs:	stairs that have a wall on both sides (also known as closed, housed, or box stairs). These can be stairs leading down to a basement or cellar.
Headroom:	The shortest clear vertical distance measured from the nosing of the tread and the ceiling.
Housed stringer:	A stringer that has been routed or grooved to accommodate the treads and risers.
Landing:	The floor area at either end of the stairs; also the area between a set of stairs, such as in an L stairs.
Newel:	The main posts of the handrail at the top and bottom or at points where the stairs change direction.
Nosing:	The rounded projection of the tread which extends past the face of the riser.

We will be adding service stairs to our deck.

Exercise 6-6:

Add Stairs

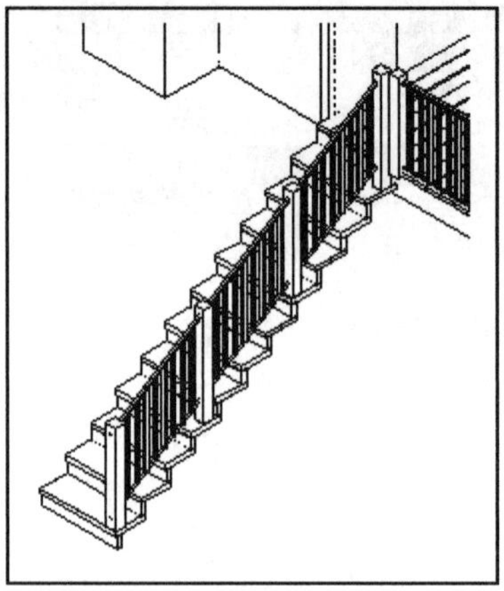

Drawing Name: Ex6-5.dwg
Estimated Time: 15 minutes

This exercise reinforces the following skills:

- Add Stairs
- Add Railing

1. 
Open *ex6-5.dwg.*
Select the Work tab.
Activate the right viewport.

2. 

Select the **Stair** tool from the Design Palette.

3. Set the Style to **Standard**.
Set the Shape to **Straight**.
Set the Vertical Orientation to **Down**.
Set the Width to **2′ 9″ [850]**.
Set the Height to **6′ 5″ [2100]**.
Set the Tread to **11″ [280]**.
Set Justify to **Left**.

BASIC		
General		
	Description	
	Layer	A240G
	Style	Standard
	Shape	Straight
	Vertical orientation	Down
	Shadow display	Casts and receives
Dimensions		
A	Width	850.00
B	Height	2100.00
	Justify	Left
	Calculation rules	Tread
C	Straight length	3080.00
D	Riser count	12
E	Riser	175.00
F	Tread	280.00
	Rise/tread calculation	630.00

Note that the Straight length is automatically calculated at **9′ 2″ [3080]**.

BASIC		
General		
	Description	
	Style	Standard
	Shape	Straight
	Vertical orientation	Down
Dimensions		
A	Width	3'-0"
B	Height	10'-0"
	Justify	Right
	Calculation rules	Tread
C	Straight length	14'-8"
D	Riser count	17
E	Riser	7"
F	Tread	11"
	Rise/tread calculation	2'-1"

4. 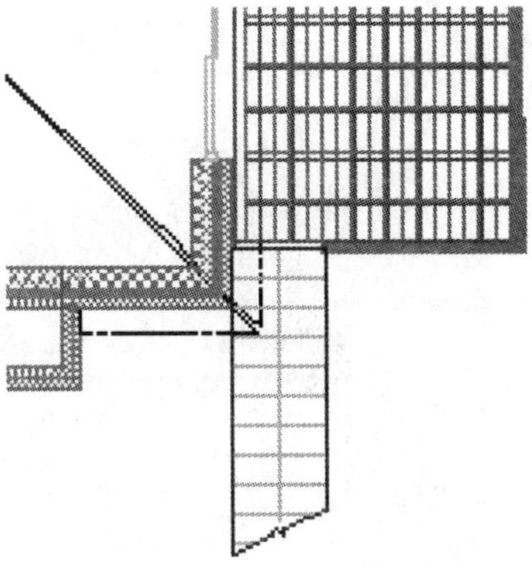

Pick an end point by the left side of the deck opening near the start of the railing.

Pick a point near the top of the deck for the end point of the stairs.

Close the dialog box.

5. We see the stair as a broken view.

6. 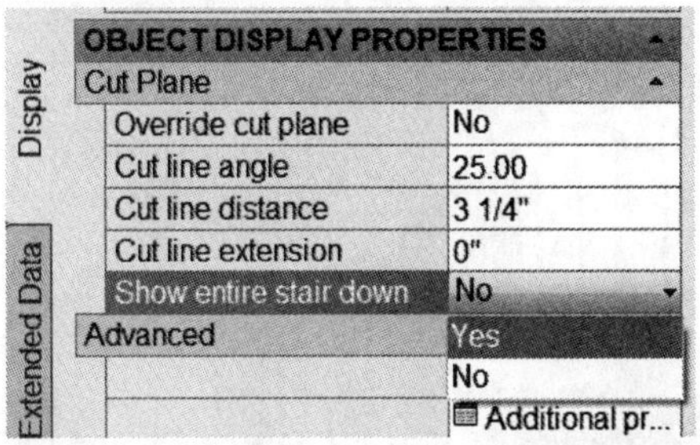

Select the stairs.
Right click and select Properties.
Select the Display tab.
Set Show entire stair down to **Yes**.

7. Type **Regen**.
The stairs now appear without a break mark.

Note: *If the view doesn't update, try switching to a different view and then switch back to Plan view.*

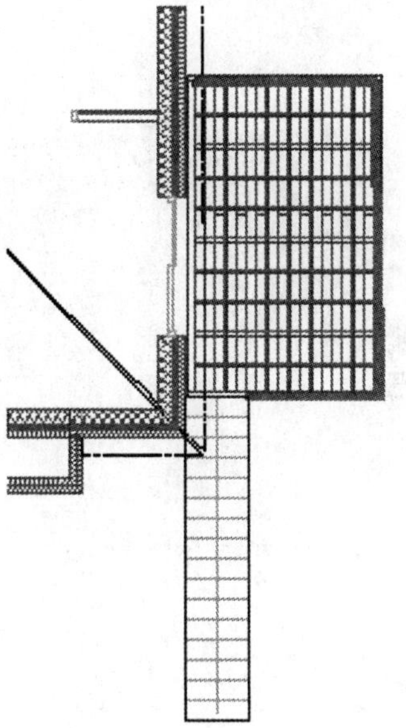

8. 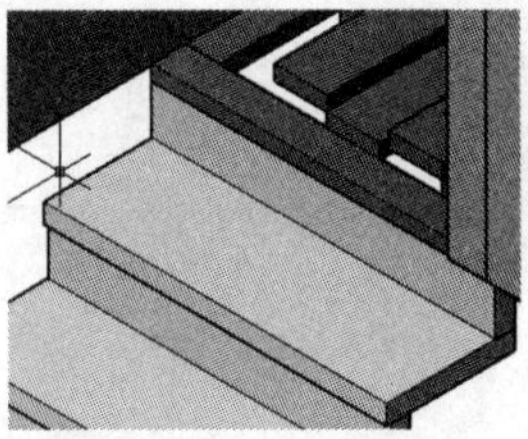

The stairs are placed, but they may need to be shifted slightly to fit with the deck.
Use the MOVE tool to position the stairs properly.
Safety regulations require a handrail down the stairs.

9. 

Select the **Railing** tool from the Design Palette.

10. 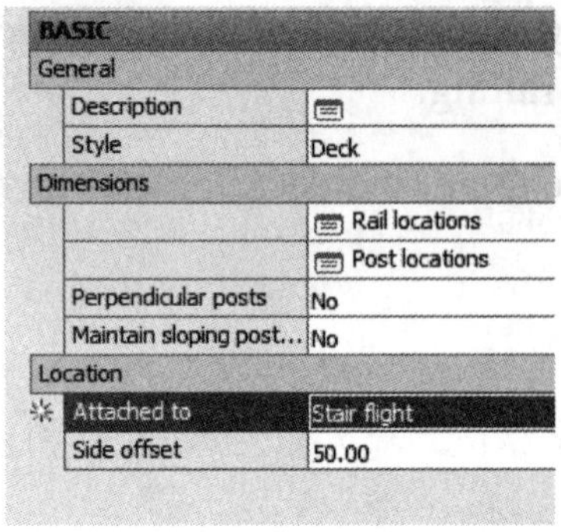

Set the Style to **Deck**.
Set Attached to: **Stair Flight**.
Set Offset to **2″ [50]**.

11. 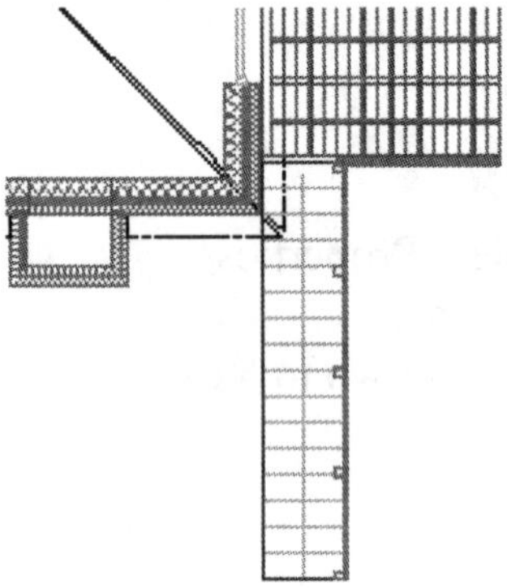

You will be prompted to select the stairs.
Pick the left side of the stair to place railing on the left side.

12. Save as *ex6-6.dwg*.

QUIZ 3

True or False

1. Custom content can be located in any subdirectory and still function properly.
2. The sole purpose of the Space Planning process is to arrange furniture in a floor plan.
3. The Design Center only has 3D objects stored in the Content area because ADT is strictly a 3D software.
4. Appliances are automatically placed on the APPLIANCE layer.
5. When you place a wall cabinet, it is automatically placed at the specified height.
6. You can create tools on a tool palette by dragging and dropping the objects from the Design Center onto the palette.

Multiple Choice

7. A residential structure is divided into:

   A. Four basic areas
   B. Three basic areas
   C. Two basic areas
   D. One basic area

8. Kitchen cabinets are located in the ______________ subfolder.

   A. Casework
   B. Cabinets
   C. Bookcases
   D. Furniture

9. Select the area type that is NOT part of a private residence:

   A. Bedrooms
   B. Common Areas
   C. Service Areas
   D. Public Areas

10. To set the layer properties of a tool on a tool palette:

    A. Use the Layer Manager
    B. Select the tool, right click and select Properties.
    C. Launch the Properties dialog
    D. All of the above

11. Vehicles placed from the Design Center are automatically placed on this layer:

A. A-Site-Vhcl
B. A-Vhcl
C. C-Site Vhcl
D. None of the above

12. The **Roof** tool is located on this tool palette:

A. DESIGN
B. GENERAL DRAFTING
C. MASSING
D. TOOLS

ANSWERS:

1) T; 2) F; 3) F; 4) F; 5) T; 6) T; 7) B; 8) A; 9) D; 10) B; 11) C; 12) A

Lesson 7

Documentation

Before we can create our construction drawings, we need to create layouts or views to present the design. AutoCAD Architecture is similar to AutoCAD in that the user can work in Model and Paper Space. Model Space is where we create the 3D model of our house. Paper Space is where we create or setup various views that can be used in our construction drawings. In each view, we can control what we see by turning off layers, zooming, panning, etc.

To understand paper space and model space, imagine a cardboard box. Inside the cardboard box is Model Space. This is where your 3D model is located. On each side of the cardboard box, tear out a small rectangular window. The windows are your viewports. You can look through the viewports to see your model. To reach inside the window so you can move your model around or modify it, you double-click inside the viewport. If your hand is not reaching through any of the windows and you are just looking from the outside, then you are in Paper Space or Layout mode.
You can create an elevation in your current drawing by first drawing an elevation line and mark, and then creating a 2D or 3D elevation based on that line. You can control the size and shape of the elevation that is generated. Unless you explode the elevation that you create, the elevation remains linked to the building model that you used to create it. Because of this link between the elevation and the building model, any changes to the building model can be made in the elevation as well.

When you create a 2D elevation, the elevation is created with hidden and overlapping lines removed. You can edit the 2D elevation that you created by changing its display properties. The 2D Section/Elevation style allows you to add your own display components to the display representation of the elevation, and create rules that assign different parts of the elevation to different display components. You can control the visibility, layer, color, linetype, lineweight, and linetype scale of each component. You can also use the line work editing commands to assign individual lines in your 2D elevation to display components, and merge geometry into your 2D elevation.

After you create a 2D elevation, you can use the AutoCAD BHATCH and AutoCAD DIMLINEAR commands to hatch and dimension the 2D elevation.

AutoCAD comes with standard title block templates. They are located in the Templates subdirectory under *Documents and Settings \<User Name>\Local Settings\Application Data\ Autodesk\ AutoCAD 2013\R18.2\enu \Template.*

If you are using VISTA or Windows 7, the templates are stored under *Users/<user name>/AppData/Local/ Autodesk/AutoCAD 2013/R18.2/enu/Template.*

Many companies will place their templates on the network so all users can access the same templates. In order to make this work properly, set the Options so that the templates folder is pointed to the correct path.

Exercise 7-1:
Creating a Custom Titleblock

Drawing Name: Architectural Title Block.dwg
Estimated Time: 30 minutes

This exercise reinforces the following skills:

- Title blocks
- Attributes
- Edit Block In-Place
- Insert Image
- Insert Hyperlink

1.  Select the **Open** tool.

2. Browse to *Documents and Settings\All Users\ Application Data\Autodesk\ACA 2013\enu\ Template\ AutoCAD Templates.*

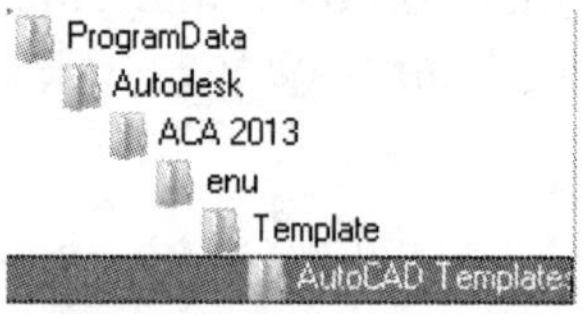

In Vista and Windows 7 machines, go to *Program Data/Autodesk/ACA 2013/enu/Template/AutoCAD Templates.*

3. 

Open the *Tutorial-iArch.dwt.*
Verify that *Files of type* is set to Drawing Template or you won't see the file.

4. Perform a **File→Save as**.

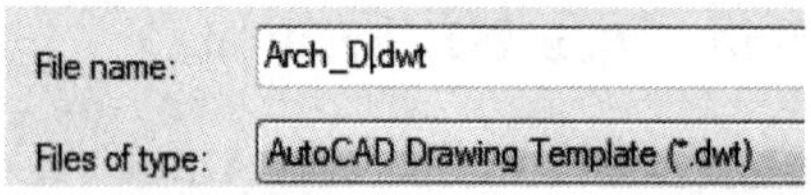

Save the file to your work folder.
Rename **Arch_D.dwt**.

5. 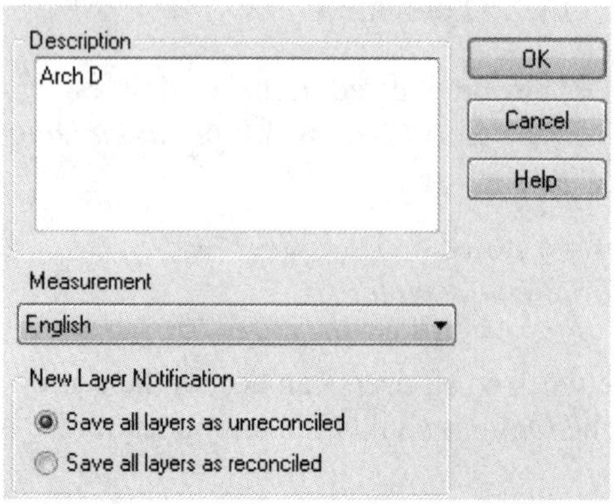

Enter a description and press **OK**.

6. 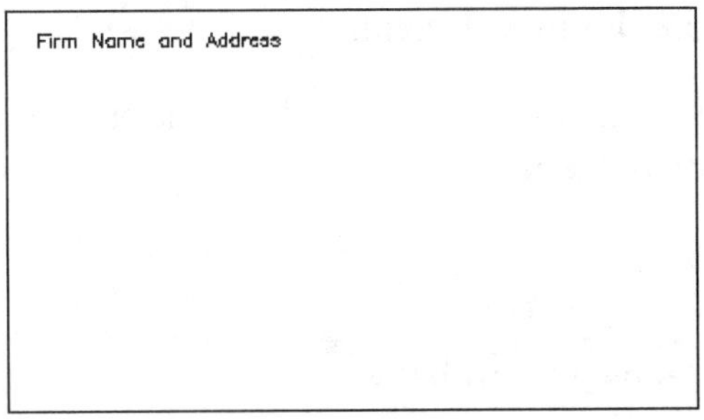

Zoom into the Firm Name and Address rectangle.

7. 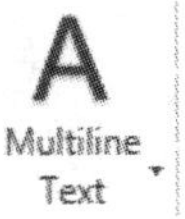

Select the **MTEXT** tool from the **Annotation** panel on the Home ribbon.

Draw a rectangle to place the text.

8. Set the Font to **Verdana.**

Hint: If you type the first letter of the font, the drop-down list will jump to fonts starting with that letter.

Set the text height to ⅛″.
Set the justification to **centered**.
Enter the name and address of your college.

9. 

Extend the ruler to change the width of your MTEXT box to fill the rectangle.

Press **OK**.

10. 

Use **MOVE** to locate the text properly, if needed.

11. 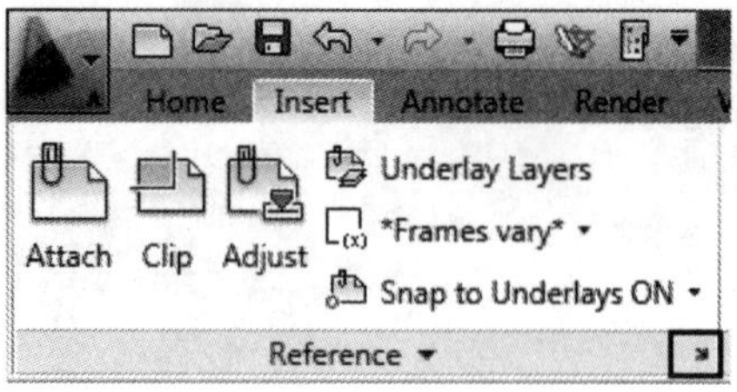

Activate the **Insert** menu.

Select the arrow located on the right bottom of the Reference panel.

12. 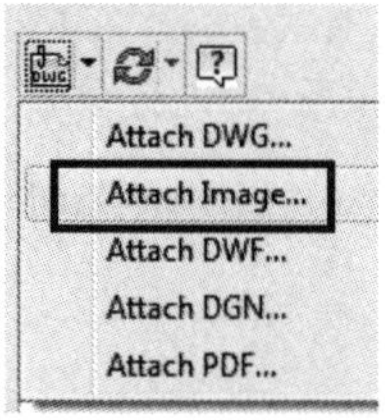

The External Reference Manager will launch.

Select **Attach Image** from the drop-down list.

13. 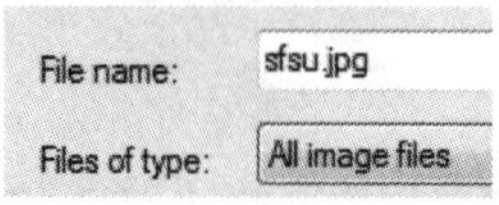

Locate the image file you wish to use.
There is an image file available for use from the publisher's website called *sfsu.jpg*.

14. 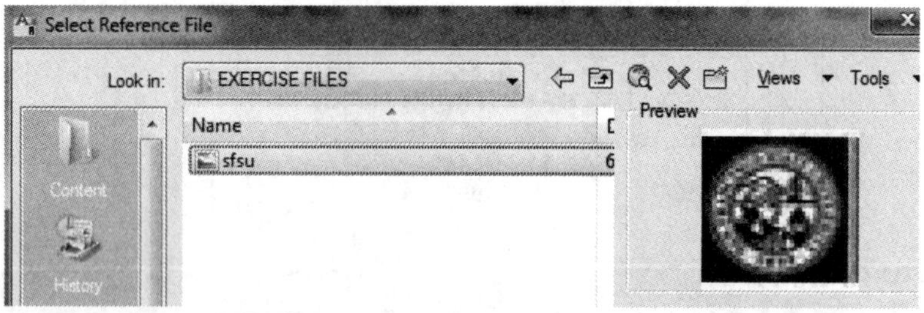

Press **Open**.

15. 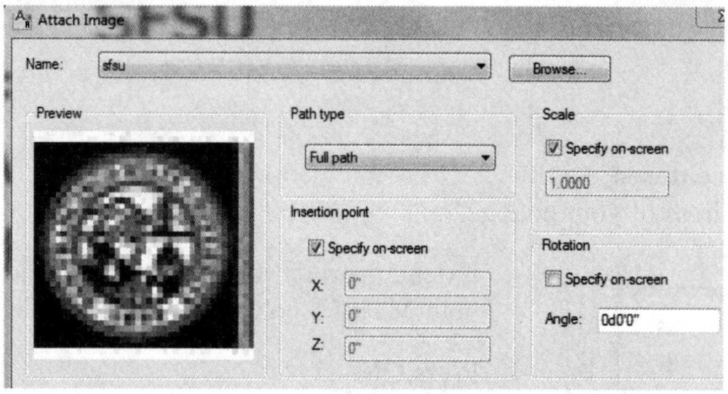

Press **OK**.

16. 

Place the image in the rectangle.

TIP: If you are concerned about losing the link to the image file (for example, if you plan to email this file to another person), you can use **INSERTOBJ** to embed the image into the drawing. Do not enable link to create an embedded object. The INSERTOBJ command is not available on the standard ribbon.

17. Select the image.
    Right click and select **Properties**.

18. 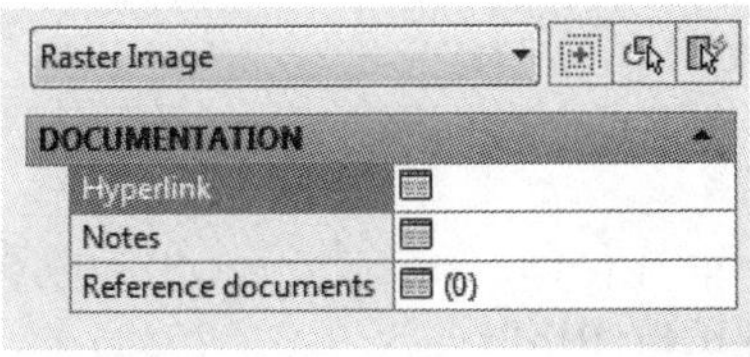

Select the **Extended** tab.
Pick the Hyperlink field.

19. 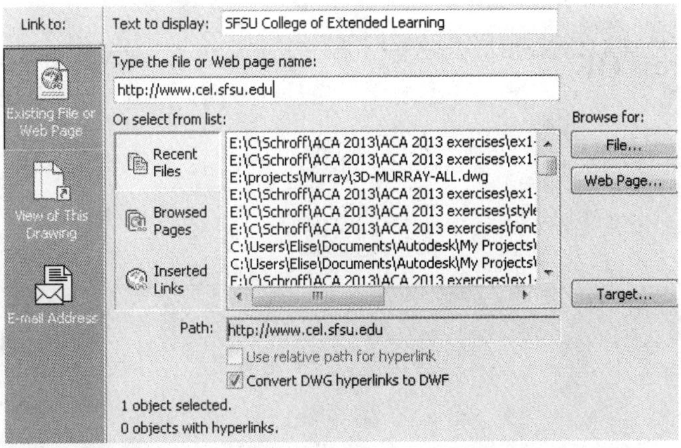

Type in the name of the school in the Text to display field.
Type in the website address in the *Type the file or Web page name* field.

Press **OK**.
Close the Properties dialog.

20. 

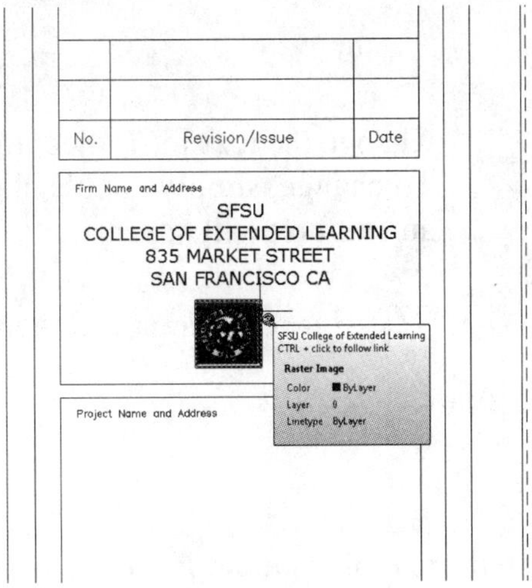

If you hover your mouse over the image, you will see a small World icon. This indicates there is a hyperlink attached to the image. To launch the webpage, simply hold down the CTRL key and left click on the icon.

TIP: If you are unsure of the web address of the website you wish to link, use the Browse for **Web Page** button.

21. 

To turn off the image frame/boundary:

Type **IMAGEFRAME** at the command line.
Enter **0**.

TIP: IMAGEFRAME has the following options:

0: Turns off the image frame and does not plot
1: Turns on the image frame and is plotted
2: Turns on the image frame, but does not plot

22. 

Select the titleblock.
Right click and select **Edit Block in-place**.

23. 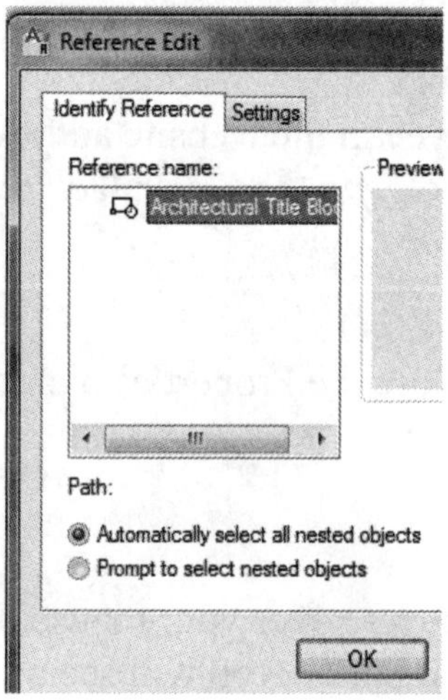

Press **OK**.

24. 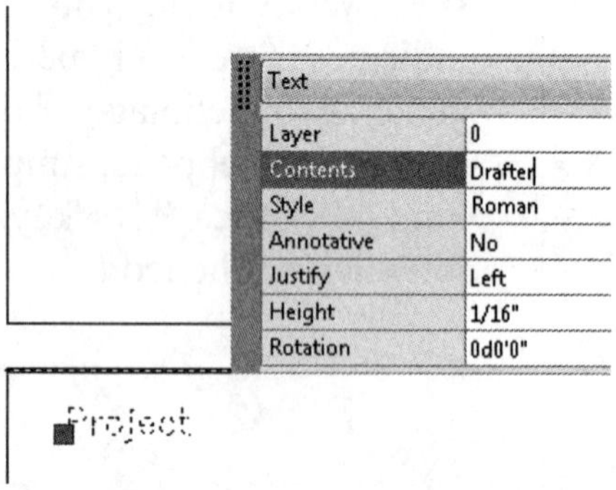

Change the text for Project to **Drafter**.
To change, simply double click on the text and an edit box will appear.

25. 

Select the **Define Attribute** tool from the Insert ribbon.

26. 

Select the **Field** tool.

27. 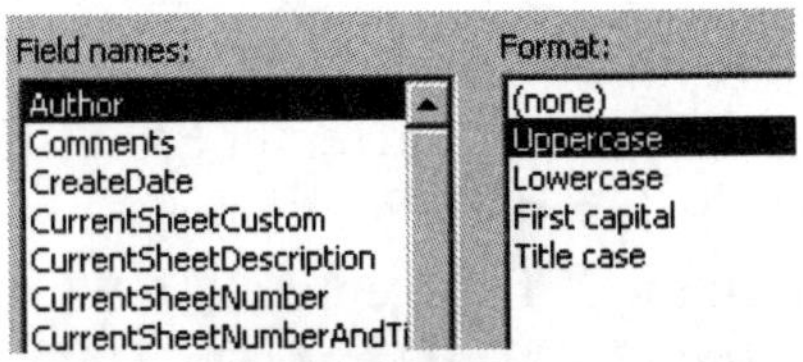

Highlight Author and Uppercase.

Press **OK**.

28. 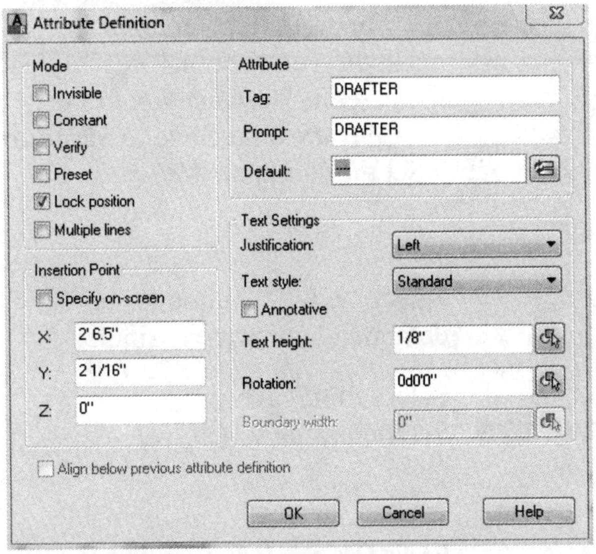

In the Tag field, enter **DRAFTER**.
In the Prompt field, enter **DRAFTER**.
The Value field is used by the FIELD property.

In the Insertion Point area:
- In the X field, enter: **2′ 6.5″**.
- In the Y field, enter: **2-1/16″**.
- In the Z field, enter: **0″**.

In the Text Options area:
- Set the Justification to **Left**.
- Set the Text Style to **Standard**.
- Set the Height to **1/8″**.

Press **OK**.

29. 

Select the **Define Attributes** tool.

30. 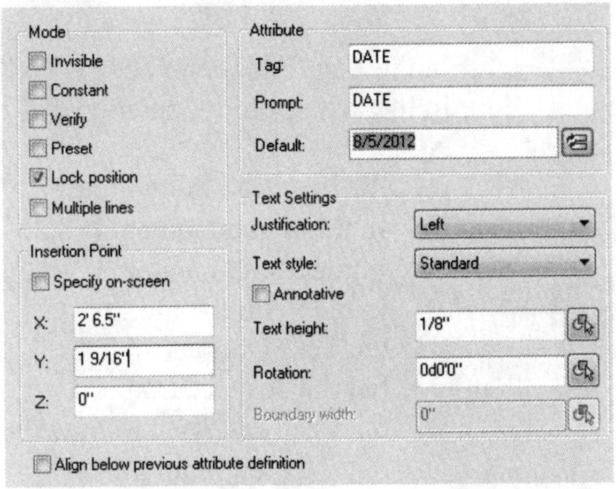

In the Tag field, enter **DATE**.
In the Prompt field, enter **DATE**.

In the Insertion Point area:
- In the X field, enter: **2′ 6.5″**.
- In the Y field, enter: **1-9/16″**.
- In the Z field, enter: **0″**.

In the Text Options area:
- Set the Justification to **Left**.
- Set the Text Style to **Standard.**
- Set the Height to **1/8″**.

31. Select the Field button to set the default value for the attribute.

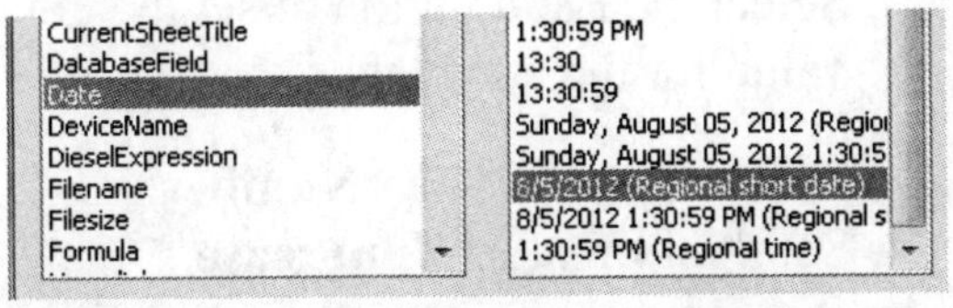

Select **Date**.
Set the Date format to **Regional short date**.

Press **OK**.

32. 

Select the **Define Attributes** tool.

33. 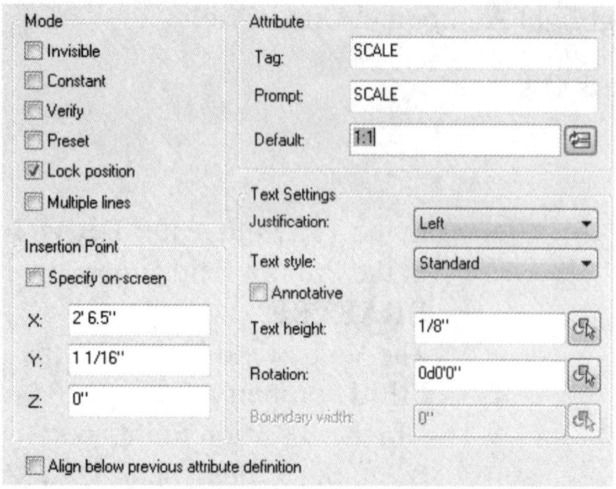

In the Tag field, enter **SCALE**.
In the Prompt field, enter **SCALE**.
In the Insertion Point area:
In the X field, enter: **2′ 6.5″**.
In the Y field, enter: **1-1/16″**.
In the Z field, enter: **0″**.
In the Text Options area:
Set the Justification to **Left**.
Set the Text Style to **Standard**.
Set the Height to **1/8″**.

34. 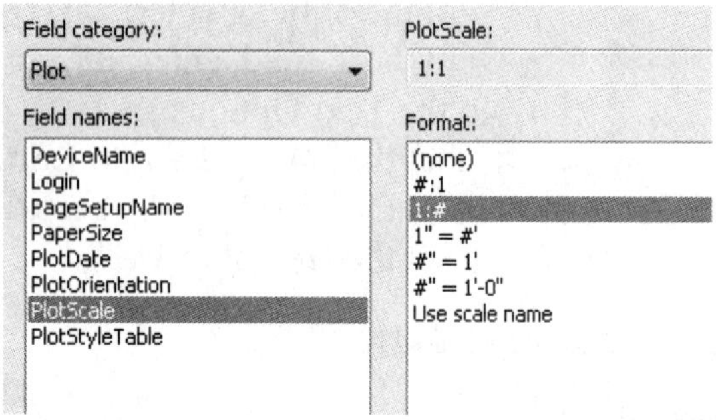

Select the Field button to set the default value for the attribute.

Select **PlotScale**.
Set the format to **1:#**.

Press **OK**.

Press **OK** to place the attribute.

35. 

Select the **Define Attributes** tool.

36. 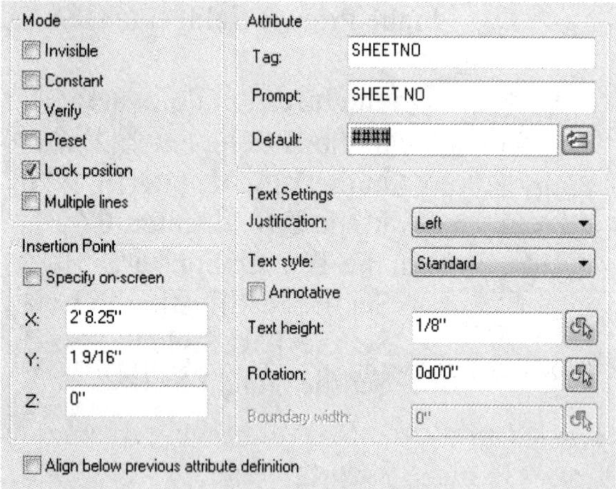

In the Tag field, enter **SHEETNO**.
In the Prompt field, enter **SHEET NO**.
In the Insertion Point area:
In the X field, enter: **2′ 8.25″**
In the Y field, enter: **1-9/16″**
In the Z field, enter: **0**
In the Text Options area:
Set the Justification to **Left**.
Set the Text Style to **Standard**.
Set the Height to **1/8″**.

37. 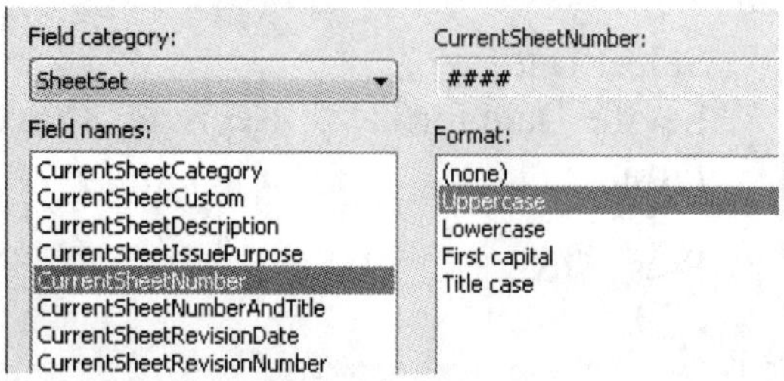

Select the Field button to set the default value for the attribute.

Select **CurrentSheetNumber**.
Set the format to **Uppercase**.

Press **OK**.

Press **OK** to place the attribute.

38. 

Select the **Define Attribute** tool.

39. 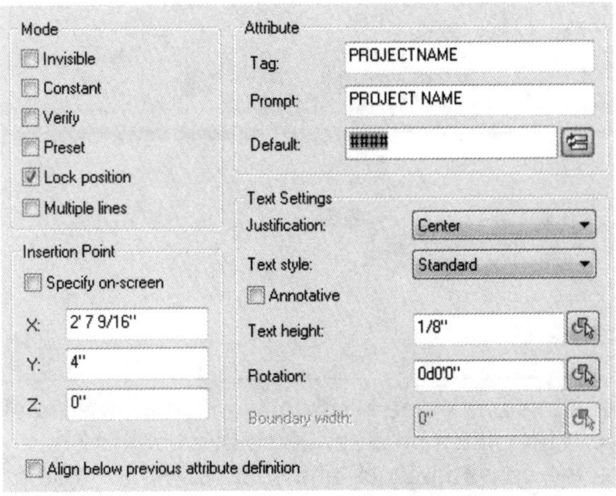

In the Tag field, enter **PROJECTNAME**
In the Prompt field, enter **PROJECT NAME**
In the Insertion Point area:
In the X field, enter: **2′ 7-9/16″**
In the Y field, enter: **4″**
In the Z field, enter: **0**
In the Text Options area:
Set the Justification to **Center**.
Set the Text Style to **Standard**.
Set the Height to **1/8″**.

40. Select the Field button to set the default value for the attribute.

Select **AEC Project** for the field category.
Set the Field Name to **Project Name**.
Set the format to **Uppercase**.

Press **OK**.

TIP: A common error for students is to forget to enter the insertion point. The default insertion point is set to 0,0,0. If you don't see your attributes, look for them at the lower left corner of your title block and use the MOVE tool to position them appropriately.

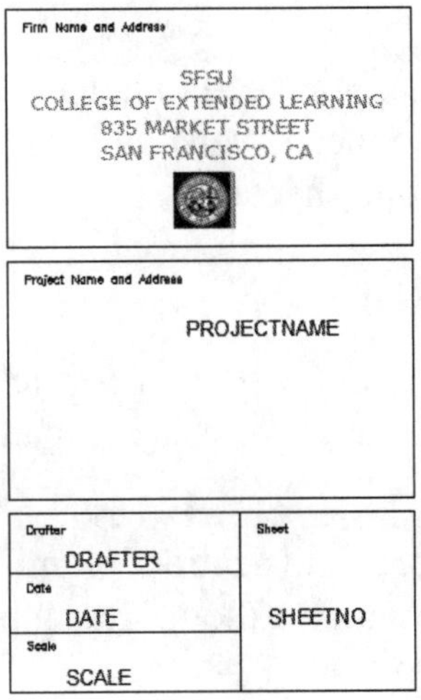

Your title block should look similar to the image shown.

If you like, you can use the MOVE tool to reposition any of the attributes to make them fit better.

41. 

Select **Save** on the ribbon to save the changes to the title block and exit the Edit Block In-Place mode.

42. 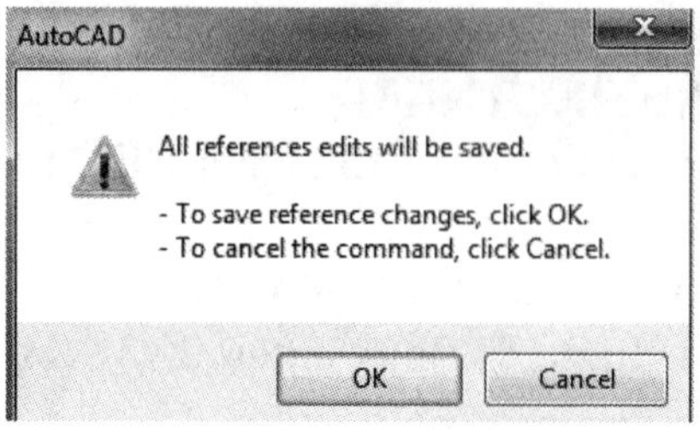

Press **OK**.

43. Save the file and go to **File→Close**.

> Tips & Tricks
>
> - Use templates to standardize how you want your drawing sheets to look. Store your templates on a server so everyone in your department uses the same titleblock and sheet settings. You can also set up dimension styles and layer standards in your templates.
> - ADT 2005 introduced a new tool available when you are in Paper Space that allows you to quickly switch to the model space of a viewport without messing up your scale. Simply select the **Maximize Viewport** button located on your task bar to switch to model space. To switch back to paper space, select the **Minimize Viewport** button.
>
> 

You use the Project Navigator to create additional drawing files with the desired views for your model. The views are created on the Views tab of the Project Navigator. You then create a sheet set which gathers together all the necessary drawing files that are pertinent to your project.

Previously, you would use external references, which would be external drawing files that would be linked to a master drawing. You would then create several layout sheets in your master drawing that would show the various views. Some users placed all their data in a single drawing and then used layers to organize the data.

This shift in the way of organizing your drawings will mean that you need to have a better understanding of how to manage all the drawings. It also means you can leverage the drawings so you can reuse the same drawing in more than one sheet set.

You can create five different types of views using the Project Navigator:

- Model Space View – a portion that is displayed in its own viewport. This view can have a distinct name, display configuration, description, layer snapshot and drawing scale.
- Detail View – displays a small section of the model, i.e. a wall section, plumbing, or foundation. This type of view is usually associated with a callout. It can be placed in your current active drawing or in a new drawing.

- Section View – displays a building section, usually an interior view. This type of view is usually associated with a callout. It can be placed in your current active drawing or in a new drawing.
- Elevation View – displays a building elevation, usually an exterior view. This type of view is usually associated with a callout. It can be placed in your current active drawing or in a new drawing.
- Sheet View – this type of view is created when a model space view is dropped onto a layout sheet.

Note: Some classes have difficulty using the Project Navigator because they do not use the same work station each class, or the drawings are stored on a network server. In those cases, the links can be lost and the students get frustrated trying to get the correct results.

Exercise 7-2:

Verifying the Project Setting

Drawing Name: ex6-1.dwg
Estimated Time: 5 minutes

This exercise reinforces the following skills:

- Project Navigator
- Project Browser

1.  Open *ex6-1.dwg.*
2. 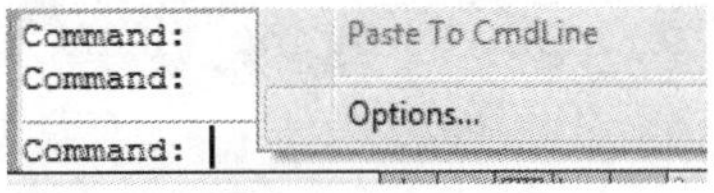

Right click in the command window and select **Options**.
3. 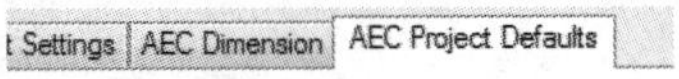

Select the **AEC Project Defaults** tab.
4. 

Verify that the AEC Project Location Search Path to the location where you are saving your files.
5. Press **OK** to close the Options dialog.
6. 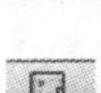 Launch the **Project Navigator** from the Quick Access toolbar.
7. 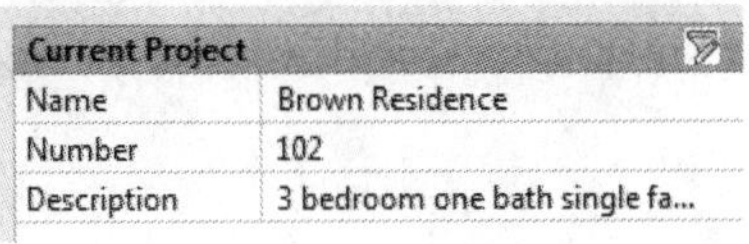

Verify that the Current Project is set to the Brown Residence project.

Tags and schedules use project information. If you do not have a current project defined, you may see some error messages when you tag elements.

Exercise 7-3:

Creating Elevation Views

Drawing Name: ex6-1.dwg
Estimated Time: 15 minutes

This exercise reinforces the following skills:

- Creating an Elevation View
- Adding a Callout
- Named Views

1.  Open *ex6-1.dwg.*

2. Switch to the Model tab.

3. 

Activate the **Top** view by clicking the top plane on the view cube.

4. 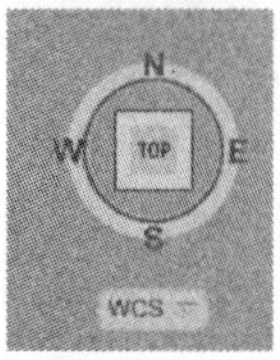

Spin the View cube so North is oriented on top.

5. 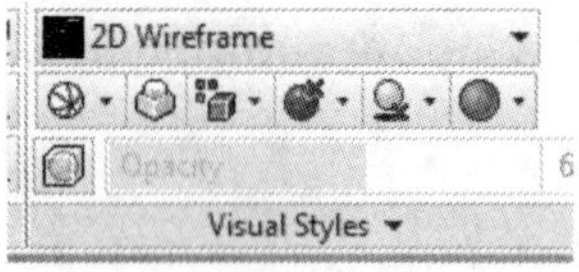

Set the view to **2D Wireframe** mode using the Visual Styles drop-down on the View ribbon.

6. 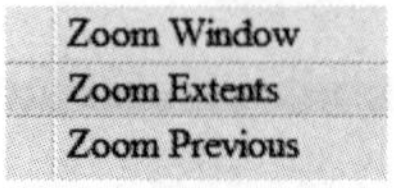

Use **Zoom Extents** to view the entire model.

7. 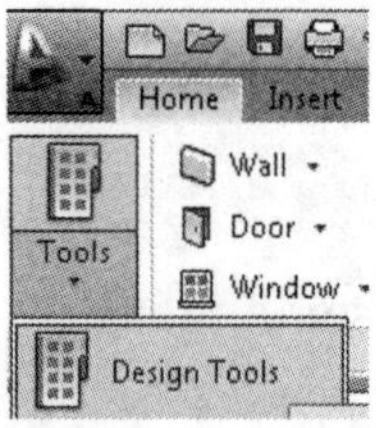

Launch the **Design Tools** palette.

8. 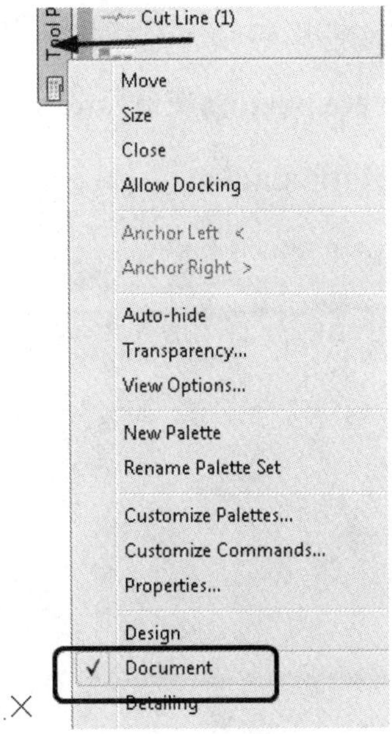

Right click on the grey bar on the left of the Design Palette.

Enable the **Document** palette.

9. 

Select the Callouts Palette on the Design Tools Palette.
Select the **Elevation Mark A2**.

10. 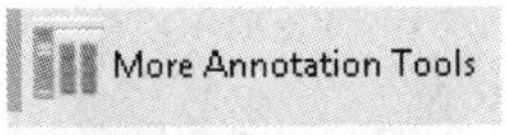

Select **More Annotation Tools**.

11. 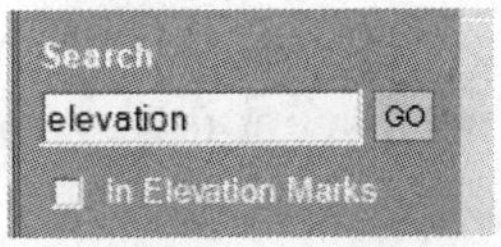

The Content Browser will launch.

Search for elevation.

12. 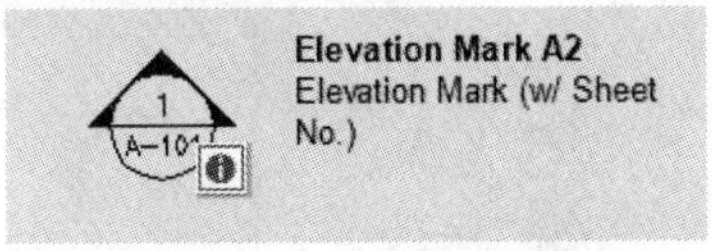

Locate **Elevation Mark A2**.

13. 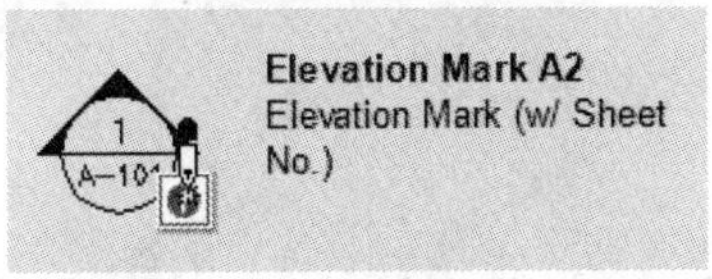

Hover the cursor over the **Elevation Mark A2** tool until you see an eyedropper.

14. 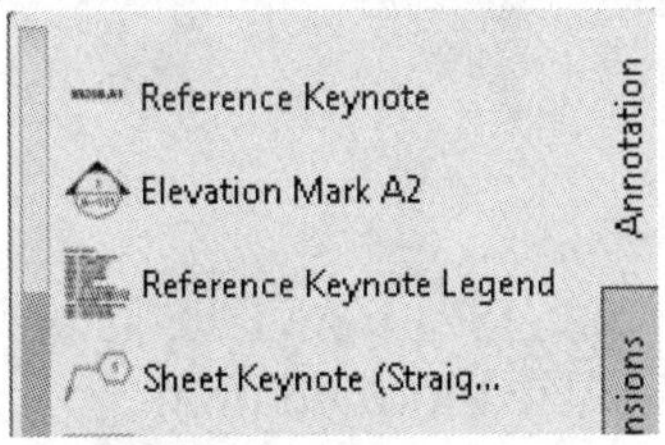

Hold down the left mouse button to drag and place the **Elevation Mark A2** on the Document Palette.

15. 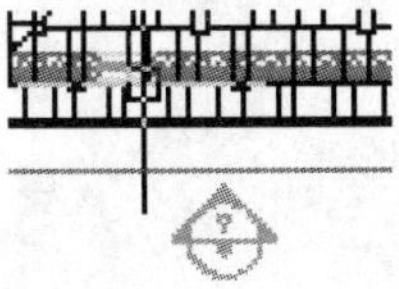

Place the elevation mark below the model.
Use your cursor to orient the arrow toward the building model.

16. 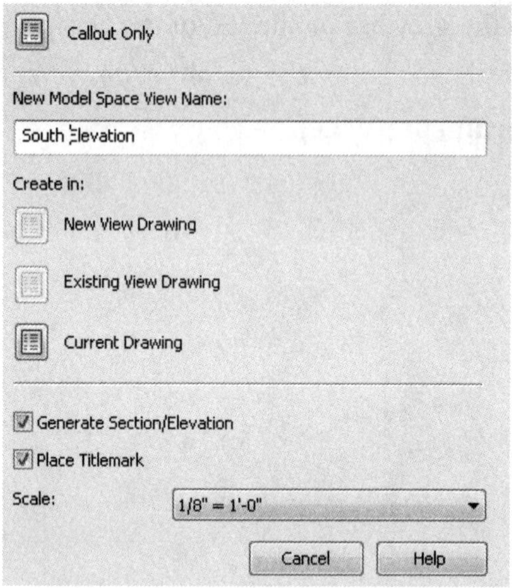

Set your view name to: **South Elevation**.

Enable **Generate Section/Elevation**.

Enable **Place Titlemark**.

Set the Scale to **1/8″ = 1′-0″**.

Press the **Current Drawing** button.

17. Window around the entire building to select it.
Select the upper left corner above the building and the lower right corner below the building.

18. 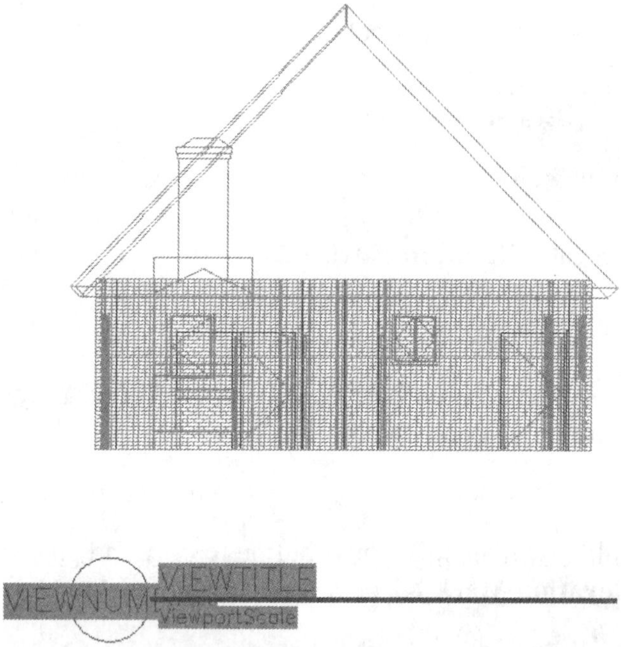

Place the elevation to the right of the view.

Zoom into the elevation view, so you can inspect it.

Zoom Extents.

19. 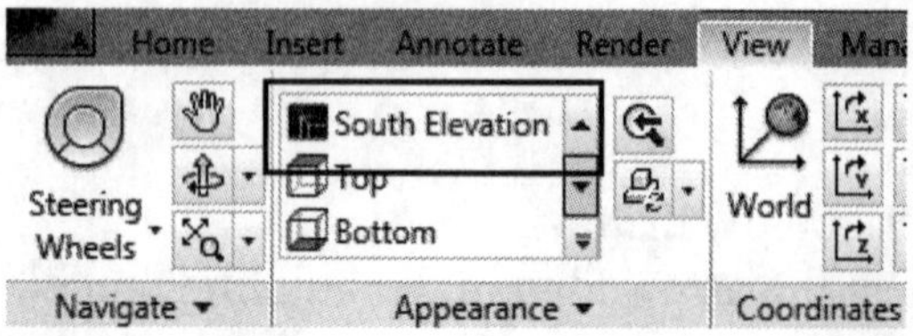

To activate the elevation view, select it from the View list located on the View ribbon.

20. Save as *ex7-3.dwg*

Exercise 7-4

Editing an Elevation View

Drawing Name: ex7-3.dwg
Estimated Time: 15 minutes

This exercise reinforces the following skills:

- Inserting a Titleblock
- Adding Keynotes
- Adding a Scale bar

1. Open *ex7-3.dwg*.

2. 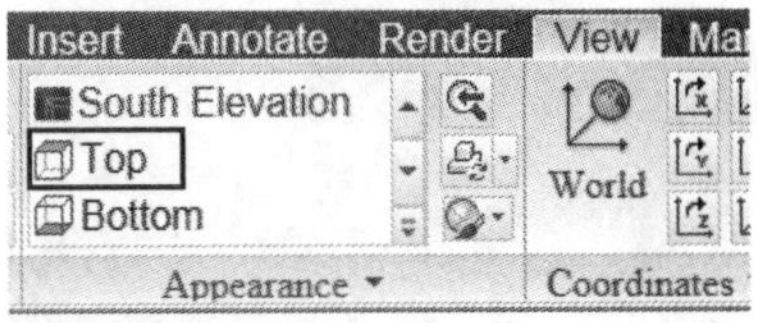

Activate the **Top** view from the View ribbon or using the View cube.

3. 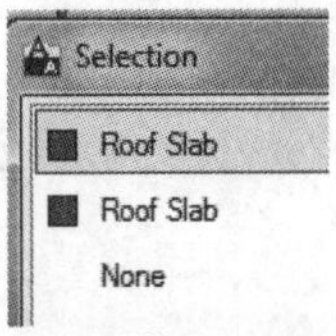

Select a roof slab.

Select one of the slabs listed in the Selection dialog.

4. 

Select **Edit Style** from the ribbon.

5. 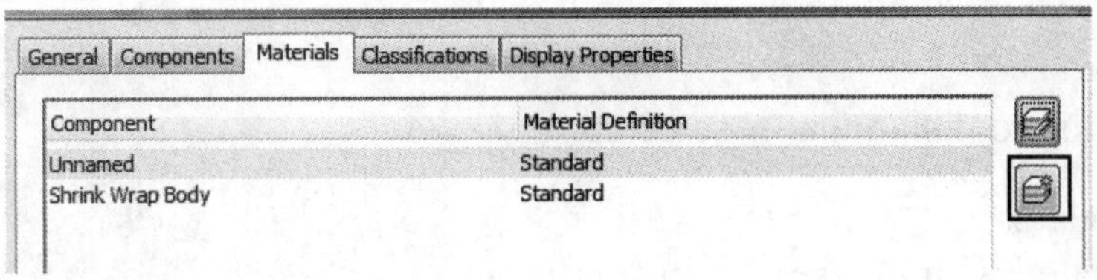

Select the Materials tab.

Select the **Add Material** Button.

6. 

Name your new material **Wood Shake**. Press **OK**.

7. 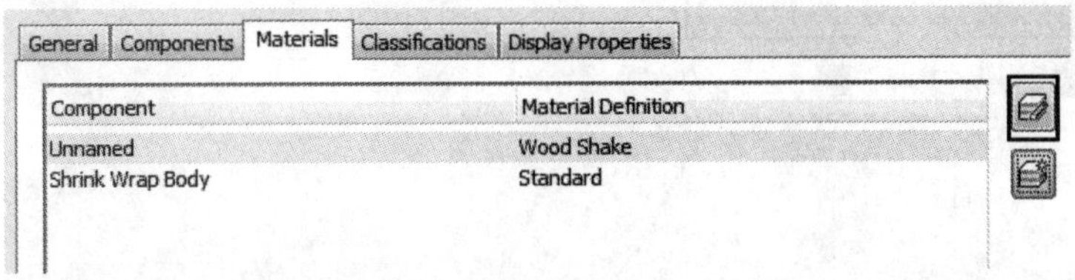

Select the **Edit Material** button.

8. 

Select the **Display Properties** tab.

9.  Select the **Properties** button.

10. 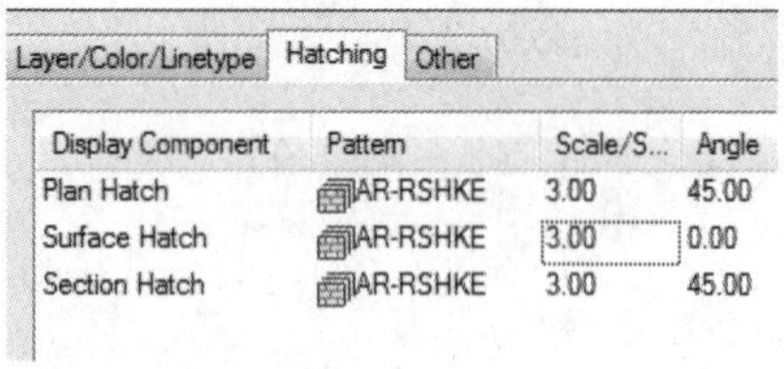

Select the **Hatching** tab.

Highlight all the Display Components.
Set the Hatch Pattern to **AR-RSHKE**.
Set the Scale to **3**.

11. 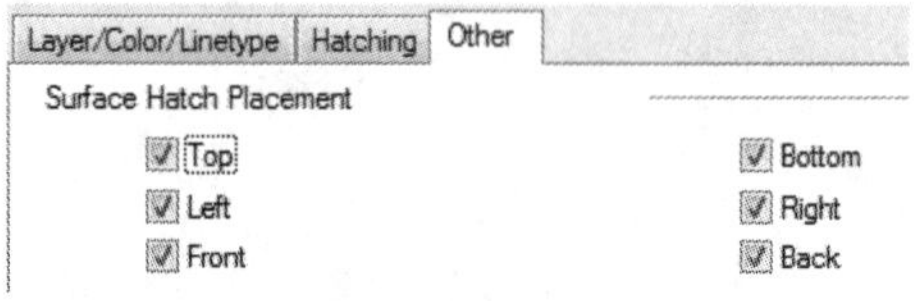

Select the Other tab.

Enable all the Surface Hatch Placement options.

12. 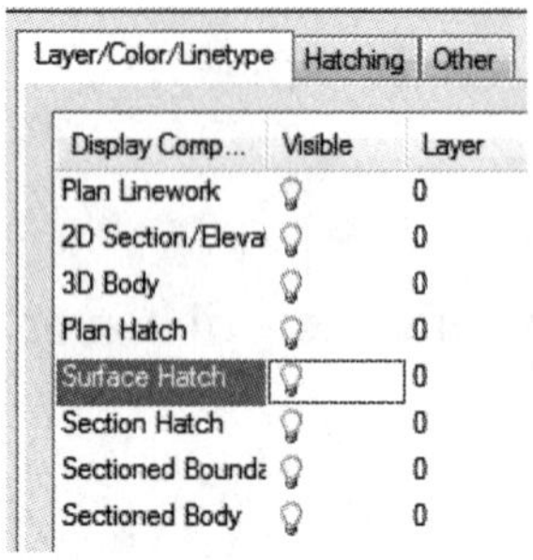

Select the Layer/Color/Linetype tab.

Turn on the layer for Plan Hatch, Surface Hatch, and Section Hatch.

13. Press **OK**.

14. 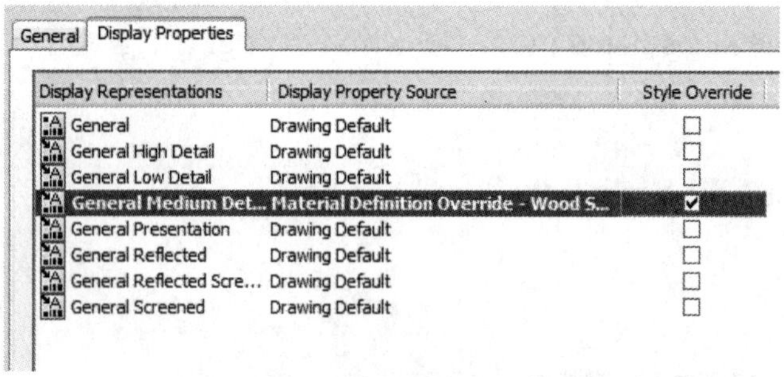

Verify that the Style Override is enabled.

15. Press **OK**.
Press ESC to release the roof slab that is selected.

The view does not update.
It needs to be regenerated with the new definition.

16. 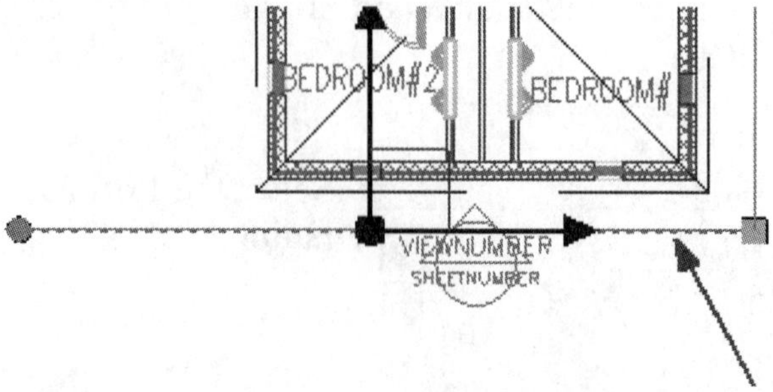

Select the elevation line in the top view.

17. 

Select **Generate Elevation** from the ribbon.

18. 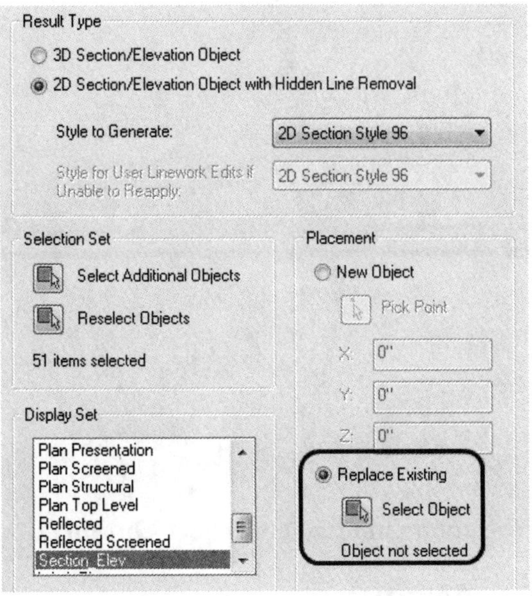

Enable **Replace Existing**.

Select the **Select Object** button.

Select the 2D Elevation placed in the previous exercise.

Press **OK**.

19. The elevation view updates.

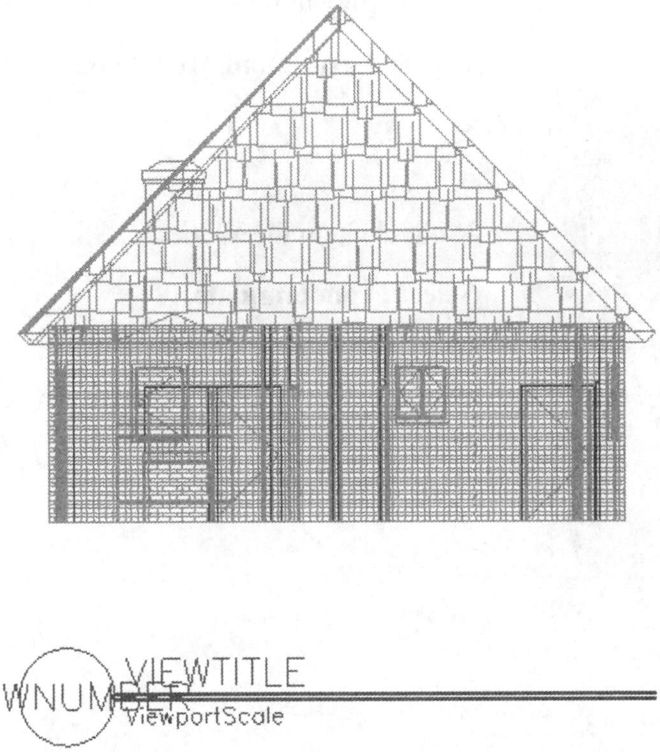

If you still do not see the shake hatch pattern, check the scale of the hatch pattern to ensure it is set low enough to be visible in the elevation view.

20. Save as *ex7-4.dwg*.

Exercise 7-5:
Creating Layouts

Drawing Name: ex7-4.dwg
Estimated Time: 25 minutes

This exercise reinforces the following skills:

- Create Layout
- Adding a View to a Layout
- Control Visibility of elements using Layers

1. Open *ex7-4.dwg*.

2. 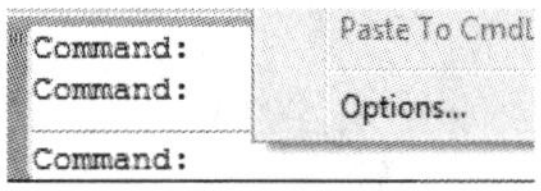

Right click on the command line and select **Options**.

   You can also type OPTIONS.

3. 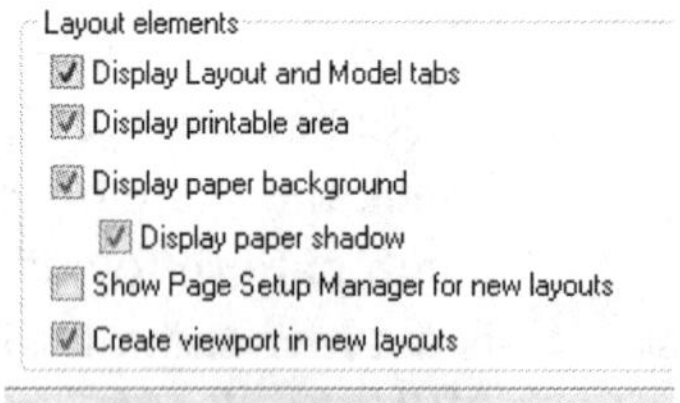

Activate the **Display** tab.

   Enable **Display Layout and Model tabs.**

   Press **OK.**

4. 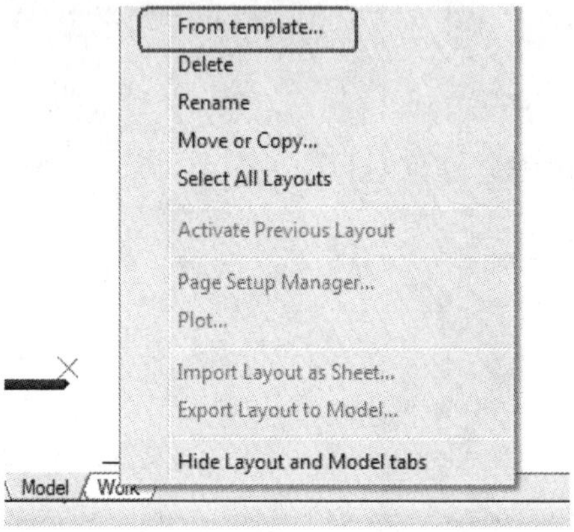

Right click on the Work tab.

   Select **From template.**

5. Browse to your exercise folder.

   Select the *Arch_D* template.
   Press **Open.**

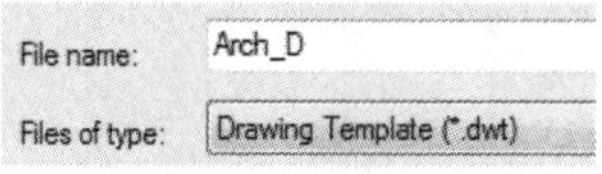

6. 

Press **OK.**

7. 

Activate the **D-Size Layout.**

8. 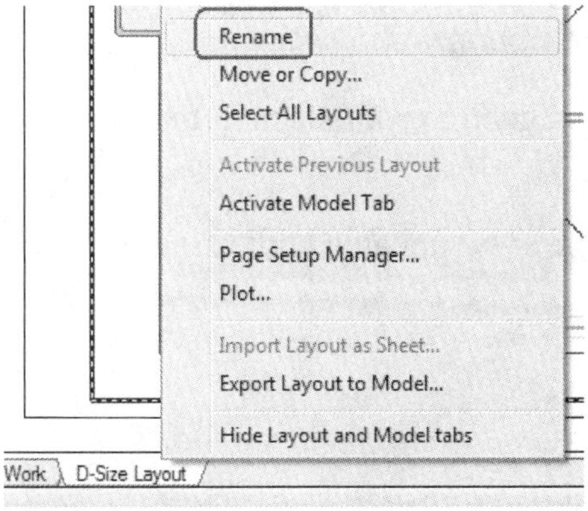

Right click on the **D-Size Layout** tab.

Select **Rename**.

9. 

Rename Floorplan.

10. 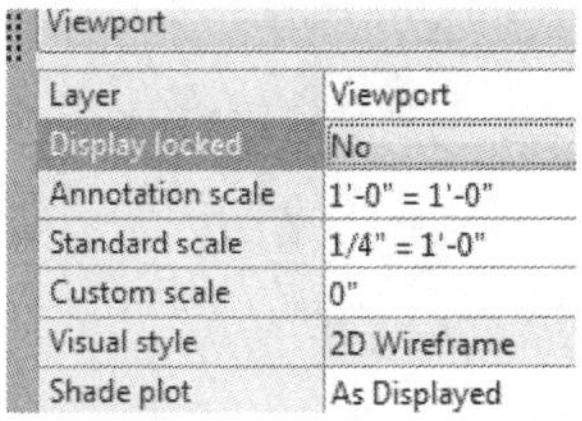

Select the viewport.

Set Display locked to **No**.

11. 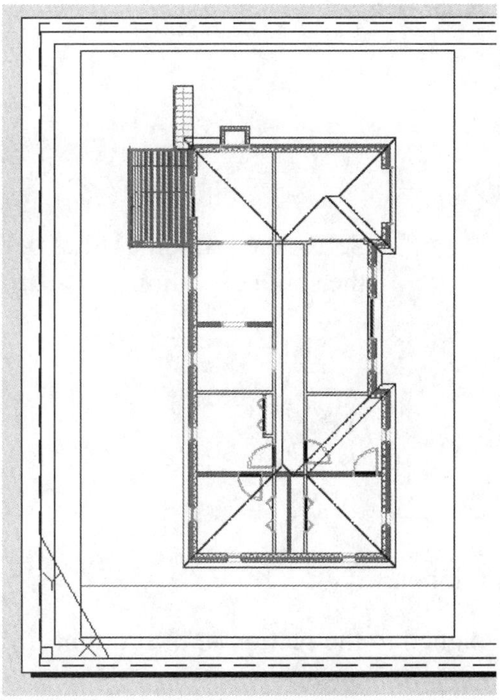

Resize the viewport to only show the floor plan.

Double click inside the viewport to activate model space.

Pan the model to position inside the viewport.

12. 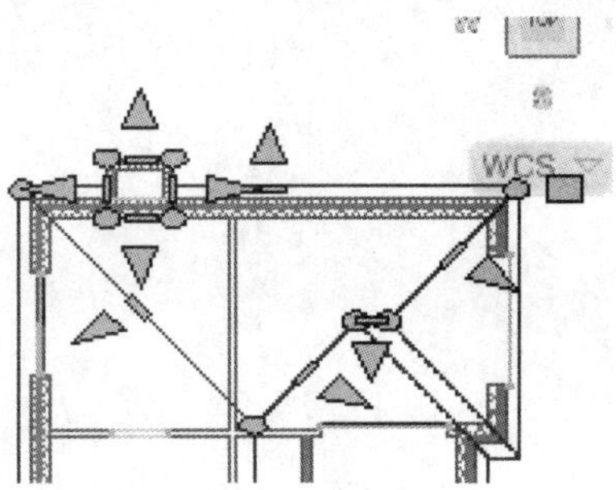

Select a roof slab.

13. 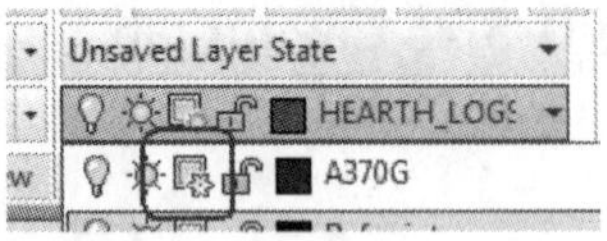

Activate the Home ribbon.

Freeze the layer assigned to roof slabs in the current viewport.

14. 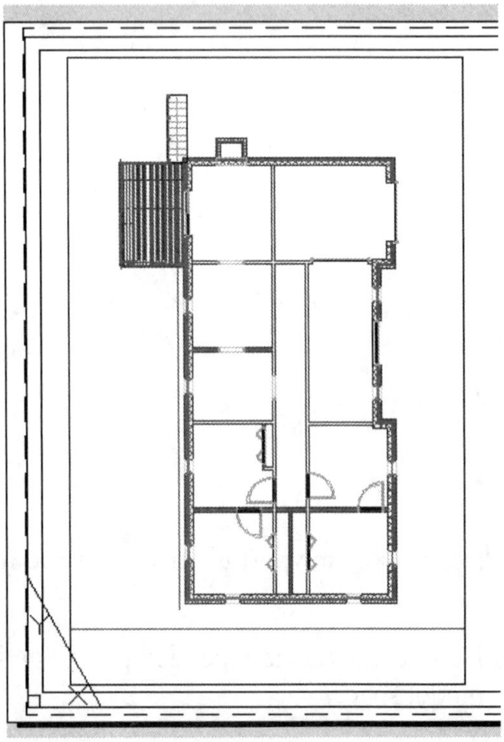

The view updates with no roof.

15. 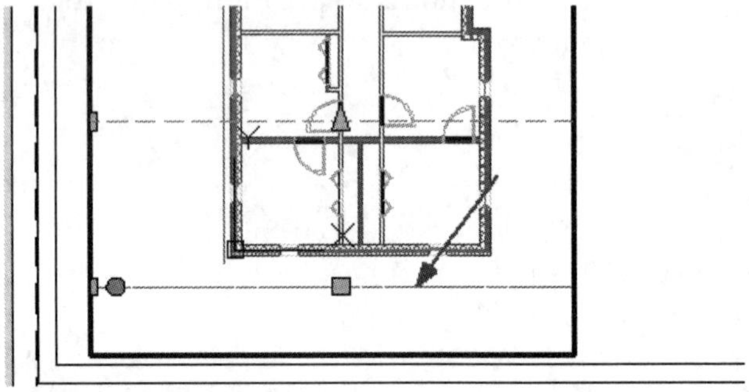

Select the section used to define the south elevation.

16. 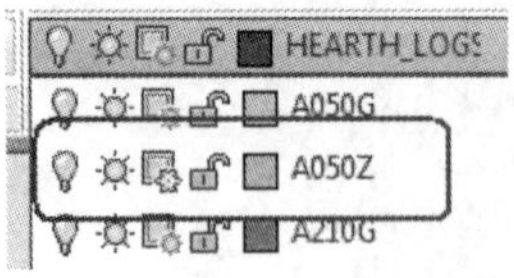

Activate the Home ribbon.

Freeze the layer assigned to the section in the current viewport.

17. 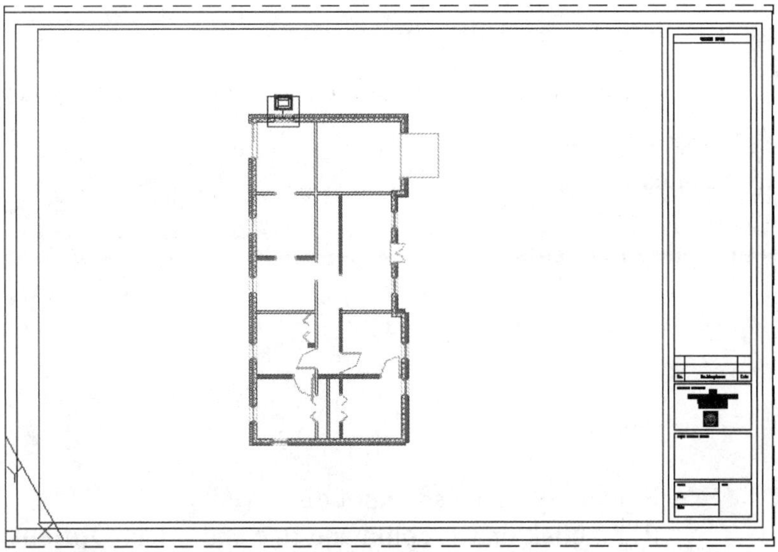

Double click outside the viewport to return to paper space.

Observe how the floor plan view has changed.

18. 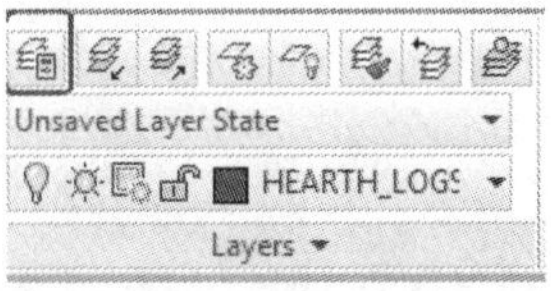

Activate the Home ribbon.

Launch the Layer Manager.

19. 

Scroll down to the Viewport layer.
Set the Viewport layer to DO NOT PLOT.

The viewports can be visible so you can adjust them but will not appear in prints.

Close the Layer Manager dialog.

20. 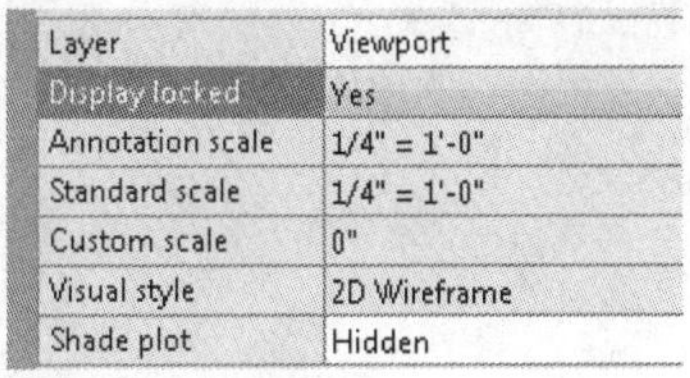

Select the viewport.
On the Properties palette:
Set the Annotation scale to **1/4″ = 1′-0″**.
Set the standard scale to **1/4″ = 1′-0″**.
Set the Shade plot to **Hidden**.
Set the Display locked to **Yes**.

21. Save as *ex7-5.dwg*.

Exercise 7-6:
Creating a Sheet

Drawing Name: ex7-5.dwg
Estimated Time: 15 minutes

This exercise reinforces the following skills:

- Layouts
- Viewports

1. Open *ex7-5.dwg*.

2. 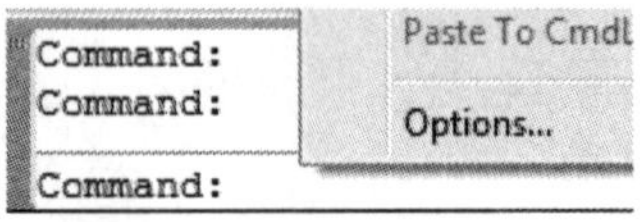

If your layout tabs are not displayed:
Right click on the command line and select **Options**.

You can also type OPTIONS.

3. 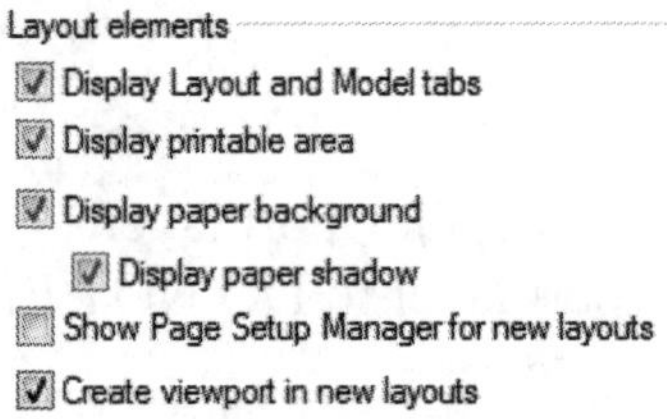

Activate the **Display** tab.

Enable **Display Layout and Model tabs.**

Press **OK**.

4. 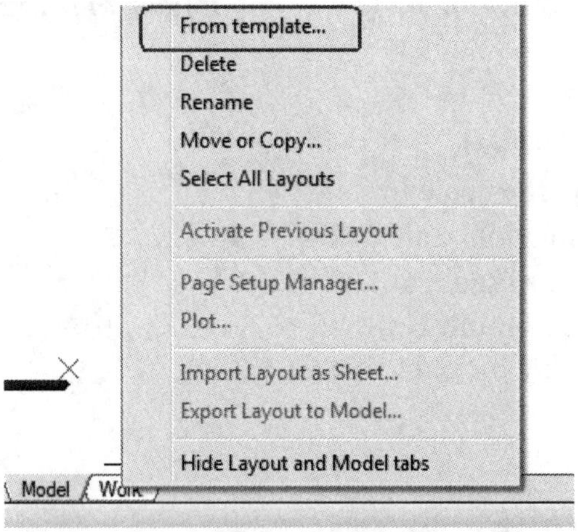

Right click on the Work tab.

Select **From template**.

5. 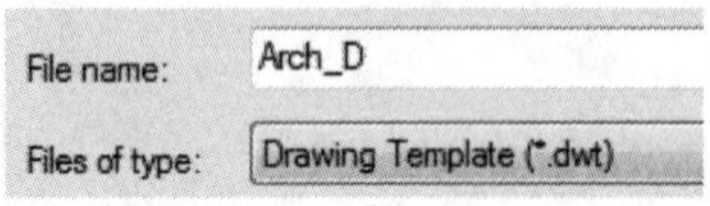

Browse to the folder where you are saving your work.
Select the *Arch_D* template.
Press **Open**.

6. 

Press **OK**.

7. 

Activate the **D-Size Layout**.

8. 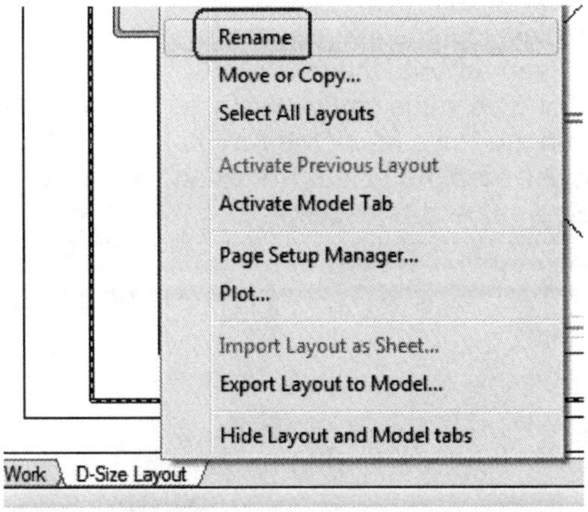

Right click on the **D-Size Layout** tab.

Select **Rename**.

9. 

Rename **South Elevation**.

10. 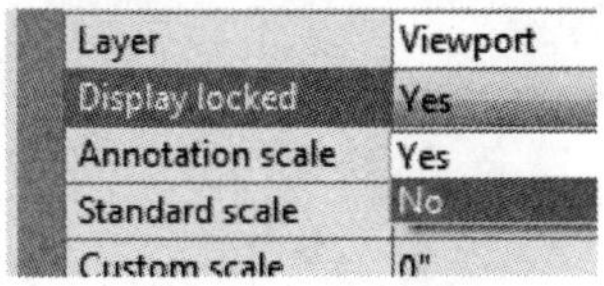

Select the viewport.
Right click and set the Display locked to **No**.

11. Double click inside the viewport to activate model space.

12. 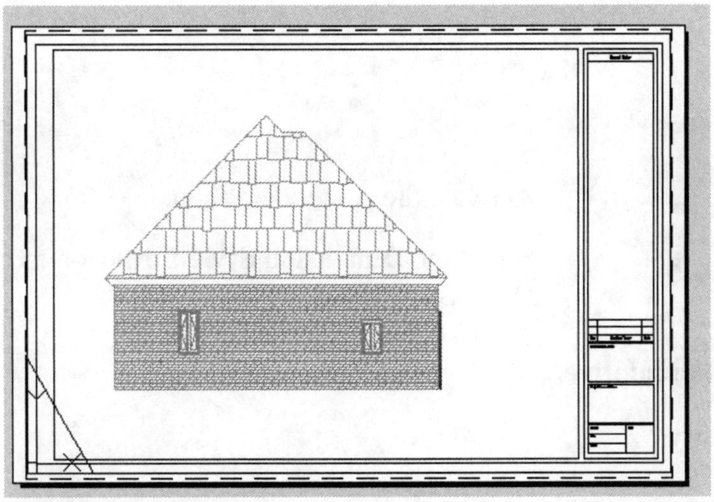

Left click inside the viewport and then position the elevation view inside the viewport.

13. 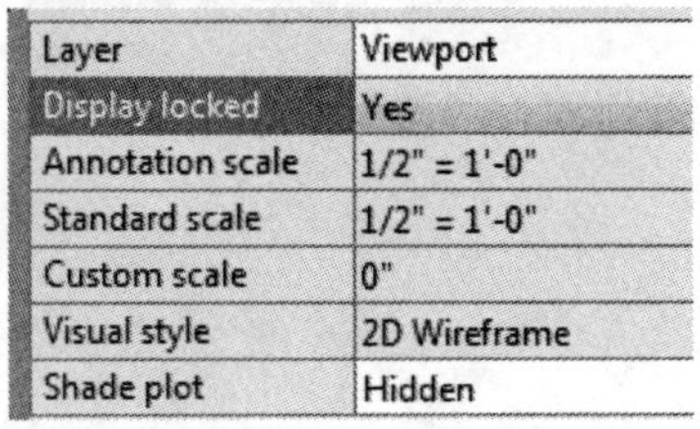

Select the viewport.
Set the Annotation scale to **½″ = 1′-0″ [1:100]**.
Set the Standard scale to **½″= 1′-0″ [1:100]**.

Set the Shade plot to **Hidden**.

You may need to re-center the view in the viewport after you change the scale. Use PAN to do this so the scale does not change.

Lock the display.

14. Save the file as *ex7-6.dwg*.

Tips & Tricks

- By locking the Display you ensure your model view will not accidentally shift if you activate the viewport.
- The Annotation Plot Size value can be restricted by the Linear Precision setting on the Units tab. If the Annotation Plot Size value is more precise than the Linear Precision value, then the Annotation Plot Size value is not accepted.

Exercise 7-7

Modify a Dimension Style

Drawing Name: ex7-6.dwg
Estimated Time: 15 minutes

This exercise reinforces the following skills:

- Dimension Styles
- AEC Dimensions

1. Open *ex7-6.dwg*

2. 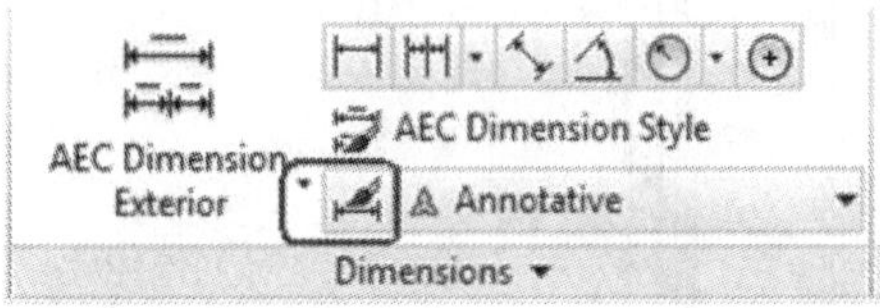

Activate the Annotate ribbon.

Select the **Dimension Style Editor** on the Dimensions panel.

3. 

Highlight **Annotative**.

4. 

Select **Modify**.

5. 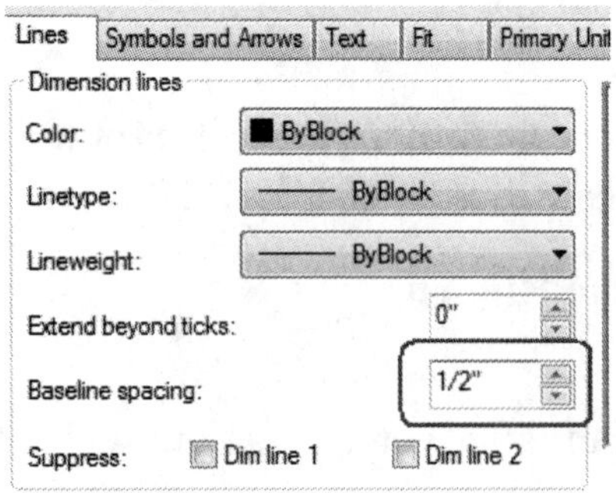

On the Lines tab:

Set the Baseline spacing to **1/2″**.

6. 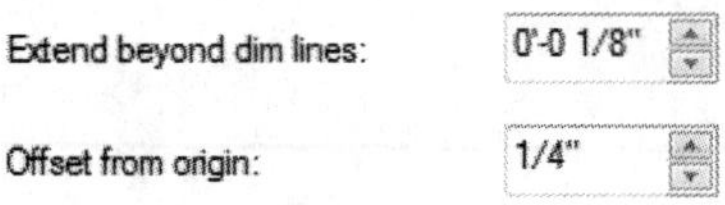

Set Extend beyond dim lines to **1/8″**.
Set Offset from origin to **1/4″**.

7. 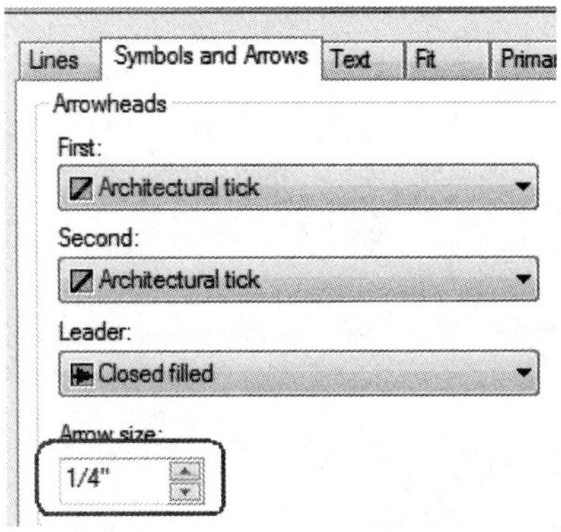

On the Symbols and Arrows tab:

Set the Arrow size to **1/4″**.

8. 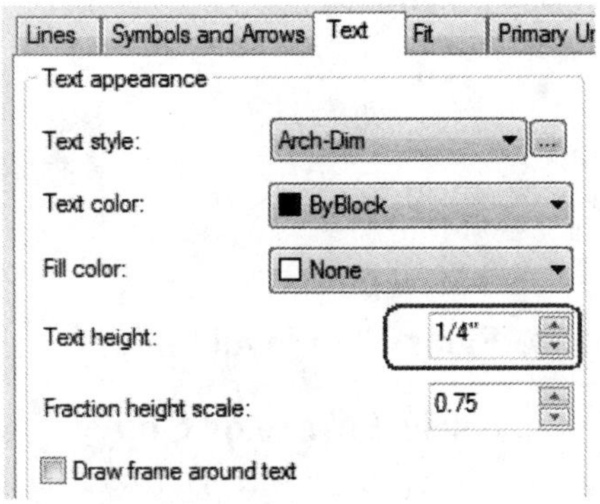

On the Text tab:

Set the Text height to **1/4″**.

9. 

Set the Offset from dim line to **1/8″**.

10. 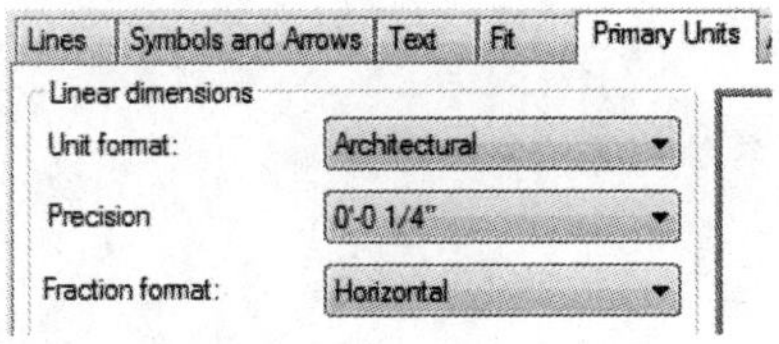

Activate the Primary Units tab.

Set the Unit format to **Architectural.**
Set the Precision to **1/4″**.

11. Press **OK** and **Close**.
12. Save as *ex7-7.dwg*.

Exercise 7-8

Dimensioning a Floor Plan

Drawing Name: ex7-7.dwg
Estimated Time: 30 minutes

This exercise reinforces the following skills:

- Drawing Setup
- AEC Dimensions
- Title Mark
- Attributes
- Layouts

1. Open *ex7-7.dwg*

2. 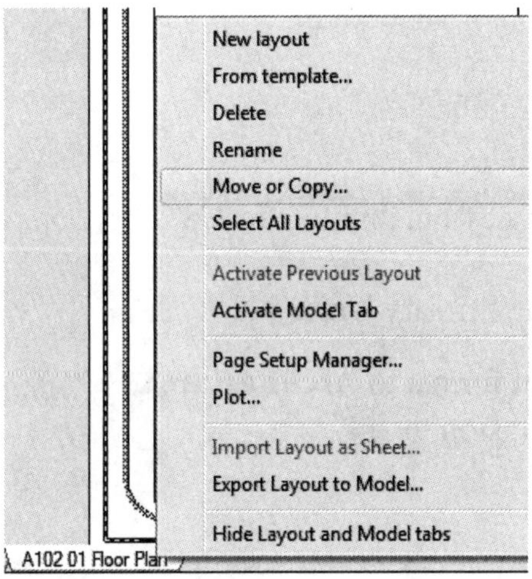

Highlight the **Floor Plan** layout tab.

Right click and select **Move or Copy**.

3. 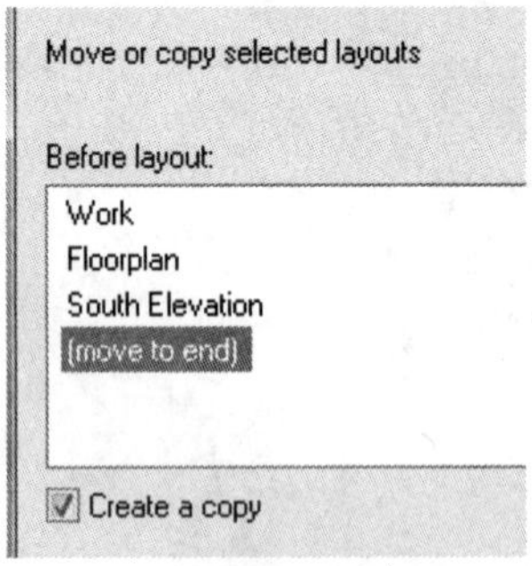

Enable **Create a copy**.

Highlight **(move to end)**.

Press **OK**.

4. 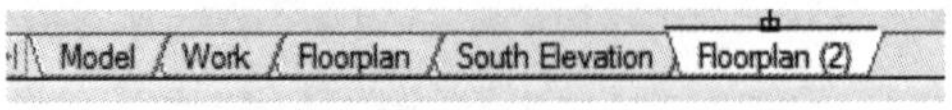

Select the second layout.

5. 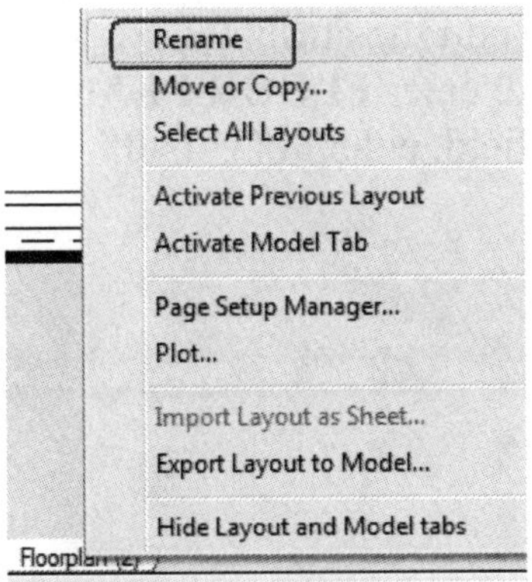

Highlight the second layout tab.

Right click and select **Rename**.

6. 

Modify the layout name to **A102 02 FLOOR PLAN**.

7. Launch the Tool Palette from the Home ribbon if it is not enabled.

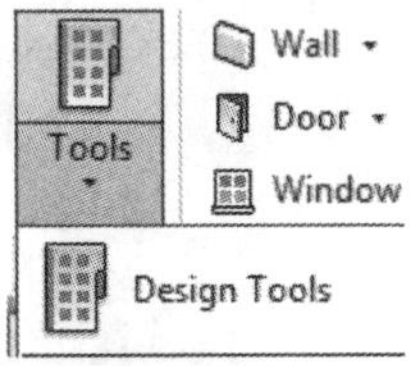

8. 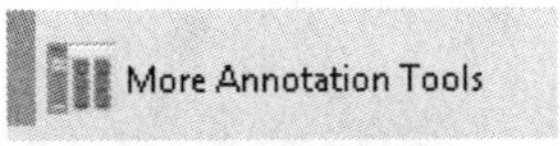

Select **More Annotation Tools** to launch the Content Browser.

9. 

Search for **title**.

10. 

Locate the **Title Mark** indicated.

11. 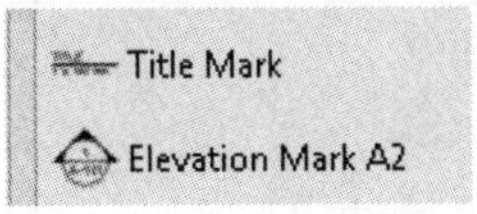

Drag and drop the Title Mark onto the Document Palette.

12. Double click inside the viewport to activate model space.

13. 

Select the **Title Mark** tool from the Callouts Palette.
Pick below the view to place the title mark.

14. 

Pick two points to indicate the start and end points of the title mark.

Place the title mark below the view.

15. 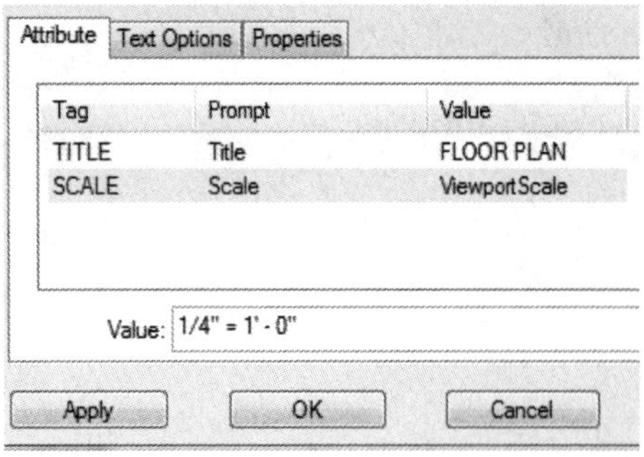

Double click to edit the attributes.
In the Title field, enter **FLOOR PLAN**.
In the SCALE field, enter **¼″ = 1′-0″**.

Press **OK**.

16. 

The view title updates.

17. 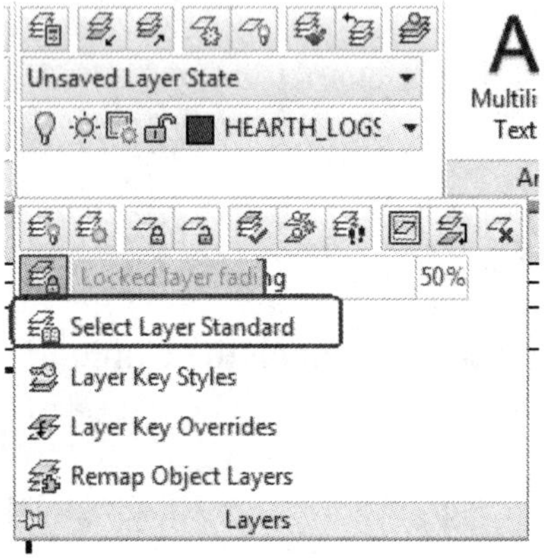

Activate the Home ribbon.

In the Layers panel drop-down:

Select **Select Layer Standard**.

18. 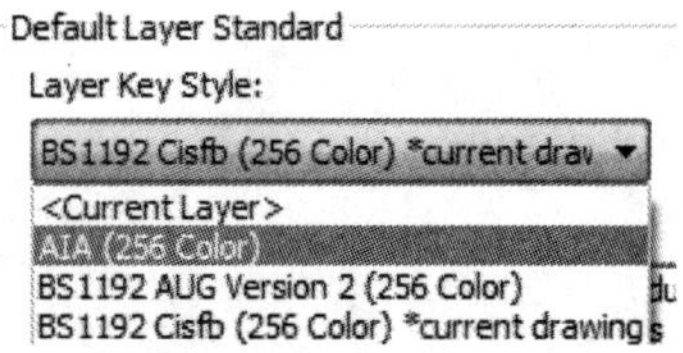

Set the Layer Key Style to **AIA (256 Color)**.

Press **OK**.

19. 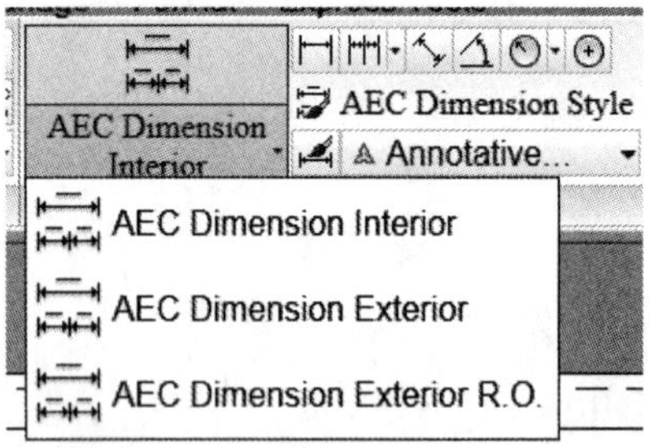

Select the **AEC Dimension - Exterior** tool on the Annotate ribbon.

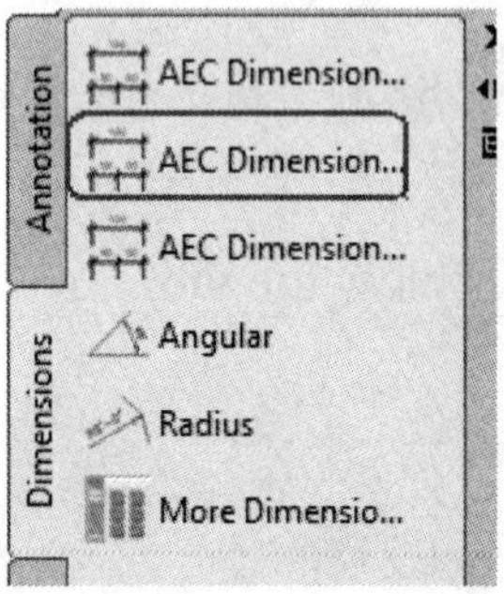

This tool is also available on the Documents tool palette on the Dimensions tab.

Add Wall Dimensions is only available in Model Space. Dimensions are automatically placed on A-Anno-Dim layer when the Layering Standard is set to AIA.

20. 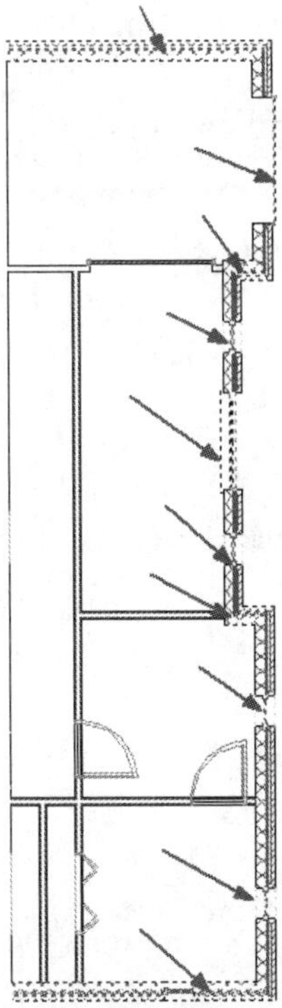

Select the walls, doors, and windows indicated on the right side of the building.

Press ENTER to complete the selection.

21. 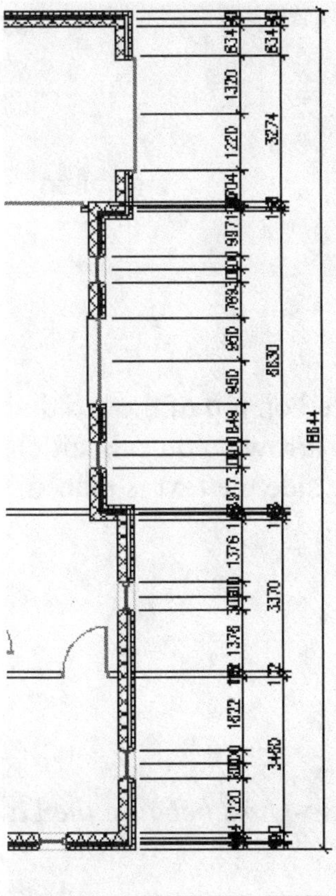

Pick to the right of the building to place the dimensions.

All dimensions relevant to the wall will be placed.

22. 

Select the Dimension you just placed.
Select **Remove Extension Lines** from the ribbon.

23. 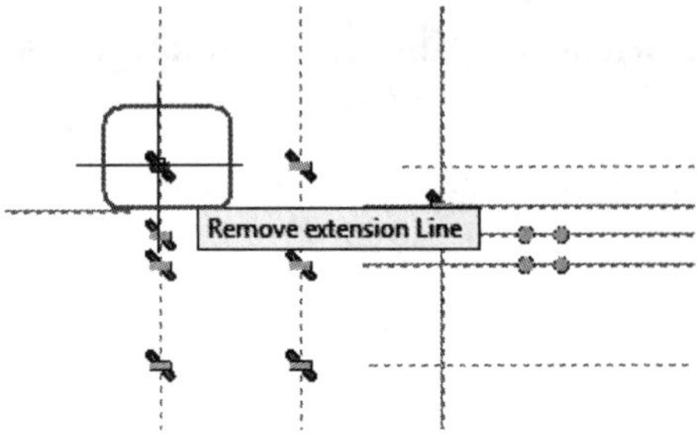

Select the grips on the extension lines that are not necessary.
You should see a tool tip indicating the extension line to remove.

The selected lines will be deleted.

24. To add an extension line:
Select the AEC Dimension.

Select the Add Extension Lines tool from the ribbon. 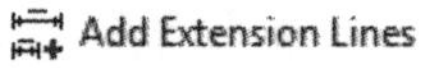

Then select the midpoint of the object to be dimensioned.
Then select the AEC Dimension.

25. 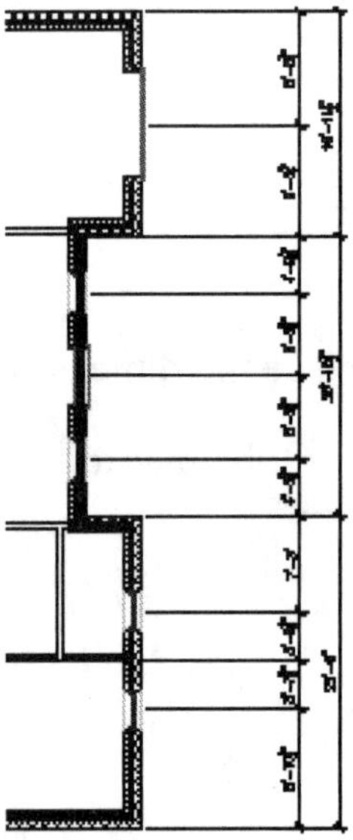
When you are done modifying the AEC Dimension, press ENTER to update the dimensions.

26. 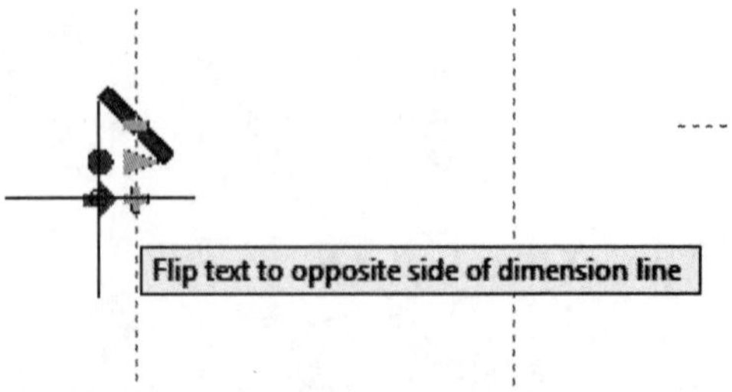

If the text landed on top of the building, look for a blue arrow. You can left click on it to flip the side the text is placed.

27. 

Select the dimension.

The dimension should automatically be placed on A-Anno-Dims because the Layer Standard was set to AIA.

28. Switch back to Paper space.

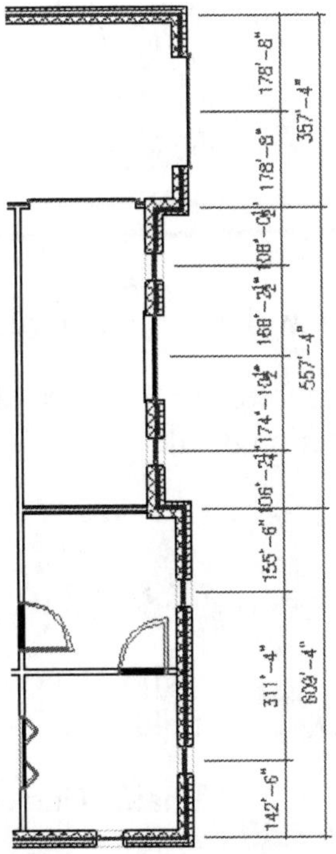

29. Save as *ex7-8.dwg.*

> **TIP:** You can insert blocks into model or paper space. Note that you did not need to activate the viewport in order to place the Scale block.

Exercise 7-9

Create a Wall Section

Drawing Name: ex7-8.dwg
Estimated Time: 15 minutes

This exercise reinforces the following skills:

- Drawing Setup
- Dimension Styles
- AEC Dimensions
- Layouts

1. Open *ex7-8.dwg.*

2. 

Activate the Model layout tab.

3.

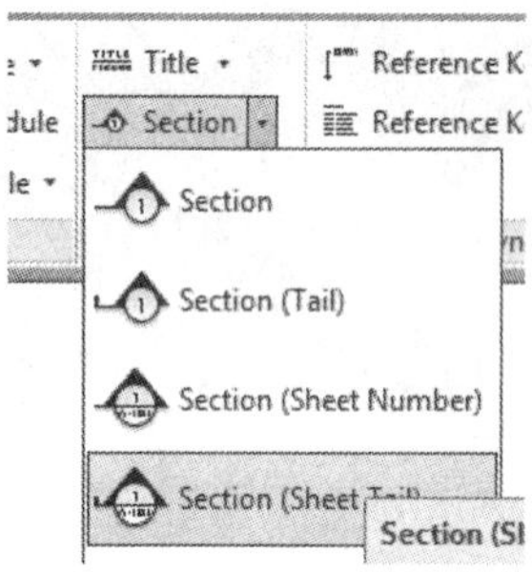

Activate the **Annotate** ribbon.

Select the **Section (Sheet Tail)** tool.

4.

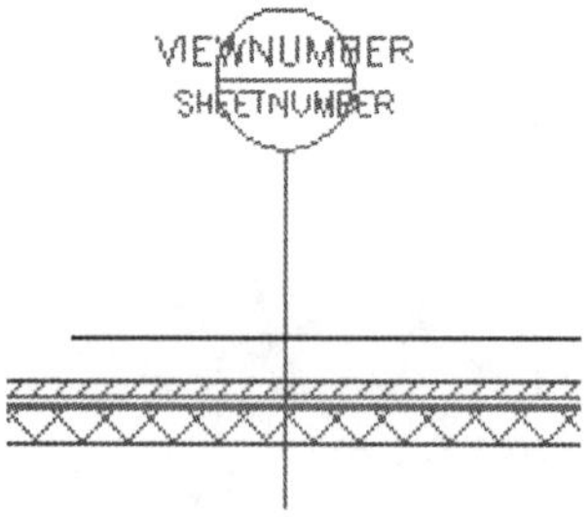

Draw the section through the north wall of the garage area.

Left click to the right of the section line to indicate the section depth.

5.

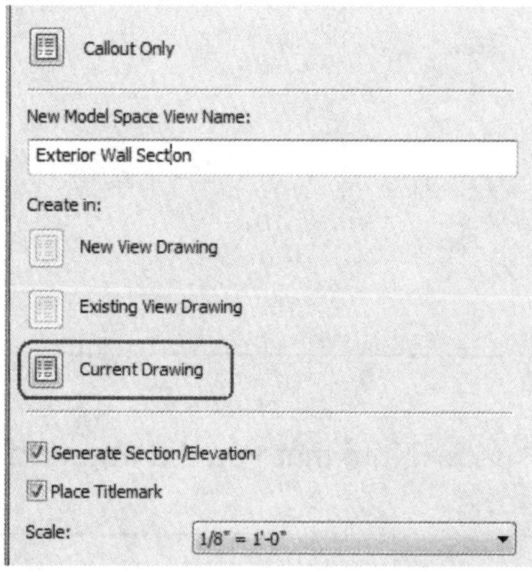

Type Exterior Wall Section in the View Name field.

Enable Current Drawing.

Enable Generate Section/Elevation.

Enable Place Title mark.
Set the Scale to 1/8″ = 1′-0″.

6.

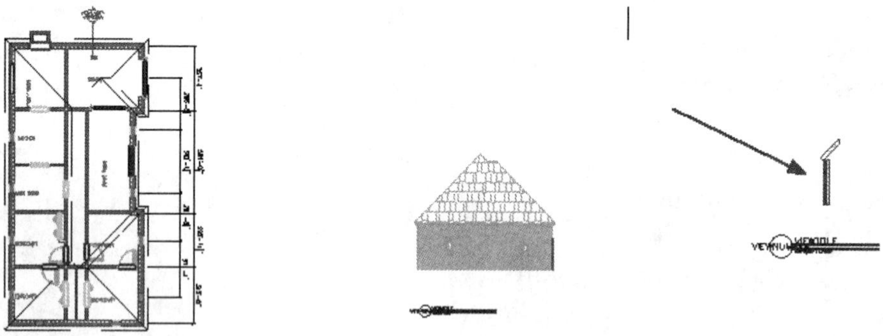

Place the view to the right of the South Elevation view.

7.

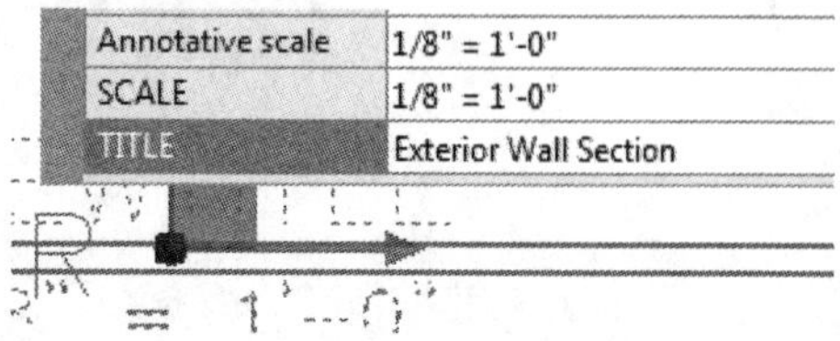

Select the view title for the wall section.

Type **1/8″ = 1′-0″** for the SCALE.

Type **Exterior Wall Section** for the TITLE.

Press ESC to release and update.

8. 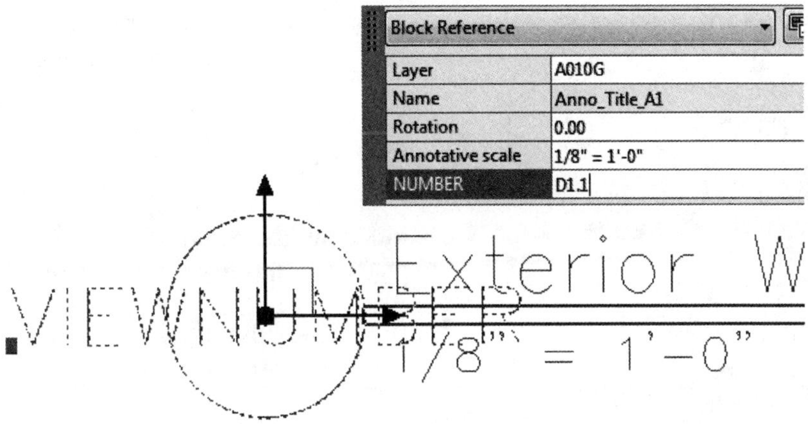

Select the View title bubble.

Type D1.1 for the NUMBER.

Press ESC to release and update.

9. 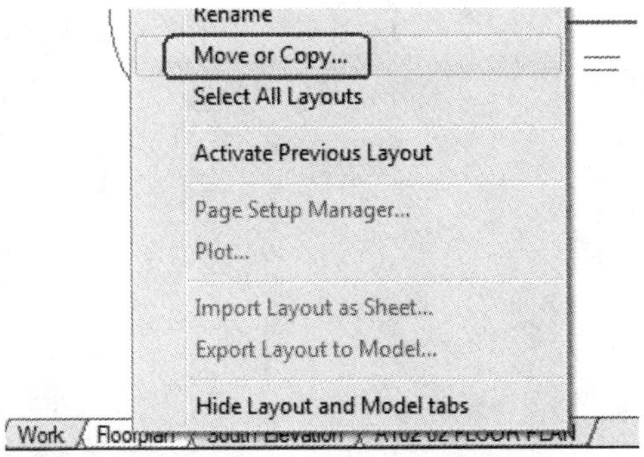

Highlight the **Floor Plan** layout tab.

Right click and select **Move or Copy**.

10. 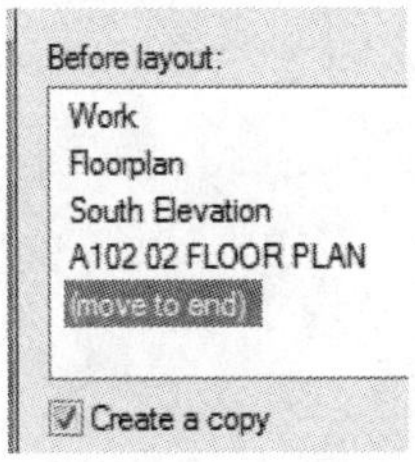

Enable **Create a copy**.

Highlight **(move to end)**.

Press **OK**.

11. 

Select the second layout.

12. 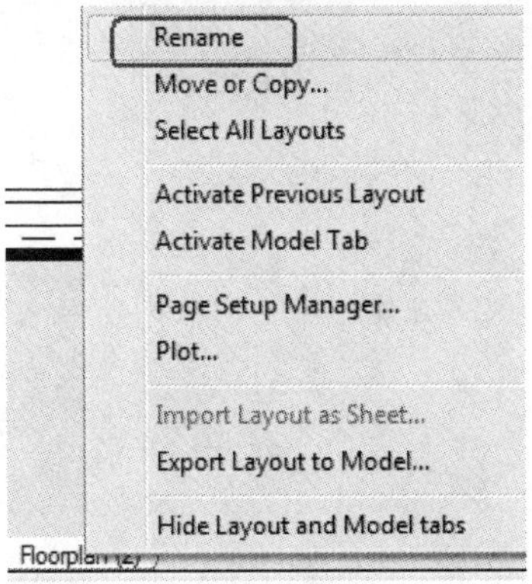

Highlight the second layout tab.

Right click and select **Rename**.

13. 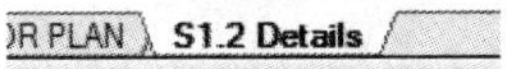

Modify the layout name to **S1.2 Details**.

14. Unlock the viewport.
Position the Exterior Wall Section in the viewport.
Adjust the size of the viewport.

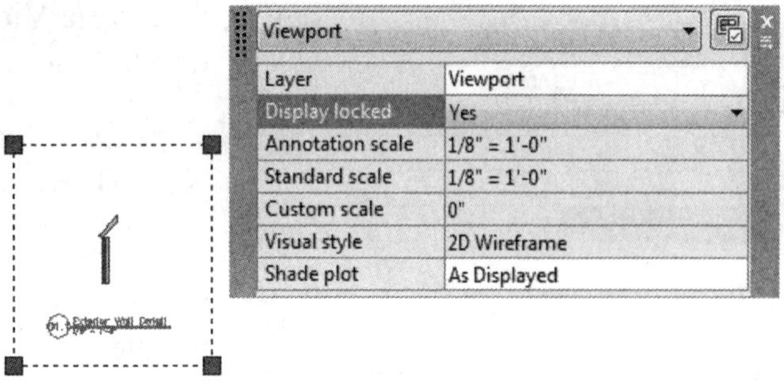

Select the viewport.
Set the Annotation scale to **1/8″ = 1′0″**.
Set the Standard scale to **1/8″ = 1′0″**.

Set the Shade plot to **As Displayed**.

Lock the display.

15. Press ESC to release the viewport.

16. Save as *ex7-9.dwg.*

Exercise 7-10

Create a Section View

Drawing Name: ex7-9.dwg
Estimated Time: 10 minutes

This exercise reinforces the following skills:

- Sections

1. Open *ex7-9.dwg.*

2. 

Activate the **Floorplan** layout tab.
Activate Model space.

3. 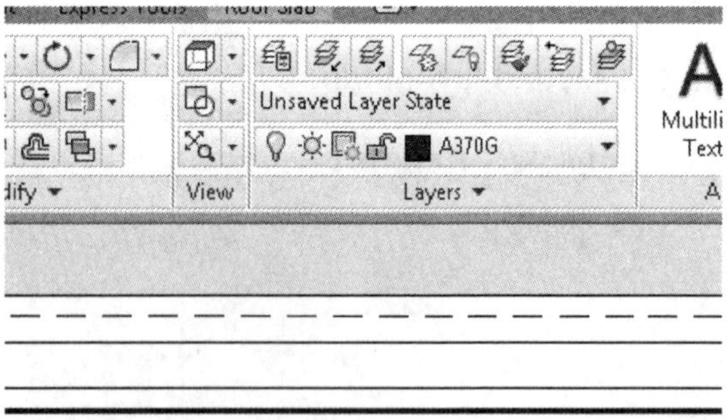

Thaw the roof slab layer.

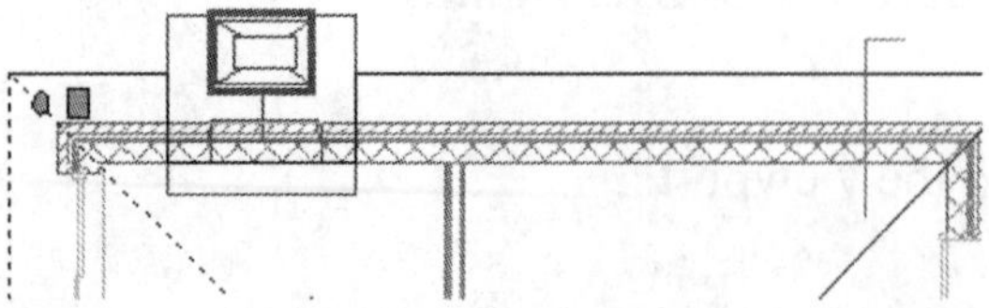

4. 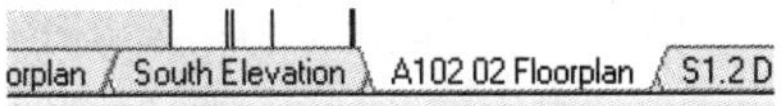

Activate the **A102 02 Floorplan** tab.

5. 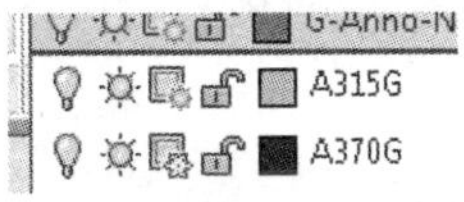

Freeze the roof slab layer in current viewport only.

6. 

Activate the **Floorplan** layout tab.
Activate Model space.

7. 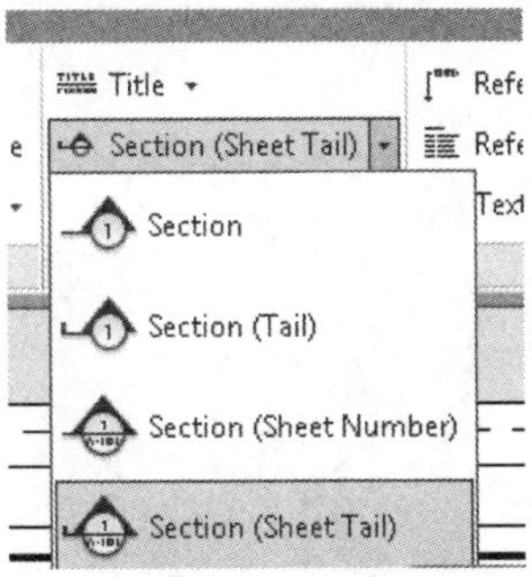

Activate the Annotate ribbon.

Select the **Section (Sheet Tail)** tool on the Callouts panel.

8. 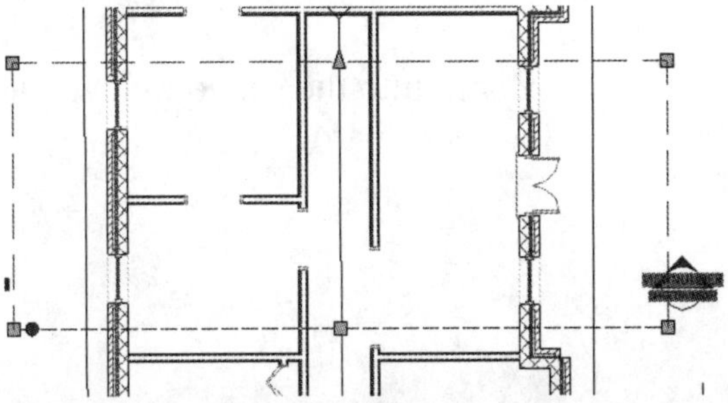
Draw a horizontal line through the walls as shown.

9. 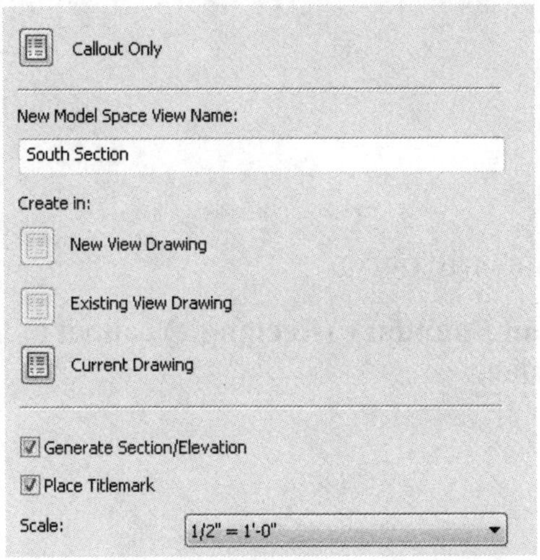

Name the View: South Section.
Enable Generate Section/Elevation.
Enable Place Titlemark.
Set the Scale to 1/2″ = 1′-0″.

Place the view in the current drawing to the right of the building.

10. 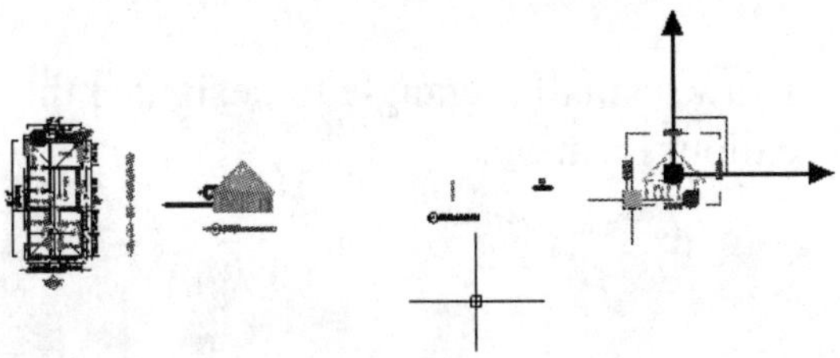
Switch to the Model tab and move the view to the right away from all the other views.

11. Save as *ex7-10.dwg*.

Exercise 7-11
Add a Callout

Drawing Name: ex7-10.dwg
Estimated Time: 45 minutes

This exercise reinforces the following skills:

- Callouts
- Wipeout
- Detail Elements
- Layouts

1. Open *ex7-10.dwg.*

2. 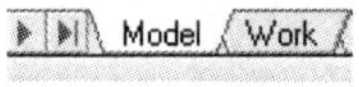

Activate the **Model** layout tab.

3. 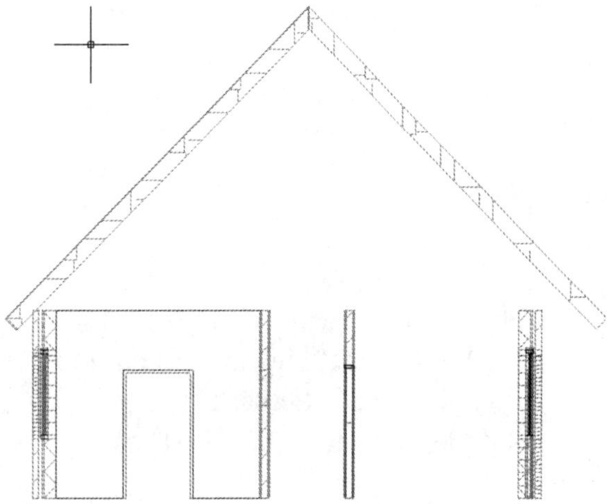
Zoom into the section view placed.

4. 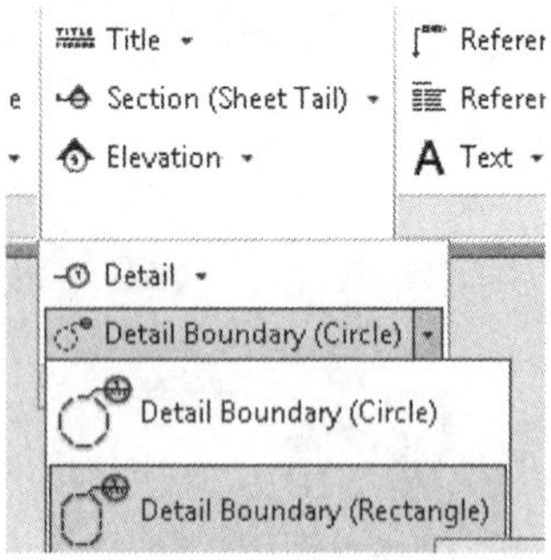

Activate the Annotate ribbon.

Select the **Detail Boundary (Rectangle)** callout tool on the Callouts panel.

5. 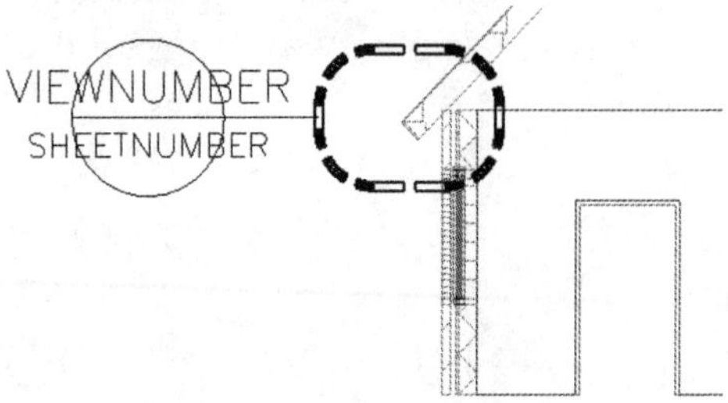

Draw a small rectangle to designate the callout location.

6. 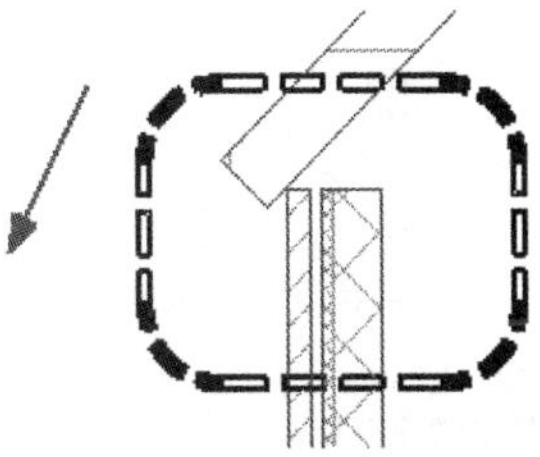

Left click to the left side of the wall section to place the label.

Press **ENTER** or right click to accept.

7. 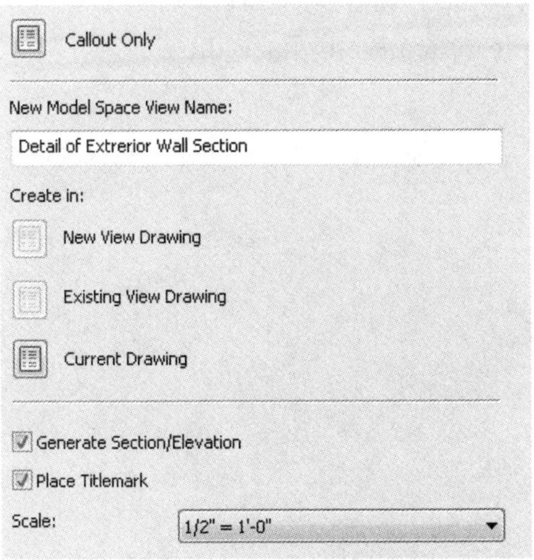

Type **Detail of Exterior Wall Section** in the View Name field.

Enable **Current Drawing**.

Enable **Generate Section/Elevation**.

Enable **Place Titlemark**.

Set the Scale to **1/2″ = 1′-0″**.

8. Place the view to the right of the elevation.

9. 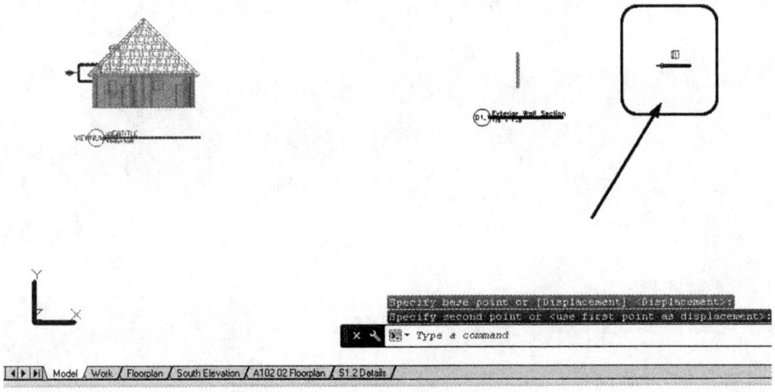

Switch to the Model tab and move the new callout view to the right of the wall section.

10. 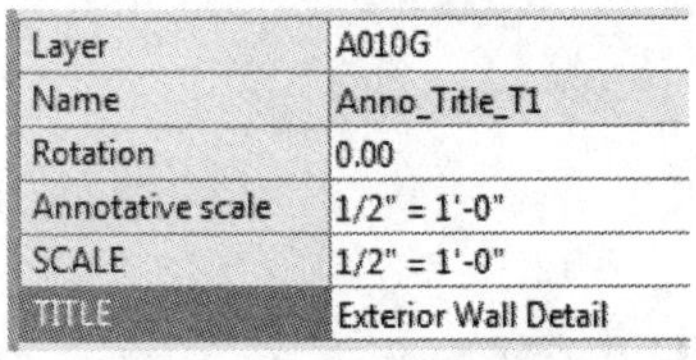

Select the view title for the wall section.

Type **1/2″ = 1′-0″** for the SCALE.

Type **Exterior Wall Detail** for the TITLE.

Press ESC to release and update.

11. 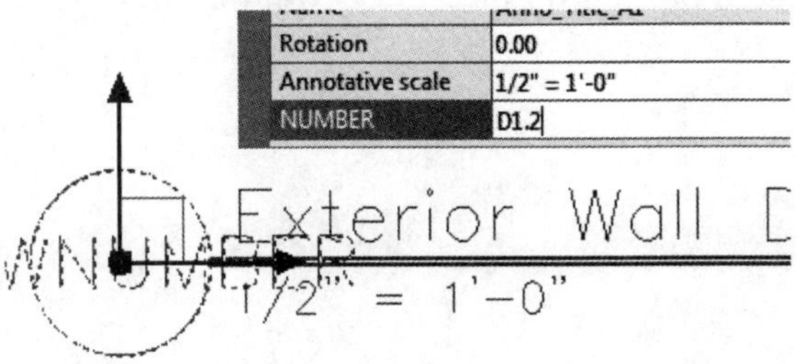

Select the View title bubble.

Type D1.2 for the NUMBER.

Press ESC to release and update.

12. 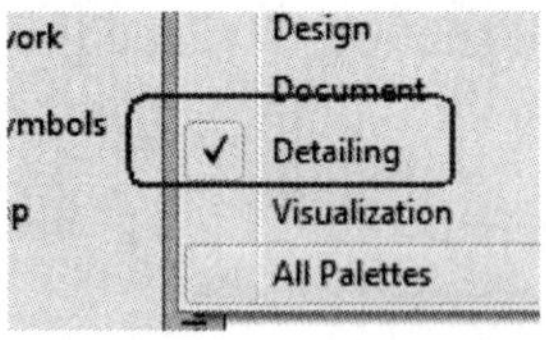

Right click on the Tool Palette's bar.

Enable the Detailing Palette.

13. 

Select the **04- Masonry** detail tool on the Basic tab.

14. 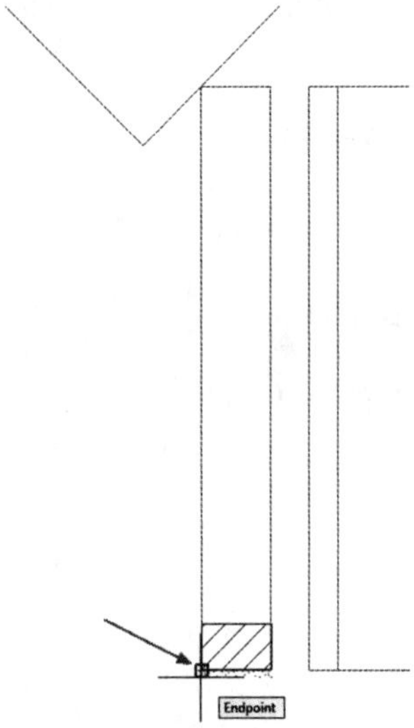

Select the endpoint indicated to place the detail.

15. 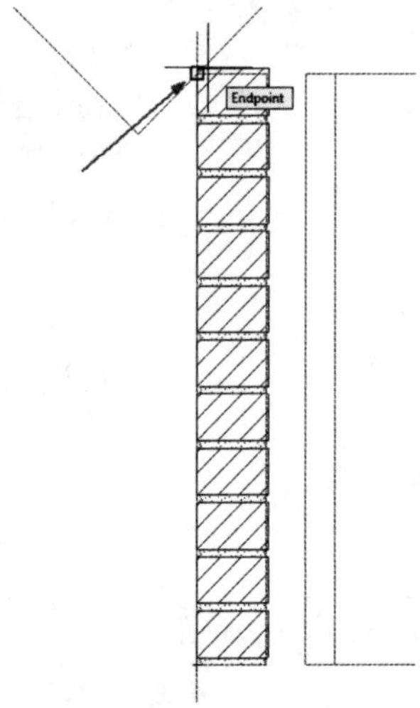

Select the top of the wall.

16. 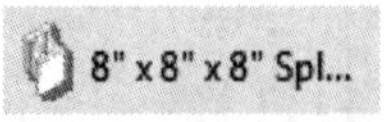

Select the Exterior tab.

Select the **8″ X 8″ X 8″ Split CMU** detail tool.

17. 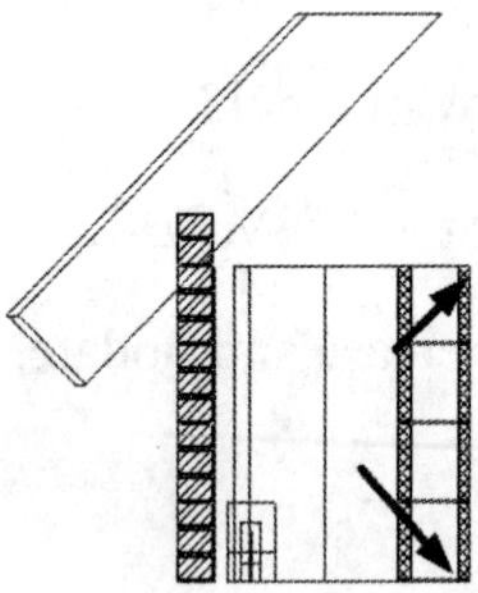

Pick the indicated points to place the CMU detail.

18. 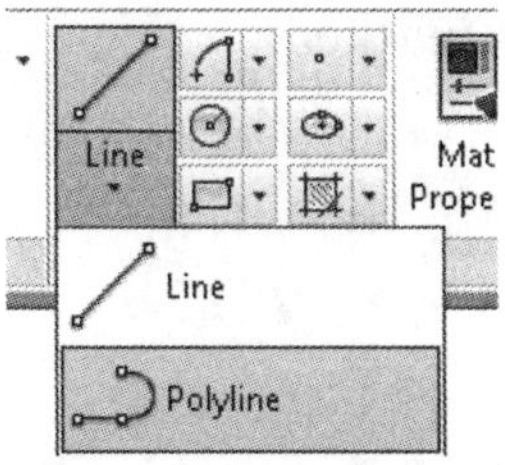

Select the **Polyline** tool from the Home ribbon.

19. 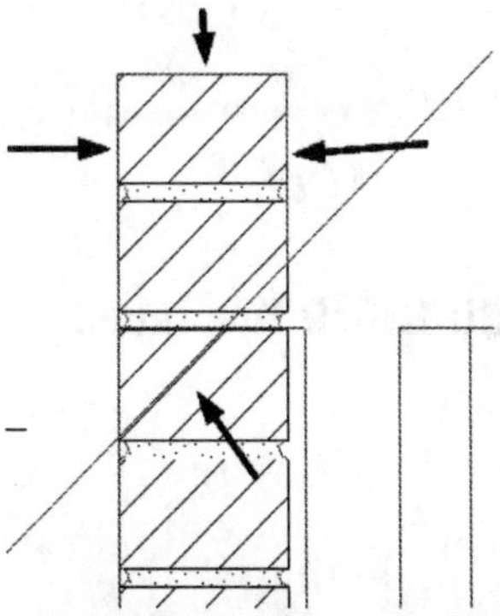

Trace around the masonry details to form a closed polygon.

20. 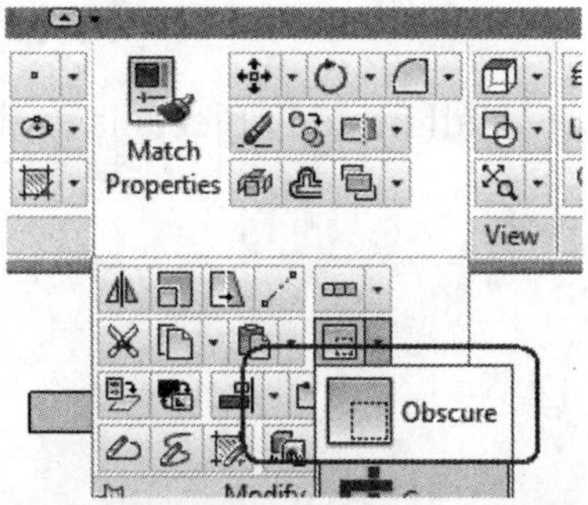

Activate the Home ribbon.

Select the **Obscure** tool on the Modify ribbon.

21. 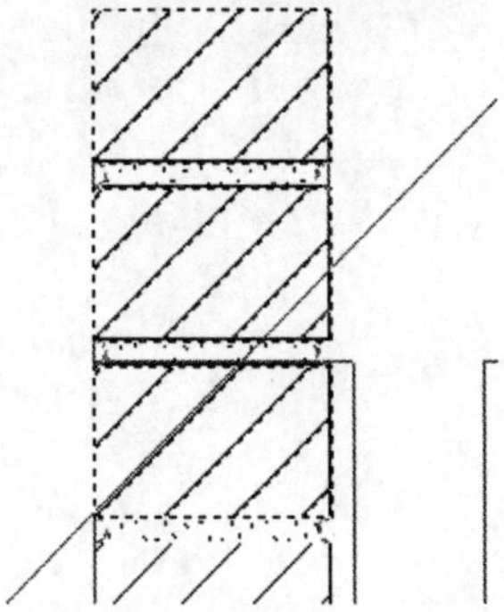

Select the details to be obscured.

Press ENTER.

22. 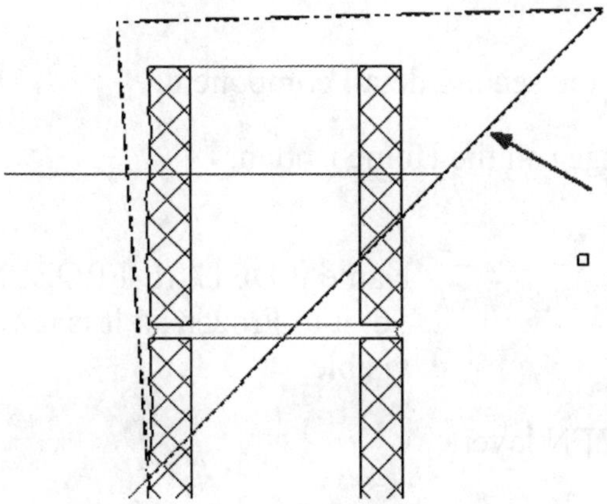

Select the polygon.

Press ENTER.

23. 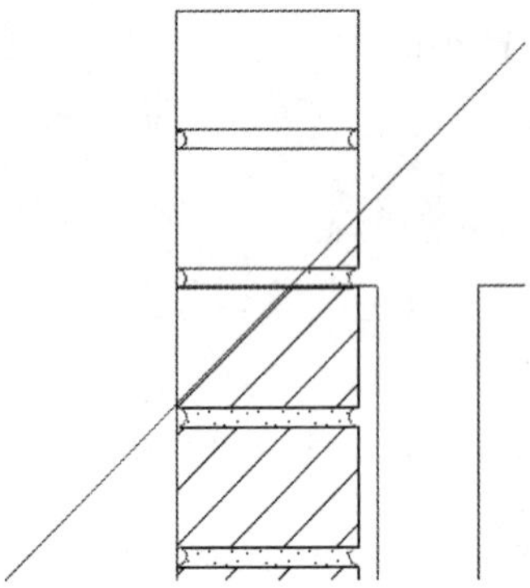

The hatch pattern on the detail is masked.

24. 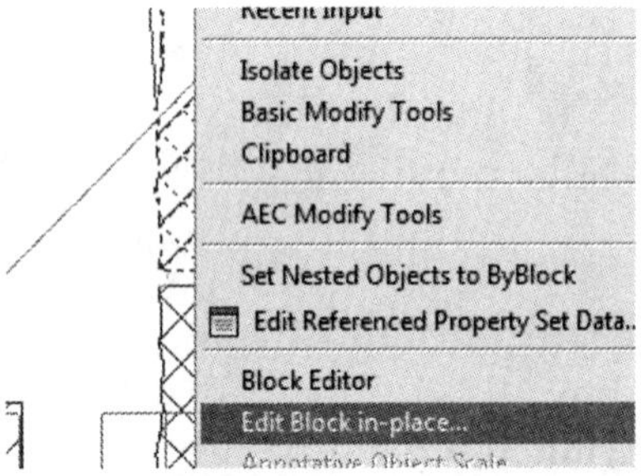

Select the detail.
Right click and select **Edit Block In-place...**

25. 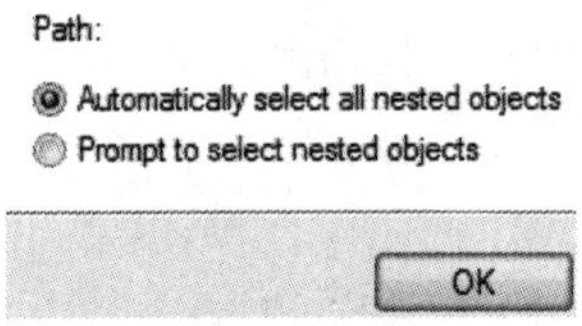

Verify that automatically select all nested objects is enabled.

Press **OK**.

26. 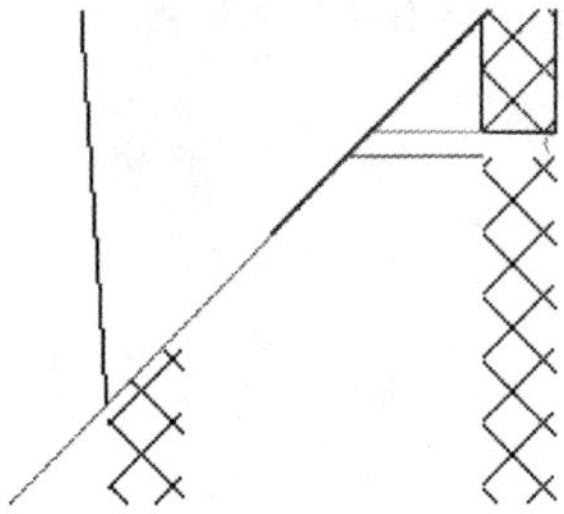

Delete the unwanted lines.

27. 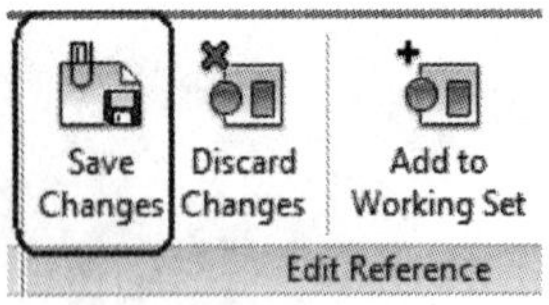

Select **Save Changes** on the ribbon.

28. 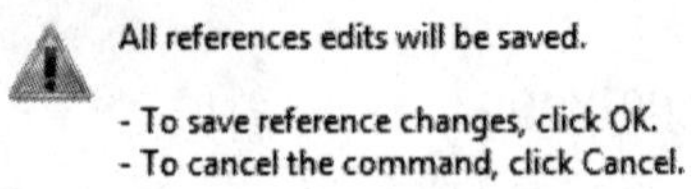

Press **OK**.

Repeat for the second detail component.

29. 

Activate the Layer Manager on the Home ribbon.
Create a new layer.

30. 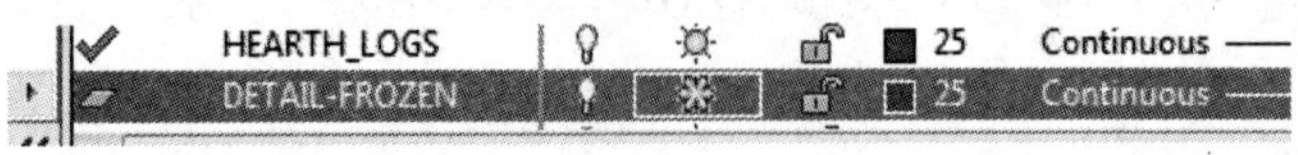

Name it DETAIL-FROZEN.
Set it to Frozen so it is not visible.

31. Place the polygon on the DETAIL FROZEN layer.

32. Our detail view so far.

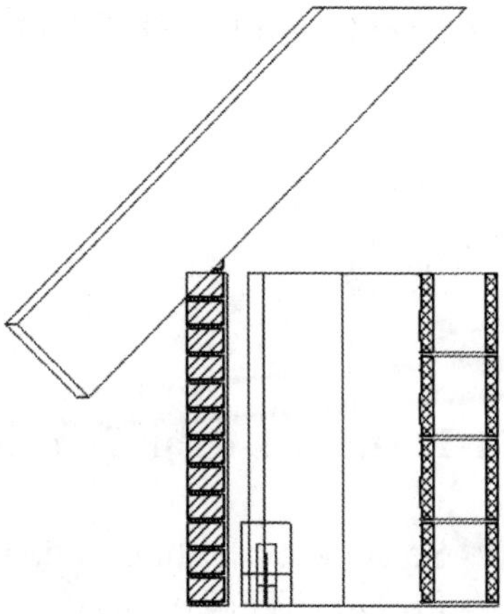

33. 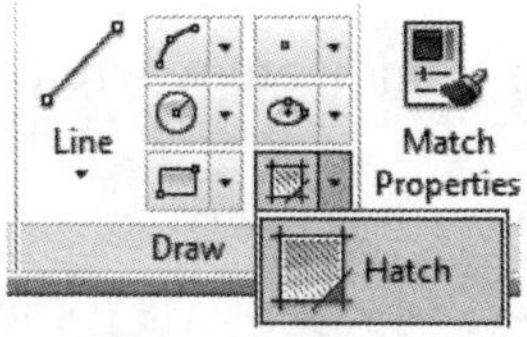

Select the Hatch tool from the Home ribbon.

34. 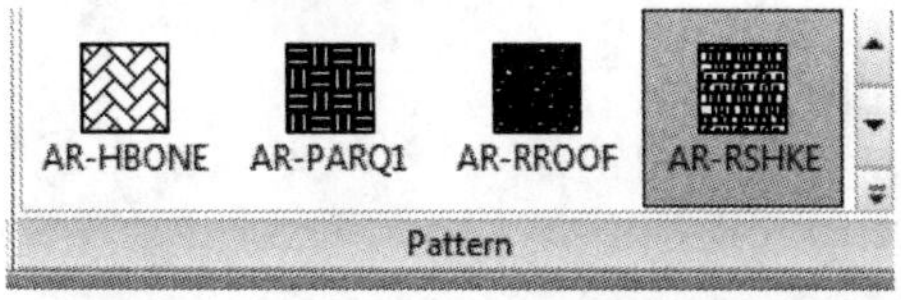

Select the **AR-RSHKE** hatch pattern.

35. 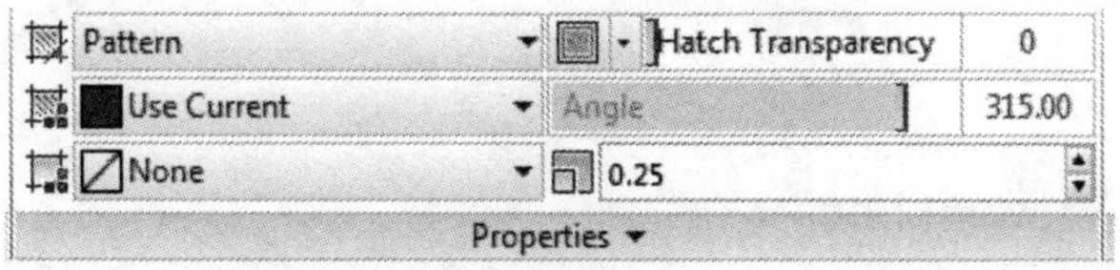

Set the angle to **315.00**.
Set the scale to **0.25**.

36. 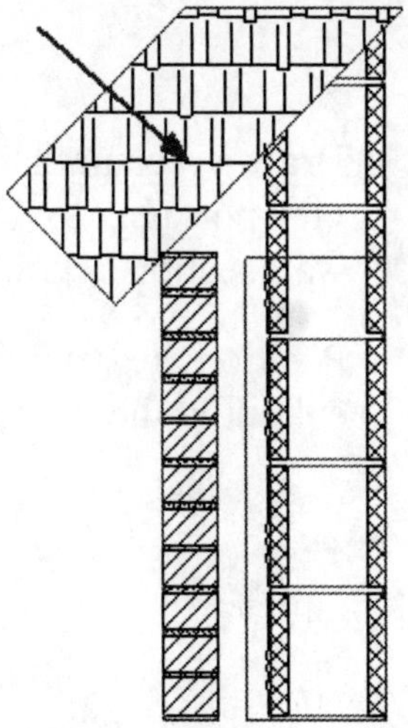
Pick a point inside the roof.

Press ENTER to place.

37. 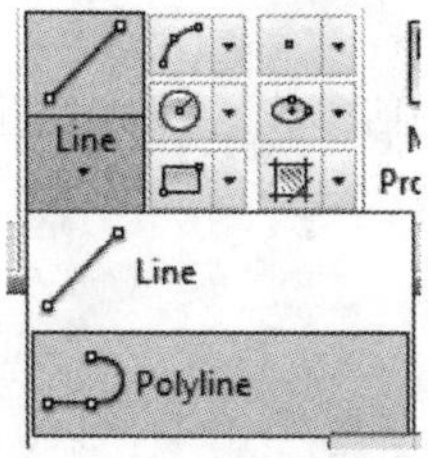

Select the **Polyline** tool from the Home ribbon.

38. 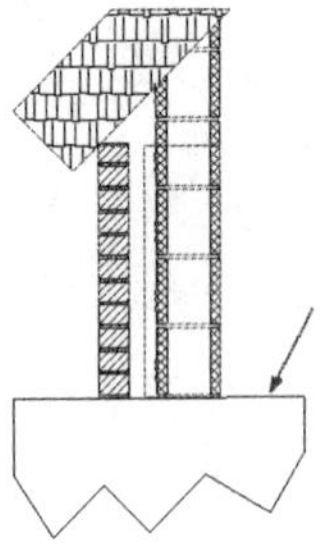

Draw a shape to approximate earthwork.

39. 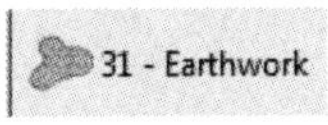

Select the **31-Earthwork** detail from the Basic tab on the Tool Palette.

40. 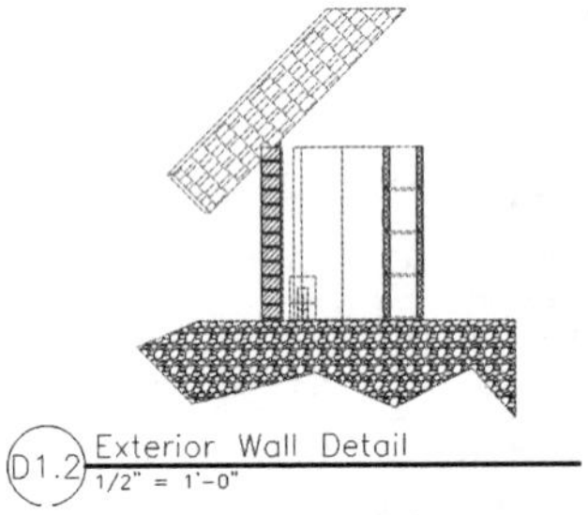

Select the polyline to be used as the boundary.
Press ENTER.

Select inside the polyline object to indicate where to place the hatch pattern.

Press ENTER.

41. 

Activate the **S1.2 Details layout** tab.

42. 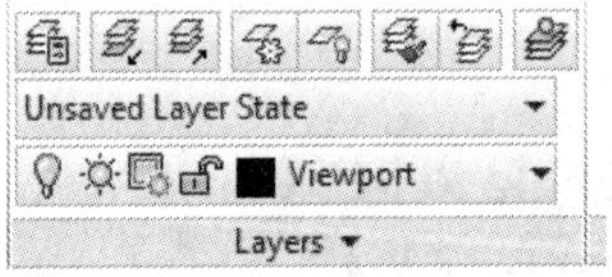

Set the current layer to Viewport.

43. 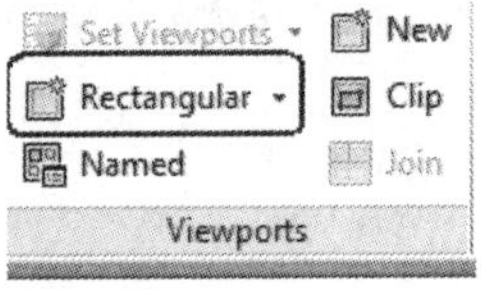

Activate the View ribbon.

Select the Rectangular viewport tool.

44. 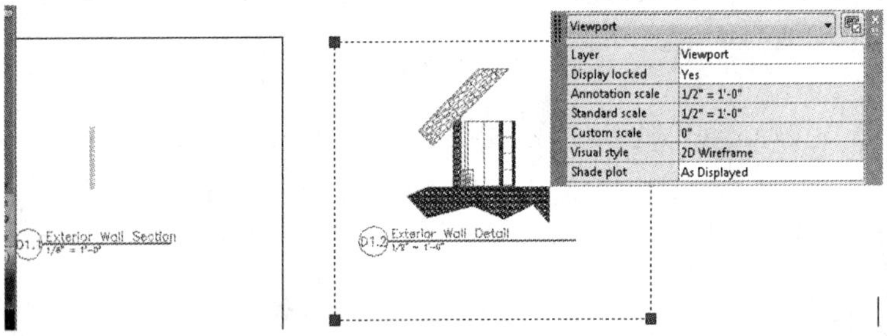

Draw a rectangular viewport next to the wall section detail.

Position the detail callout in the viewport.

45. Select the viewport.
Set the Annotation scale to **1/2″ = 1′0″**.
Set the Standard scale to **1/2″ = 1′0″**

Set the Shade plot to **As Displayed**.

Lock the display.

46. Press ESC to release the viewport.

47. Save as *ex7-11.dwg*.

Exercise 7-12
Creating Space Styles

Drawing Name: Ex7-11.dwg
Estimated Time: 10 minutes

1. Open *ex7-11.dwg.*

2. 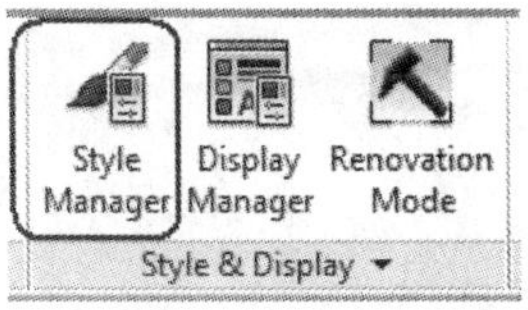

Activate the **Manage** ribbon.

Select the **Style Manager**.

3. 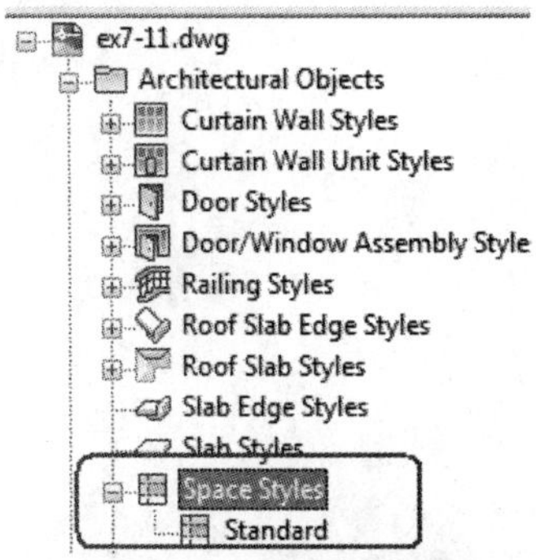

Locate the *Space Styles* drawing.

Make sure you set the Files of Type to dwg or you won't see it.

Note that there is only one space style currently available.

4. 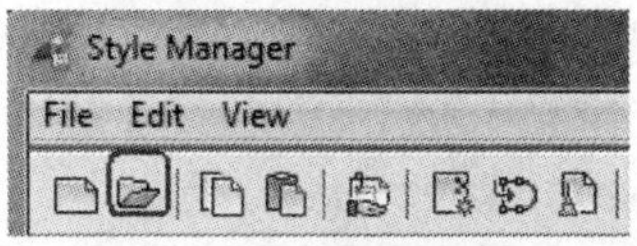

Select the **Open Drawing** tool.

5. 

Browse to the exercise folders for this text.
Change the files of type to **Drawing (*.dwg).**
Open the *space styles.dwg.*

6. 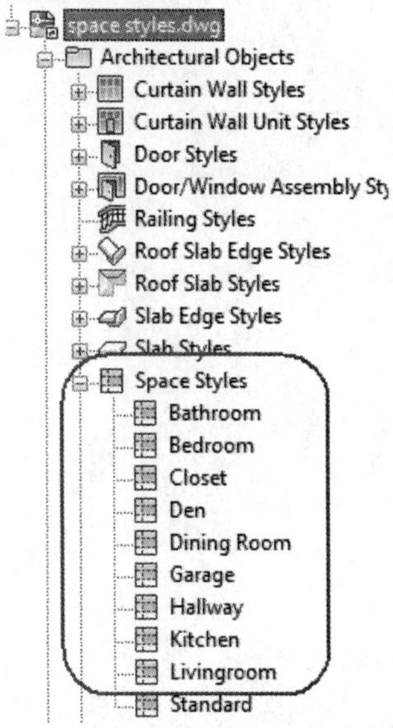

Expand the *space styles.dwg* in the Style Manager.

Note several space styles have been defined.

7. 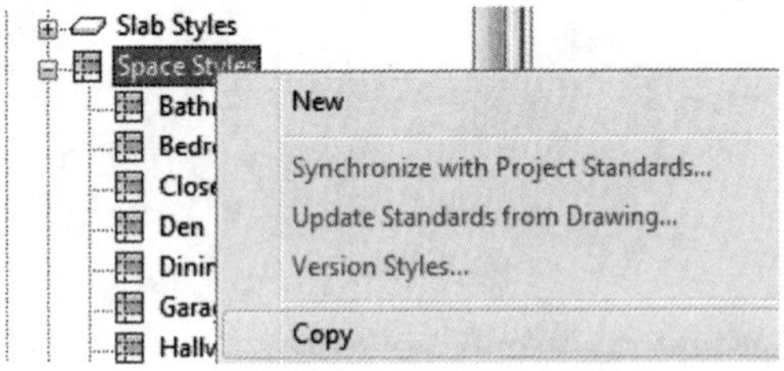

Highlight the **Space Styles** in the *space styles.dwg*.
Right click and select **Copy**.

8. 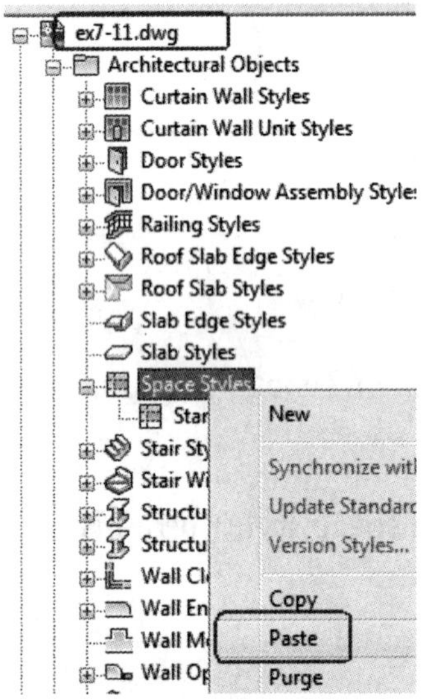

Scroll up to the *ex7-11.dwg*.

Highlight **Space Styles**.

Right click and select **Paste**.

9. 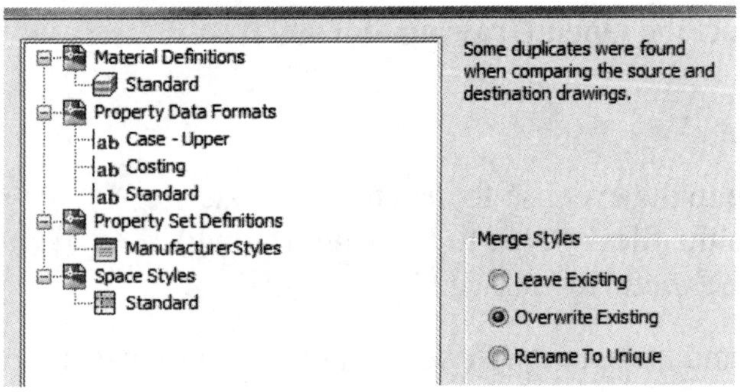

If this dialog appears advising of duplicate definitions:
Enable **Overwrite Existing**.
Press **OK**.

10. 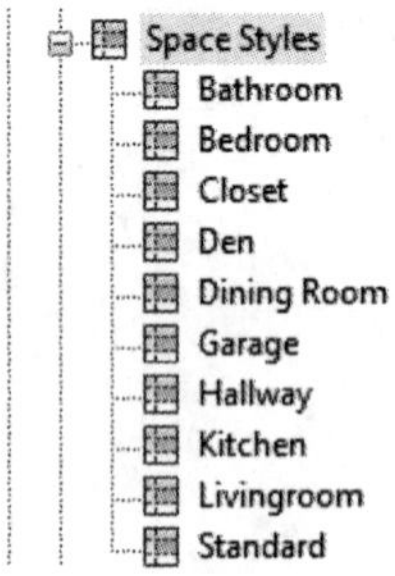

The space styles are now copied into your project.

Close the Style Manager.

11. Save as *ex7-12.dwg*.

Exercise 7-13

Adding Spaces

Drawing Name: Ex7-12.dwg
Estimated Time: 15 minutes

This exercise reinforces the following skills:

- Layouts
- Spaces

1. Open *ex7-12.dwg.*
2. Select the Model tab.
3. 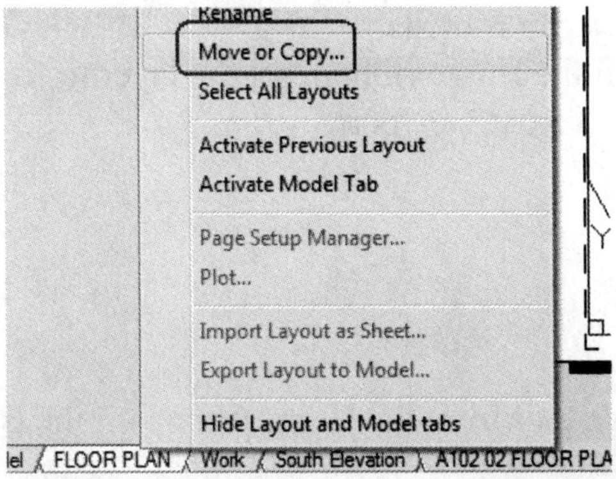

   Highlight the **Floor Plan** layout tab.

   Right click and select **Move or Copy**.
4. 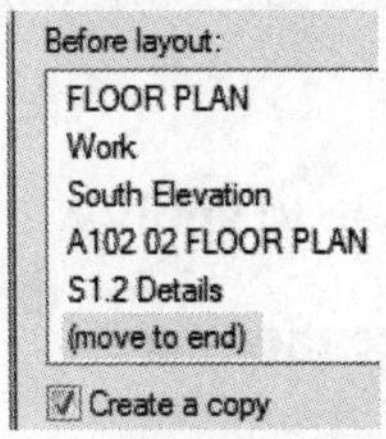

   Enable **Create a copy**.

   Highlight **(move to end)**.

   Press **OK**.
5. 

   Select the second layout.
6. 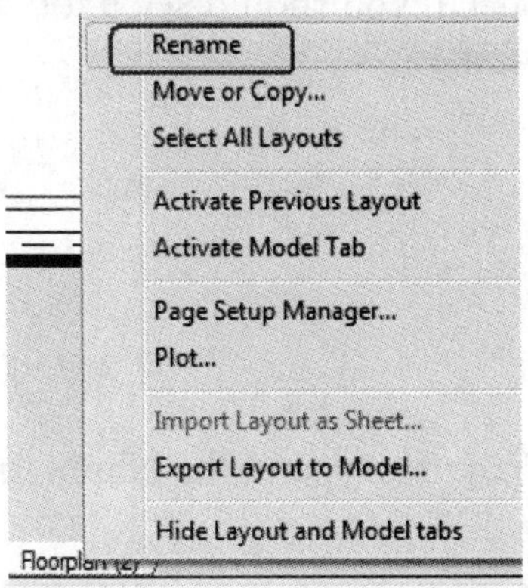

   Highlight the second layout tab.

   Right click and select **Rename**.
7. 

   Modify the layout name to **A102 03 ROOM PLAN**.

8. 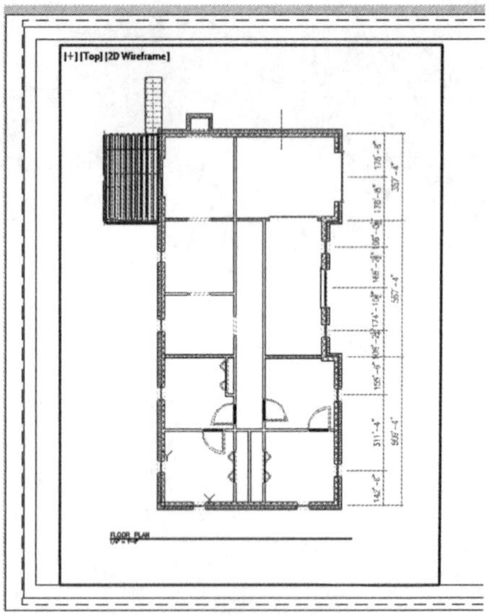

Double click inside the viewport to activate model space.

9. 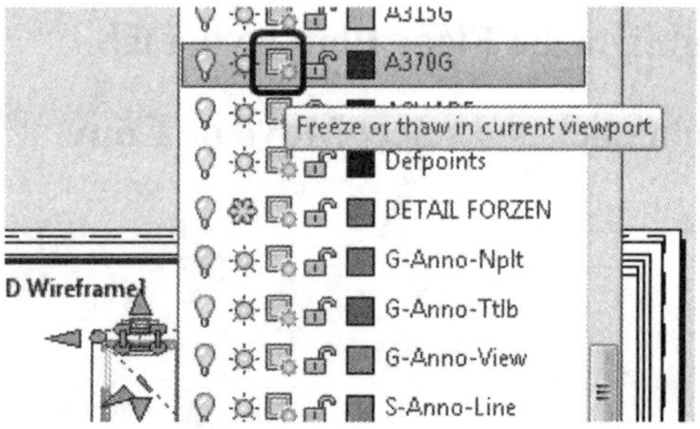

Select a roof slab.
On the Home ribbon, set the layer to freeze in current viewport.

10. 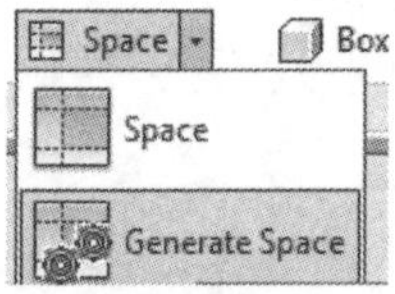

Select the **Generate Space** tool from the Home ribbon on the Build panel.

11. 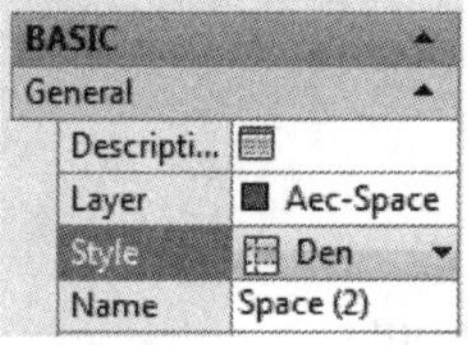

On the Properties palette, select the space style to apply.

Left click inside the designated space to place the space.

12. 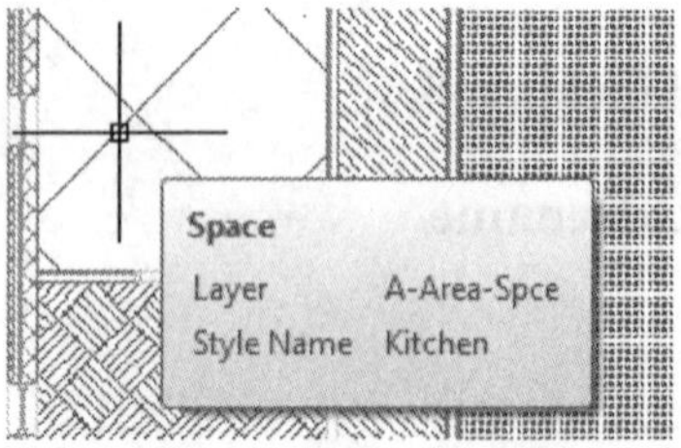

If you hover over a space, you should see a tool tip with the space style name.

13. 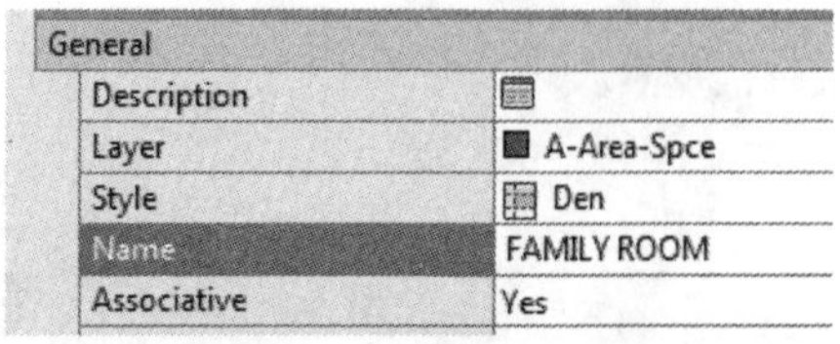

Select a space.

In the Properties palette: type in the Name for the SPACE.

This is the name that will appear on the room tag.

14. Repeat for all the spaces.
    Press ESC to release the selection of each space before moving on to the next space.

    Verify that only one space is selected to be renamed each time or you may assign a name to the wrong space unintentionally.

15. Save as *ex7-13.dwg*.

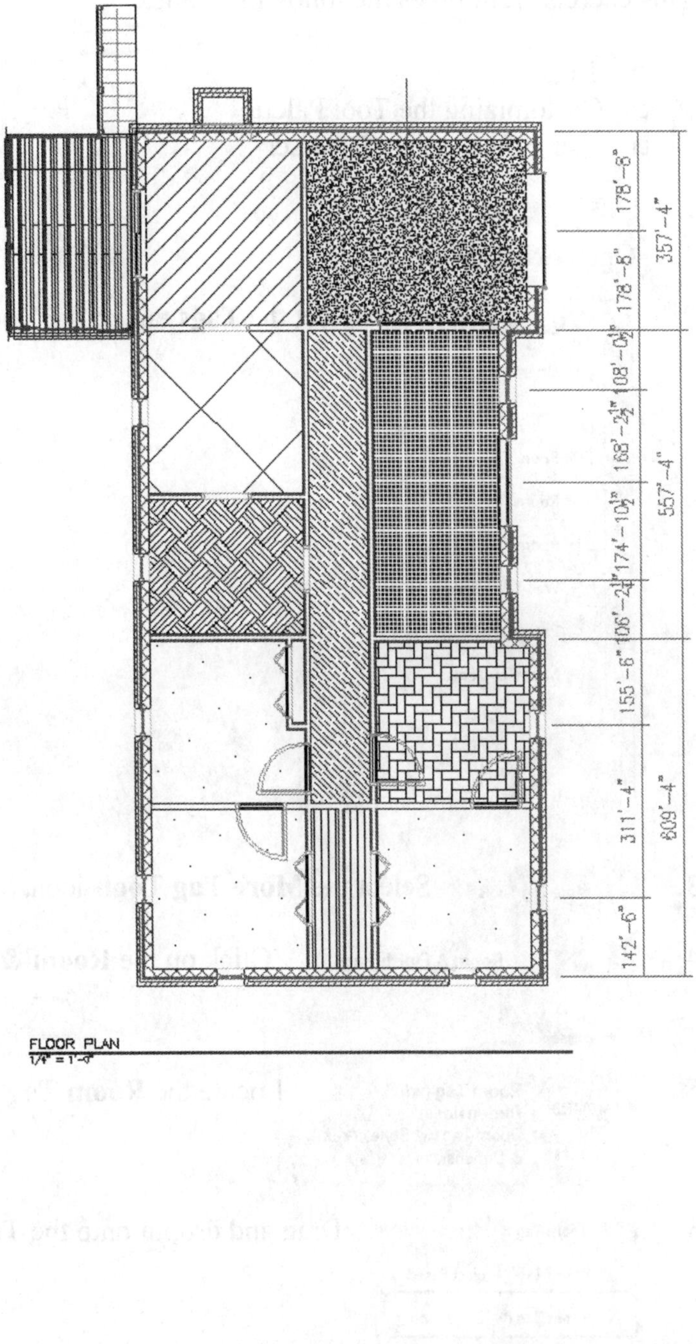

Exercise 7-14

Adding Room Tags

Drawing Name: ex7-13.dwg
Estimated Time: 15 minutes

This exercise reinforces the following skills:

- Tags
- Customizing the Tool Palette
- Using the Content Browser

1. Open *ex7-13.dwg.*

2. 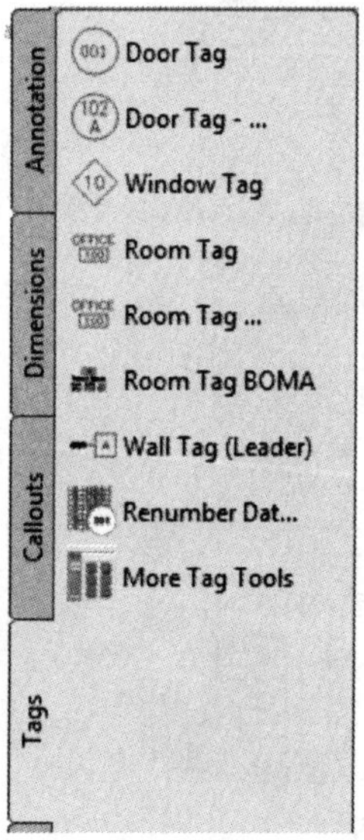

Select the **Tags** tab on the Document Tool Palette.

3. 

Select the **More Tag Tools** icon.

4. 

Click on the **Room & Finish Tags**.

5. 

Locate the **Room Tag (w/Dimensions)**.

6. 

Drag and drop it onto the Tool Palette.

7. 

Select the **A102 03 ROOM PLAN** layout tab.
Double click in the viewport to activate model space.

8. 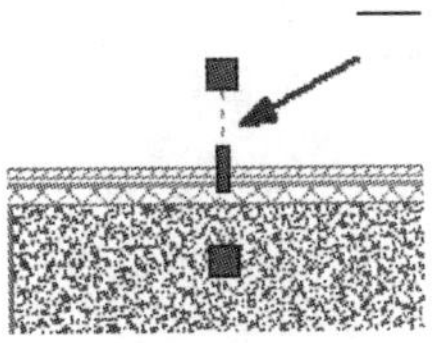
Select the section line on the north wall used to define the wall section.

9. 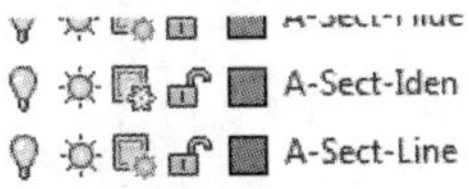

Set to **Hide in the current viewport** using the Layer drop-down on the Home ribbon.

10. 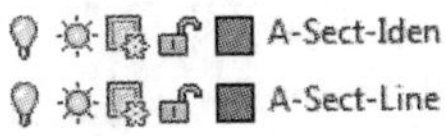

Set A-**Sect-Iden** to **Hide in the current viewport**.

11. 

Select the **Room Tag (w/Dimensions)**.

12. 

Select the family room space.
Press **ENTER** to place the tag centered in the room.

13. 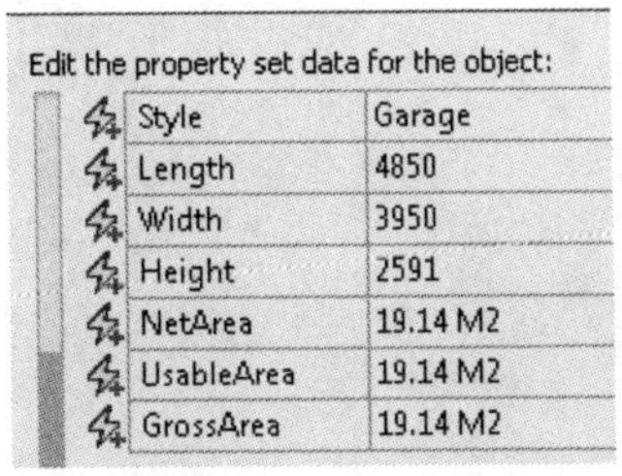
Edit the property set data for the object:

Style	Garage
Length	4850
Width	3950
Height	2591
NetArea	19.14 M2
UsableArea	19.14 M2
GrossArea	19.14 M2

A small dialog will appear showing all the data attached to the space.

You can modify any field that is not grayed out.

Press **OK**.

14. 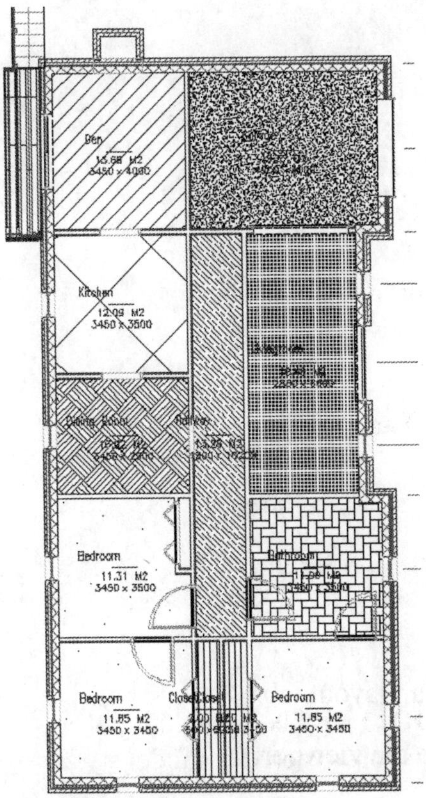

Repeat to tag all the spaces.

15. 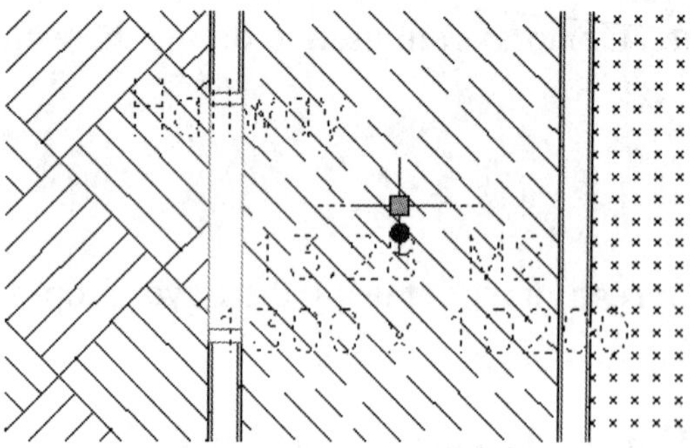 Select the Hallway tag.

16. 

On the Properties palette:
Select **Anchor**.

17. 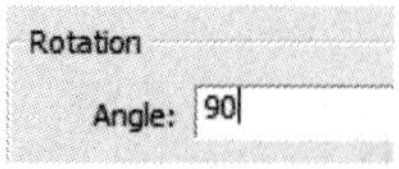

Set the Rotation angle to **90**.
Press **OK**.

18. Press ESC or left click outside the building model to release the selected tag.

19. 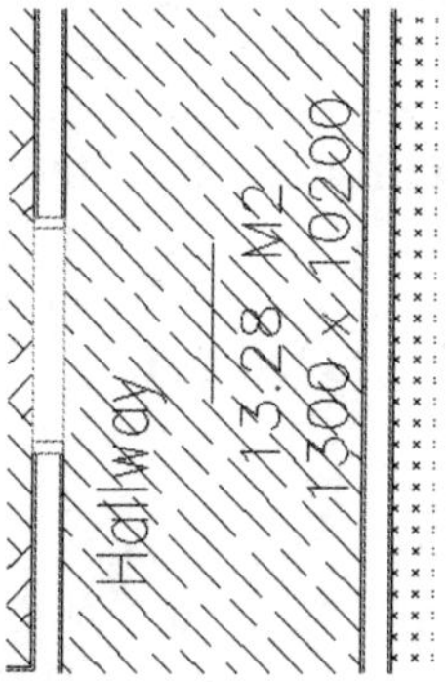

The tag is rotated 90 degrees.

20. Save as *ex7-14.dwg*.

Exercise 7-15

Adding Door Tags

Drawing Name: ex7-14.dwg
Estimated Time: 10 minutes

This exercise reinforces the following skills:

- Tags

1. Open *ex7-14.dwg.*
2. 

Activate the A102 02 Floor plan layout tab.
3. Activate model space by double-clicking inside the viewport.

4. 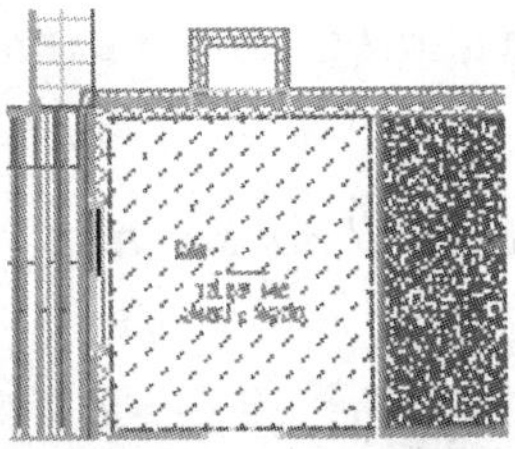

Select the DEN space so it is highlighted.

5. 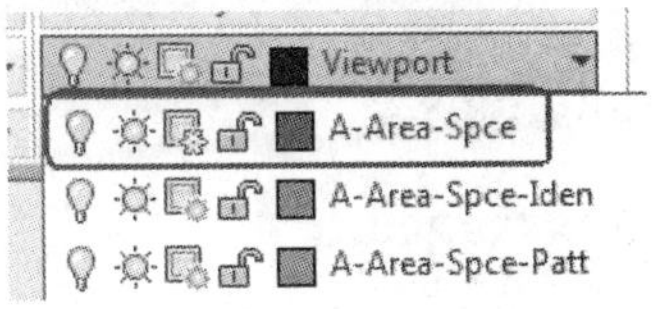

Activate the Home ribbon.
The A-Area-Spce layer should be shown.
Freeze the layer in the current viewport.

6. 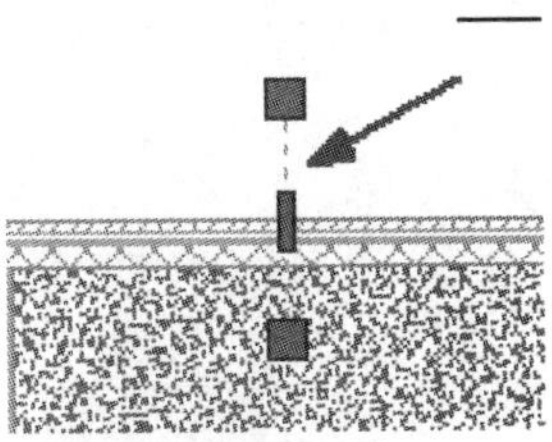

Select the section line on the north wall used to define the wall section.

7. 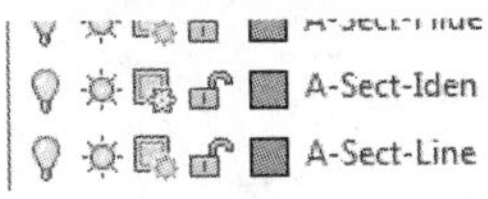

Set to **Hide in the current viewport** using the Layer drop-down on the Home ribbon.

8. 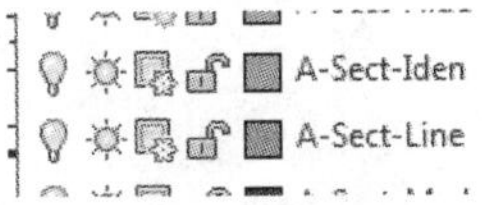

Set A-**Sect-Iden** to **Hide in the current viewport.**

9. Activate the Document palette.
Activate the Tags tab.

Select the Door Tag tool. 

10. 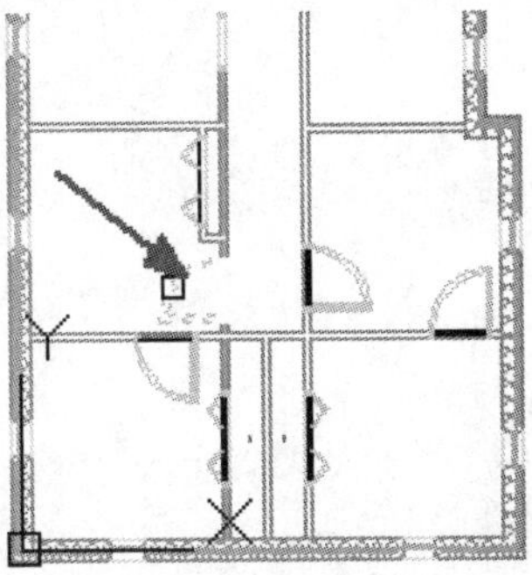

Select a door.

Press ENTER to center the tag on the door.

11. 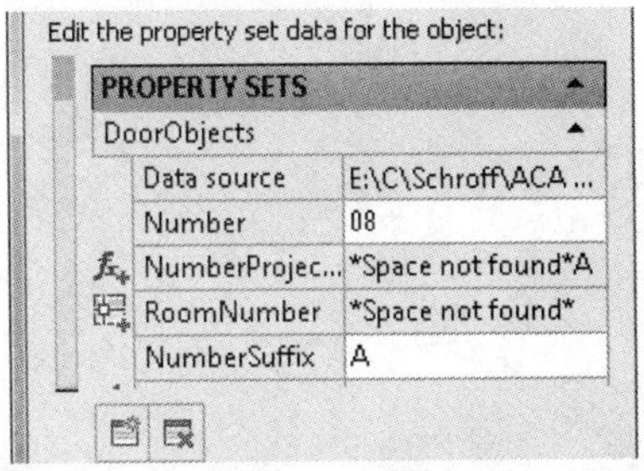

Press **OK**.

Some students may be concerned because they see the Error getting value next to the Room Number field.

If you tag the spaces with a room tag assigning a number, you will not see that error.

12. Right click and select **Multiple**.
Type All.
Select the remaining doors in the floor plan to add the door tags.

13. 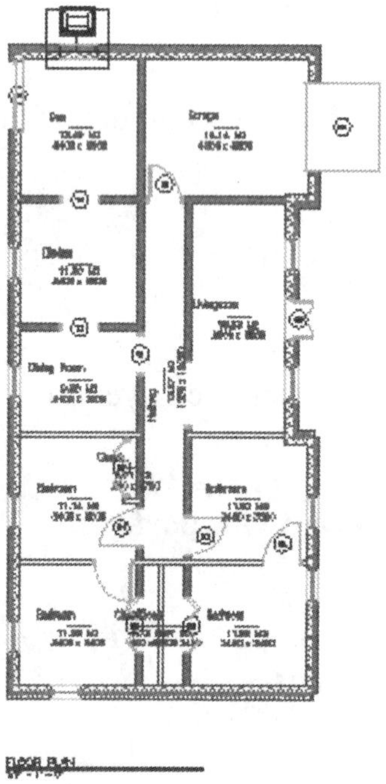

There should be thirteen doors tagged.

Save as *ex7-15.dwg.*

Exercise 7-16

Create a Door Schedule

Drawing Name: ex7-15.dwg
Estimated Time: 10 minutes

This exercise reinforces the following skills:

- Schedules

1. Open *ex7-15.dwg.*

2. 

Activate the Model layout tab.

3. 

Select the Door Schedule tool.

The Door Schedule tool can be found on the Annotate ribbon or on the Document Tool Palette on the Scheduling tab.

4. Type **ALL** on the command line.

   ACA will automatically filter out any non-door entities and collect only doors.

   Press **ENTER**.

5. 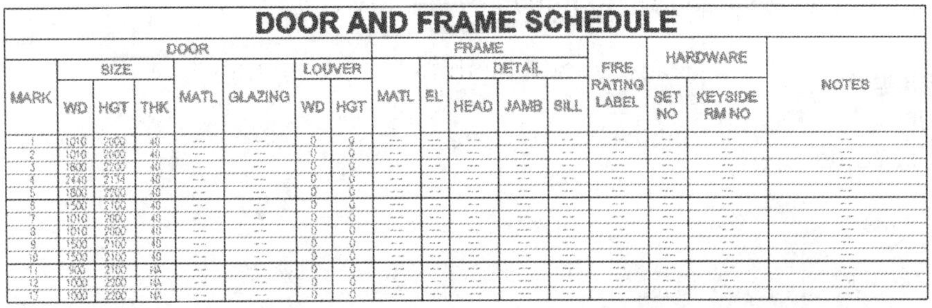

   Left click to place the schedule in the drawing window.

   Press **ENTER**.

6. 

   Activate the **A102 02 Floor Plan** layout tab.

7. 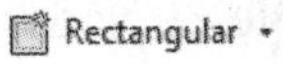

   Activate the View ribbon.
   Select the **Rectangular** viewport tool.

8. 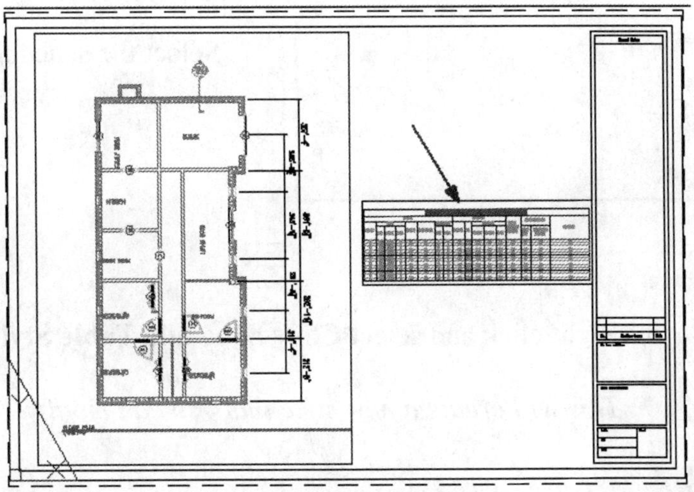

   Draw a rectangular viewport.

   Position the door schedule in the viewport.

9. 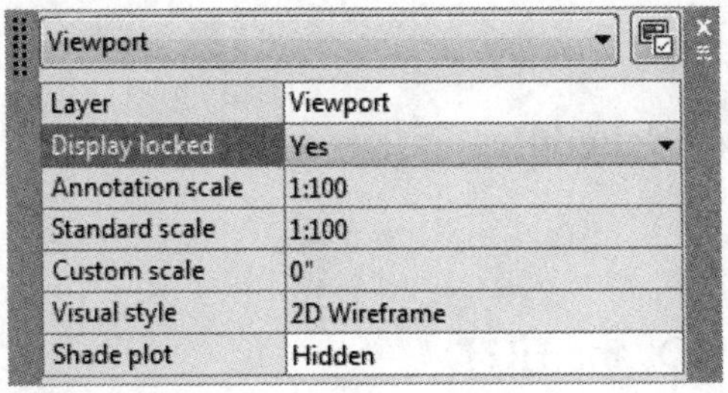

   Select the viewport.

   Verify that it is on the Viewport layer.

   Set the Standard scale to **1:100.**

   Set the Display locked to **Yes**.

10. Save as *ex7-16.dwg*.

Exercise 7-17

Create a Door Schedule Style

Drawing Name: ex7-16.dwg
Estimated Time: 30 minutes

This exercise reinforces the following skills:

- Schedules
- Style Manager
- Text Styles
- Update Schedule

1. Open *ex7-16.dwg.*

2. 

Activate the **A102 02 Floor Plan** layout tab.

3. 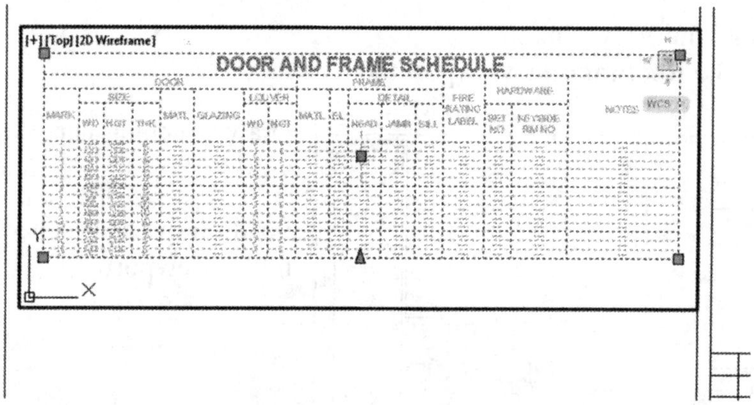

Double click inside the viewport with the door schedule.

   Select the schedule.

4. 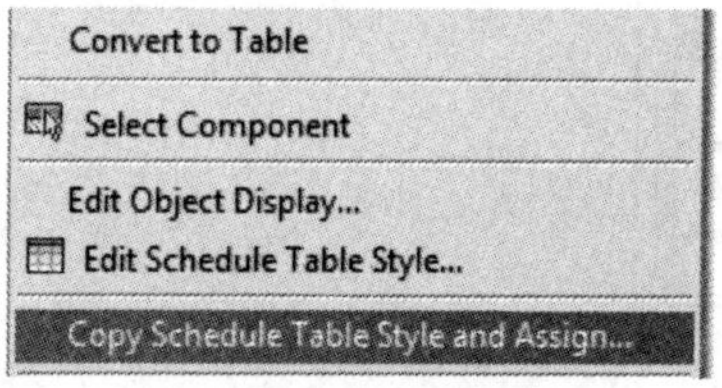

Right click and select **Copy Schedule Table Style**.

   This will create a new style that you can modify.

5. 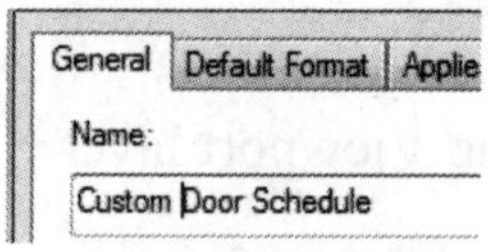

Select the **General** tab.

   Rename **Custom Door Schedule**.

6. 

Select the **Columns** tab.

7. 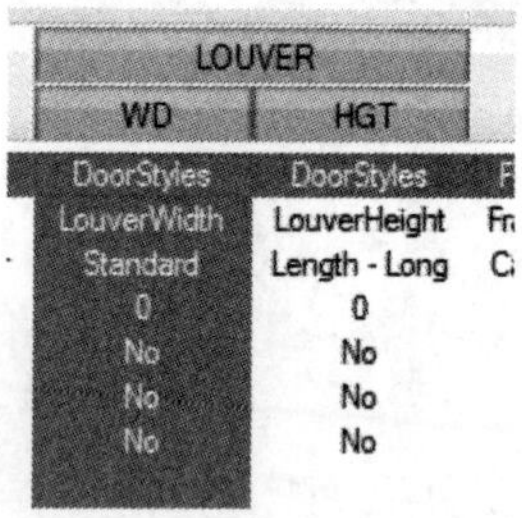

Highlight Louver, WD, and HGT.

8. 

Press **Delete**.

9. 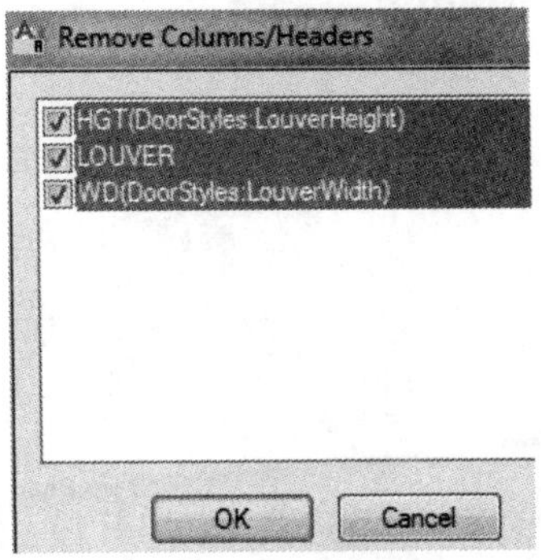

You will be asked to confirm the deletion.

Press **OK**.

10. 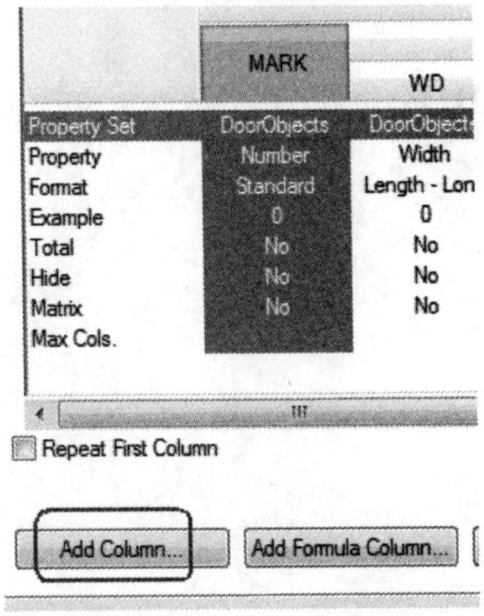

Highlight **MARK**.

Select the **Add Column** button.

11. 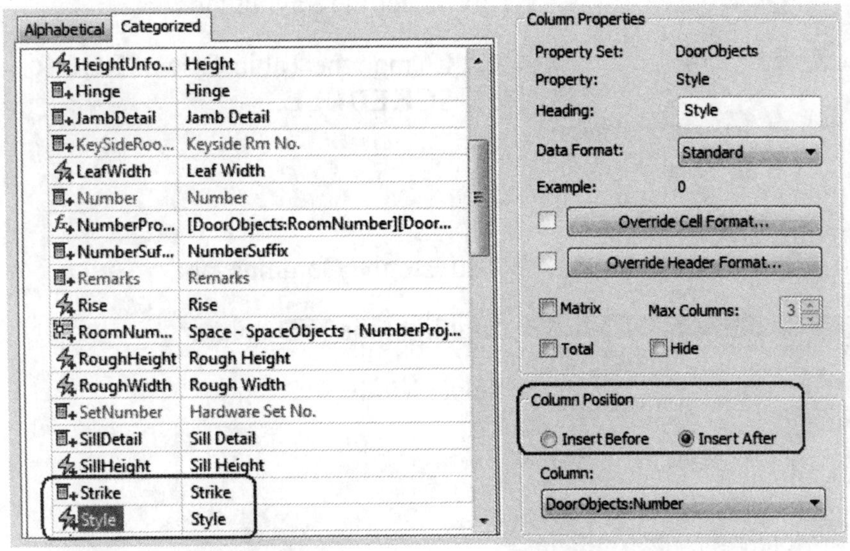

Scroll down until you see Style.

Highlight **Style**.

Confirm that the Column Position will be inserted after the DoorObjects: Number.

Press **OK**.

12. 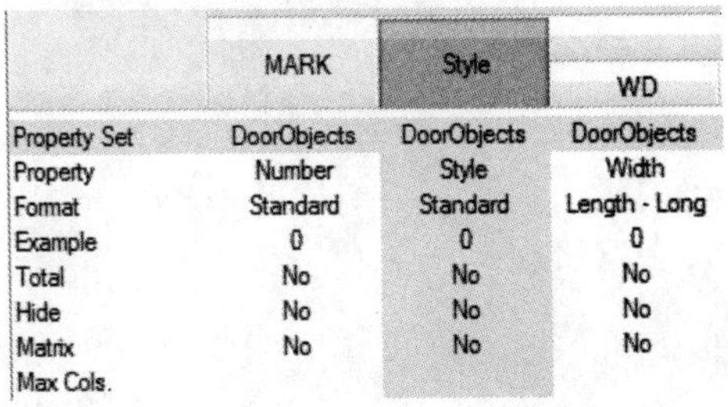

The new column is now inserted.

13. 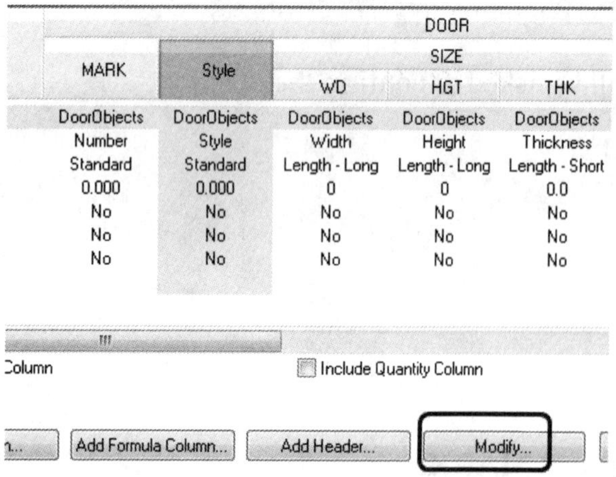

Highlight the **Style** Column and select **Modify**.

14. 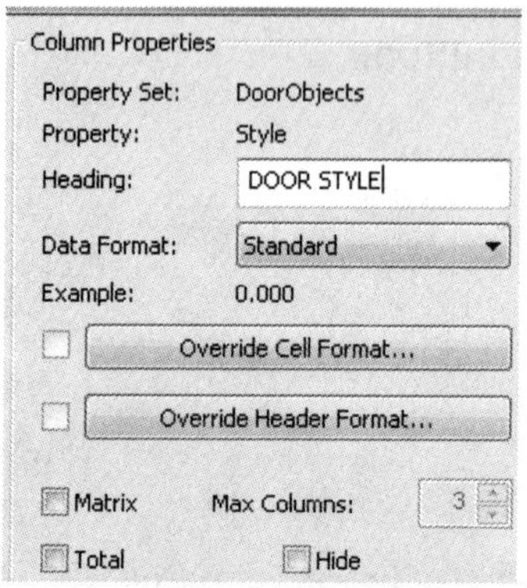

Change the Heading to **DOOR STYLE**.

Press **OK**.

15. 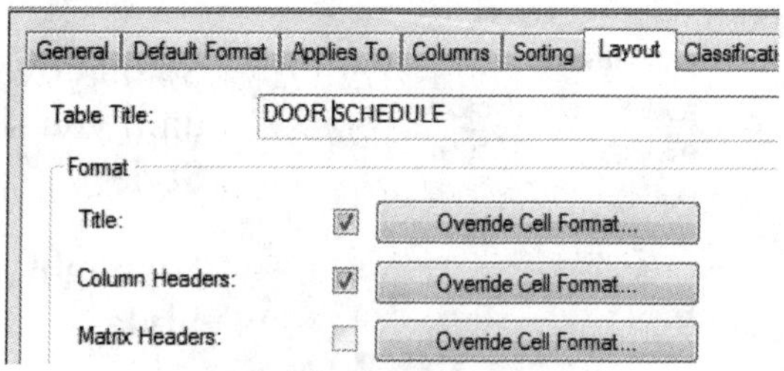

Select the Layout tab.

Change the Table Title to **DOOR SCHEDULE**.

16. 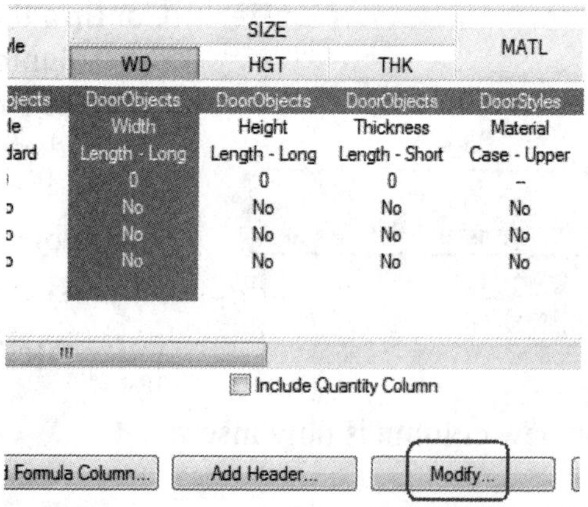

Activate the Columns tab.

Highlight the **WD** column.

Select **Modify**.

17. 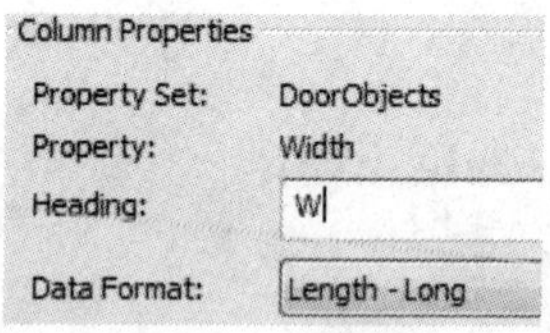

Change the Heading to **W**.

Press **OK**.

18. 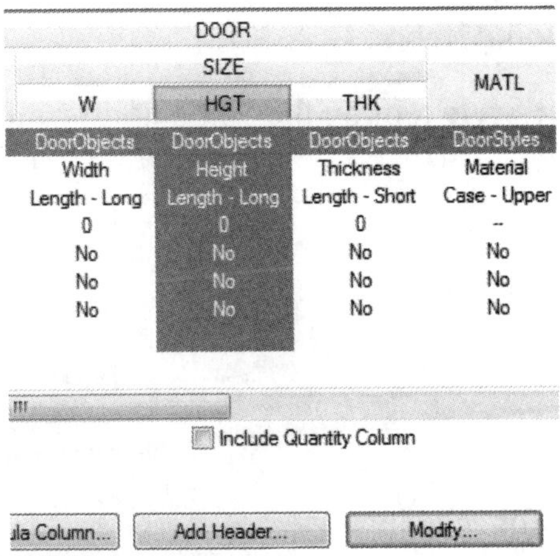

Highlight the **HGT** column.

Select **Modify**.

19. 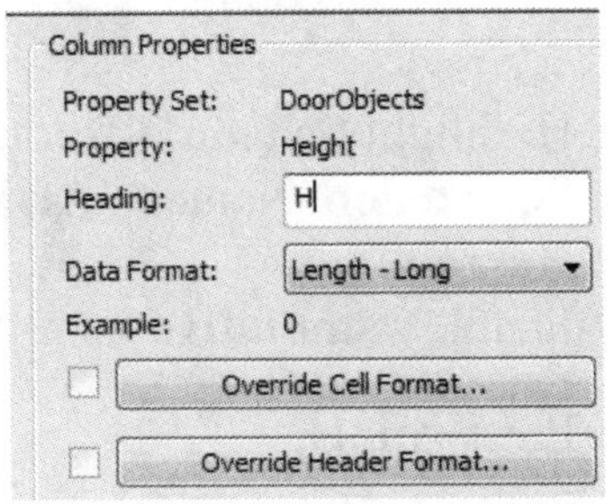

Change the Heading to **H**.

Press **OK**.

20. Press **OK** to close the dialog.

21. 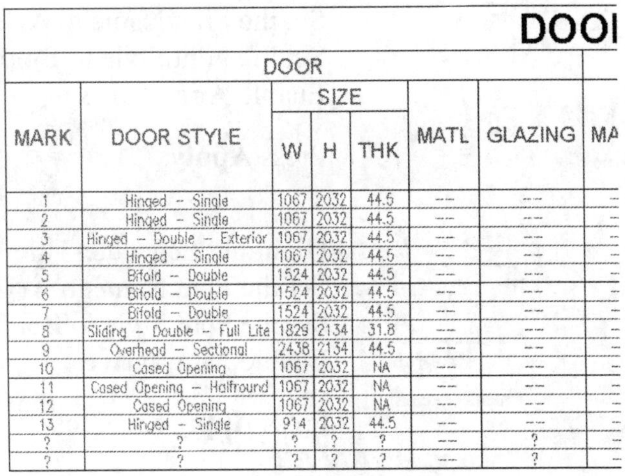

DOOI

MARK	DOOR STYLE	W	H	THK	MATL	GLAZING	MA
1	Hinged - Single	1067	2032	44.5	--	--	-
2	Hinged - Single	1067	2032	44.5	--	--	-
3	Hinged - Double - Exterior	1067	2032	44.5	--	--	-
4	Hinged - Single	1067	2032	44.5	--	--	-
5	Bifold - Double	1524	2032	44.5	--	--	-
6	Bifold - Double	1524	2032	44.5	--	--	-
7	Bifold - Double	1524	2032	44.5	--	--	-
8	Sliding - Double - Full Lite	1829	2134	31.8	--	--	-
9	Overhead - Sectional	2438	2134	44.5	--	--	-
10	Cased Opening	1067	2032	NA	--	--	-
11	Cased Opening - Halfround	1067	2032	NA	--	--	-
12	Cased Opening	1067	2032	NA	--	--	-
13	Hinged - Single	914	2032	44.5	--	--	-
?	?	?	?	?	--	?	-
?	?	?	?	?	--	?	-

The schedule updates.

If there are question marks in the schedule, that indicates doors which remain untagged.

22. 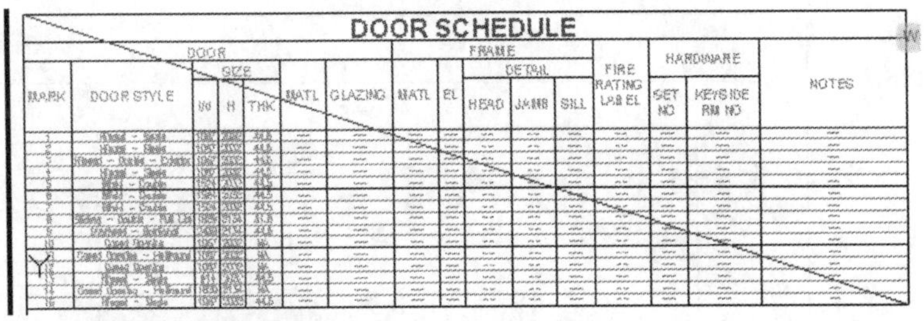

A diagonal line through the schedule indicates it requires updating.

23. 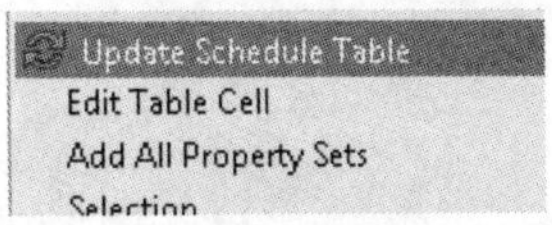

Select the schedule.
Right click and select **Update Schedule Table**.

24. 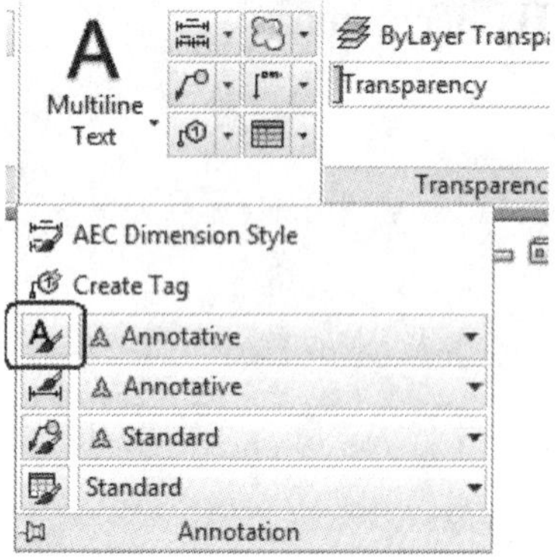

Activate the Home ribbon.

Select the **Text Style** tool on the Annotation panel.

25. 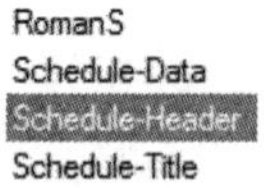

Notice there are text styles set up for schedules. Highlight each one to see their settings.

26. 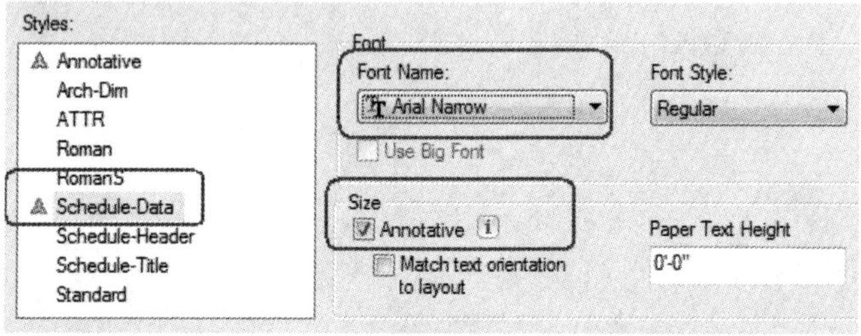

Highlight **Schedule-Data.**
Set the Font Name to **Arial Narrow**.
Enable **Annotative**.

Press **Apply**.

27. 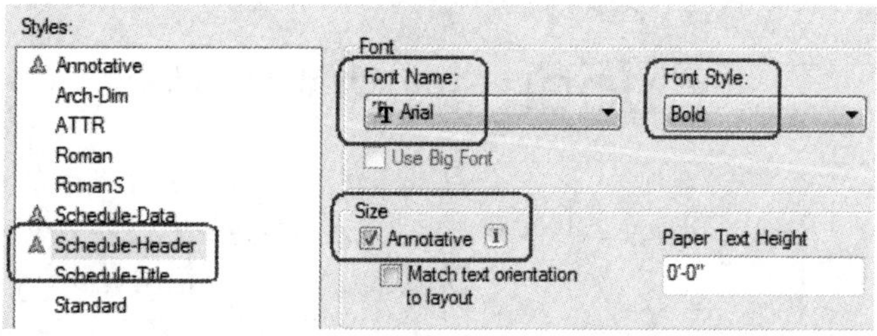

Highlight Schedule-Header.
Set the Font Name to **Arial**.
Set the Font Style to **Bold**.
Enable **Annotative**.

Press **Apply**.

28. 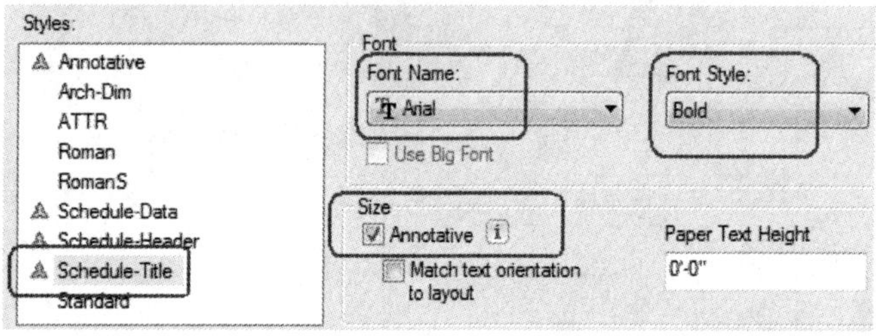

Highlight Schedule-Title.
Set the Font Name to **Arial**.
Set the Font Style to **Bold**.
Enable **Annotative**.

Press **Apply** and **Close**.

29. Note that the schedule automatically updates.

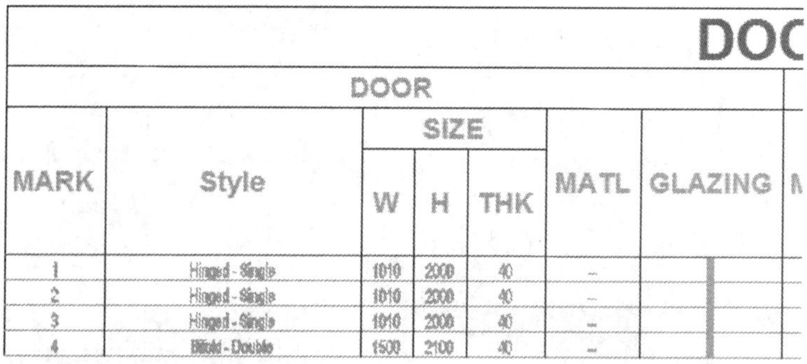

30. Save as *ex7-17.dwg*.

QUIZ 4

True or False

1. Columns, braces, and beams are created using Structural Members.
2. When you isolate a Layer User Group, you are freezing all the layers in that group.
3. You can isolate a Layer User Group in ALL Viewports, a Single Viewport, or a Selection Set of Viewports.
4. When placing beams, you can switch the justification in the middle of the command.
5. Standard AutoCAD commands, like COPY, MOVE, and ARRAY cannot be used in ACA.

Multiple Choice

6. Before you can place a beam or column, you must:

   A. Generate a Member Style
   B. Activate the Structural Member Catalog
   C. Select a structural member shape
   D. All of the above

7. Select the character that is OK to use when creating a Structural Member Style Name.

   A. -
   B. ?
   C. =
   D. /

8. Identify the tool shown. 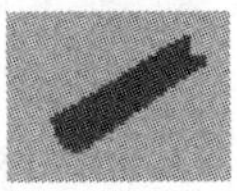

   A. Add Brace
   B. Add Beam
   C. Add Column
   D. Structural Member Catalog

9. Setting a Layer Key

   A. Controls which layer AEC objects will be placed on.
   B. Determines the layer names created.
   C. Sets layer properties.
   D. All of the above.

10. There are two types of stairs used in residential buildings:

    A. INSIDE and OUTSIDE
    B. METAL and WOOD
    C. MAIN and SERVICE
    D. FLOATING and STATIONARY

11. Select the stair type that does not exist from the list below:

    A. Straight-run
    B. M Stairs
    C. L Stairs
    D. U Stairs

12. The first point selected when placing a set of stairs is:

    A. The foot/bottom of the stairs.
    B. The head/top of the stairs
    C. The center point of the stairs
    D. Depends on the property settings

ANSWERS:

1) T; 2) F; 3) T; 4) T; 5) F; 6) D; 7) A; 8) A; 9) A; 10) C; 11) B; 12) D